SUETONIUS

THE
CAESARS

GAIUS SUETONIUS TRANQUILLUS

THE
CAESARS

TRANSLATED, WITH
INTRODUCTIONS AND NOTES, BY

DONNA W. HURLEY

Hackett Publishing Company, Inc.
Indianapolis/Cambridge

15 14 13 12 11   1 2 3 4 5 6 7

For further information, please address:
Hackett Publishing Company, Inc.
P.O. Box 44937
Indianapolis, IN 46244-0937

www.hackettpublishing.com

Cover image: Known as the Eid Mar denarius, this silver coin was issued by Brutus in 42 B.C., before the fateful battle at Philippi against Mark Antony and Octavian, to celebrate the assassination of Caesar on the Ides of March 44 B.C. The coin shows the cap of liberty, which was given to released slaves, between two Roman daggers. Image courtesy of the Roman Numismatic Gallery, © Andreas Pangerl, www.romancoins.info.

Cover design by Abigail Coyle
Text design by Meera Dash
Maps by William Nelson
Composition by William Hartman
Printed at Sheridan Books, Inc.

Library of Congress Cataloging-in-Publication Data
Suetonius, ca. 69–ca. 122
      [De vita Caesarum. English]
      The Caesars / Gaius Suetonius Tranquillus ; translated,
with introductions and notes, by Donna W. Hurley.
          p. cm.
      Includes bibliographical references and index.
      ISBN 978-1-60384-313-3 (pbk.) — ISBN 978-1-60384-314-0 (cloth)
      1. Emperors—Rome—Biography—Early works to 1800.
      2. Rome—History—Julio-Claudians, 30 B.C.–68 A.D.
      3. Rome—History—Flavians, 69–96. I. Hurley, Donna W.
      II. Title.
      DG277.S83 2010
      937'.070922—dc22

                                                      2010015764

The paper used in this publication meets the minimum requirements of American National Standard for Information Sciences—Permanence of Paper for Printed Library Materials, ANSI Z39.48–1984.

CONTENTS

PREFACE

Robert Kaster (the recent editor of Suetonius' *De grammaticis et rhetoribus*) once joked that although he admired Suetonius' work, he would not invite him to dinner. The past thirty years have seen increasing interest in the diligent and conscientious biographer, and longer acquaintance with the *eruditissimus* scholar has had its rewards. It allows an appreciation not only of what he achieved but also of what he did not attempt. It grants him permission not to be Tacitus. Not every word that Suetonius wrote is golden. Still, his preservation of Augustus' correspondence alone makes the *Caesars* a worthy candidate for the one book allowed a shipwrecked survivor on a desert island. Dinner invitations? Yes, maybe often.

Hackett's professional support for this translation project has been reassuring. I thank Deborah Wilkes for her patient editing and Meera Dash for seeing it to publication. The publisher's reader, Allan Kershaw, has saved me some embarrassing errors although I am responsible for others that have surely survived the editing process. Thanks are also due John Ramsey for his close reading of the lives of the Divine Julius and the Divine Augustus. Katharina Volk has helped by expanding my library resources, and I am deeply grateful for the continuing encouragement of Professor Emerita Elaine Fantham. My husband has been generous in welcoming Tranquillus into our home.

Donna W. Hurley
New York, New York

INTRODUCTION

Suetonius' *Books on the Life of the Caesars* (*Libri de vita Caesarum*) offer an intriguing stew of sober doings and trivial details. On the one hand, we find speculation about Caesar's rationale for starting a bloody civil war (*Jul.* 30). On the other, we learn that wits at the court of Gaius (Caligula) put slippers on the hands of Claudius, the future emperor, when he dozed off at table so that he would rub his face with them when he awoke (*Cl.* 8). These biographies of the first Roman emperors and their forerunner, Julius Caesar, are rich in information and detail, but what relationship do they have to reality? Suetonius preserves much that was said and written about the emperors during the time in which they lived and not long afterward, but as our own experience tells us, much that is said and written is not impartial. The *Caesars* contain a mass of material to be sifted and weighed. We can be grateful that Suetonius preserved the quantity of information that he did, for the biographies provide a window, as vivid as any from ancient Rome, of the world as it was then. The reader is left to determine whether they constitute a satisfying literary achievement or provide the emperors with believable personalities.

Suetonius

Gaius Suetonius Tranquillus was born around 70 CE into a well-off and at least moderately political family. He describes himself as a "young man" in reference to an event of 88 CE (*Ner.* 57.2) as well as to an unknown point in the reign of Domitian (81–96 CE; *Dom.* 12.2). His family was equestrian, members of the order that stood just below senators in social distinction. Suetonius' grandfather had been sufficiently intimate with the court of Gaius (Caligula) to report insider gossip about one of the emperor's wild enterprises (*Cal.* 19.3), and his father had served as a military tribune, an officer with the legions who fought for the emperor Otho in 69 CE (*Oth.* 10.1). An equestrian could pursue a military career as one option, but Suetonius followed a civilian path that included the law and, in his case, scholarship.

The literary *Letters* of Pliny the Younger (Gaius Plinius Caecilius Secundus, c. 61–112 CE) provide glimpses of Suetonius' progress. These may seem few and slight, but they are, in fact, more revealing than the evidence often available for ancient personalities. Pliny was a somewhat older contemporary of Suetonius and a fellow equestrian, but he climbed the ladder of elected office, entered the senate, and in the year 100 was appointed suffect (replacement) consul by the emperor Trajan (emperor 98–117 CE). The climax of his career came with his governorship of Bithynia-Pontus in Asia Minor, where he apparently died in about 112. Pliny was a man of letters and a political figure, not an unusual pairing, and he appears to have made Suetonius his protégé, advising and assisting him in both his scholarly efforts and the public arena.

At a fairly young age (around 97 CE),[1] Suetonius receives encouragement from Pliny when he is nervous about pleading a case in court. Pliny rallies him but will try to have the case postponed if Suetonius cannot recover his nerve (*Letters* 1.18). When Suetonius is trying to buy a small estate near Rome, Pliny intervenes to get him a good price, calling it a property particularly suitable for a scholar (*scholasticus; Letters* 1.24). A little later (101–3 CE) Pliny arranges a commission for him as military tribune, but Suetonius, apparently uninterested in a military career, asks that it be transferred to a cousin. Pliny applauds the tact with which Suetonius has made the request and praises him for his family loyalty (*Letters* 3.8).

By about 105 CE Pliny is urging Suetonius to introduce to the public a literary work that he has been slow to publish. It is already "finished and perfect," Pliny writes, and he calls on their "good friendship" to strengthen his argument (*Letters* 5.10). But then it is Pliny who asks for advice. Should he have his freedman read his poetry for him at a public recitation or should he read it himself, even if he reads badly? (*Letters* 9.34) Finally, perhaps around 110, Pliny uses his influential position to intervene for Suetonius in order to obtain for him a significant favor. At this time he was governor of Bithynia and probably had Suetonius on his staff. He petitions the emperor Trajan to grant the childless Suetonius, "a very learned man," the "right of three children" (*ius trium liberorum*), the considerable rights and privileges given to all men with that credential (*Letters* 10.94). Trajan does grant the request but writes that it is

---

1. Dates here come from the publication dates of Pliny's *Letters*.

something that he does "sparingly" and stresses how unusual a bene-
faction it is (*Letters* 10.95). Pliny's *Letters* expose a world in which
political and literary circles were closely joined and patronage was
indispensable.

These were encouraging beginnings for Suetonius, but the success that he later achieved could not have been anticipated. He rose
to hold the most important and influential positions available to an
equestrian, service in the imperial secretariat. The *Historia Augusta*,
a fourth-century compilation of imperial biographies, reports that
he served as *ab epistulis*, secretary in charge of imperial correspondence, under the emperor Hadrian (emperor 117–38 CE; *Hadrian*
11.3). The *Historia Augusta* is a highly imaginative work of dubious
authority, but confirmation of Suetonius' position at court came
in 1950 when a damaged inscription, plausibly from a statue base,
turned up in Algeria at the site of the ancient seaport Hippo Regius.
The inscription confirms that Suetonius served as *ab epistulis* and
provides additional information about his career. It lists a priesthood, appointment to the juror roll by Trajan, another priesthood,
and then three secretarial positions: *a studiis* (a kind of adviser on
cultural affairs), *a bybliothecis* (presumably in charge of libraries and
records), and finally *ab epistulis* by appointment of Hadrian. Damage
to the inscription prevents certainty about who appointed him to
the first two secretarial positions. It may have been with the blessing of Trajan that he entered the imperial service. Pliny, as we have
seen, had called him to Trajan's attention. If so, his responsibilities
may have continued under Hadrian, who made the last appointment.
Alternatively, Hadrian named him to all three posts. The African
provenance of the inscription suggests that Suetonius' family had its
roots there. Such a connection is not inconsistent with Suetonius'
own testimony that he was in Rome as a young man and was educated in the city (*Lives of the Grammarians* 4.6). A statue at Hippo
Regius might honor a favorite son who had made good.

The date that Suetonius left Hadrian's court is as uncertain as
the date of his arrival. His departure is said to have been connected
with that of the praetorian prefect Gaius Septicius Clarus, commander of the elite praetorian guard that served the emperor. This
was the most important equestrian military position, and Septicius
held it under Hadrian at the same time that Suetonius served as his
ab epistulis, a top civilian position. Septicius was also a protégé of
Pliny, who had dedicated the first book of his *Letters* to him, and

Suetonius would dedicate at least the first book of his *Caesars* to him.
Their interlocked careers indicate a circle of patronage. The *Historia
Augusta* reports that both Suetonius and Septicius were dismissed
from the court in 122 CE because they were "too familiar" with the
empress. Some lack of respect or disregard of protocol should be
imagined. But this collection of biographies is notoriously wrong
about dates, and the inscription at Hippo Regius offers a possible
later time for Suetonius' departure. Hadrian toured the province
of Africa in 128 CE, and if Suetonius was still connected with the
court, he would have accompanied him. The inscription in the
African town might then have commemorated imperial generosity
with his secretary instrumental in its award. No more is known of
Suetonius after this, but the length of his service to the emperor has
been thought to bear on the composition of the *Caesars*. Whatever
its duration, he had spent time as an insider at the center of power
and knew how the emperor worked, and he was equipped to add his
opinion to current assumptions about what made a good emperor
good and a bad one bad.

Suetonius' Writings and Ancient Biography

That Suetonius was a prolific author can perhaps be inferred from
Pliny's letters, but explicit evidence is found in the *Suda*, a Byzantine
historical encyclopedia compiled near the end of the tenth century.
This has an entry on Tranquillus (as Suetonius was sometimes called
in antiquity) that attributes to him a large number of titles. From
the *Suda* and a few other random references a dozen titles emerge.
These writings appear to be compilations, encyclopedic works themselves, with titles such as "On the Names and Types of Clothes,"
"On Roman Spectacles and Games," and "On Physical Defects."[2]
Two of these, in Greek and abridged, turned up in the nineteenth
century: "On Words of Insult" and "On Greek Games." Only one
title among these nonbiographical works seems to be an outlier; "On
Cicero's *Republic*" was evidently a polemic against a detractor of the
republican orator.

Rome inherited much of its literary culture from its Greek intellectual masters, including ideas about genre and the boundaries
between categories of literary composition. Epic poetry was not to

---

2. For the complete list, see Wallace-Hadrill, 43 n. 22.

be confused with lyric; each had a distinct meter and its own appropriate content. Prose had its genres, too: philosophical dialogues, history, oratory, literary letters, and so forth. These types also followed rules, although perhaps not so clearly defined as those for poetry. History dealt with events broadly, with events that concerned nations, and with kings and battles. It used a narrative structure and formal language, but it necessarily included persons too, and this at least in part gave biography its beginnings. Thucydides introduces his readers to Pericles as Homer does Achilles, but there is a difference between biographical elements embedded in history and epic and the recognition of biography as a separate genre with its own limitations and possibilities. The modern scholar Arnaldo Momigliano defined it simply as "an account of the life of a man from birth to death,"[3] more than a person's involvement in public affairs. The origin of "lives" (what the Greeks called biographies) as a genre is obscure, but by the end of the fourth century BCE, Greeks had begun to produce collections of lives in series—the lives of poets or generals or philosophers, for instance. Such collections indicate an interest in the type of individual as opposed to the particular individual himself. Juxtaposed examples ask the question, "What is a good (and by implication bad) poet (or general or philosopher)?"

Biography had roots in Rome as well. Romans took their ancestors seriously, proud to ride the coattails of their forbearers' accomplishments. A long tradition of funeral orations listed the attainments of the dead, and grave tablets and public monuments preserved lists of offices held and responsibilities fulfilled. The inscription for Suetonius at Hippo Regius, posthumous or not, fits the model. The best known of these is Augustus' own detailed cataloging of his achievements, his *Res gestae*, his "things done," his deeds.[4] Augustus intended to have this record inscribed in bronze and posted outside his Mausoleum, the tomb that he built for himself and his family. It recorded his accomplishments arranged by category: wars won, games sponsored, benefactions bestowed, public works constructed—categories to be revisited in Suetonius' *Caesars*.

---

3. Momigliano, *Greek Biography*, 11.

4. The document is properly called the *Monumentum Ancyranum* because a copy of it was found inscribed on the wall of a temple of Rome and Augustus in Ancyra in Galatia (modern Turkey).

The first truly unambiguous statement of a biographical tradition comes not in Greek writings where it might be expected but from Cornelius Nepos (c. 100–24 BCE), a Roman who lived and worked in the late Republic and into the reign of Augustus. Among Nepos' many writings was *De viris illustribus*, "On Famous Men," some part of which survives. In this work Nepos not only advanced the practice of offering lives in series (philosophers, orators, and so forth) but made a second distinction as well; he divided his subjects into Roman and non-Roman to create an additional point of comparison. In one of the biographies in his series on foreign generals (a portion of his work that is extant), he states that he is writing biography and makes it clear that biography is different from history: "I fear that if I begin to set forth the deeds [of my subject], I will seem not to be narrating a biography but rather writing a history" (*Pelopidas* 1.1). He has already apologized for biography in his preface, apparently acknowledging that he saw it as a poor cousin to history. He writes, "I do not doubt that there will be many readers who will judge this kind of writing trivial and unworthy of the characters of great men"—and here he expands the content permitted to biography— "when they read the report of who taught music to Epaminondas or find it among his virtues that he danced well or played the pipes with skill" (*Preface* 1).

Late in the first century CE, Plutarch (Mestrius Plutarchus, c. 50–120 CE), a Greek very much integrated into the larger Roman world, chose to follow Nepos' lead in comparing lives across cultures. He wrote twenty-three pairs of biographies that juxtaposed prominent public figures, Greek and Roman. He also wrote a series of lives of Roman emperors, two of which, those of Galba and Otho, have survived. Plutarch, like Nepos, states clearly, "I am writing not history, but lives" (*Alexander* 1.1). He intended to instruct by presenting good and bad behaviors.

Biography was thus a genre choice available to Suetonius in the early second century, and he, like Nepos, also wrote volumes titled *De viris illustribus*, "On Famous Men"—his own extensive collection of lives. Suetonius' subjects were Roman poets, orators, historians, philosophers, grammarians, and rhetoricians, probably well over a hundred entries all told. A partial list and an estimate of the scope of the series has been extracted from the work of the fourth-century Christian scholar Jerome, who used Suetonius as his source for his own encyclopedic *Chronicle*. Some few remnants of Suetonius' biographies of poets (Terence, Horace, Lucan, and Virgil) have survived in abbreviated and edited form because ancient scholars appropriated them and attached them to commentaries on their works. Bits about one orator, Passienus Crispus, and one historian, Pliny the Elder, have also come down to us. But two categories, grammarians and rhetoricians, have survived, the first complete, the second in part. These lives are quite brief; Suetonius probably found no great quantity of information on which he could draw. But his very choice of teachers, grammarians and rhetoricians, the fact that he did not limit himself to the types that Nepos and his Greek predecessors had chosen, points to the particular interests of the *scholasticus*. All of his categories, in fact—poets, orators, historians, and philosophers, as well as these less obvious two—bear on literature and education. Emperors would come later in the *Caesars* and have more in common with Nepos' kings and generals and Plutarch's public men. The publication date of Suetonius' *De viris illustribus* is unknown, and it may not all have been put before the public at the same time. When Pliny wrote of something already "finished and perfect" in about 105 CE (*Letters* 5.10), he may have had it or some part of it in mind. It plausibly preceded the *Caesars* and Suetonius' entry into the imperial service and would surely have enhanced his literary reputation; perhaps it was what allowed Pliny to recommend Suetonius as a "very learned man" (Pliny, *Letters* 10.94). *De viris illustribus* may have been a bridge between his encyclopedic writings and the *Caesars*, an ambitious collection in which Suetonius cataloged the deeds and attributes of the early Roman emperors as he had cataloged games and insults, and compared his emperors as he and earlier biographers had compared poets, orators, and philosophers.

Libri de vita Caesarum

Background

Suetonius almost certainly published his *Caesars*, at least in part, when he was serving in his official capacity at court. The opening pages of the biography of Julius Caesar, his first subject, are lost, but they contained a dedication to Septicius Clarus, Pliny's protégé and Hadrian's praetorian prefect. This information was reported by John Lydus, a sixth-century Byzantine scholar, who saw the complete text. The dedication strongly suggests that this first of the *Caesars* was published while both Suetonius and Septicius were connected to the court, before they were dismissed in 122 CE—if that was truly the case.

By the time in which Suetonius wrote, emperors and the empire were a fact. The coalescence of powers that was the principate had turned into a job that never did acquire a job description but for which there were nonetheless hopes and expectations of performance and character. Suetonius' sponsor, Pliny the Younger, had set these criteria out clearly. When Pliny became suffect consul by the grace of Trajan in the year 100 CE, he thanked the emperor with the customary fulsome speech in the senate. This speech he later revised and expanded, and it has survived as a literary document referred to as his *Panegyricus*, an elaborate flattery that catalogs all the good things that Trajan did and all of the qualities that he exemplified. Negative examples from past reigns are included for comparison. The aptness of such praise is irrelevant, and the message that it delivered was in any case more prescriptive than descriptive, since Trajan had been emperor for less than two years.

But the rhetorical artifact did describe an ideal. Pliny lists Trajan's consulships, military achievements, financial generosity, building projects, administration of justice, sound governance, and the entertainments that he sponsored for the populace. Personal qualities are gathered into virtues, abstractions such as generosity, clemency, citizenlike behavior, self-restraint, and so on. Many of his virtues are peculiarly "imperial" in that they fit a man acting from a position of superior power. The *Panegyricus* assumes that an emperor's private persona lay behind his public achievement, that private and public behaviors were interlocked. And so we learn about Trajan's table manners and sleeping habits, the pleasure he took in hunting, and even the modesty of his wife and sister. The same assumption had allowed Nepos to contemplate a music master and dance skills in his biography of a general. An emperor should furthermore look the part. Trajan was tall and carried himself handsomely. His white hair added to the impression of maturity. Physiognomy, the pseudoscience of determining character from physical characteristics, was thought a useful tool.

Pliny, the suffect consul, and Suetonius, the imperial secretary, were both insiders who ostensibly subscribed to the value system of the *Panegyricus*. Suetonius seems almost to have adopted it as his handbook when he wrote the *Caesars*. He singles out many of the same actions for praise or blame and includes a fair sampling of the virtues that Pliny describes, using them not only as criteria for judgment but as organizing motifs for important segments of his work. Biography by definition looks to the past, and it would have been presumptuous for Suetonius to suggest that his *Caesars* were intended to educate the reigning emperor. But both they and the *Panegyricus* are similarly prescriptive by implication since they introduce the concept of the ideal emperor. Emperors were an ambitious category to take on—even though Plutarch had shown the way.

Sources and Composition

Suetonius found most, although not all, of his information in written sources, in histories and memoirs that have not survived. This is clear from correspondences between the content of his *Caesars* and the content of the histories that cover the same period, those of his somewhat older contemporary Cornelius Tacitus, and Cassius Dio, who wrote a history of Rome in Greek a hundred years later. Suetonius augmented sober historical sources with pamphlet literature as his collection of invective against Julius Caesar suggests (*Jul.* 49, 73) and with hearsay such as he tapped in reference to Claudius' behavior in the law courts ("I used to hear from my elders . . ." *Cl.* 15.3). He did something else that appeals to modern standards for serious research: he relied on original documents. He consulted the "public record," a posted list of happenings in Rome, for evidence about Gaius' birthplace (*Cal.* 8.2), and he was able to judge the originality of Nero's poetry because he had seen the manuscript in the emperor's handwriting (*Ner.* 52). He quoted from Tiberius' addresses to the senate (*Tib.* 28). Most impressively, he accessed the correspondence of Augustus and used it to illustrate the emperor's problem in dealing with his wife's unpromising grandson, the future emperor Claudius (*Cl.* 4), and to show that Augustus, contrary to the received tradition, did indeed value his adopted son Tiberius (*Tib.* 21.4–7). Such investigations were not wholly unique. The historian Tacitus retrieved senatorial records and petitioned Pliny to tell him about his uncle's death during the eruption of Mount Vesuvius in 79 CE (Pliny, *Letters* 6.16, 20). But a historian would digest and rework this information. Suetonius, on the other hand, copied Augustus' engaging letters directly into his text. The emperor's letters about his gambling and snacks are priceless, as is the amazingly intimate correspondence with Mark Antony about their sex partners.

Some scholars have thought that Suetonius' status as court insider gave him particular access to imperial correspondence, speeches, and manuscripts and that he was especially conversant with archival materials because he served as *a bybliothecis* (whatever duties that position covered). It has also been thought that such special access to privileged materials was relevant to the composition of the *Caesars* because when Suetonius was no longer at court, he lost this access. We do not, however, really know what imperial archives were or if any even existed as such. Other documents went unpublished; for example, Augustus did not want Julius Caesar's youthful writings made public (*Jul.* 56.7). Because other ancient authors cited Augustus' correspondence as well, it must have been available somewhere, with some degree of access.[5] Perhaps one needed to move in acceptable political or literary circles or be known as a friendly commentator in order to see it, but one did not have to be a ranking court official.

The issue of access to unpublished materials arises because of the apparent difference in the care taken with the first of the *Caesars*, Julius Caesar, compared to the last, Domitian. The lives appear to have been written more or less in the order in which they stand, that is, in the chronological order in which the emperors reigned. The dedication to Septicius Clarus indicates that the Julian life was published first, and since the life of the Divine Augustus is intact but does not have its own introduction, it was probably published at the same time. But was the dedication only for these first two? Did it introduce the first six, perhaps—those of the emperors through Nero? Or was it for all twelve as we have them? It would be helpful to have those opening pages of the life of the Divine Julius if Suetonius included in them, along with the dedication, a statement about the scope of his project.

The biographies of Julius Caesar and Augustus are long and detailed. Suetonius names his sources and identifies individuals. The lives of the other Julio-Claudian emperors (Tiberius, Gaius, Claudius, and Nero) are less expansive; sources are hinted at rather than named ("Reliable authors have added . . . " *Ner.* 34.4), and many names have become "a certain man" or "a man of praetorian rank." But extensive and careful research remains in the genealogies of the Claudii (*Tib.* 1–4) and the Domitii (*Ner.* 1–5) and most conspicuously

---

5. Tacitus, *Dialogus de oratoribus* 13.2; Quintilian, *Institutio oratoria* 1.6.19; Pliny the Elder, *Naturalis historia* 13.83.

in the investigation of the birthplace of Gaius (*Cal.* 8). The letters of Augustus still appear as long as they are available. Care is taken with the finished product. This is less the case with the last six *Caesars*, those of the interregnum emperors of the civil war that followed the death of Nero (Galba, Otho, Vitellius) and the Flavians (Vespasian, Titus, Domitian). Investigations into genealogy (always an interest) persist, but these biographies are much shorter. A number of these emperors did not reign long (neither did Gaius), but Vespasian and Domitian ruled for longer periods and still their biographies fill fewer pages proportionally than do those of the Julio-Claudians. Gaps seem to indicate cutting from a fuller text. Otho leaves Rome, but where is he going? (*Oth.* 8.3) Vitellius' parents are horrified at the prophecy that their son will one day govern a province, but why? (*Vit.* 3.2) The life of the Divine Titus seems inserted into a transplanted eulogy. This cursory treatment has been difficult to explain since Suetonius lived through the reigns of the Flavian emperors as a child and young adult and would have known individuals who had experienced the civil war years of 68 and 69 CE. More eyewitness reports would have been welcome.

Suetonius' own biography has been used to explain this increasing loss of focus. One supposition has been that when he and Septicius were made to leave the court, he lost access to the imperial archives and could no longer write with the detail that he had lavished on Julius and Augustus and, to a lesser extent, on the other Julio-Claudians. But this explanation is not convincing, since access to the sources he used seems to have been fairly widely available. Alternatively, dismissal could have dimmed his enthusiasm as he plodded through his project to the end. But Andrew Wallace-Hadrill has noted that Suetonius' *De viris illustribus* focused on the grammarians and rhetoricians of the late Republic and the Augustan years, precisely the period covered in the first two *Caesars*. He has further suggested that this was the period that the scholarly Suetonius found truly interesting. Suetonius appears to have been much less concerned with more recent history, especially with the emperors who came after Nero.[6]

The difference between the life of Julius Caesar and that of Domitian can also be explained by competition from a contemporary. Tacitus, suffect consul and governor of Asia in 111–12 CE, had published his historical books called *Histories* in 109 or 110. These

---

6. Wallace-Hadrill, 61–66.

covered the years of the civil wars after the death of Nero and the reigns of the Flavians, the emperors Galba through Domitian in all. In 110 or shortly thereafter, Tacitus probably began working on his *Annals*, books that covered the reigns of the emperors Tiberius through Nero. We cannot know when Suetonius conceived the idea of his imperial biographies, but the facts of his biography suggest that it could have been at about this same time or perhaps somewhat later. As a member of the Roman literary world, he would have known that Tacitus' new work started with the reign of Tiberius and did not deal with the time of Julius Caesar and Augustus. These figures were free, so to speak, and available for expansive treatment. With the other Julio-Claudians, Suetonius would compete with Tacitus on his own terms; he would write biography and not history, digging into family histories not found in the *Annals*, tapping his own primary sources and adding the personal detail appropriate to a different genre. But why write about the last six Caesars at all if he found them uninteresting? The biographies of Galba through Domitian parallel the matter of Tacitus' *Histories*, a work that covered the history of the period under the same six emperors. Suetonius felt it important to conform to the parameters defined by the renowned consular historian and plausibly to accept them as the boundary for the series of biographies that he had begun.

Organization

Suetonius chose to organize most elements of his biographies by topics or rubrics, as they are often called.[7] Arrangement under headings was not unlike the method he would have used in his works that listed and cataloged games and insults. At the turn of the twentieth century a German scholar, Friedrich Leo, proposed that such an organization had been developed for the biographies of literary men specifically and that Suetonius had transferred it to his biographies of Roman emperors.[8] He further suggested that this method did not work very well for political figures. Although Leo has been judged overly accepting of the idea that the ancients relied inflexibly on genre distinctions, as well as excessively speculative in thinking that arrangement by rubric

---

7. "Rubric" derives from the red letters with which key words can be written to distinguish them from the body of a text.

8. F. Leo, *Die griechisch-römische Biographie* (Leipzig: B. G. Teubner, 1901).

had developed exclusively for biographies of literary figures, he was correct in thinking that Suetonius had set himself a difficult task. It was challenging to find a place for provincial government, military achievement, and judicial style in a text that also described the color of an emperor's eyes and his food preferences.

Despite Suetonius' choice to proceed by rubric, chronology is implicit in biography if it is to trace the whole of a man's life "from birth to death." Suetonius does begin with birth and end with death, and he even reaches back before birth to ancestry. After that comes the emperor's life before his accession. Suetonius arranges each emperor's reign by topic or rubric, allotting space for physical description and personal habits. Some rubrics are concrete—Julius Caesar's eccentric dress, for instance (*Jul.* 45.3). Others are abstract, such as Claudius' fearfulness (*Cl.* 35.1–37.2) or Vespasian's cupidity (*Ves.* 16). Omens may predict death, and chronology returns with death itself and perhaps a coda of some sort. Rubrics are nested in chronology. The *Caesars* trace this pattern in a very general way, but each life presented an organizational challenge.

The life of the Divine Augustus conforms to the pattern most closely. Ancestry, birth, and a very short summation of Augustus' life are followed by a statement that his reign is to be presented by topic (*Aug.* 9). First comes a rubric of the wars that brought him to sole power. Rubrics of administration follow and reach a climax with the honors awarded him. A second transitional statement announces a turn to private life (*Aug.* 61), and this is followed by family relationships, friendships, his habits and amusements, his temperance, simplicity, and generosity, and after that his sleeping habits, physical appearance, even his idiosyncratic spelling conventions—the complete list is long. Religious practices and dreams make an apt preamble to omens predictive first of his lifelong greatness and then of his death. At the end comes the death narrative and Augustus' will. Rubrics nested in chronology, indeed, within a carefully controlled structure. It is tempting to think that Suetonius wrote this well-ordered biography of Augustus before tackling the life of Julius Caesar, a less obvious candidate for inclusion in the series.

Julius Caesar had a long run to sole power, and so chronology persists until his return to Rome after the civil war. Suetonius treats his dictatorship as the equivalent of an imperial reign. The lost portion at the beginning surely contained his ancestry, birth, and early years. Narrative turns unannounced into rubrics related to public life:

triumphs, the reform of the calendar, and building projects, to name a few. Next should come the events that lead to his death, but Suetonius postpones them and announces that he will describe the private man (*Jul.* 44.4). Personal rubrics follow: physical appearance, sexual behavior, food intake, military skill, and (as with Augustus) much, much else. Concrete rubrics evolve into rubrics of abstract qualities: loyalty, kindness, mercy, moderation—but finally arrogance, and it is this last rubric that returns the biography neatly back to chronology, for in Suetonius' judgment it was Caesar's arrogance that prompted his assassination. Rubrics again lie nested in chronology. These first two lives are not only the most thorough; they also call attention to their structure and represent the most satisfying execution. Suetonius clearly expended considerable thought and effort on both.

Chronology and rubrics continue to be juggled for the remaining *Caesars*, and attention is still called to structure even if not as thoroughly as with Julius Caesar and Augustus. With three evil emperors, Suetonius makes a central division not between public and private, as with Augustus and Caesar, but between good and evil. The reign of Gaius (Caligula) is organized first around neutral actions: consulships, entertainments, and public works. Then Suetonius writes, "So far, this has been about an emperor . . . what is left is about a monster" (*Cal.* 22.1), and he arranges Gaius' deviant behavior under arrogance, sexual misbehavior, and cruelty. In the life of Nero the strategy is similar, for Suetonius writes that he first collected "irreproachable" actions and those "worthy of praise to some degree" but then moves on to speak of "disgusting acts and criminal deeds" (*Ner.* 19.3). The life of Domitian has a good–bad division too but lacks clarity in that it occurs twice (*Dom.* 3.2, 10.1).

Like Julius Caesar, Tiberius had long experience with public affairs before he became emperor at the age of fifty-five, and chronology persists similarly in his biography. Suetonius perceives Tiberius as taking a turn for the worse with his self-exile on Capri midway through his reign (*Tib.* 39–41). As a result, good–bad and public–private distinctions are subsumed to a degree within a chronological structure. Nor is the life of the Divine Claudius so tidy. Here Suetonius separates the public emperor and the private man as with Julius Caesar and Augustus, but as a transition he describes Claudius as the perennial toady of his wives and freedmen (*Cl.* 25.5). Suetonius makes generally positive remarks about the public figure, but overall his statements about the man are negative. The well-intentioned

Vespasian was easier to deal with, and the public–private dichotomy works better in this abbreviated biography. But the structure of rubrics within chronology comes close to disappearing with the three emperors whose brief reigns followed that of Nero and with the quasi-eulogistic treatment of the Flavian Titus. Birth and death do, of course, surround other material; Suetonius continues to honor the emperors' genealogy; and some rubrics survive, even though an abbreviated narrative form occupies more space. Of course, these emperors reigned so briefly that they executed scarcely any administrative measures that could be described in distinct rubrics.

This imperative toward clear organization continues on the paragraph level as well. Suetonius takes pains to help his readers follow his intent, and so topic sentences serve as careful and precise outlines. "Some terrible disasters happened while [Titus] was emperor," writes Suetonius, and he lists three: the eruption of Vesuvius, a huge fire in Rome, and an unprecedented plague. He then describes each with some detail in the same order (*Tit.* 8.3). On a larger scale, Gaius' innate cruelty is introduced (*Cal.* 27.1). Indiscriminate cruelty expands to include verbal cruelty (29.1) and is further particularized as cruelty while at rest, at play, and at dinner (32.1–3). But complex goals can make clarity a struggle. Suetonius announces (in a single sentence) that he will describe Claudius' dealings with religious, civilian, and military customs and with all social classes both in Rome and abroad, as well as his reforms and revivals of old practices and his introduction of new ones (*Cl.* 22). Categories, geography, and time overlap, and Suetonius works hard to organize disparate material.

Another imperative appears to have been a desire to be thorough, to include all the information that he had, to get it all in somehow. It is impossible, to be sure, to know when something has been left out, but odd facts in odd places seem to betray an effort to find a place in which to put everything, to have no bits left over when he had finished. In his account of Tiberius' young manhood, Suetonius notes his first marriage to Vipsania, then moves on to their divorce and his second marriage to Julia, daughter of Augustus, their deteriorated relationship, and the death of their child. What had begun in chronology has turned into a marriage rubric. Next, rather awkwardly, comes Tiberius' attentive piety toward his dead brother Drusus (*Tib.* 7.2–3). Suetonius could apparently find no more closely related material to which to join this information about the relationship between the brothers, and a marriage rubric has in the end become a rubric of family relationships. In a rubric of dinner parties in the life of the Divine Claudius, the emperor is said to have liked to give large banquets, and two examples illustrate the point. Next comes his inclusion of children at his dinners to portray his old-fashioned values, then his treatment of a guest who supposedly stole a golden goblet to demonstrate his clever management, and then an edict excusing farts at the table to exemplify his trivial and eccentric concerns (*Cl.* 32). The dinner table is a hook on which to hang essentially disparate items.

But do Suetonius' rubrics as they stand generate lifelike portraits of human beings? The *Caesars* inspire comparison with cubist painting. Virtues and vices stick out at odd angles, a bit like arms and legs in a Picasso. He did not intend to make his subjects come alive by any modern literary standard, and it is unfair to ask it of him. The thorough *scholasticus* tapped into a tradition valued for its presentation of facts, and apparently his temperament, talent, and experience motivated him to pursue this goal in as orderly a fashion as he could. The reader is invited to assemble his or her own emperor.

Style

The word "style" in the same sentence with "Suetonius" will seem an oxymoron to those who accept the conventional judgment that Suetonius' style is abominable, or more accurately, that he has none. "He is no real writer," wrote a commentator in the early twentieth century.[9] Although much of his writing is indeed inelegant, this statement is not quite true.

Since Suetonius was writing biography, his *Caesars* had license to break the rules for historical composition and include technical terms normally not found in literature. A procurator with a salary of 200,000 sesterces is a *ducenarius* (*Cl.* 24.1), and an ersatz military appointment is *supra numerum* (*Cl.* 25.1). Both terms occur in inscriptions from this period but not in literature. The Greek words and phrases pervasive in conversation but out of place in proper Latin prose appear in the *Caesars*. Suetonius includes lampoons verbatim (*Jul.* 49; *Tib.* 59; *Ner.* 39), quotes edicts and addresses directly (*Tib.*

---

9. G. Funaioli under "Suetonius," in *Real-Encyclopädie der classischen Altertumswissenschaft*, vol. IV A (Stuttgart: J. B. Metzler, 1931), column 621.

28; *Dom.* 11.3), and copies in Augustus' letters, as has been noted (*Aug.* 71, 76; *Tib.* 21; *Cal.* 8.4; *Cl.* 4). The modern reader welcomes these anomalies as vivid additions, although contemporary readers might have found them odd. Less pleasing is his descent into pedantry: he inspects variants of the title of a speech by Julius Caesar (*Jul.* 55.3), digresses on the linguistic history of the Latin words for "boy" and "girl" (*Cal.* 8.3), and comments on Augustus' idiosyncratic word choices (*Aug.* 87.2).

Suetonius often seems disinterested in how he puts his mass of information on the page. On the one hand (ostensibly to hurry his story along), he can be brief to the point of being cryptic: "[Claudius] suppressed a section of the *lex Papia Poppaea* that had been added under Tiberius on the assumption that men over sixty could not father children" (*Cl.* 23.1). It takes effort to understand that Claudius adjusted the law to forgive penalties imposed on childless men over sixty because the earlier assumption had been that they were unable to father children, but the new assumption was that they could still fulfill their obligation to procreate beyond that age and so were subject to penalty if they did not do so.

On the other hand, many sentences are packed full of the circumstantial information that provides context for his central argument, plausibly from the same impetus to hurry things forward. Participles and all variety of subordinate constructions pile on to set the scene for the main verb that reports what the emperor did or intended to do. In a single packed sentence, Suetonius tells us that Gaius arbitrarily sent away criminals (as lunch for hungry beasts) after a preamble recognizes the fact that the cattle necessary to feed beasts being readied for the arena were expensive, that he had looked the prisoners over but ignored the charges against them, and that he had done this while standing in the center of a colonnade (*Cal.* 27.1). Tiberius' neglect of his sick mother, her death, the postponement of her burial leading to the putrefaction of her body, and the refusal of divine honors for her are all dependent on verbs that express the emperor's not caring and prohibiting (*Tib.* 51.2). Such sentences read like the tactic of someone pushing through circumstantial information quickly before he loses his reader's attention. Sentences may pile on top of one another, each adding a fact of its own. The choppy sequence gives a disconnected and unsatisfactory feel. This is especially true with the chronological narrative of Julius Caesar's career.

   This charge—that Suetonius did nothing more than cram information onto the page—can often be maintained, but stylistic grace notes occasionally occur: Titus dismisses his paramour Berenice— "both he and she were unwilling"; the short Latin sentence ends with two forms of the word "unwilling" juxtaposed (*invitus invitam; Tit.* 7.2). Conjunctions and their absence supply variation: a literal translation of the Latin would make the offspring of Germanicus "Agrippina, Drusilla, Livilla," and then "Nero and Drusus and Gaius Caesar" (*Cal.* 7). Claudius' lack of solid research embarrasses him when he charges "bachelorhood and childlessness and poverty" against those who turn out to be "husbands, fathers, wealthy men" (*Cl.* 16.3); in the Latin, three abstract nouns (with conjunctions) return as three concrete nouns (without conjunctions). This may not be subtle elegance, but such devices are clearly studied efforts.

   The chief ingredient of Suetonius' style, however, derives from the organizational imperative already noted, his drive toward order and tidiness; what occurs in larger units works on the sentence level as well. Rubric sentences are often balanced internally. One of the sentences that marks the change from Domitian's positive to negative actions reads: "He continued on a path neither of mercy nor of restraint in his financial dealings, but he plunged rather more quickly into cruelty than into greed" (*Dom.* 10.1). The Latin contains four abstract qualities, two positive, two negative, two in each half of a balanced sentence. Mercy will become cruelty and financial responsibility will turn into greed. Two look back to what has already been described; two look forward. Suetonius continues: Domitian "killed a number of senators" (*Dom.* 10.2), and the names of ten victims march through the paragraphs that follow, in the Latin each at or near the beginning of its sentence, each the object of a verb, as the murders are detailed. Such sentences are crafted to make his message clear. The dismissive treatment of the young Claudius is illustrated in successive sentences, each beginning in the Latin with the relationship and name of a family member as the subject: mother Antonia, grandmother Livia, sister Livilla. The name of a fourth family member, great-uncle Augustus, is brought to a forward position in the next sentence to be parallel to the other three although he is not the subject of the main clause (*Cl.* 3.2). Even the repeated (and monotonous) third-person singular past-tense verbs with the emperor as their subject maintain focus.

Historical Value

Suetonius has not only been judged "no real writer." He has also been accused of being nothing but a gossipmonger, a purveyor of juicy scandal. Sadism and debauchery do find a place among more benign behaviors, but it is not the inclusion of these elements that were permitted in biography that decreases the value of the *Caesars* as a historical source. Rather, the most significant impediment to the reconstruction of events is Suetonius' use of rubrics to carry much of his information. Chronology is not totally absent, as has been noted, and narrative sequence is sometimes present, but outside evidence is necessary to locate the contents of rubrics in time.

Suetonius would have assumed that his readers could follow the sense when he pulled events apart and inserted them variously, but it scarcely mattered since history was not his aim. The siege at Dyrrachium (of major importance in the war between Julius Caesar and Pompey the Great) surfaces a number of times, but its significance is never explained. Instead, the siege was of long duration and the siege walls were high (*Jul.* 35.1), and Pompey did not follow up on his advantage (*Jul.* 36). The siege was a reason for Caesar's daring to cross the Adriatic in winter (*Jul.* 58.2), and Dyrrachium was where Caesar's men showed hardihood (*Jul.* 68.2) and where a rare Caesarean defeat took place (*Jul.* 68.3). In the life of the Divine Augustus the triumvir Marcus Aemilius Lepidus is dead at *Aug.* 31.1 but rather disconcertingly present in an anecdote at *Aug.* 54.

Suetonius sometimes turns a single action into a generalization; if one of his emperors does something once, the action is said to be habitual. Claudius forced a freedman back into slave status in 46 CE; Suetonius implies that he made it a rule (*Cl.* 25.1). Domitian had a habit of watching staged naval battles during torrential rains (*Dom.* 4.2), but only one such downpour is known.

Furthermore, Suetonius' close focus on his imperial subjects makes him rigorous in excluding everything not directly pertinent to them as individuals. The progress of a war in the provinces might be crucial for a historian. Nero's general Gnaeus Domitius Corbulo, for instance, settled affairs in Armenia and kept that geographically strategic state a client kingdom within the empire, but because Nero was not personally involved in Asia Minor, Suetonius ignores events there. His only notice of this campaign is the arrival of Armenia's King Tiridates in Rome, an opportunity for Suetonius to describe

Nero's obsession with extravagant spectacle (*Ner.* 13). He does make exception for ancestors, especially Drusus the Elder, the father of Germanicus (*Cl.* 1), and Germanicus himself, the father of Gaius (*Cal.* 1–6). These two figures have their own minibiographies.

Despite these obstacles to the reconstruction of events, the modern historian can find much of value in the *Caesars*. Suetonius has sometimes recorded facts and details when others have not. He is our only source for a second conspiracy against Nero (*Ner.* 36.1) and for the existence of a daughter of Claudius who was exposed and left to die (*Cl.* 27.1). Ordinary error may occur, but in general, what Suetonius offers can be accepted, or rather, more accurately, made subject to the same scrutiny required for all ancient historical material, an important caveat. The cliché that history is written by winners is literally true in the case of wars, of course, but the idea can be extended more broadly to include survivors of an unpopular regime or those pleased to have the past validate the present. As Tacitus acknowledged, history was written out of flattery or hatred.[10]

Bias figures in all historical texts from this period, those extant and also those that have been lost. The Flavian dynasty viewed Nero's theatrics from their more restrained perspective. Claudius had to dissociate himself from the erratic Gaius, who had preceded him and whose legitimate successor he, in a sense, was. Once these interpretations became layered in the historical tradition, they might be doubted or modified but were difficult to dislodge. Interestingly, Suetonius' work offers exceptions, since his use of Augustus' letters to correct misconceptions represents genuine revision. But the bias inherent in his sources nonetheless plays a role in the *Caesars* and joins the template for expressions of approval and disapproval of imperial behavior found in Pliny's *Panegyricus*.

More consistently reliable as historical value is the background information that Suetonius provides for his judgments. The offhand statement that Augustus imported attractive boys to play games with him because "he detested dwarfs and misshapen people and all grotesques of that kind" can be taken as evidence of how such individuals might be devalued (*Aug.* 83). Gaius started some races casually in response to the crowd as he was looking down on the Circus Maximus from a house on the Palatine Hill (*Cal.* 18.3); clearly, one could watch races from the comfort of a private house. In order

---

10. Tacitus, *Annals* 1.1; *Histories* 1.1.

to illustrate Galba's competency as a general, Gaius is said to have reviewed the legions of Upper Germany and pronounced them the best trained of all the assembled forces (*Gal.* 6.3). This statement affirms that the troop buildup for a campaign in Germany was real and that Gaius' much maligned military efforts were not the joke that they were usually alleged to be.

Yet the most valuable contribution to our historical understanding of the age from the gossipmonger Suetonius may lie in the gossip, the prejudiced material itself. Gaius probably did not cut through his victims with a saw, something that all tyrants were said to do (*Cal.* 27.3). Tiberius may not have indulged in so much innovative sex play on Capri (*Tib.* 43–45); what goes on behind closed doors (or on an island) is to be imagined. The specifics of Vitellius' gluttony may not be accurate, but they are good in the telling (*Vit.* 13). Suetonius, the careful scholar, anxious to record all that he knew, did not invent these stories. Others, however, did; their invention is a fact. It is worthwhile to ask who might have told them and when and whose interest they served. We can be grateful that Suetonius was the inclusive collector that he was.

Afterlife

As the Roman emperor became the dominant factor in governance, it was increasingly natural to view history as a series of personalities. A focus on the emperor was true even in Tacitus' annalistic writing, and a hundred years later Cassius Dio would organize the books of his *Roman History* by imperial reigns. Suetonius' *Caesars* spawned sequels. In the third century, Marius Maximus wrote about the twelve emperors who followed Domitian. Although this text is lost, traces of it in other writings reveal that its author was not shy about including notorious personal scandal. In the fourth century, the spurious *Historia Augusta* imagined the biographies of still more emperors on the Suetonian model. In the ninth century, the monk Einhard wrote *The Life of Charlemagne*, using Suetonius' life of the Divine Augustus as a model.

We know that a complete text of the *Caesars* existed in the sixth century because the scholar John Lydus was able to report the dedication to Septicius Clarus. But by the ninth century the one manuscript from which all known later manuscripts were derived had lost the first pages of the life of the Divine Julius and whatever preamble or introduction accompanied its dedication. The text began to be copied, and a number of manuscripts from the eleventh century exist. Interest accelerated during the later Middle Ages, and during the Renaissance the *Caesars* became extremely popular. The *Caesars* informed the Robert Graves novels of the 1950s, *I Claudius* and *Claudius the King*.

This Translation

This translation of Suetonius' *Caesars* is based on the 1908 edition of Maximilian Ihm (Teubner); significant textual difficulties are few. The translation has not attempted to impose more style on the text than the Latin has but to offer a readable and serviceable text in contemporary American English. The structure of most Latin sentences has not been imported into English, for to do so would make it cumbersome and awkward to read. Suetonius' sentences are often crowded in a way that only works in a highly inflected language such as Latin can be. However, as the discussion of his organization and style has tried to make clear, he made great efforts to set forth his material clearly and to present it neatly, and this orderliness has been transplanted into the English whenever it could be done without sacrificing readability. Topic sentences outline paragraphs as they do in the Latin.

The *Caesars* touch on about 180 years of particularly interesting Roman history, the period of change from republic to empire and the developing institutions of the altered government. The scope and the variety of material included make it a challenge to provide the background against which a reader in the twenty-first century can access it. The material in "What the Romans Knew," which follows, can be no more than a brief introduction to the history and social context dealt glancing blows by the text. This discussion is supplemented by a Glossary that extracts unfamiliar terms. The Index of Historical Names is intended to help the reader navigate the wealth of proper names; it includes people who make multiple appearances in the text and differentiates between people who have the same name, which happened frequently in ancient Rome. A Chronology of Major Events and family trees of the intermarried imperial families are provided. Place names receive ample attention in the maps and in the footnotes that identify, date, and synthesize events. The notes explain things (jokes, for instance) that would

otherwise be incomprehensible to the reader of a translation. But
they do not open the Pandora's box of interpretation by evaluating
Suetonius' contribution to historical understanding or commenting
on the accuracy of details. It is left to the reader to decide whether
Claudius was poisoned or died of natural causes.

Abbreviations appear throughout this volume as follows:

Julius	*Jul.*
Augustus	*Aug.*
Tiberius	*Tib.*
Gaius (Caligula)	*Cal.*
Claudius	*Cl.*
Nero	*Ner.*
Galba	*Gal.*
Otho	*Oth.*
Vitellius	*Vit.*
Vespasian	*Ves.*
Titus	*Tit.*
Domitian	*Dom.*

WHAT THE ROMANS KNEW: ROME AND ITS INSTITUTIONS

Suetonius wrote for contemporaries who understood what he was talking about. They knew what a *pontifex maximus* was and could recognize a Thracian gladiator and a *retiarius* from their armaments. What follows here is the barest minimum of the background necessary for an understanding of the late republican and early imperial periods of Rome as reflected in Suetonius' detail-crammed text. This material is of necessity simplified and limited to issues that arise in the *Caesars*. Furthermore, institutions and practices changed over the 180 or so years covered in the biographies. But it is hoped that these paragraphs, together with the Glossary and other aids, will provide some understanding of why Suetonius approves and disapproves of an emperor's behavior.

Geography

Rome was located on the Tiber River, about fifteen miles from where it flows into the Tyrrhenian Sea. The Tiber is not navigable by large vessels, so ships had to be offloaded at the port of Ostia at its mouth. But Ostia had no safe natural harbor, and most cargo came to the city through Puteoli on the Bay of Naples. Claudius tried to remedy this inconvenient transport by building a port at the Tiber's mouth.

The city was built among seven hills that divided it into discrete quarters. On low ground was the Forum, the political center of the city during the Republic, an open space surrounded by temples and other public buildings. Emperors built additional forums as time went on. The senate might meet in the senate house (*curia*) but could be convened elsewhere. The Campus Martius, the "field of Mars," was a flat area suitable for exercise and voting that could be used as a military parade ground. It increasingly filled with statues, trophies, and structures, including temples, theaters, and the Mausoleum of Augustus.

The most important hill was the Capitoline, the site of the temple of Jupiter Optimus Maximus ("Jupiter Best and Greatest"), the destination of triumphant generals. Wealthy and influential families had lived on the nearby Palatine Hill for a long time. Emperors made their homes there and annexed more property until their residential complex covered the entire hill and the Palatine was turned into the imperial palace. As such, it displaced the Capitoline as the symbolic site of power in the city. Nero built extravagantly, and his buildings extended even beyond this.

Social Distinctions

Society in ancient Rome was highly stratified. In the dim and distant history of the Republic, a formal distinction between patricians (distinguished families) and plebeians (commoners) had emerged. Benefits and responsibilities for patricians varied during the course of the Republic, but by the time of the principate, inherited patrician status conferred no more than the kind of standing that "old families" enjoy. Emperors would also sometimes grant this status. Some priesthoods were reserved for patricians, and the office of tribune was reserved for plebeians, but no significant difference between the two remained. Plebeian status did not preclude election to high office or membership in the senate, and there were wealthy and distinguished plebeian families. But "plebeian" also came to mean "ordinary citizen" as well as "nonpatrician."

Senators were at the top of the social hierarchy. Then came equestrians (Roman knights), then plebeians, freedmen, and slaves. A minimum property qualification of one million sesterces was required for members of the senatorial order, and they were forbidden to engage in trade. The equestrian order took its name from its original function as a cavalry force. It stood just below that of the senate in wealth and distinction and together with it comprised the upper class. Despite the hierarchical nature of Roman society, a degree of mobility was possible, and equestrians might rise to become senators, especially with the help of patronage and family connections. The property requirement for Roman knights was 400,000 sesterces, and they could engage in the business activity that was inappropriate for senators. In the Republic, censors performed surveys to confirm compliance with the financial requirements and address issues of character. Emperors later assumed the censorship role.

Slaves, at the bottom of the social ladder, did not all suffer the same treatment. Some labored in agriculture and did other heavy or dangerous work whereas others served in households and were even secretaries and personal assistants or teachers. Freedom was possible, and the population of freedmen (freed slaves) was large. Freedmen continued to have obligations to their former masters, now called their patrons, but after another generation passed, these obligations disappeared, and the sons of freedmen joined the rest of the ordinary free population. Some freedmen became indispensable to their patrons, and conservative members of society frowned on their influence.

Governmental Institutions and Practices

Elected Officials and Magistrates

The empire inherited from the Republic the tradition of electing magistrates to hold annual offices in a prescribed order. Each year twenty *quaestors*, twelve to eighteen *praetors*, and two *consuls* were elected. The offices of *aedile* and *tribune* fell between quaestor and praetor; patricians were not required to serve as aediles in order to climb the ladder further, and the tribunate was reserved for plebeians. Once elected quaestor, a man entered the senate and was a senator for life, barring malfeasance or the loss of his property requirement. The emperor might, however, adlect (appoint) someone to the senate or to a higher level within it. The minimum age requirement for each office was excused for favored people, such as members of the imperial family. The emperor determined eligibility for any of these offices; appointment to the Board of Twenty (with token duties in Rome) allowed a young man to stand for the quaestorship and so embark on a "senatorial career." The two consuls who took office on the first of January gave their names to the year, but they were often replaced with *suffect consuls* (substitute consuls) for later parts of the year.

The consuls presided over the senate. Praetors retained the responsibility for the criminal courts that they had had during the Republic, and they also oversaw major public games and had other duties. Aediles initially retained some of the responsibilities for city management that they had had earlier, but these duties came to be performed by imperial appointees. The ten tribunes no longer had the important powers they had exercised during the Republic, the veto, the right to call the senate into session, and sacrosanct status. These too were subsumed by emperors, who held "tribunician power." Quaestors had various assignments as financial aides to higher officials, but two or more who were most favored served as personal assistants to the emperor, as "his" quaestors.

Election was by the popular assembly until 14 CE, when selection was transferred to the senate. After that, the people merely ratified their choice. A degree of competition remained for lower offices, although the candidates favored by the emperor were guaranteed election. But the election of consuls (regular or suffect) became a formality since the emperor selected only two candidates in each instance. This put these fortunate men under heavy obligation to him. Many sons of senators and some equestrians pursued the prestige of the higher offices, the goals of a senatorial career, because they were stepping stones to further imperial appointment.

Imperial Governance

The dysfunctional Republic that Julius Caesar encountered when he embarked on his career evolved by stages into what was essentially a monarchy, although it was never defined as such. When Augustus was the only strongman left standing after the bloody struggle that followed Caesar's assassination, stability was achieved by a charade that republican institutions had been retained, though in reality affairs were directed by one man. The emperor never had a job description. The consuls functioned as his political allies; the senate followed his lead. The balance was difficult to manage. In time the principate (as the new form of government was called, deriving from *princeps*, "first man," "leading citizen") became a tradition of its own—the fading facade of republican institutions notwithstanding.

A *consular* (former consul) might hope to become governor in a province as a *proconsul*. Appointees of praetorian rank were called *propraetors*. During the Republic it had been the senate that appointed former consuls to govern provinces and command the legions based there, but in the empire it made appointments only for provinces that did not have legions. The emperor kept provinces with military contingents under his control and appointed their governors. This obligated them to him and so made them ostensibly no threat when entrusted with the command of armies. (The strategy did not, however, prevent the unrest that broke out after Nero's death, when a number of imperial appointees used their military resources to make their own bids for the principate.) Other business was increasingly handled by imperial *procurators*, personal appointees of the emperor, often men of equestrian status and (like the provincial governors) responsible to him and to him alone. They managed his broad financial interests and increasingly operated as his representatives in all areas. The emperor could govern by edict, although he might choose to have his directive come through the senate.

The state treasury amassed revenues from various taxes, but the emperor became personally very wealthy from gifts, foreign and domestic, and from legacies and inheritances, as well as from the estates of those who died intestate or were condemned on criminal charges. These sources supplemented the properties that had accrued, first to the Julian family, the first ruling family, and then to the principate itself. The early emperors willed their estates to their successors—or attempted to. But as time passed, the emperor's private wealth simply went with the job. His gifts to the military and the populace allowed him to court popularity. State assets and the imperial purse became entangled.

Family

A family was headed by an adult male who had a father's power (*patria potestas*) until his death. The authority of the head of household was absolute in theory and included power over life and death but was exercised most often in regard to property. Children might, however, sometimes be emancipated. When a child was born, the father chose whether or not to accept it as his own, give it his name, and rear it in the family. Alternatively, he could reject it and leave it to die by exposure. Adoption, even the adoption of adult males, was relatively frequent. It allowed a family name to continue when it had no male offspring, or it could be a political tool. For example, Augustus adopted his forty-five-year-old stepson Tiberius for dynastic purposes.

Marriage was another political tool. It strengthened interfamily alliances and was especially important for the imperial family. Divorce took little more than a statement of intent and could be used politically as well. Extramarital sex with a freedwomen, freedman, or slave (female or male) was incidental for an upper-class male. However, adultery with a woman of privileged family was a serious matter because it threatened to destroy the web of family alliances. Sex between men was socially acceptable for the partner who played the active role but never for the one who played the passive role, which indicated subservience.

Fertility was encouraged for the upper classes, especially by Augustus, who came to power after civil war had totally erased many prominent families. The marriage law enacted during his reign, the *lex Papia Poppaea*, penalized bachelorhood and freed married citizens with three legitimate children from some restrictions on inheritance and on the age at which they could seek public office.

Names

Roman men generally had three names (for example, Gaius Julius Caesar or Gnaeus Calpurnius Piso). The second of these, the hereditary family or clan name, was called the *nomen* (name) and was the most important. In the period covered by the *Caesars* only about fifteen first names (*praenomina*) were in use (Marcus, Lucius, Quintus, and so forth). These were so few that they were not very useful for identifying individuals outside of a man's family. And because they were so few, they were almost always abbreviated (M, L, Q), including in inscriptions. This small choice expanded somewhat, especially in the imperial family, to make room for other more prestigious names. The third name, the *cognomen*, may have originated as a nickname but came to identify a branch of the larger family. Although *cognomina* were not universal (for example, Marcus Antonius, or Mark Antony, had no cognomen), they were the rule by the early empire. Honorific cognomina were sometimes added; the son of the emperor Claudius was Britannicus after the conquest of Britain. Such honorific names might also be passed on. It was possible to have a number of cognomina. Men were often called by their cognomen.

Women usually had a single name, the feminine form of their father's family name (Julia, Claudia, Domitia), sometimes combined with the feminine form of a family cognomen (Livia Drusilla, Vipsania Agrippina). Daughters might be distinguished by their order of birth (Antonia Major, Antonia Minor).

Adoptees took the name of their new father but retained their original *nomen* in adjectival form. For example, the emperor Augustus, born Gaius Octavius, became Gaius Julius Caesar Octavianus after his adoption by Gaius Julius Caesar.

Slaves had a single name that they retained as a cognomen if they were freed and enfranchised. They chose a *praenomen* and *nomen* for themselves, frequently that of their former master or the ruling emperor.

Justice, the Courts, and Inheritance

During the Republic, elected magistrates and praetors in particular were responsible for the dispensation of justice. In civil suits, a praetor arranged the terms for settlement between plaintiff and defendant and appointed judges to decide the case. The plaintiff was forced to post a bond in order to discourage frivolous suits, but courts were crowded with a logjam of cases nonetheless. In criminal cases the praetor assigned cases to standing courts designated to deal with particular laws that had penalties specifically prescribed.

These procedures continued during the empire with appeal to the emperor possible. But there developed an alternate system: senior magistrates and especially the emperor held "examinations" or "hearings" on their own. The senate could function as a court presided over by a consul or the emperor. Such hearings were more flexible than the praetor's courts because they were not restricted to cases defined by specific laws, and they left the door open to arbitrary justice. Treason trials took place in these extraordinary courts, and we read of emperors holding hearings in private and not allowing defendants to present their cases.

Judges and juries for the traditional courts were drawn from jury panels. One's name on a list of available jurors was confirmation of citizenship, but jury duty was considered onerous. Emperors added extra panels to spread the burden and made alterations in the court sessions. The presiding officer sat on a raised platform or tribunal. Courts had no designated sites but frequently were held in the Forum, and civil cases would later find a home in the nearby Basilica Julia. A defendant might wear mourning clothing to gain sympathy.

Punishments varied according to the social class of the guilty. Criminals of the lower classes could be sent to the mines, executed by being thrown to the beasts in the arena, or punished in some other barbaric way. Noncitizens or slaves could be crucified. But members of the upper classes were executed by beheading or sent into exile. These class-based punishments became law in the second century CE but operated during the period covered by the *Caesars*. Imprisonment was always intended to be temporary.

Only a Roman citizen could make a will. Those listed as second-ary heirs received inheritance if those named first could not, and heirs in the third degree were very unlikely to benefit, their inclu-sion being little more than a complimentary gesture. Witnesses were required, and the elaborate sealing of the document guarded against forgery. It had long been a custom for testators to remember friends in their wills, and the practice developed to include naming the emperor. He might generously refuse to accept a legacy from a testator who had children, but a greedy emperor insisted that he be included. If he were not, the will could be termed "ungrateful" and declared invalid. The property in invalid wills defaulted to the treasury and found its way into state funds or funds controlled by the emperor. This was also the case with estates of those found guilty of crimes.

Laws recommended by the senate were named for the person who proposed them and could be enacted to deal with quite specific issues.

The Military

The heavy-armed infantry legion was the principal unit of Rome's professional standing army. Consisting of about 4,800 men at full strength and augmented by cavalry, there were twenty-five to thirty legions during the period covered by the *Caesars;* some were destroyed or disbanded as new ones were raised. Each had a silver eagle that represented its integrity as a unit. Legions were under the command of imperial appointees (generals) but under the overall command of the governor of the province in which they were stationed. A governor's loyalty to the emperor was always at issue because of the significant number of troops that he controlled. Troops saluted their successful general as *imperator,* and emperors came to bear this honorific title by virtue of their position.

Each legion was divided into ten cohorts and further divided into centuries of eighty men led by a centurion. The well-paid centurion of the first century of a legion's first cohort was called the *primi-pilaris,* the equivalent of a modern army unit's most senior enlisted man. Legionary soldiers were supposed to be citizens, but as they increasingly began to be recruited from the provinces, they may have received citizenship on enlistment. In the time of Augustus the term of service was sixteen years, but it increased to twenty and then to twenty-five. Annual pay was low in comparison with the generous discharge bounty. Winter quarters were permanent encampments in safe positions distant from the frontier; summer camps were temporary encampments in the field. When on the march legionaries set up a fortified position every day. Decimation, the execution of one out of every ten men in a unit chosen by lot, was a traditional means of discipline, more often threatened than enforced at the time about which Suetonius wrote.

Auxiliary units (infantry cohorts and cavalry wings) supported the legions. Conscripted locally from the non-Roman population and not paid as well as legionary soldiers, the men were given Roman citizenship on discharge. The loyalty of these units was sometimes in question. They were commanded by junior officers, military tribunes who were young men drawn from the senatorial and the equestrian orders.

The praetorian guard was a special unit of nine cohorts stationed in Rome. It historically served as the general's bodyguard detail, and when emperor and commander in chief became one and the same, it protected his position in Rome. Praetorians received higher pay than did other legionaries, and their permanent stationing in Rome gave them extraordinary power in the creation and retention of an emperor. Originally scattered about the territory near the city, they were collected into a camp adjacent to the city wall during the reign of Tiberius.

The navy did not have the long military tradition of the army, but there were two major fleets, one based at Misenum on the Bay of Naples and another at Ravenna on the Adriatic. Their crews, both marines and rowers, were non-Romans and freedmen, but they were not slaves.

Life and Culture

Religion

Religion was a matter for the state, and the colleges of priests were state officials. The most important priest was the *pontifex maximus*, a position that the emperor came to assume along with his other offices. The Vestal Virgins, who served Vesta, the goddess of the hearth, formed the only female priesthood. Drawn from daughters of the senatorial class, Vestals vowed sexual abstinence for thirty years; infraction was punished harshly. A proper respect for state rituals was thought admirable in an emperor; contempt for the gods was frowned on.

Priests performed animal sacrifice on behalf of the people, and this practice together with the celebration of holidays honoring the gods formed the center of religious observance. Sacrifices could go wrong. The animal might not go down quietly or could escape, and this boded ill. "Taking the auspices" meant observing natural events, primarily the behavior of birds, to determine the gods' approval or disapproval of a venture. No one without the proper authority could do this. A commanding general fed the sacred chickens before a battle; if they ate hungrily, it was believed that success would follow. A *haruspex* was an Etruscan soothsayer who interpreted signs, especially those that were evident in the examination of the entrails of animals.

Individuals might donate valuable objects (the spoils of war) in temples or build new temples. *Lares* and *Penates*, the gods who protected households, were revered in shrines in private homes, and the state had its own version of these tutelary deities. Belief in signs from heaven, portents and omens, was almost universal. Horoscopes in particular were trusted.

Education and Literary Culture

Boys might be sent to modest schools to learn to read and write, but the education of an upper-class boy began at home with tutors. Girls might also receive an elementary education. Probably by his early teens a boy was sent to a *grammaticus* in whose school he applied himself to the "liberal studies" of law, philosophy, mathematics, and music but primarily language and literature. Greek culture was pervasive, and much education was bilingual with the goal of literacy in both Greek and Latin. In his mid-teens the boy would be put under the tutelage of a *rhetor* to learn public speaking.

Students practiced their rhetorical skills by declaiming, presenting arguments on set subjects. Once a boy had received the *toga virilis* ("toga of manhood") and his rhetorical education was thought complete, he was apprenticed to a prominent civilian figure, perhaps a relative, who would introduce him into public life in the Forum, and he learned to plead cases in the courts. Selection to the Board of Twenty might precede another apprenticeship, a year as a military tribune.

Declamation and public recitations (readings) of poetry and prose were popular entertainments, and it was common for educated men to compose literary works.

Ceremony, Regalia, and Clothing

Rituals and outward marks of distinction were important. Lictors carrying *fasces*, bundles of rods, accompanied magistrates in public. Twelve attended a consul, six a praetor. In the empire the numbers varied, but the emperor and other men of importance merited them. Outside Rome, axes were bound into the rods in order to represent the power of life and death.

The toga, a wrapped garment of white wool (heavy, restrictive, and uncomfortable) represented formal civilian dress and was required for senators and in some contexts. Boys were awarded the *toga virilis* at the age of about fifteen when they were escorted to the Forum by their male relatives in a coming-of-age ceremony. Until that time they wore togas bordered with a broad purple band, the *toga praetextata*, a garment worn by elected officials as well. But togas were cumbersome and ceased to be worn much unless they were required. Underneath was a tunic worn belted. Senators, their sons, and apparently those allowed to stand for office had a tunic with a broad purple stripe down the front. Other equestrians wore tunics with narrow stripes. "Greek dress" was acceptable in some contexts, but informal, "at-home" wear was frowned on in public. Silk clothing and other extravagances were always suspect as effeminate. Dark clothing was for mourning. A knight was distinguished by the gold ring that he was permitted to wear.

The military triumph was an ancient and elaborate tradition in which the successful general entered the city wearing a specially embroidered tunic and with a laurel wreath held above his head. He was conveyed in a chariot drawn by white horses to his destination, the temple of Jupiter on the Capitoline Hill. A full triumph came to be reserved for the emperor, to whom as commander in chief all victories belonged, or for his close family. The senate might, however (with the emperor's approval), confer the regalia of triumph (*ornamenta triumphalia*), a statue and the right to wear the triumphator's distinctive clothing. Ovations were lesser celebrations awarded for less important victories. Ovations progressed to the temple of Jupiter Latiaris on the Alban Mount outside the city.

An emperor might also award the regalia of a consul or a praetor. As with triumphal regalia, this was the right to wear the clothing and enjoy the privileges of a magistrate without the honor of the office itself. Crowns were military decorations, the most important of which was the civic crown, a crown of oak leaves, awarded for saving a citizen's life. The emperor received it as a matter of course. There was also a naval crown, a turreted crown for the first man to scale an enemy wall, and so forth.

Protocol was important. To rise to one's feet in the presence of rank was an obvious token of respect. The senate utilized a formal established order for speaking, and at public entertainments seating arrangements were increasingly ordered by social class. The orchestra in the theater was reserved for senators and the first fourteen rows for equestrians, and other venues had seating rules as well. Senators and equestrians were expected to behave with the dignity thought appropriate to their status.

Houses

The city houses of wealthy Romans faced inward and centered on the atrium, an open space that had a reservoir to catch rainwater. Here were kept the death masks (*imagines*) of ancestors, which advertised the importance of the family and were carried in funeral processions. The atrium was the site of the morning audience at which the clients and associates of a great man and those who wished to petition his favors came to the house to pay their respects. The portion of the house's outside perimeter that abutted the street might be rented, often to shopkeepers. The wealthy also had gardens in the city and multiple houses in the country.

The less wealthy population of Rome rented living space, often in multistoried apartment blocks. These crowded quarters on narrow streets made the city susceptible to fires that could easily spread out of control. After a massive fire in 64 CE, the emperor Nero attempted to rebuild the city with broader streets and with structures provided with balconies to facilitate firefighting.

Entertainment

The population of Rome especially, but also the empire in general, was entertained by shows ("games") put on for them at great expense. Gladiatorial combats were the most notorious. Gladiators came in several varieties, outfitted with heavier or lighter armor. Most fought individually. A Thracian, for example, might be paired against a *murmillo*. But *retiarii* fighting in groups tried to net their opponents. Fights were rarely to the death, at least not in the combat itself. A defeated gladiator lay down his weapons and appealed for mercy to the official who was presiding over the entertainment. If he had fought well and pleased the crowd, he might be spared; if not, he was dispatched on the spot. The crowd made its choice known, but it was the presider, the person who had arranged the games and paid for them, often the emperor, who made the decision. He was courting popularity if he followed the crowd's lead. Gladiators were of low status, prisoners of war or criminals or slaves, but some became famous and even the objects of erotic attention. Members of the upper classes sometimes fought in the arena, although this was considered inappropriate and even forbidden.

Beast hunts, contests between men and animals, were another variety of violent spectacle. The combatants in these enjoyed less prestige than did gladiators. Staged battles on land and sea were essentially mass executions, and actual executions, in the arena or elsewhere, were considered entertainment.

Races between chariots drawn by teams of horses were extremely popular. There were four racing clubs, the Blues, Greens, Whites, and Reds, the last two apparently subordinate to the first two. The clubs had rabid fans, emperors among them.

Many kinds of entertainments were called games. Plays, pantomime dancing, and musical offerings took place in theaters, especially in the theater of Pompey, which had been built in the mid-first century BCE. Nero instituted new entertainments that featured contests in which he could display his musical talent. Secular Games were intended to be rare, seen by a person only once in his lifetime, but Augustus, Claudius, and Domitian all staged them. Atellan farce (low comedy) had stock characters and could be used as a vehicle for ridiculing the emperor. Games gave the emperor a rare opportunity to interact with his subjects, and he sometimes threw tokens to the crowd that could be exchanged for prizes. At the races the imperial family had a conspicuous box from which they could not only watch but also be viewed.

Chariot races took place in "circuses" (racecourses), especially in the capacious Circus Maximus. Beast hunts and battles were staged there, too. Immense basins for the enactment of naval battles were dug near a source of water. Gladiatorial games and hunts took place in amphitheaters, some of them temporary and improvised, and in the stone amphitheater of Statilius Taurus, which was built during the reign of Augustus. The Flavian amphitheater (known later as the Colosseum) was dedicated by the emperors Vespasian and Titus in 79 and 80 CE.

Gambling, especially with dice, was extremely popular. It was supposedly allowed only during the Saturnalia, the December holiday when many freedoms were permitted, but it was impossible to control. The emperors Augustus and Claudius, we are told, played a great deal.

Units of Measurement

The Roman foot was slightly less than twelve inches. Five feet made a pace and a thousand paces a mile, which was a little more than nine-tenths of a modern mile. A cubit was also a measure of length, about the equivalent of a modern foot and a half, the distance from a man's elbow to his fingertips.

Money

The basic monetary unit that Suetonius names is the *sestertius* ("sesterce" as rendered in English; plural "sesterces"). It was a silver coin of relatively slight value, the equivalent of two and a half asses, coins made from bronze and then later from copper. Four sesterces were equal to a silver denarius, and twenty-five denarii were equal to a gold aureus. It is impossible to give a modern equivalent for a sestertius, but 400,000 (the census requirement for an equestrian) made a man wealthy, and a million (the requirement for a senator) made him quite wealthy. There was no paper money.

Time and the Calendar

Years were reckoned by consulships; Augustus was born, for instance, "in the consulship of Marcus Tullius Cicero and Gaius Antonius," 63 BCE. The year was given the name of the consuls who took office on January 1. Dates were calculated from three named days: the Kalends, the first day of the month; the Nones, the fifth; and the Ides, the thirteenth. But in March, May, July, and October, the Nones fell on the seventh and the Ides on the fifteenth. Dates were calculated backward from these three points, and days at both ends of the count were included. Three days before the Ides of June was June 11; ten days before the Kalends of November was October 21.

The year had a total of only 355 days prior to the calendar reform of Julius Caesar, but after that the number of days in each month became the same as we have today. By the earlier system the months had ceased to correspond to the season as time passed, and annual festivals began to fall in the wrong season of the year. Extra (intercalary) months were inserted in an attempt to bring the calendar and the solar year into concert again.

A day was divided into twelve "hours" from sunrise to sunset with the sixth hour falling at noon. The length of each hour and the divisions between them depended on the time of year. The night was divided into four quarters or "watches" with the end of the second watch falling at midnight.

SUGGESTIONS FOR FURTHER READING

Baldwin, B. *Suetonius*. Amsterdam: Hakkert, 1983.

Barrett, A. A. *Caligula: The Corruption of Power*. New Haven, CT: Yale University Press, 1990.

———. *Agrippina: Sex, Power, and Politics in the Early Empire*. New Haven, CT: Yale University Press, 1996.

———. *Livia: First Lady of Imperial Rome*. New Haven, CT: Yale University Press, 2002.

———, ed. *Lives of the Caesars*. Oxford: Blackwell, 2008.

Bradley, K. R. "The Significance of the *Spectacula* in Suetonius' *Caesars*." *Rivista Storica dell'Antichità* 11 (1981): 129–37.

———. "The Imperial Ideal in Suetonius' 'Caesares'." *Aufstieg und Niedergang der römischen Welt* II 33.5 (1991): 3701–32.

Champlin, E. *Nero*. Cambridge, MA: Belknap Press of Harvard University Press, 2005.

Coleman, K. M. "Fatal Charades: Roman Executions Staged as Mythological Enactments." *Journal of Roman Studies* 80 (1990): 44–73.

———. "Launching into History: Aquatic Displays in the Early Empire." *Journal of Roman Studies* 83 (1993): 48–74.

Dorey, T. A., ed. *Latin Biography*. London: Routledge, 1967.

Eck, W. Translated by D. L. Schneider with additional material by S. A. Tacács. *The Age of Augustus*. 2nd ed. Malden, MA: Blackwell, 2007.

Edwards, M. J., and S. Swain, eds. *Portraits: Biographical Representation in the Greek and Latin Literature of the Roman Empire*. Oxford: Oxford University Press, 1997.

Fantham, E. *Julia Augusti: The Emperor's Daughter*. London: Routledge, 2006.

Galinsky, K. *Augustan Culture*. Princeton, NJ: Princeton University Press, 1998.

Garnsey, P. *Social Status and Legal Privilege in the Roman Empire*. Oxford: Oxford University Press, 1970.

Ginsburg, J. *Representing Agrippina: Constructions of Female Power in the Early Roman Empire*. Philadelphia: American Philological Association, 2006.

Goldsworthy, A. *Caesar: Life of a Colossus.* New Haven, CT: Yale University Press, 2006.

Griffin, M. T. *Nero: The End of a Dynasty.* London: Routledge, 1987.

Jones, A. H. M. *The Criminal Courts of the Roman Republic and Principate.* Oxford: Blackwell, 1972.

Jones, B. W. *The Emperor Titus.* New York: St. Martin's Press, 1984.

———. *The Emperor Domitian.* London: Routledge, 1992.

Levick, B. *Claudius.* New Haven, CT: Yale University Press, 1990.

———. *Tiberius the Politician.* 2nd ed. London: Routledge, 1999.

———. *Vespasian.* London: Routledge, 1999.

Lewis, R. G. "Suetonius' 'Caesares' and Their Literary Antecedents." *Aufstieg und Niedergang der römischen Welt* II 33.5 (1991): 3623–74.

Millar, F. *The Emperor in the Roman World.* Ithaca, NY: Cornell University Press, 1977.

Millar, F., and E. Segal, eds. *Caesar Augustus: Seven Aspects.* Oxford: Clarendon Press, 1990.

Momigliano, A. Translated by W. D. Hogarth. *Claudius: The Emperor and His Achievement.* 2nd ed. Oxford: Oxford University Press, 1961.

———. *The Development of Greek Biography.* Expanded ed. Cambridge, MA: Harvard University Press, 1993.

Morgan, G. *69 AD: The Year of Four Emperors.* Oxford: Oxford University Press, 2006.

Murison, C. L. *Galba, Otho, and Vitellius: Careers and Controversies.* Hildesheim: Georg Olms, 1993.

Saller, R. "Anecdotes as Historical Evidence for the Principate." *Greece & Rome* (ser. 2) 27 (1980): 69–83.

Seager, R. *Tiberius.* 2nd ed. Oxford: Blackwell, 2005.

Shotter, D. C. A. *Nero Caesar Augustus: Emperor of Rome.* Harlow, UK: Longman, 2008.

Syme, R. "Biographers of the Caesars." *Museum Helveticum* 37 (1980): 104–28 = *Roman Papers* vol. 3: 1251–75.

———. "The Travels of Suetonius Tranquillus." *Hermes* 109 (1981): 105–17 = *Roman Papers* vol. 3: 1337–49.

Talbert, R. J. A. *The Senate of Imperial Rome.* Princeton, NJ: Princeton University Press, 1984.

Tatum, W. J. *Always I Am Caesar.* Oxford: Blackwell, 2008.

Wallace-Hadrill, A. *Suetonius, the Scholar and His Caesars.* New Haven, CT: Yale University Press, 1983.

Wardle, D. "Suetonius and His Own Day." In *Studies in Latin Literature and Roman History,* edited by C. Deroux. Brussels: Latomus, 1998, 425–47.

Wellesley, K. *The Year of the Four Emperors.* 3rd ed. with a new introduction by B. Levick. London: Routledge, 2000.

Wiedemann, T. *Emperors and Gladiators.* London: Routledge, 1995.

Wilkes, J. "Julio-Claudian Historians." *Classical World* 65 (1972): 177–203.

Wilkinson, S. *Caligula.* London: Routledge, 2004.

Commentaries on the Text

Bradley, K. R., ed. *Suetonius'* Life of Nero: *An Historical Commentary.* No. 157. Brussels: Latomus, 1978.

Butler, H. E., and M. Cary, eds. *C. Suetoni Tranquilli Divus Julius.* Oxford: Clarendon Press, 1927. Reissued with a new introduction, bibliography, and additional notes by G. B. Townend. Bristol, UK: Bristol Classical Press, 1982.

Carter, J. M., ed. *Suetonius: Divus Augustus.* Bristol, UK: Bristol Classical Press, 1982.

Hurley, D. W., ed. *An Historical and Historiographical Commentary on* Suetonius' "Life of C. Caligula." American Classical Studies 32. Atlanta: Scholars Press, 1993.

———. *Suetonius: Divus Claudius.* Cambridge: Cambridge University Press, 2001.

Jones, B. W., ed. *Suetonius: Vespasian.* London: Bristol Classical Press, 2000.

Jones, B. W., and R. D. Milns, trans. *Suetonius: The Flavian Emperors, A Historical Commentary with Translation and Introduction.* London: Bristol Classical Press, 2002.

Kaster, R. A., ed. and trans. *C. Suetonius Tranquillus: De grammaticis et rhetoribus.* Oxford: Oxford University Press, 1995.

Lindsay, H., ed. *Suetonius: Caligula.* London: Bristol Classical Press, 1993.

———. *Suetonius: Tiberius.* London: Bristol Classical Press, 1995.

Mooney, G. W., ed. *C. Suetoni Tranquilli de vita Caesarum libri VII–VIII.* London: Longman, 1930.

Mottershead, J., ed. *Suetonius: Claudius.* London: Bristol Classical Press, 1986.

Murison, C. L., ed. *Suetonius: Galba, Otho, Vitellius.* London: Bristol Classical Press, 1992.

Shotter, D. C. A., ed. and trans. *Suetonius: Lives of Galba, Otho, Vitellius.* Warminster, UK: Aris and Phillips, 1993.

Wardle, D., ed. *Suetonius'* Life of Caligula: *A Commentary.* No. 225. Brussels: Latomus, 1994.

Warmington, B. H., ed. *Suetonius: Nero.* 2nd ed. London: Bristol Classical Press, 1999.

CHRONOLOGY OF MAJOR EVENTS

BCE

107–100   Gaius Marius is the dominant military figure.

100–83   Political struggles in Rome. War with Italian cities. Fighting between the factions of Marius and Lucius Cornelius Cinna against the faction of Lucius Cornelius Sulla.

88–63   A series of wars against Mithridates VI of Pontus.

83   Sulla returns to Rome after fighting in the East and defeats the forces of Cinna. Proscriptions.

82–79   Sulla dictator in Rome.

72   Julius Caesar is military tribune.

69   Caesar is quaestor.

65   Caesar is aedile.

63   The conspiracy of Catiline; the consulship of Cicero.

62   Caesar is praetor.

61   Caesar is governor in Spain.

60   The First Triumvirate is formed, made up of Caesar, Gnaeus Pompeius (Pompey the Great), and Marcus Licinius Crassus. Caesar stands for the consulship.

59   Caesar is consul.

58–50   Caesar's command in Gaul.

50   Pressure to remove Caesar from his command.

49   Caesar is ordered to disband his troops, but he crosses the Rubicon and civil war begins.

48   Caesar defeats Pompey at Pharsalus. Pompey murdered at Alexandria.

47   Caesar defeats Ptolemy in Egypt. Affair with Cleopatra.

46   Caesar defeats Scipio and Juba in Africa.

45   Caesar defeats the sons of Pompey at Munda in Spain (the end of the opposition) and returns to Rome.

44 Caesar named dictator for life. He is assassinated on March 15. In his will his great-nephew Gaius Octavius is named his heir, is adopted, and becomes Gaius Julius Caesar Octavianus (later Augustus).

43 War at Mutina. The Second Triumvirate is formed, composed of Octavius, Mark Antony, and Marcus Aemilius Lepidus.

42 War at Philippi; the assassins of Caesar are defeated.

41–40 War at Perusia.

38 Octavius marries Livia Drusilla.

38–36 Naval war against Sextus Pompey.

36 Lepidus removed from the triumvirate.

32 Break between Octavius and Antony.

31 Battle of Actium; Octavius defeats the forces of Mark Antony and Cleopatra.

30 Deaths of Antony and Cleopatra at Alexandria.

29 Octavius celebrates a triple triumph at Rome.

27 Octavius receives the name of Augustus.

25 Marriage of Augustus' daughter Julia and Marcellus.

23 Illness of Augustus. Conspiracy against Augustus. Death of Marcellus.

21 Marriage of Julia and Marcus Agrippa.

18–17 Laws encouraging marriage are enacted.

17 Secular Games. Augustus adopts his grandsons Gaius and Lucius Julius Caesar.

12 Death of Marcus Agrippa.

11 Marriage of Julia and Tiberius.

6 Tiberius retires to Rhodes.

2 Julia is exiled.

1 Gaius Caesar is sent to the East with proconsular authority.

CE

2 Tiberius returns to Rome. Lucius Caesar dies.

4 Gaius Caesar dies. Augustus adopts Tiberius and Agrippa Postumus; Tiberius adopts Germanicus.

6–8 Agrippa Postumus disinherited and exiled.

8   Julia the Younger is exiled.

9   Massacre of the legions of Publius Quinctilius Varus in Germany.

14   Death of Augustus. Tiberius becomes emperor.

14–16   Germanicus campaigns in Germany.

17   Triumph of Germanicus, who is sent to the East with supreme command.

19   Death of Germanicus.

23   Death of Tiberius' son Drusus.

26   Tiberius leaves Rome for Capri.

29   Death of Livia. Exile of Agrippina the Elder and death of Germanicus' son Nero.

31   Fall and execution of Sejanus.

33   Death of Agrippina the Elder and Germanicus' son Drusus.

37   Death of Tiberius. Gaius (Caligula) becomes emperor. Death of Tiberius Gemellus.

39–40   Gaius campaigns in Gaul and Germany.

41   Assassination of Gaius. Claudius becomes emperor.

42   Attempted coup against Claudius.

43   Successful invasion of Britain.

47   Secular Games.

47–48   Claudius' censorship.

48   Marriage and execution of Messallina and Gaius Silius.

49   Marriage of Claudius and Agrippina the Younger.

50   Claudius' adoption of Nero.

53   Marriage of Nero and Octavia.

54   Death of Claudius. Nero becomes emperor.

55   Death of Britannicus.

59   Murder of Agrippina the Younger. Nero establishes the Juvenalia.

60   Nero establishes the Neronia.

62   Death of Sextus Afranius Burrus and exile of Lucius Annius Seneca. Execution of Octavia. Marriage of Nero and Poppaea Sabina.

64   Nero's first appearance on the stage in Naples. Fire at Rome.

65 Pisonian conspiracy. Death of Poppaea. Nero's debut in Rome at the second Neronia.

66 Marriage of Nero and Statilia Messallina. Tiridates in Rome.

66–67 Nero's tour of Greece.

68 Revolt of Vindex. Suicide of Nero. Galba recognized as emperor.

69 (January) Vitellius proclaimed emperor. Galba murdered. Otho proclaimed emperor.

69 (April) Otho defeated at first battle of Betriacum. Suicide of Otho.

69 (July) Vespasian proclaimed emperor in the East.

69 (October) Vitellius defeated in the second battle of Betriacum.

69 (December) Death of Vitellius in Rome.

70 Vespasian arrives in Rome.

79 Death of Vespasian. Titus becomes emperor. Eruption of Mount Vesuvius.

79–80 Dedication of the Flavian amphitheater (Colosseum).

81 Death of Titus. Domitian becomes emperor.

88 Secular Games.

96 Assassination of Domitian. Nerva becomes emperor.

98 Death of Nerva. Trajan becomes emperor.

117 Death of Trajan. Hadrian becomes emperor.

The Roman World

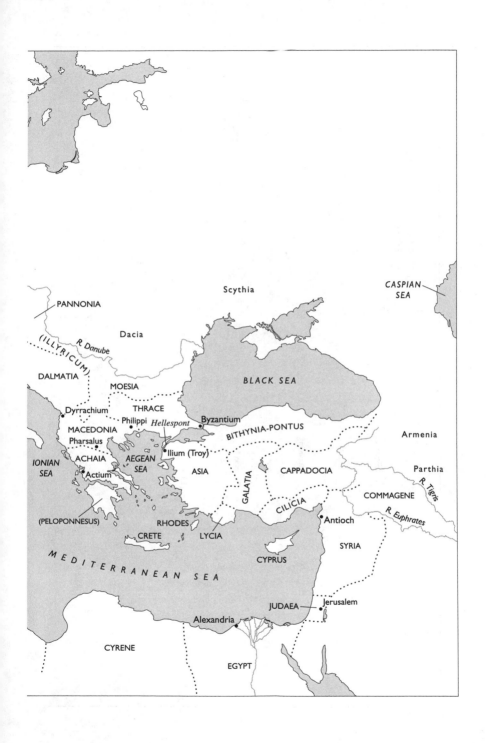

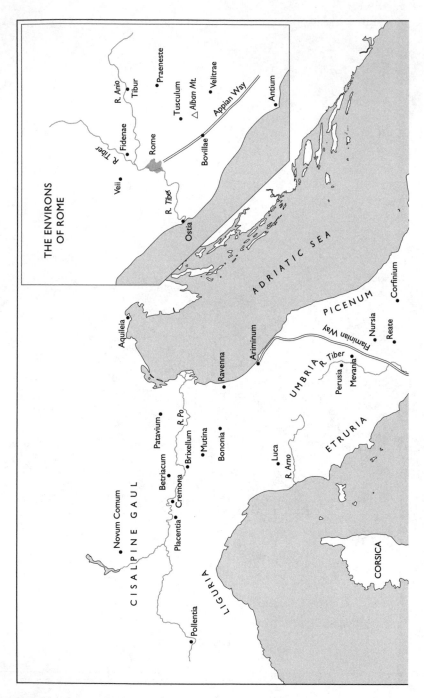

Italy

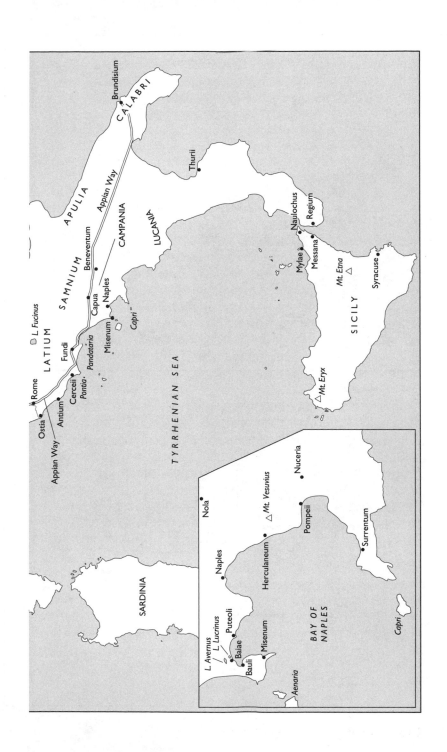

APULIA

CALABRI

Brundisium

Thurii

Appian Way

Naulochus
Regium

Beneventum

CAMPANIA

Mylae
Messana

SAMNIUM

LUCANIA

Mt. Etna
Syracuse

Capua
Naples

L Fucinus

Capri

SICILY

LATIUM

Fundi
Misenum

Pandataria

Mt. Eryx

Rome
Cerceii
Pontia

Ostia
Antium

Appian Way

TYRRHENIAN SEA

Nuceria

Nola

Mt. Vesuvius

Pompeii

Naples

Herculaneum

Surrentum

SARDINIA

Puteoli

L Avernus
L Lucrinus
Baiae
Misenum

Bauli

Aenaria

BAY OF
NAPLES

Capri

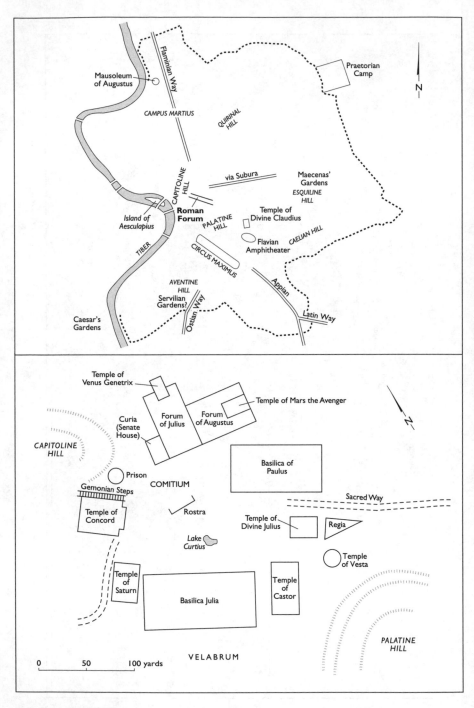

The City of Rome and the Roman Forum

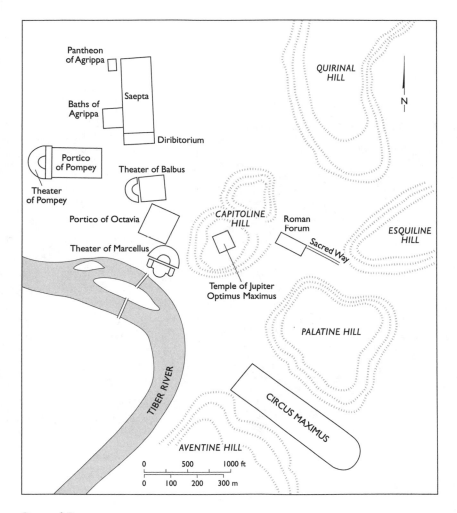

Pantheon
of Agrippa

Saepta

Baths of
Agrippa

Diribitorium

Portico
of Pompey

Theater of Balbus

Theater
of Pompey

Portico of Octavia

CAPITOLINE
HILL

Roman
Forum

Sacred Way

ESQUILINE
HILL

QUIRINAL
HILL

N

Theater of Marcellus

Temple of Jupiter
Optimus Maximus

PALATINE HILL

TIBER RIVER

CIRCUS MAXIMUS

AVENTINE HILL

| 0 | 500 | 1000 ft |
| 0 | 100 | 200 | 300 m |

Central Rome

THE CAESARS

THE DIVINE JULIUS

100–44 BCE

*The life of Gaius Julius Caesar, republican general and dictator, opens
Suetonius' series of imperial biographies. Caesar was not a Roman
emperor. The empire traditionally begins with the reign of Augustus. But
Caesar set the stage for new developments in the power structure of Rome,
and in Suetonius' eyes this contribution qualified him for inclusion in the
Caesars.*

*Suetonius begins each of the lives with the ancestry of his imperial
subject. But the opening chapters are missing from the life of the Divine
Julius. They would have contained information about Caesar's family, his
birth in 100 BCE, and his early life, including perhaps anecdotes or omens
that predicted the larger-than-life figure he would become. In the surviving
chapters, Suetonius begins by following Caesar's career chronologically,
from his rise to power during the difficult and dangerous years of the late
Roman Republic to his conquest of Gaul, civil war, his return to Rome,
and his dictatorship.*

*At the end of chapter 44, however, when the next event to be reported
is Caesar's death, Suetonius breaks away from his chronology and begins
to present Caesar by rubrics describing his physical appearance, his habits,
his oratory and writing, his military skill and bravery, and aspects of his
character. The final trait is arrogance, and the anecdotes that illustrate it
prompted his assassination on the Ides of March in 44 BCE. Accordingly,
Suetonius returns to his chronological narrative in chapter 80 to conclude
with Caesar's death and its aftermath.*

*Caesar's reputation was, and still is, a mixed one. He was a towering
figure, competent, energetic, and intelligent, but his raw ambition
overwhelmed all else. Suetonius measures him against what he believes
is the ideal emperor and comes up with the same judgment. Thus his
biography captures the complexity of its subject.*

1

[1.1] . . . Caesar lost his father in his sixteenth year. The next year, when he was named *flamen dialis*,[1] he dismissed Cossutia, who was from an equestrian family but very rich and betrothed to him before he received the adult toga. He married Cornelia, a daughter of Cinna, four times consul, and she later bore him a daughter, Julia. The dictator Sulla could find no way to force him to divorce her.[2] [1.2] Caesar was therefore considered a member of the rival party and made to forfeit his priesthood, his wife's dowry, and his family property and even to abandon the political scene at Rome. Despite the fact that his malaria was getting worse, he had to change his hiding place almost every night, and he avoided arrest by paying off the men who were hunting him down. This was his situation until the Vestal Virgins and his relatives Mamercus Aemilius and Aurelius Cotta[3] helped him attain pardon. [1.3] Everyone knows how Sulla finally relented: for a long time he had refused to listen to his political allies, prominent men who were pleading on Caesar's behalf and pressing his case stubbornly. In the end he stated (either with divine insight or by human inference), "You have won your point and will get what you want—so long as you know that this man, about whose welfare you are so very concerned, will someday be the death of the party of the *optimates*, which you, as well as I, have acted to preserve. For in Caesar there are many Mariuses."[4]

[2] Caesar's first military service was in Asia, on the staff of the governor Marcus Thermus. When his commander sent him to Bithynia to bring back the fleet, he stayed there for a time with Nicomedes, and there was talk of shameful sex acts with the king.[5] The story was reinforced when he went back to Bithynia a second time a few days later, on the excuse of collecting money owed to a freedman client. His reputation fared better during the remainder of his service, and Thermus awarded him the civic crown at the

---

1. A priest of Jupiter, who was required to be married and for whom divorce was forbidden. Caesar evidently never became priest.

2. Lucius Cornelius Cinna and Lucius Cornelius Sulla were archenemies in the bloody and highly partisan political struggles of the 80s BCE.

3. Mamercus Aemilius Lepidus and Gaius Aurelius Cotta.

4. The populist Gaius Marius opposed Sulla and the *optimates*, the party of the traditional ruling families.

5. The accusation that he played the female in a homosexual union continued to dog him; see 22.2, 49.1–3, 52.3.

capture of Mytilene.[6] [3] Caesar also served for a short time under Servilius Isauricus in Cilicia.[7] When word came that Sulla was dead, he hurried to Rome in anticipation of a new insurgency being initiated by Marcus Lepidus. Although Lepidus encouraged Caesar to join his cause by offering generous rewards, Caesar refrained, for he distrusted the man's character and even more his prospects, which were less promising than he had thought.[8]

[4.1] In any case, after this civil unrest was suppressed, Caesar prosecuted for extortion Cornelius Dolabella, a man of consular rank who had been awarded the honor of a triumph. When Dolabella was found innocent, Caesar chose to withdraw to Rhodes in order to avoid the ill feeling that followed and to have time and leisure to study with Apollonius Molo, a very famous teacher of rhetoric at that time. Crossing to the island after the beginning of winter, he was taken prisoner by pirates near the island of Pharmacussa[9] and, to his great irritation, held captive for almost forty days with only his doctor and two personal slaves for company. [4.2] As soon as he was taken, he had sent off his companions and the other servants to raise the money for his ransom quickly. After fifty talents had been paid and he was set on shore, he instantly got ships into the water, pursued the pirates as they sailed away, and, when he had them in his power, inflicted the punishment on them that he had often threatened as a joke.[10] Since Mithridates[11] was ravaging the nearby region, Caesar did not want to seem indifferent to threats against Rome's allies, so he proceeded to Rhodes and from there crossed over to the province of Asia. He raised auxiliary forces, forced the king's representative out of the province, and strengthened the loyalty of the states that were wavering and uncertain in their allegiance.

[5] As a military tribune—the first elected position that he held when he came back to Rome—he adopted, with great enthusiasm,

---

6. The chief city on the island of Lesbos, off the province of Asia.

7. The south coastal area of modern Turkey.

8. 78 BCE. The consul Marcus Aemilius Lepidus tried unsuccessfully to repeal some of Sulla's laws.

9. A small island off the province of Asia.

10. Crucifixion; see 74.1.

11. King Mithridates VI of Pontus on the Black Sea. Rome confronted him in a series of wars between 88 and 63 BCE.

the cause of those who were trying to restore the tribunes' authority
that Sulla had reduced. Also, he used a bill introduced by Plotius to
restore the citizenship of his brother-in-law Lucius Cinna, as well
as that of those who had supported Lepidus with him in the time of
civil unrest and had escaped to Sertorius after the consul's death.[12]
He addressed the issue himself before the popular assembly.

[6.1] When he was quaestor,[13] Caesar delivered the customary
eulogies from the rostra for his aunt Julia and his wife Cornelia
when they died. In the speech for Julia, he had this to say about the
ancestry that his aunt and father shared: "On her mother's side, my
aunt Julia's family arose from kings, and on her father's, it was linked
to the immortal gods. For the Marcius Rex family—her mother's
name was Marcia—is descended from Ancus Marcius. The Julians,
the clan to which our family belongs, are descended from Venus.[14]
And so in her family there are present both the solemn respect due
kings, who have the greatest power among men, and the reverence
due gods, in whose power the kings themselves abide."

[6.2] Caesar married Pompeia to take Cornelia's place. She was the
daughter of Quintus Pompeius[15] and granddaughter of Lucius Sulla.
He divorced her later on suspicion of adultery with Publius Clodius.
Clodius had allegedly had access to Pompeia when he slipped into an
officially sanctioned religious observance in woman's clothing; the
story was so persistent that the senate opened an inquiry about the
defilement of the sacred rites.[16]

------

12. Caesar was military tribune in 72 or 71 BCE. Lepidus died shortly after
he failed to overturn Sulla's laws in 78. Cinna and others joined Quintus
Sertorius, who held out in Spain in support of the Marian cause until 72.
Plotius (otherwise unknown) introduced a law that provided for Cinna's
recall.

13. 69 BCE.

14. Ancus Marcius was an early king of Rome. The Julians had begun to
claim descent from the goddess Venus through Julus (Ascanius), son of
Venus' son Aeneas, the Trojan hero.

15. Consul with Sulla in 88 BCE.

16. This scandal happened in 62 BCE when Clodius entered Caesar's house
while the rites of the Bona Dea (Good Goddess) were being celebrated.
Men were strictly excluded from this ritual. Publius Clodius Pulcher was
later adopted into a plebeian family in 59 so that he could become tribune,
a position that would allow him to attack Cicero; see 20.4 and *Tib.* 2.4.

[7.1] When he was quaestor, the province of Further Spain fell to him by lot. When the governor ordered him to travel around the district courts to administer justice and he arrived at Gades, he noticed the statue of Alexander the Great at the temple of Hercules and groaned as though disgusted with his own idleness—he had done nothing worth remembering at an age when Alexander had already conquered the world. He immediately asked to be released from his assignment so that he could take advantage of the greater opportunities available in Rome as soon as he could. [7.2] Soothsayers further incited him to pursue his most extravagant ambitions. The night after he saw the statue he was troubled in his sleep by a dream in which he had raped his mother. They interpreted this as portending rule over all the world, since his mother, whom he saw lying there at his mercy, was none other than the earth, which is considered the parent of all humankind. [8] He left Spain before his time in office was over and went to the Latin colonies that were claiming citizenship.[17] He would have incited them to take action if the consuls had not anticipated unrest and kept the legions that they had raised for Cilicia stationed there for a time.

[9.1] Nonetheless, Caesar soon made more ambitious plans in Rome. A few days before becoming aedile, he was suspected of conspiring with the former consul Marcus Crassus and also with Publius Sulla and Lucius Autronius, who had been convicted of illegal canvassing when they were elected to the consulship.[18] Their plan was to attack the senate at the opening of the year[19] and then, after they had killed those that they had decided on, Crassus would become dictator and name Caesar his master of the horse.[20] Sulla and Autronius were to be reinstated to the consulship after the conspirators had put the state in order according to their design. [9.2] This conspiracy appears in the history of Tanusius Geminus, the edicts of Marcus Bibulus, and the orations of the elder Gaius

---

17. Towns in Italy north of the Po River.

18. In 66 BCE. Marcus Licinius Crassus, consul in 70 and again in 55, was influential because of his wealth. He would later be a member of the triumvirate; see 19.2. Publius Cornelius Sulla was the nephew of the dictator Sulla.

19. 65 BCE.

20. A dictator was a temporary supreme magistrate chosen at a time of crisis. He appointed a master of the horse as second in command.

Curio. Cicero also appears to refer to it in a letter to Axius when he
says that Caesar established in his consulship the monarchy that he
had contemplated when he was aedile. Tanusius adds that Crassus,
either from a change of heart or from fear, did not appear on the day
chosen for the killings, and for that reason Caesar did not give the
signal on which they had agreed. Curio says that he was to let his
toga slip from his shoulder. [9.3] Curio and Marcus Actorius Naso[21]
are also responsible for the story that Caesar conspired with the
young Gnaeus Piso as well.[22] Piso had been awarded the province of
Spain by an irregular procedure and without his asking, because he
was suspected of hatching a plot in the city. Piso abroad and Caesar
in Rome agreed to incite revolution simultaneously with the help of
the Ambrani and the Transpadanes.[23] These plans were abandoned
when Piso died.

[10.1] When he was aedile, Caesar fitted the Capitoline (also the
Comitium and the Forum and its public buildings) with temporary
covered arcades in which to display some of the large quantity of
stage machinery that he had ready. He presented beast hunts and
games both with a colleague and by himself, but he did it in such a
way that he alone received thanks for what had been done at shared
expense. His colleague Marcus Bibulus did not let this pass but said,
"What happened to Pollux has happened to me: for when the temple
to the twin brothers was raised in the Forum, it was called only the
'Temple of Castor.' In like fashion, the bounty that Caesar and I
provided together is called Caesar's alone." [10.2] Caesar also presented a gladiatorial show but with somewhat fewer pairs of fighters
than he had planned. Because the huge gang of gladiators that he had
collected from all parts intimidated his enemies, legal remedies were
taken as to the maximum number of gladiators that any one person
was permitted to have in Rome.

---

21. This paragraph lists several writers hostile to Caesar: on Gaius
Scribonius Curio (the elder), see also 49.1, 50, 52. Marcus Bibulus would
share offices with Caesar several times; see 10.1, 19.1–2. Quintus Axius
was a correspondent of Cicero. Tanusius is known only here. Naso wrote a
history of the period.
22. Gnaeus Calpurnius Piso; the Calpurnii Pisones played prominent roles
in the early empire.
23. The Ambrani lived on the coast of northwest Italy and what is today
southeast France; the Transpadanes lived north of the Po.

[11] Once Caesar was certain that he was popular with the common people, he tried with the help of some of the tribunes to have Egypt awarded to him as a province by popular vote. He recognized the opportunity that this special command offered; the citizens of Alexandria had driven out their king, who had been named a friend and ally by the senate, and their action was widely disapproved. Opposition from the *optimates* rendered him unsuccessful. In retaliation and in order to reduce that party's influence in every way he could, he again set up the trophies of Gaius Marius that Sulla had torn down earlier, trophies that commemorated victories over Jugurtha and over the Cimbri and the Teutones.[24] When Caesar was presiding over the court that tried murder cases, he included in his definition of "murderer" those who had received payment from the state for the heads of citizens that they had brought in during the proscription, despite the fact that they were immune according to the Cornelian laws.[25] [12] He also suborned someone to bring a charge of high treason against Gaius Rabirius, who had been the senate's principal agent some years earlier when it was reining in the subversive tribune Lucius Saturninus.[26] It fell to Caesar by lot to pronounce sentence in this case, and he was so eager to find him guilty that when Rabirius appealed his case to the people, nothing did him more good than the harshness of his judge. [13] Caesar abandoned hope of obtaining the province and campaigned for the office of *pontifex maximus*, distributing very generous bribes in the process. When he calculated the size of the debt he had run up as a result, he is said to have told his mother, when she kissed him good-bye the morning he left for the polling place, "I won't come home unless I come home *pontifex*." He defeated two very powerful competitors for the priesthood, both of whom were much older and more distinguished than he, and he did this so decisively that he received more votes in their tribes than either of them did all told.

[14.1] Caesar was praetor elect when the conspiracy headed by Catiline was exposed and the entire senate was determined on the death penalty for his coconspirators. Caesar alone took the position

---

24. Marius' (1.3) military successes were against Jugurtha in Africa and Germanic tribes in the north.

25. These laws made Sulla's agents exempt from prosecution.

26. 63 BCE. Old business: Rabirius was accused of killing Lucius Appuleius Saturninus thirty-seven years earlier.

that their property should be confiscated by the state and that they should be imprisoned in different towns.[27] Indeed, by pointing out over and over again how much the common people would come to hate them, he instilled such fear into those urging draconian measures that Decimus Silanus, the consul designate, was not ashamed to moderate the proposal he had made (it would have been disgraceful to change it), giving the excuse that it had been understood as harsher than he had intended. [14.2] Caesar would have carried his point, since many were already on his side (among them Cicero, the consul's brother),[28] if a speech by Marcus Cato[29] had not strengthened the resolve of the senators who were having trouble reaching a decision. Not even then did Caesar stop putting obstacles in the way, not until the armed band of Roman knights standing guard around the senate threatened to kill him as he continued to press his case. They even pointed their drawn swords at him, and this led those who were closest to him to leave him sitting alone. The few who shielded him had difficulty getting their arms around him and throwing their togas over him. He was obviously frightened at that point, and he not only called off the fight but kept away from the senate meetings for the rest of the year.

[15] On the first day that he was praetor, Caesar summoned Quintus Catulus to render an account to the people about the restoration of the Capitol, and he introduced a bill in which responsibility for the project was transferred from Catulus to someone else.[30] But he could not stand up to the united opposition of the *optimates*. When he saw that they had immediately stopped attending to the new consuls and had gathered in large numbers to resist him, he dropped the proceedings. [16.1] But he offered himself as a very tenacious backer and defender of the tribune Caecilius Metellus, who, in spite of his colleagues' veto, was proposing laws that would be extremely disruptive. Caesar stopped when a decree

27. The participants in the conspiracy headed by Lucius Sergius Catilina were arrested in late 63 BCE. The renowned orator Marcus Tullius Cicero was consul that year and took the lead in advocating for the death penalty.

28. Quintus Tullius Cicero.

29. Marcus Porcius Cato (Uticensis), Caesar's conservative archenemy.

30. January 1, 62 BCE. Quintus Lutatius Catulus Capitolinus belonged to the *optimates*.

of the senators relieved both Metellus and himself of their responsibilities.[31] But he had the audacity to carry on with his duties and
preside over the courts until he learned that some were ready to
bar him by force of arms. He then dismissed his lictors, took off his
magistrate's toga, and sought refuge quietly at home, intending to
lie low as the situation required. [16.2] Two days later he restrained
the crowd that had gathered spontaneously and was enthusiastically
promising to support him in an attempt to restore his influence.
This temperate response was unanticipated, and the senate that had
been hastily called into session because of the mob sent its most
prominent members to thank him. They summoned him to the
senate house, praised him generously, and, canceling the earlier
decree, restored him to office.

[17.1] Caesar found himself in danger once again when he was
named as one of Catiline's associates. An informer, Lucius Vettius,
made the charge before the quaestor Novius Niger, and in the senate it was brought by Quintus Curius, to whom the state had voted
a reward because he was the first to uncover the conspirators' plans.
Curius claimed that he had learned about Caesar's complicity from
Catiline himself. Vettius even promised to produce a document
given to Catiline that was in Caesar's handwriting. [17.2] There was
no way that Caesar would allow this allegation to stand. Appealing
to Cicero's testimony, he explained that he had, on his own, reported
certain details of the conspiracy to Cicero, and he saw to it that
Curius was not given his reward money. As for Vettius, the bond he
had posted was forfeit,[32] his home was ransacked, and he was badly
beaten and almost torn to pieces in front of the rostra at a public
assembly before Caesar threw him into prison. He treated Novius
the same way because the quaestor had allowed a magistrate of superior rank to be arraigned in his court.

[18.1] After his praetorship, the province of Further Spain fell to
his lot. Financial guarantors helped him rid himself of the creditors
who were trying to keep him in Rome, and he set out before provincial appointments were fully arranged, conduct that was neither
usual nor legal. It is unclear whether his haste derived from fear

---

31. Quintus Caecilius Metellus was evidently proposing drastic measures in
response to the crushing of the Catilinarian conspiracy the previous year.

32. A plaintiff had to put up a bond, a requirement that discouraged frivolous lawsuits.

of the legal proceedings in store for him now that he was a private citizen or from a desire to be more prompt in his support of the allied states that were begging for help. He put the province in order and went back to Rome just as quickly as he had left, without waiting for the arrival of his successor. He wanted a triumph and a consulship. [18.2] But since the elections had already been announced, he could not be added to the list of candidates unless he entered the city as a private citizen. Many opposed his petition to be exempt from this law, and he had to forgo the triumph so as not to be denied the consulship. [19.1] Of his two competitors, Lucius Lucceius and Marcus Bibulus, he made common cause with Lucceius and arranged for him (he was less popular than Caesar but had more funds) to promise the voting blocks money in both their names. When the *optimates* learned of this, they saw to it that Bibulus promised the same amount, for they were afraid that once Caesar reached the highest office, he would stop at nothing if he had a like-minded colleague in league with him. Many contributed money; even Cato agreed that this time bribery was for the good of the state.

[19.2] And so Caesar was elected consul along with Bibulus. The *optimates* continued to be apprehensive and assigned the least important provinces to the consuls at the time when they entered office—supervision of the forests and the public pasturelands.[33] Caesar was deeply insulted by this slight and made all manner of friendly overtures to Gnaeus Pompey, who was at odds with the senate because it had been too slow to ratify the arrangements he had made after defeating King Mithridates. Caesar reconciled Pompey with Marcus Crassus, who had been Pompey's enemy ever since their serious quarrels when they shared the consulship. He entered into a compact with both of them with the object that nothing be done in the state that displeased any one of the three.[34]

[20.1] Caesar's very first act on entering office[35] was to ensure that the daily register of affairs, not only those of the senate but of the people as well, was written up and made public. He reinstated

---

33. These were the assignments that they would have after their terms in office; forests and pasturelands did not come with armies.

34. The alliance of Caesar, Gnaeus Pompeius Magnus (Pompey the Great), and Crassus (9.1), consuls in 70 BCE, became known as the First Triumvirate.

35. He became consul on January 1, 59 BCE.

the ancient custom by which, in a month when he did not have the *fasces*, an attendant went before him and the lictors followed behind.[36] When a land reform bill was being brought forward and his coconsul Bibulus announced that the omens were unfavorable for the transaction of official business,[37] Caesar used force to eject him from the Forum. The next day Bibulus complained in the senate, but no one could be found who had the courage to speak to the matter or even express an opinion about the disturbance, although often in the past decrees had addressed cases of civil disorder that were similar but less troubling. Bibulus was rendered so desperate that until he left office, he did nothing but hide in his house and issue edicts about unfavorable omens. [20.2] From then on, one man and one man alone ordered all the business of the state in accordance with his own desires. When some clever wags made a joke about witnessing a document, they wrote that something was done "in the consulship of Julius and Caesar," instead of "in the consulship of Caesar and Bibulus," dating it twice with the same person by giving both his family name and his cognomen. And these verses made the rounds:

> What was done just now was done in Caesar's consulship—not Bibulus'.
> I don't remember anything that was done when Bibulus was consul.

[20.3] Caesar divided up the plain called Stellas,[38] an area that our forefathers had set aside as inviolable, and the Campanian land that had been left as a revenue-producing property for the state, and he distributed it, not by lot but directly, to twenty thousand citizens who had three or more children. For the relief of the tax contractors who were seeking abatement, he reduced the amount they had to pay by a third but warned them publicly not to bid irresponsibly when new contracts were awarded. And he granted anything anyone wanted; no one objected, or if anyone tried to, he was frightened off. [20.4] When Marcus Cato interfered, Caesar ordered him hauled out of the senate house by a lictor and taken to prison. When Lucius

---

36. The two consuls for the year ruled in alternate months. Twelve lictors with *fasces* went before the consul in the month when he served.

37. Public business was interrupted when a magistrate observed an adverse sign in the sky.

38. In northern Campania.

Lucullus[39] opposed him too audaciously, Caesar made him so afraid that false charges would be brought against him that Lucullus fell on his knees before him unprompted. At the ninth hour of a day when Cicero was speaking in court and deploring the current state of affairs, Caesar moved Publius Clodius from patrician to plebeian status. Clodius was Cicero's enemy, and he had struggled unsuccessfully for a long time to make the change.[40] [20.5] Finally, in order to challenge the opposing faction as a group, he bribed an informer to confess that certain people had tried to get him to kill Pompey, and it was agreed that the man would name them before the rostra. When the informer had offered one or two names to no effect and had aroused suspicion that he was making false accusations, Caesar abandoned this plan as ill conceived and poisoned the informer—or so it is believed.

[21] At about this time Caesar married Calpurnia, the daughter of Lucius Piso, consul elect, and he arranged for his own daughter Julia to marry Gnaeus Pompey. Her earlier engagement to Servilius Caepio was broken off despite the fact that Servilius had been especially helpful to Caesar in his recent attack on Bibulus. After this new relationship came into being, he began to ask Pompey to give his opinion in the senate first, although it had been his practice to ask Crassus to speak first and it was customary for the consul to adhere throughout the year to the order that he had established on the first day of January.

[22.1] And so, with the support of his father-in-law and his son-in-law,[41] Caesar chose Gaul from all the available provinces. It offered financial prospects and provided convenient possibilities for triumphs. In the beginning he received Cisalpine Gaul and Illyricum under provision of the Vatinian law.[42] Then the senate granted him

---

39. Lucius Licinius Lucullus, known for his luxurious living at the end of his life; see *Tib.* 73.1.

40. The adoption into a plebeian family was put through hastily after the close of the normal business day. Clodius (originally Claudius) wanted to be a tribune in order to attack Cicero; only plebeians could be tribunes.

41. Piso and Pompey.

42. A law proposed by the tribune Publius Vatinius, a supporter of Caesar. Laws might address a specific case.

Gallia Comata[43] as well, because they were afraid that if they did not, the people would give him this, too. [22.2] Caesar was overjoyed and could not keep from boasting a few days later in the crowded senate house, "I got exactly what I wanted despite the moans and groans of my reluctant rivals; from now on I will be mounting the heads of all of them." And when someone insulted him by saying that this would not be easy for a woman to do, he answered with a joke: "Semiramis reigned in Syria, and the Amazons once controlled a large part of Asia."[44]

[23.1] When his term as consul ended and the praetors Gaius Memmius and Lucius Domitius[45] were beginning to look into his activities of the previous year, he handed the investigation over to the senate. But when the senate did not address it and wasted three days in meaningless arguments, he left for his province. His quaestor was immediately detained for a preliminary proceeding on a number of charges, and then the tribune Lucius Antistius indicted Caesar himself. Caesar appealed to the board of tribunes as a whole and avoided a trial on the argument that he was away from Rome on the state's business. [23.2] Learning from this experience, Caesar resolved to protect himself in the future and always made a great effort to put the annually elected magistrates in his debt. He did not support a candidate or allow anyone to reach high office who did not agree to fight his battles for him when he was away from Rome. He did not hesitate to make some of them seal this bargain with an oath and even execute a written contract. [24.1] But when Lucius Domitius, a candidate for the consulship, threatened openly to do as consul what he had been unable to do as praetor (that is, deprive Caesar of his army), Caesar summoned Crassus and Pompey to Luca, a city in his province,[46] to persuade them to seek second consulships in order to force Domitius out of the contest. He also made sure that their influence would be

---

43. "Hairy Gaul," Gaul beyond the Alps, so called because it was uncivilized.

44. "Mounting the head" meant forcing someone to perform oral sex. The slur of his being a woman comes from Caesar's alleged relationship with Nicomedes; see chapter 2. Semiramis was a legendary queen and the Amazons legendary female warriors.

45. Memmius continued to attack Caesar; see 49.2, 73. Lucius Domitius Ahenobarbus was an ancestor of the emperor Nero; see *Ner.* 2.2–3.

46. Cisalpine Gaul. This conference took place in 56 BCE.

used to extend his command for five years.[47] [24.2] This arrangement
increased his confidence, and he added legions to the number that
he had been given by the state, and he paid for them himself. One
was raised in Transalpine Gaul and had a Gallic name, Alauda.[48]
He awarded citizenship to every soldier in the legion, once it had
the benefit of Roman training and was equipped with Roman arms.
[24.3] After that, he did not let pass any excuse to make war, not even
unjust or dangerous war, and he harassed Rome's allies as well as the
brutal and hostile tribes. It was for this reason that on one occasion
the senate decided to send representatives to look into the situation
in the Gallic provinces; some thought that Caesar should be handed
over to the enemy. But things went well for him, and he earned more
celebrations of thanksgiving for his military successes than anyone
ever before, and they were of longer duration.

[25.1] The following are more or less the wars that he waged in
the nine years that he held his command. With the exception of
some allied states that had served him well, he reduced all of Gaul
to provincial status, the land bounded by the high mountains of
the Pyrenees and by the Alps and by Mount Cebenna[49] and by the
Rhine and Rhone rivers, an area 3,200 miles in circumference. He
imposed on it an annual payment of 40 million sesterces to defray
the cost of his occupying army. [25.2] Caesar was the first Roman to
build a bridge and advance against the Germans who lived across the
Rhine, and he inflicted devastating casualties on them. He attacked
the British people, who had been unknown up to then, and when
he had conquered them, he ordered them to hand over tribute and
hostages. He suffered reverses only three times in the course of
all these successful engagements: while he was in Britain his fleet
was almost destroyed in a storm, in Gaul a legion was routed near
Gergovia,[50] and in the German territories his lieutenants Titurius
and Aurunculeius were killed in an ambush.

[26.1] During this period, he lost first his mother, then his daughter, and shortly thereafter his grandchild. Meanwhile, when there

---

47. Caesar's initial command in Gaul had been from 58 to 54 BCE. This
arrangement added five more years.
48. "Crested lark," from the shape of the crests on their helmets.
49. The Cévennes; southeast France.
50. In central Gaul.

was great confusion in the state because of the murder of Publius Clodius,[51] the senate voted that there be only one consul and named Gnaeus Pompey to the position. The tribunes intended that Caesar be Pompey's colleague, but Caesar persuaded them to propose an alternative to the people, that he be permitted to stand for a second consulship in absentia when his command was nearing its end. This would prevent his having to leave Gaul prematurely to run for office with his military objectives still unrealized. [26.2] When Caesar had gotten what he wanted, he was filled with optimism and focused on more ambitious projects. He let slip no opportunity to bribe or do favors for anyone, either in his public capacity or as a private citizen. With spoils from his campaigns, he began to build a forum in Rome on ground that cost more than 100 million sesterces. He proclaimed the unprecedented honors of a gladiatorial show and a public banquet in memory of his daughter.[52] So that people would eagerly look forward to these events, he had his private staff prepare some of the food for the banquet, although arrangements had been made through the markets. [26.3] When celebrated gladiators fought before unfriendly crowds, he ordered them rescued by force and held for his own games.[53] He saw to it that novice combatants were trained, not in the gladiatorial school or by professionals, but in private homes by Roman knights and even by senators who had experience in armed combat. He pleaded earnestly with these sponsors (this can be seen in his letters) to give their personal attention to the trainees and to instruct their practice themselves. He doubled legionary pay permanently. Whenever grain was available, he offered it to the soldiers without limit or measure and sometimes gave each a slave from his private booty.

[27.1] To retain Pompey's goodwill and keep him as his kinsman, Caesar offered him marriage with Octavia, his sister's granddaughter who was married to Gaius Marcellus.[54] His own plan was to marry

---

51. Clodius (6.2) was killed in January of 52 BCE by a gang employed by his political enemy Milo (30.3).

52. Unprecedented for a woman.

53. Defeated gladiators who displeased the spectators were normally killed.

54. Pompey refused the offer. Gaius Claudius Marcellus would be consul in 50 BCE (29.1). His cousins were Marcus, who was consul in 51 (28.2–3), and another Gaius, who was consul in 49. All three were hostile to Caesar.

Pompey's daughter, who was intended for Faustus Sulla.[55] He put
all of Pompey's associates and even a large part of the senate under
obligation to himself by giving them free or low-cost loans. He made
extremely generous bequests to members of the other orders, both
those whom he sought out and those who came to him on their own,
and also to their freedmen and young slaves in proportion to the favor
that they enjoyed with their master or patron. [27.2] Furthermore,
he was the only one genuinely willing to help people accused of
crimes or in debt or who were profligate young men. He helped
them unless their criminal charges, poverty, or level of extravagant
living pressed more heavily on them than he could remedy. To these
he stated explicitly, "Civil war is clearly a necessity." [28.1] He was
just as eager to win over kings and provinces throughout the world.
To some he offered the enticement of thousands of captives; to others he sent military aid—when they wished it and as often as they
wished it—without the authorization of the senate and the Roman
people. He also made beautiful with splendid public works the most
important cities of Italy and of the Gallic and Spanish provinces, and
also those of Asia and Greece.

[28.2] At this point everyone was awed by his activity and won-
dering where it would end. Finally the consul, Marcus Claudius
Marcellus, introduced a proposal to the senate and prefaced it with
the announcement that he was about to set forth a matter of great
importance to the state. He proposed that Caesar be replaced before
the term of his command had ended. The war was over, peace had
been established, and the victorious army ought to be discharged. He
further proposed that a candidate who was not in the city should not
be on the ballot, since Pompey had not, despite subsequent legislation, annulled the decree of the people. [28.3] (It had happened that
when Pompey proposed a law concerning the rights and privileges
of magistrates, he forgot to make an exception for Caesar in the
section barring candidacy in absentia. He corrected his error later
after the law had already been engraved in bronze and stored in the
aerarium.) Marcellus was not content to seize Caesar's provinces and
take away his special privileges; he also proposed that the colonists
whom Caesar had settled at Novum Comum by provision of the

---

55. A daughter of Pompey by an earlier wife; Faustus Cornelius Sulla was
the son of the dictator (also at 75.3). These plans came to nothing.

Vatinian law[56] be deprived of citizenship on the grounds that the privilege had been granted to curry favor and had exceeded the law's intent. [29.1] Caesar was incensed at this turn of events; as he was often heard to say, "It will be more difficult to push me from the first position in the state to the second than from the second to the lowest." He used all of his resources to oppose the measures taken against him; he sometimes had the tribunes intervene with vetoes on his behalf and sometimes the other consul, Servius Sulpicius.

When Gaius Marcellus, who had followed his first cousin Marcus in the consulship, tried to introduce the same bill the following year,[57] Caesar extended a huge bribe to secure the support of the other consul, Aemilius Paulus, and of Gaius Curio, the most aggressive of the tribunes.[58] [29.2] But when he saw that everything was inevitably going to go against him and that even the consuls for the coming year were lined up with his enemies, he wrote a letter to the senate asking that the benefit conferred by the people not be taken from him[59] or, alternatively, that other generals divest themselves of their armies as well. He was confident (or so it is thought) that it would be easier for him to assemble his veterans when he wanted than for Pompey to enlist new soldiers, and so he suggested to his opponents that, until he became consul, he give up eight legions and Transalpine Gaul but keep two legions and the province of Cisalpine Gaul, or even a single legion along with Illyricum. [30.1] But when the senate did not intervene in this dispute, and his enemies declared that they would not bargain with the state's well-being, he crossed into Nearer Gaul,[60] completed his circuit of the courts, and took up a position at Ravenna. He was ready to claim his entitlement by war if the senate came down too harshly on the tribunes who were interceding on his behalf.[61]

---

56. Modern Como, in Cisalpine Gaul. On the Vatinian law, see 22.1.

57. 50 BCE.

58. Gaius Sempronius Curio (the younger), son of Curio (the elder); see 9.2, 36, and 50.1.

59. That is, permission to stand for the consulship in absentia, without disbanding his army; see 26.1–2.

60. Cisalpine Gaul.

61. As was their right, two tribunes vetoed the decree that required Caesar to disband his army. The senate ignored their veto, and the two were forced to flee.

[30.2] This was, to be sure, the rationale Caesar gave for civil war, but it is thought that he had had other motives: Gnaeus Pompey said repeatedly that Caesar's personal wealth was insufficient either to complete the projects he had taken on or to fulfill the expectations of the people when he returned home; as a consequence, he wanted to throw everything into confusion and create chaos. [30.3] Others say that he was afraid that he would be forced to render an account of what he had done in his first consulship when he had flouted the auspices and ignored the vetoes of the tribunes. Marcus Cato had declared repeatedly under oath that he would initiate criminal proceedings against Caesar just as soon as he let his army go, and it was widely predicted that if Caesar returned as a private citizen, he would plead his case in court surrounded by armed men as Milo had.[62] [30.4] Pollio[63] lent further credence to this explanation when he reported the exact words that Caesar spoke at the battle at Pharsalus[64] as he looked out on his enemies, dead and dying: "This is what they wanted. They would have found me, Gaius Caesar, guilty, despite my magnificent achievements, if I had not turned to my army for help." [30.5] There are some who think that, seduced by the habit of command, he assessed his strength and that of his enemies and seized the opportunity to grasp the absolute power that he had wanted from an early age. Cicero, among others, apparently attributed this motive to him when he wrote in the third book of *De officiis* that lines of Euripides were always on Caesar's lips.[65] Cicero translates them like this:

> If justice must be outraged, it must be done
> To rule. In other things, respect the good.

[31.1] And so, as soon as he learned that the tribunes' veto had not been sustained and that they had fled the city, he quickly sent cohorts on ahead in secret, and so as not to arouse suspicion and to conceal

---

62. Titus Annius Milo, supporter of Cicero and notorious opponent of Clodius, was convicted of Clodius' murder in 52 BCE; see 26.1.

63. Gaius Asinius Pollio lived into the empire; he was an orator and author of a history of the civil war. Suetonius cites him as a source again at 55.4 and 56.4.

64. The battle of the civil war in which Caesar defeated Pompey in 48 BCE.

65. *De officiis* 3.82. The quotation is from *Phoenician Women* 524–25.

what he was going to do, he was present at a public entertainment, gave his attention to plans for the school for gladiators that he was intending to build, and, as he often did, attended a dinner party with a large number of guests. [31.2] Then, after sunset, he took mules from a nearby mill, harnessed them to his carriage, and set out with a small company by a very obscure route. When their torches went out and he lost the road, he wandered about for a long time until, near daybreak, he found a guide and walked back to the road along narrow paths. When he joined his cohorts near the river Rubicon, the boundary of his province,[66] he stopped for a short time and thought about the enormity of what he was about to set in motion. He turned to those closest to him and said, "We can still turn back. But once we cross this little bridge, everything will have to be settled by arms." [32] While he paused, he saw something wonderful: a figure of remarkable size and beauty was suddenly sitting nearby, playing on a pipe. The shepherds came running to listen to him, and the soldiers too from their posts, and with them came the trumpeters. The apparition seized a horn from one of them and, rushing toward the river, raised the call to battle with a mighty blast and pressed forward to the opposite bank. Then Caesar said, "Let us go where we are summoned by the miracles sent by the gods and by the wrong done us by our enemies. The die is cast." [33] And so when the army had crossed over and was joined by the tribunes who had been forced out of Rome, Caesar held an assembly, and weeping and tearing the clothing from his breast, he summoned forth allegiance from his soldiers. Some think that he even promised equestrian status to each and every one of them. But this is incorrect, for while he was speaking to them and exhorting them, he kept showing them the finger of his left hand and professing that he would gladly tear the ring from it to reward all those who were with him in his effort to uphold his position of honor. Those who were at the far edge of the assembly could see him as he spoke more easily than they could hear him and believed that he had said what they guessed from what they saw. The story spread that he had promised the right to the ring together with a gift of 400,000 sesterces.[67]

[34.1] Here in order are the most important things that Caesar did after that: He seized Picenum, Umbria, and Etruria. He took into

---

66. A small river that was the boundary of Cisalpine Gaul. It was an act of treason to bring an army into Italy.

67. The gold ring of the senatorial and equestrian orders.

custody and then released Lucius Domitius, who had been named
his successor after the outbreak of hostilities and was defending
Corfinium with a garrison. He proceeded along the Adriatic to
Brundisium where Pompey and the consuls had retreated so that
they could cross to Greece as soon as possible. [34.2] He tried without success to block their escape by creating obstacles of all sorts. He
returned to Rome, summoned the senate to discuss state business,
and then moved against Pompey's strongest forces, which were in
Spain under the command of three lieutenants, Marcus Petreius,
Lucius Afranius, and Marcus Varro. But before he left he said to
his close associates, "I am going to face an army without a general
and will return to a general without an army." And although he was
delayed by laying siege to Massilia,[68] a town in his path that had
closed its gates to him, and by a severe shortage of provisions, he
nonetheless quickly gained supremacy everywhere.

[35.1] From Spain, Caesar returned to Rome and then crossed
over to Macedonia to confront Pompey. For almost four months he
blockaded him with massive siege works and kept him shut up in
camp, but he finally routed him on the battlefield at Pharsalus and
followed him when he fled to Alexandria. When he learned that
Pompey had been killed, he made war against King Ptolemy,[69] who
he understood was also planning to entrap him. This war was truly
very difficult since it was fought neither in a place nor at a time of
year that gave the Romans equal odds, but in the winter within the
walls of a city that was home to a very large and well-trained enemy
force. Caesar was unprepared and in need of provisions of every
kind. After the war was won, he turned the kingdom of Egypt over
to Cleopatra and her younger brother. He did not make it into a
province because he feared that it offered potential for revolution if
at some time in the future it should have an ambitious governor.

[35.2] From Alexandria, he went to Syria and from there to
Pontus in response to urgent news regarding Pharnaces, the son of
Mithridates the Great. Pharnaces had been making war whenever
the opportunity presented, and his great success had made him reckless. Within five days of arriving, within four hours of catching sight
of the enemy forces, Caesar crushed them in a single battle. He often
remarked upon the good fortune that had been granted Pompey, who

---

68. Modern Marseilles.
69. Ptolemy XIII, boy king of Egypt married to his sister Cleopatra.

was praised for his exceptional military skill when he fought weak enemies like this one. Next he defeated Scipio and Juba,[70] who commanded remnants of the enemy faction that was reviving in Africa, and Pompey's sons in Spain.

[36] The only losses that Caesar suffered in all the campaigns of the civil war were those that befell his lieutenants. Gaius Curio died in Africa. Gaius Antonius fell into enemy hands in Illyricum. Publius Dolabella[71] lost a fleet also near Illyricum, and Gnaeus Domitius Calvinus an army in Pontus. Caesar himself was always very successful when he fought, and only twice was the outcome of an engagement in doubt. Once when he was in retreat at Dyrrachium[72] and Pompey did not press his advantage, Caesar's comment was that his opponent did not know how to win. The second time was in the final battle in Spain when the situation seemed so hopeless that he even contemplated suicide.

[37.1] Caesar celebrated five triumphs after the wars, four of them in the same month after the defeat of Scipio but with several days in between, and one after the defeat of Pompey's sons. The first and most elaborate was his triumph over Gaul, the second, his triumph over the Alexandrians, then over Pontus and the one after that his triumph over Africa and the last over Spain. The display was different for each. [37.2] When he was passing through the Velabrum[73] on the day of the Gallic triumph, his chariot axle broke and he was almost thrown out. He ascended the Capitoline by torchlight with forty elephants supporting lamps on his right and left. At the Pontic triumph he displayed among items in the procession a placard on which three words were written:

VENI VIDI VICI[74]

---

70. Quintus Caecilius Metellus Pius Scipio, consul in 52 BCE and a diehard supporter of Pompey. Juba was a prince of Numidia. The final battle in Africa took place in 46 BCE.

71. See Curio at 29.1. Publius Cornelius Dolabella was not the Dolabella whom Caesar prosecuted; see 4.1, 55.1.

72. A town in Macedonia near the coast at the border of Dalmatia, the site of the siege that was described at 35.1.

73. A busy passage near the Forum through which the triumphal parade passed.

74. "I came. I saw. I conquered." This placard referred to his victory over Pharnaces; see 35.2.

This did not illustrate deeds done in the war as did other placards but signified that the battle had been completed quickly.

[38.1] Caesar gave each foot soldier 24,000 sesterces, calling it booty due his veteran legions. This was in addition to the 2,000 sesterces that he had paid them at the beginning of the civil war. He allocated land but not in contiguous parcels, so that none of the owners would be forced out. He distributed to each citizen, in addition to ten measures of grain and the same number of pounds of oil, the 300 sesterces that he had promised in the beginning, along with another hundred to compensate for the delay. [38.2] He waived a year's rent in Rome up to the amount of 2,000 sesterces, and in Italy, up to 500. He added a public banquet and a distribution of meat, and after his victory in Spain, he gave two dinners. Deciding that he had provided the first banquet on the cheap and in a manner inconsistent with his generosity, he gave a second, very lavish one five days later.

[39.1] He sponsored an assortment of entertainments: a gladiatorial show, theatrical productions in all the wards of the city (these featured actors of all languages), races in the Circus, athletic contests, and a staged sea battle. In the gladiatorial contest in the Forum, Furius Leptinus, descended from praetors, fought with Quintus Calpenus, formerly a senator who had argued cases before the court. The sons of the leading men of Asia and Bithynia performed a Pyrrhic dance.[75] [39.2] In the theater the Roman knight Decimus Laberius acted in a pantomime that he had written, and when he was awarded 500,000 sesterces and the gold ring, he crossed from the stage through the orchestra and sat in the fourteen rows reserved for knights.[76] For the races the Circus was lengthened at each end and a ditch dug to encircle it; young men of high rank drove their four-horse and two-horse chariots there and exhibited the skill of jumping between horses. The Game of Troy was performed by two squadrons of boys, older and younger. [39.3] Beast hunts took place for five days straight, and for a finale, a battle was staged with combatants drawn up in two battle lines, each with five hundred foot soldiers, twenty elephants, and thirty horsemen. To give them more space to fight, the turning posts were removed from the Circus, and in their place

---

75. A ritual dance with armor.

76. The first fourteen rows beyond the orchestra were reserved for knights. With his pay, Laberius retrieved the equestrian status that he had forfeited by appearing on the stage.

twin military camps were constructed facing one another. Athletes competed for three days on a track laid out for this purpose in the confines of the Campus Martius. [39.4] In a mock naval battle, ships from the Tyrian and Egyptian fleets with two, three, or four sets of oars and carrying a large number of combatants clashed in a lake that had been dug in the Lesser Codeta.[77] The crowd that converged on Rome for all these entertainments was so large that many of the visitors stayed in tents pitched in the city streets or along the roads, and several times a large number were crushed to death in the crowd, two senators among them.

[40.1] Caesar turned next to ordering the affairs of state. He made corrections to the calendar that had long been in disarray because the priests had been too generous in allowing extra days and months to be inserted. The festival that celebrated the harvest did not fall in the summer nor did that for the gathering of grapes fall in the autumn. He made the year 365 days long so that it was congruent with the course of the sun. He got rid of the extra month that could be inserted but added one day every fourth year. [40.2] To make his calendar fit better with the upcoming Kalends of January, he inserted two extra months between November and December; the year in which the adjustments were made therefore had fifteen months, including the already established intercalary month that had fallen that year.[78]

[41.1] Caesar filled vacancies in the senate, admitted new people to the ranks of patricians, and increased the number of praetors, aediles, and quaestors as well as of less important officials. He restored those whom the censors had deprived of their rank or a jury had found guilty of bribery. [41.2] He shared election responsibilities with the populace. Except for the consulship, half of the other candidates nominated were chosen by the people; the other half were those whom Caesar had named. He made his selections known in brief written notices sent to each tribe: "Caesar Dictator to such and such a tribe: I commend so-and-so to you so that with your vote they may retain the respect due them." He also allowed the sons of men who had been proscribed to seek office. He reduced participation in the

---

77. A low marshy area near the Tiber in the Campus Martius.

78. Before Caesar's reform, the year had consisted of 355 days with an extra ("intercalary") month inserted intermittently after February. Special arrangements were necessary to phase in the new calendar.

courts to two classes of jurors, equestrians and senators. He removed
a third class, that of the treasury tribunes.[79]

[41.3] Caesar took a census of the general populace, but one not
organized in the usual way or by the customary localities. He did
it instead street by street with the help of the owners of apartment
blocks, and he reduced the number of those eligible to receive free
grain from 320,000 to 150,000. To prevent a new assembly from
being convened for the revision of this roll in the future, he made
provision for a drawing of lots every year under a praetor's supervision to determine who not on the list should take the places of those
who had died. [42.1] In order to maintain the population of the city
after eighty thousand of its citizens had been settled in overseas
colonies, he ruled that no citizen older than twenty or younger than
forty,[80] not in military service, should be away from Italy for three
years in succession and that no senator's son should go abroad except
as a military attaché or as an aide to a magistrate. He further ruled
that cattle farmers should have young men of free birth make up at
least a third of their herdsmen. He made citizens of all the medical
doctors in Rome as well as all the instructors in the liberal arts. His
idea was that this would make them more content to settle in the city
and make others come there.

[42.2] With regard to borrowed money, Caesar put an end to the
hope for the debt cancellation that had frequently been demanded,
and in the end he decreed that debtors must satisfy the claims of
their creditors according to the value of their property at the price
they had paid for it before the civil war, after deducting any interest
that had either been paid or promised. This solution erased about a
quarter of the debt. [42.3] He disbanded all the guilds except for the
long-established ones. He increased punishments for breaking the
law. Since the rich found it easier to commit crimes because they
could live as exiles with their fortunes intact, he made murderers
of family members forfeit all their property (as Cicero writes) and
other criminals, half. [43.1] He was most painstaking and strict in
the administration of justice. He took senatorial rank from those
convicted of extortion. He dissolved the marriage of a man of praetorian rank because he had married a woman a mere two days after she
had been divorced by her former husband, even though adultery was

---

79. They had lower financial qualifications.
80. Forty may not be correct; the Latin text is unclear.

not suspected in the case. He created a port tax on foreign imports. He took away the use of a litter and the privilege of wearing purple clothing and pearls from everyone except certain people of certain ages on certain days. [43.2] He was especially careful about enforcing sumptuary laws and placed guards around the market to confiscate the cooked food that had been banned and to bring it to him. And he sometimes sent lictors and soldiers to take from the dining room food that had already been served—in case the guards had missed something.

[44.1] When it came to beautifying and building the city and to protecting and expanding Rome's supremacy, Caesar's plans grew more numerous and more grandiose with each passing day. First of all, he proposed to erect a temple for Mars, the largest ever, by filling in and leveling the lake where he had presented his sea battle,[81] and to build a huge theater in the space next to the Tarpeian Rock.[82] [44.2] He wanted to reduce the corpus of civil law to reasonable size by collecting in a small number of books the essential and best instances from the huge and wide-ranging mass of legal precedents. He wanted to open the most important of the Greek and Latin libraries to the public, and he gave Marcus Varro[83] the responsibility of gathering and organizing the materials. [44.3] He planned to drain the Pomptine marshes, let the water out of Lake Fucinus, build a road from the Adriatic through the spine of the Apennines all the way to the Tiber, dig through the Isthmus of Corinth,[84] check the Dacians who had overrun Pontus and Thrace, and then wage war against the Parthians, approaching them through Lesser Armenia and not engaging their forces in battle before he had assessed their strength.

[44.4] Death prevented him from carrying out these projects and from planning others. Before I tell about his end, it will not

---

81. See 39.4.

82. A steep cliff on the side of the Capitoline Hill; criminals were executed by being thrown from it.

83. Marcus Terentius Varro, a literary figure who was formerly one of Pompey's lieutenants; see 34.2.

84. Almost legendary impossible tasks. The Pomptine marshes lay near the coast south of Rome. Lake Fucinus was a shallow lake in the mountains about fifty miles east of Rome. Claudius would take on the lake project; see *Cl.* 20.1–2.

be inappropriate for me to describe the conspicuous features of his appearance and the way he took care of himself and his lifestyle, his character, and, equally important, the way he thought about civilian and military matters.

[45.1] Caesar is said to have been a tall man with a pale complexion, well-proportioned limbs, a mouth that was a little too large, bright dark eyes, and vigorous good health, except that near the end of his life he would faint suddenly and also suffered nightmares. Twice while engaged in public business he had epileptic seizures. [45.2] He was quite particular about his grooming. He not only had his hair cut and his beard shaved meticulously but even had unwanted hairs plucked, a practice of which some disapproved. He also had a great deal of trouble resigning himself to his baldness, which he thought unsightly because it often exposed him to jokes from his detractors. And so he got into the habit of combing his thinning hair forward from the top of his head, and of all the honors voted him by the senate and the people, there was none that he accepted or made use of with greater pleasure than the permanent right to wear the laurel crown.

[45.3] They say that his dress was striking as well. His senator's tunic had fringed sleeves that came down to his hands, and he always wore it rather loosely belted. This habit gave rise to Sulla's warning the party of the *optimates* to watch out for "the boy with the loose belt."

[46] At first Caesar lived in ordinary accommodations in the Subura, but after he became *pontifex maximus*, he lived in the official residence on the Sacred Way.[85] Many have written about his extravagant passion for elegance and luxury: When still a poor man and in debt, he had a villa near the sacred grove of Diana at Lake Nemi that he had built from the ground up and completed at great expense; he destroyed it totally because it was not exactly what he had had in mind. When he was on campaign, he took with him paving stones of mosaics and marble. [47] He invaded Britain in hope of finding pearls, and these he sometimes held in his hand to assess their size and test their weight. He was always very enthusiastic about collecting precious stones, embossed metalwork, statues, and paintings by artists of the past. He purchased slaves that were attractive and well

---

85. The Subura was a modest district in Rome. The Sacred Way was an important street that ran through the Forum.

trained but so expensive that it embarrassed even him, and he did not allow their purchase price to be entered in his accounts. [48] In the provinces he would hold banquets in two dining rooms; in one, guests wearing soldiers' cloaks or Greek dress reclined at table, in the other, well-born Romans in togas together with the more important provincial dignitaries. He maintained discipline in his household, paying attention to detail, and he exercised great rigor in matters both large and small. He put in chains a baker who served his guests different bread from the bread that he served Caesar, and he executed a favorite freedman who had committed adultery with the wife of a Roman knight, despite the fact that no complaint had been lodged.

[49.1] There was, to be sure, nothing to damage his reputation for accepted sexual behavior—except his sharing a bed with Nicomedes.[86] This, however, was a serious scandal that persisted and exposed him to widespread ridicule. I leave out of consideration the notorious verses of Licinius Calvus[87]—"Everything that Bithynia and Caesar's buggerer ever had"—not to mention the speeches of Dolabella and the elder Curio.[88] Dolabella says, "Caesar was the mistress rival of the queen, the one who slept on the inside in the royal litter." Curio calls him "Nicomedes' brothel" and a "Bithynian whorehouse." [49.2] I ignore as well the edicts that Bibulus released in which he wrote, "My fellow consul was Bithynia's queen; he had once desired a king, but now he desires a kingdom."[89] At that time, as Marcus Brutus[90] tells it, a certain Octavius, a deranged man who talked too freely, addressed Pompey as "King" at a large gathering and then greeted Caesar as "Queen." Gaius Memmius' contribution is that Caesar served as cupbearer to Nicomedes[91] and took his place with other young male prostitutes at a large dinner party where the guests included Roman merchants whom he names. [49.3] Cicero was

---

86. For Nicomedes, see chapter 2.

87. Gaius Licinius Calvus; Suetonius also mentions his verses at 73.

88. The Dolabella whom Caesar prosecuted; see 4.1, 55.1. For Curio, see 9.2.

89. On Bibulus' edicts, see 9.2, 20.1.

90. Marcus Junius Brutus, one of the leaders of the conspiracy that assassinated Caesar; see 80.4.

91. For Memmius, see 23.1. Ganymede, the cupbearer of the gods, signifies a handsome young boy in the sexual service of his master.

not content with stating in some letters that the king's attendants had escorted Caesar to the royal bedchamber where, dressed in purple, he had lain down in a golden bed and that the chastity of the youth descended from Venus was tainted in Bithynia. When Caesar was defending Nicomedes' daughter Nysa in the senate and recalling the favors that the king had tendered him, Cicero said, "Spare us those details, please. Everyone knows what he gave you and what you gave him." Finally, at his Gallic triumph,[92] his soldiers shouted out this tasteless bit among the jokes that they chant when they follow the chariot:

> Caesar rubbed out the Gauls; Nicomedes rubbed down Caesar:
> Look! Caesar rides now in triumph! (He rubbed out the Gauls.)
> No triumph for Nicomedes! (He rubbed down Caesar.)[93]

[50.1] Caesar is generally thought to have been disposed to extra-marital affairs and unrestrained in his quest for them. He damaged the reputations of a large number of distinguished women, among them Postumia, the wife of Servius Sulpicius;[94] Lollia, the wife of Aulus Gabinius;[95] Tertulla, the wife of Marcus Crassus; and even Pompey's wife, Mucia. One thing is certain: the two Curios, father and son, and many others criticized Pompey because his desire for power later prompted him to marry the daughter of the man on whose account he had divorced his wife after she had borne him three children. Pompey had been in the habit of sighing deeply and calling Caesar "Aegisthus."[96] [50.2] But Caesar loved Servilia best of all. She was the mother of Marcus Brutus, and in his last consulship he bought her a pearl that cost 6 million sesterces. During the civil war, in addition to other presents, he made large estates over to her at auction for next to nothing. Many were truly astonished at how

---

92. See 37.1.

93. The meanings of the verb include "massage" and "subjugate" and allow a pun.

94. Servius Sulpicius Rufus, consul in 51 BCE; see 29.1.

95. Consul in 58 BCE.

96. When the Greek general Agamemnon returned home after the end of the Trojan War, he learned that his wife was in an adulterous relationship with Aegisthus. Mucia was unfaithful with Caesar when Pompey was absent on campaign.

cheap they were, and Cicero cleverly quipped, "It was even a better bargain because a third was knocked off." (Servilia was thought to have procured her daughter Tertia for Caesar.)[97]

[51] It is clear from these verses that his soldiers shouted during the Gallic triumph that he did not steer clear of married women, even in the provinces:

> Men of the city! Protect your wives!
> We are bringing the bald adulterer home!
> In Gaul you fucked away all the money
> That you borrowed here in Rome!

[52.1] He loved foreign queens, too, among them Eunoe of Mauretania, wife of Bogudes.[98] According to Naso,[99] Caesar gave her and her husband a large number of generous gifts. But most of all he loved Cleopatra.[100] He often feasted with her until daybreak and would have traveled with her on her luxurious sailing ship deep into Egypt, almost as far as Ethiopia, if his army had not refused to follow. Finally, he brought her to Rome and did not send her away again until he had made her a wealthier and more powerful woman by giving her important honors and rich rewards. And he allowed her to call her son by his name. [52.2] Some Greeks have described this boy as looking and walking like Caesar. Mark Antony[101] told the senate that Caesar himself had claimed the boy and that Gaius Matius, Gaius Oppius,[102] and the rest of Caesar's friends knew this. Gaius Oppius, thinking that the matter clearly needed to be explained and put right, published a book that claimed the boy was not Caesar's son, even though Cleopatra said he was. [52.3] The tribune Helvius Cinna let a number of people know that he had a law, written and in

---

97. The joke lies in the fact that Tertia means "a third."

98. Caesar made Bogudes king in Mauretania to oppose King Juba, who was allied with Pompey; see 35.2.

99. Marcus Actorius Naso; see also 9.3.

100. Cleopatra became coruler of Egypt with her brother Ptolemy XIII in 51 BCE. She was about twenty-one when Caesar met her a few years later.

101. Marcus Antonius, heir apparent after Caesar's assassination; see 82–84.

102. Oppius was particularly close to Caesar (see 72) and assisted him when he was dictator.

hand, that Caesar had directed him to see passed while he was out of the city. It permitted Caesar to marry any wives that he wanted and as many as he wanted for the purpose of siring children. But so that no one may doubt the depths to which his reputation for indecency and adultery had sunk, the elder Curio in one of his speeches called him "a man for every woman and a woman for every man."

[53] Not even his enemies deny that he drank very little wine. Marcus Cato says, "Caesar was the only one who ever tried to overthrow the state sober." Gaius Oppius informs us that Caesar was so uninterested in what he ate that on one occasion he helped himself liberally to the rancid oil that his host had served in place of first-quality olive oil; everyone else refused it, but Caesar did not want to appear to accuse his host of carelessness or bad manners.

[54.1] Caesar did not show this kind of self-control when he commanded armies or when he held office. As some have substantiated in their writings, as proconsul in Spain he solicited money from allied states to pay off his debts and plundered some of the towns in Lusitania as though they were enemy settlements, despite the fact that they had been willing to obey his orders and had opened their gates to him when he arrived. [54.2] In Gaul he looted the offering-filled shrines and temples of the gods. He destroyed cities more often for plunder than as punishment. As a consequence, he amassed a huge quantity of gold that he offered for sale throughout Italy and the provinces at 3,000 sesterces a pound. [54.3] In his first consulship he stole 3,000 pounds of gold from the Capitol and replaced it with an equal weight of gold-covered brass. He conferred allied status and kingdoms for a price, taking from Ptolemy alone almost 6,000 talents in his name and Pompey's. Later on he sustained the burdens of civil wars and met the expenses of his triumphs and gladiatorial contests with patent thievery and by looting sacred sites.

[55.1] When it came to skill in oratory and prowess in the art of war, Caesar's renown equaled or outstripped that of the very best. There is no doubt that he was considered among the preeminent advocates after he prosecuted Dolabella.[103] In any case, when Cicero makes a list of orators in his dialogue *Brutus*, he writes that he sees no one to whom Caesar ought to yield first place and that his manner of speaking is skillful and vivid, and even grand and noble in

---

103. See 4.1.

a way. This is what he wrote to Cornelius Nepos[104] about Caesar: [55.2] "What do you say to this? What orator will you rank ahead of him, of those, that is, who have pursued no other occupation? Whose ideas are clearer or more concise? Whose words are more carefully chosen or more apt?" It seems that Caesar imitated Caesar Strabo's rhetorical style,[105] at least when he was a young man, and took some expressions verbatim from a speech of his titled *On Behalf of the Sardinians* and included them in a legal argument of his own. Caesar is said to have spoken in a piercing voice and used strong movements and gestures and to have made a pleasing impression. [55.3] He left behind a number of speeches, but some are attributed to him on poor grounds. Augustus thinks with good reason that his speech *On Behalf of Quintus Metellus* was not his own publication but had been transcribed by shorthand writers who did a bad job of following what he said. I agree, for I find in some copies that it does not even have the title *On Behalf of Metellus* but rather *Which He Wrote for Metellus*, although it is written from Caesar's viewpoint and exonerates both Metellus and himself of charges from their common enemies. [55.4] Augustus also has difficulty thinking that *Before His Soldiers in Spain* is his own. The speech has survived in two sections; one portion was delivered in the earlier battle, the second in the later battle, when Asinius Pollio[106] says that Caesar did not have time to address the troops at all because the enemy attacked so quickly.

[56.1] Caesar also left commentaries that covered his successes in the Gallic war and in the civil war that he fought against Pompey. It is unknown who wrote the commentaries on the Alexandrian, African, and Spanish wars. Some think that it was Oppius but others that it was Hirtius, who also completed the last unfinished book of the Gallic war.[107] Cicero has this to say about Caesar's *Commentaries* in his *Brutus*: [56.2] "He wrote commentaries that must be regarded very favorably indeed. They are unadorned, direct, and pleasing; every rhetorical embellishment has been stripped away as though it

---

104. Poet, historian, and biographer of the late Republic and the first years of the empire.

105. Gaius Julius Caesar Strabo, a distant cousin of Caesar, active in the 80s BCE and killed in the political chaos at that time; see *Cal.* 60.

106. See 30.4.

107. For Oppius, see 52.2. Aulus Hirtius was with Caesar in Gaul and died fighting as consul at Mutina in 43 BCE; see *Aug.* 10.3, 11.

were a piece of clothing. But although he wanted others to have material available from which to draw if they wanted to write history, he has perhaps done a favor for unskilled writers who want to tease the contents with a curling iron and has truly discouraged men with good sense from writing."[108] [56.3] Hirtius praises Caesar's *Commentaries* like this: "Everyone regards them so highly that it is clear that they have stolen an opportunity from writers rather than provided one. Yet I, more than other men, admire this work. Others know how well and accurately he wrote, but I, how easily and quickly."[109] [56.4] Asinius Pollio considers them written too carelessly with too little regard for plain truth, since Caesar accepted many things that others did on blind faith and related things that he did himself inaccurately, either on purpose or because he forgot. Pollio also thinks that Caesar would have rewritten and corrected them.

[56.5] Caesar left behind *On Analogy*, a work in two books,[110] two *Diatribes against Cato*,[111] and also a poem titled *The Journey*. He wrote the first of these while he was crossing the Alps on his way back to his army from Nearer Gaul[112] after discharging his responsibilities with the circuit courts. He wrote the next two around the time of the battle of Munda[113] and the last on his way from Rome to Further Spain, where he arrived after a journey of twenty-four days. [56.6] His communications to the senate are also extant. Caesar was apparently the first to write them in columns and change their form to that of a small book that could be preserved; earlier consuls and generals only sent dispatches written across the roll.[114] There are also letters to Cicero and to his close friends about private concerns. If he had anything confidential to say in these, he wrote in code;

---

108. *Brutus* 262.

109. *On the Gallic War*, Book 8, preface.

110. A work on standardizing grammar.

111. For Cato, see 14.2. After he died, Cicero wrote in his praise; Caesar countered.

112. Cisalpine Gaul.

113. A town in the south of Spain, the site of Caesar's final victory in the civil war, 45 BCE.

114. Proper books were written in columns that appeared side by side on the scroll as it was unrolled horizontally. It seems to have been the custom for field dispatches to be written straight across a scroll, turned to be unrolled vertically, or on a single sheet.

The Divine Julius 33

that is, he disposed the order of the letters so that words could not be recognized. In case anyone wants to explore this matter and solve his system, Caesar exchanged the fourth letter of the alphabet (D, that is) for A, and the rest of the letters in the same way. [56.7] Some writings from his boyhood and youth have also survived: *Praises of Hercules, Oedipus* (a tragedy), and *Collected Sayings*. Augustus prevented the publication of all of these in a very short, direct letter he sent to Pompeius Macer, whom he had trusted to put his libraries in order.

[57] Caesar was highly skilled in the use of arms, was a fine horseman, and had unbelievable tolerance for physical exertion. On the march he went ahead of his force, sometimes on horseback, more often on foot, his head uncovered in sun or rain. Traveling unencumbered by baggage, he covered extremely long distances with incredible speed, a hundred miles a day in a hired carriage. If there were rivers in the way, he swam across them or floated across on inflated skins. As a result, he quite often reached his destination before his arrival was announced.

[58.1] It is hard to know whether his operations in the field were inspired more by caution or by audacity. He never led his army along routes where ambush was likely to occur unless he had scouted the terrain thoroughly. Nor did he send it to Britain before he had investigated for himself the harbors, the passage, and the approach to the island. On the other hand, when he heard that a camp in Germany was under siege, he disguised himself as a Gaul and made his way to his men through enemy guard posts. [58.2] He ran the enemy fleet's blockade to cross from Brundisium to Dyrrachium in the winter. And when the force that he ordered to follow him failed to appear, despite his sending for them repeatedly with no success, he finally, at night, concealed his face and secretly boarded a small boat. He did not reveal his identity or allow the pilot to turn back in face of the strong headwind until he was close to drowning in the heavy sea.[115]

[59] Caesar was never fearful or hesitant about undertaking a new venture—not even when faced with divine disapproval. When he was offering sacrifice and the victim bolted, he did not postpone

---

115. In the winter of 49–48 BCE, Caesar had landed in Macedonia with a contingent of his force, but when reinforcements failed to appear, he disguised himself as a slave and tried to return to Italy for them. A storm turned him back.

setting out against Scipio and Juba.[116] Even when he slipped and fell on leaving his ship, he spun the omen into something positive and said, "Africa, I have you in my possession." And in order to ridicule prophecies in which the gods labeled the name Scipio lucky and invincible in that province, he kept a totally despicable member of the Cornelian clan in his camp, a man whom they called Salvitio because of his scandalous life.[117]

[60] Caesar not only fought battles that had been planned ahead of time but also fought when occasion offered, often directly from the march and sometimes in extremely wild weather, when he was least expected to initiate action. It was only at the end of his fighting career that he delayed engaging the enemy; he thought that the victories he had won so often gave him reason to court disaster less, that he would not gain nearly so much by victory as he would lose by defeat. He never drove the enemy from the field without depriving them of their camp as well, a tactic that left them no place of retreat in panic. When a battle hung in the balance, he let the horses go, his own first of all, so that his men would have to hold their ground with no means of escape. [61] Caesar's own horse was extraordinary. Its feet were almost human, its hooves divided like toes. It had been born in his stables, and after the soothsayers announced that the animal was a sign that its master would rule the whole world, Caesar took good care of it. He was the first person to ride it, and it allowed no one else on its back. He later even dedicated a statue of it in front of the temple of Venus Genetrix.

[62] If the line of battle gave way, Caesar would often restore it single-handedly. He stood in the way of the men who were turning their backs, took hold of them individually, and twisted them around by the throat to face the enemy. Sometimes they were panic stricken: once a standard-bearer threatened him with the spike on the end of his standard when Caesar tried to hold him back; another time one left his standard in Caesar's hand when he stopped him.

[63] Caesar's self-confidence was as great as his determination, and examples of it are even more impressive. After the battle at Pharsalus, when he had sent his force on to Asia and was crossing the Hellespont in a small merchant vessel, he encountered the enemy

---

116. See 35.2 for Scipio and Juba in Africa.

117. Scipio was a name in the Cornelian family. This man was evidently nicknamed Salvitio after a disreputable actor in mimes.

in the person of Lucius Cassius with ten warships. Caesar did not try to get away. On the contrary, he drew close, pressed Cassius to surrender, and took him on board when he begged for mercy. [64] During an assault on a bridge at Alexandria, a sudden incursion of the enemy forced Caesar into a small boat. When a great many others tumbled headlong into the same vessel, he jumped into the sea and escaped by swimming two hundred paces to the nearest ship. He kept his left hand above water so that the papers he was holding would not get wet, and he dragged along his cloak with his teeth so that the enemy would not have it as a trophy.

[65] Caesar's men won his approval, not by their character in private life or by their standing in Rome but solely on their ability to fight. His treatment of them was harsh and lenient to the same degree. He kept them under close control, not everywhere or at all times but always when the enemy was close at hand. Then, especially, he enforced very strict discipline. He did not let them know in advance when they would march or commence fighting but had them fully prepared and focused so that he could lead them out wherever he wanted at any time without warning. He often did this for no reason, particularly when it was raining or on feast days. And he would sometimes advise them to keep a close eye on him and then slip away suddenly day or night and make a longer march than usual to wear out those who were lagging behind slowly. [66] If his troops were frightened by a report of enemy forces, he boosted their confidence, not by denying or minimizing the danger but by exaggerating it further. For instance, when they waited in dreadful apprehension for Juba to appear, Caesar called them to assembly and addressed them as follows: "Know you this! Within a few days the king will be here with ten legions, three thousand horsemen, a hundred thousand lightly-armed troops, and three hundred elephants. Therefore, let those in doubt stop asking further questions or expressing an opinion and let them believe me, who have full knowledge. If they do not, I shall, you can be sure, order them loaded onto an old, worn-out ship and carried off by whatever wind to whatever land."

[67.1] On the other hand, Caesar did not pay attention to every transgression or match every punishment to the magnitude of the offense. He collected evidence against deserters and traitors zealously and punished them severely but turned a blind eye to other wrongdoing. Sometimes after an important victory, he would release his men from their duties and remove restrictions on their behavior.

He would brag, "My soldiers can fight even smeared with perfumed ointments." [67.2] When he addressed them in assembly, he did not call them soldiers but by the more flattering name comrades-in-arms. And he kept them well outfitted, equipping them with weapons that flashed with gold and silver. He did this for appearance but also to make them grasp them more tightly in battle for fear of losing them. He cared so deeply for his men that, when he heard about the disaster that Titurius had suffered,[118] he let his beard and hair grow and did not cut them until he had punished those responsible. [68.1] With these tactics Caesar rendered his men wholly devoted to him and made them tough as well.

At the beginning of the civil war, every centurion of every legion offered to take on the expense of a horseman from the money he had saved. Absolutely all of his soldiers served without rations or pay, those who were better off assuming the support of their less fortunate comrades. Not a single one deserted during the long course of the war. When those who were captured were allowed to live on condition that they be willing to fight against him, many refused. [68.2] They tolerated hunger and other hardships, not only when they were under siege themselves but when they were laying siege to others. When Pompey was at the defensive works at Dyrrachium and saw the sort of bread made from grass that was keeping Caesar's men alive, he said, "I am fighting against wild animals," and he ordered the bread taken away quickly and not shown to anyone. He did not want knowledge of the enemy's stamina and its ability to endure privation to break the fighting spirit of his own men.

[68.3] Proof of their courage in battle comes in the fact that at Dyrrachium, on the one occasion when the fight went against them, they took the lead in asking to be punished; in consequence, their commander thought they should be comforted rather than punished. In other battles they easily defeated vast numbers of enemy forces even when their own numbers were many times smaller. In one battle a single cohort of the Sixth Legion left in charge of an outpost held off four of Pompey's legions for several hours. Almost every man had been shot by the overwhelming number of enemy arrows, 130,000 of which were discovered inside the palisade. [68.4] His army's success comes as no surprise if one takes note of individual acts of bravery— those of the centurion Cassius Scaeva, for instance, or the ordinary

---

118. See 25.2.

soldier Gaius Acilius, not to mention others. Scaeva continued to guard the gate of the outpost assigned to him even after he had lost an eye, his thigh and shoulder had been pierced through, and his shield had 120 holes in it. Acilius had his right hand cut off when he put it on the deck of an enemy ship in a naval battle near Massilia. But following the example of the Greek Cynegirus, a well-known paradigm for conduct, he jumped onto the ship and used the knob on his shield to push back those who stood in his way.

[69] Caesar's men never mutinied during the ten years of wars in Gaul. There was some unrest during the civil war, but the men quickly returned to duty, not so much because of their commander's lenience toward them but from the force of his authority. He never shrank from troops who were rioting but always faced them. He even dismissed the whole Ninth Legion in disgrace at Placentia,[119] although Pompey still had a force under arms. He restored them grudgingly after they begged and pleaded but not until he had punished the guilty. [70] And although his friends tried to discourage him, he did not hesitate to confront the soldiers of the Tenth Legion in Rome. They were making threats that endangered the city and demanding discharge and payment, even though war was raging in Africa at the time. Nor did he hesitate to dismiss them from his service. But with a single word (he called them citizens instead of soldiers) he brought them around and caused them to relent.[120] They immediately shouted back that they were soldiers, and they followed him to Africa on their own initiative, although he refused to call for their service. He punished those who were most guilty of inciting insurrection by taking away a third of their reward money and a third of the land set aside for them.

[71] Caesar was attentive to his clients even when he was young, and he served them faithfully. He defended Masintha, a young man of noble descent, against King Hiempsal with such spirit that he grabbed the beard of Juba, the king's son.[121] When the young man was declared responsible for paying tribute, he quickly spirited him away from the people who were dragging him off into custody. He kept him hidden in his house for a long time and then, when he set out

---

119. In Cisalpine Gaul, 49 BCE.

120. See 67.2 for Caesar's manipulation of his troops by terms of address.

121. Masintha may be the son of the Numidian king whom Pompey deposed in favor of Juba's son Hiempsal. On Juba, see 35.2.

for Spain after his praetorship, he took Masintha with him in his litter, where his escort of retainers and the *fasces* of his lictors hid him.

[72] He always treated his friends with kindness and consideration. When he was traveling with Gaius Oppius through a wooded
area and Oppius suddenly fell sick, Caesar halted at a lodging that
had room for only one person. It was he who slept on the ground
in the open air. Once in power, he advanced people of the lowest
rank to the most important positions. When this drew criticism,
he openly acknowledged, "If highway robbers and murderers had
helped me defend my honor, I would have returned such men the
same favor."

[73] On the other hand, the grudges he nursed were never so serious that he did not willingly set them aside when occasion required.
He replied to Gaius Memmius' vicious speeches with language
that was equally harsh, but he later supported his candidacy for
the consulship.[122] With Gaius Calvus, who was seeking reconcili-
ation through friends after writing his notorious epigrams, Caesar
took the initiative and wrote to him first.[123] Valerius Catullus, who
Caesar acknowledged had stained his character indelibly with his
poems about Mamurra, he invited to dinner the very day the poet
apologized, and he continued to enjoy the company of the poet's
father as always.[124] [74.1] Even when he took vengeance, he showed
great moderation. When he got hold of the pirates who had held him
prisoner,[125] he ordered them crucified (he had sworn earlier to put
them on the cross), but he had their throats slit first. He could never
bear to harm Cornelius Phagita. He was the man who had laid a trap
for him when he was sick and in hiding. He bribed him not to hand
him over to Sulla and barely escaped.[126] Philemon, his secretary, who
had promised Caesar's enemies that he would poison him, he put to
death without torture. [74.2] When he was called to bear witness
against Publius Clodius, who had committed adultery with his wife
and was charged with defiling religious rites in connection with that

122. In 54 BCE; for Memmius, see 23.1, 49.2.

123. An example of Gaius Licinius Calvus' epigrams appears at 49.1.

124. The poet Gaius Valerius Catullus wrote several obscene poems about
Caesar and his aide Mamurra.

125. See 4.1–2.

126. See 1.2.

affair, he testified that he knew nothing, although his mother Aurelia and sister Julia had reported the entire episode faithfully before the same judges.[127] And when asked why he had divorced his wife if this were the case, he said, "Since it is my opinion that my family should be as free from suspicion as from criminal charges."

[75.1] There is no doubt that Caesar showed admirable restraint and compassion in his conduct both during the civil war and after his victory. Whereas Pompey proclaimed that he would consider those who were not on the side of the government to be enemies of the state, Caesar announced that those who were neutral and belonged to neither party he would count his own. He also gave all whom he had promoted to the rank of centurion on Pompey's recommendation the opportunity to join Pompey's camp. [75.2] When terms of surrender were being discussed at Ilerda and the two armies were socializing on a regular basis, Afranius and Petreius had a sudden change of heart and killed the Julian soldiers that they seized within their camp.[128] Caesar was unwilling to retaliate in kind against this betrayal. At the battle of Pharsalus he declared that citizens should be spared, and he later allowed each of his men to save the life of one man of his choice on the opposing side. [75.3] The only ones said to have died other than in battle were Afranius, Faustus, and the younger Lucius Caesar,[129] and not even these are thought to have been killed on his order. The first two resumed fighting after they had been pardoned. Lucius Caesar had cruelly butchered Caesar's freedmen and slaves and had slaughtered animals that Caesar had ready for the public games. [75.4] Finally, when the war was over, Caesar allowed everyone, even those not yet pardoned, to return to Italy and assume public office and command armies. He even put back the statues of Lucius Sulla and Pompey that the populace had smashed and scattered. Later on, if any serious plots were devised against him or he was the subject of verbal attacks, he preferred to put a stop to such hostile acts rather than punish the people responsible. [75.5] And so he did not pursue even the conspiracies that he learned had been hatched in nighttime meetings; the only thing he

---

127. The Bona Dea affair at 6.2.

128. Caesar defeated the Pompeians in 49 BCE near Ilerda, a town in northeast Spain. For Afranius and Petreius, see 34.2.

129. On Faustus Sulla, see 27.1. Lucius Julius Caesar was a cousin of Caesar's who sided with Pompey.

did was publish an edict making it known that he was aware of them. He considered it an adequate reprimand for those who attacked him viciously to warn them publicly not to continue. He tolerated with composure the savaging of his reputation in Aulus Caecina's angrily accusatory book and in the abusive poetry of Pitholaus.[130]

[76.1] But Caesar did and said other things that outweighed these liberal acts. As a result it is thought that he was killed justly because he abused his power. Not only did he accept too many tokens of distinction—continuous consulship, the dictatorship for life, control over the behavior of citizens, and also *imperator* as his first name, the cognomen Father of His Country, his statue placed among those of kings, and a raised platform among the seats in the theater—he also permitted honors to be given him that were greater than were appropriate for a human being: a golden chair in the senate house and in the law court, a carriage and a ceremonial litter for the circus procession, temples, altars, statues placed next to those of the gods, a *pulvinar*, a *flamen*, another college of priests for the Lupercalia, and a month named after him. There were no honors that he did not accept or bestow as he chose.

[76.2] The third and fourth times Caesar was consul, it was in title only;[131] he was content with the power of the dictatorship that had been conferred on him along with the consulships. In both years he named suffect consuls to replace him for the last three months. The only elections he held during this time were for tribunes and aediles. He appointed prefects to take charge of city affairs while he was away and gave them praetorian rank. When a consul died suddenly on the day before the Kalends of January, Caesar gave the meaningless position to someone who asked for it to hold for a few hours. [76.3] With the same willfulness he disregarded tradition and lined up magistrates for a number of years in the future. He gave consular regalia to men of praetorian rank and brought into the senate men who were not citizens from birth, some of them half-civilized Gauls. Furthermore, he put his own slaves in charge of the mint and of collecting taxes for the state. He handed over the care and command of the three legions he had left behind at Alexandria to Rufio, one of his favorites, who was the son of a freedman. [77] He

---

130. Writers who favored Pompey and attacked Caesar.
131. 46 and 45 BCE.

was equally intemperate in his public statements; Titus Ampius[132] reports these: "The Republic is nothing—only a name without shape or substance." "Sulla did not know his ABC's when he resigned the dictatorship." "Men ought to speak more carefully with me now and consider what I say as law." His arrogance was such that once when a *haruspex* announced that the organs of the sacrificial beast boded ill and that it had no heart, he said, "The signs will be more favorable since I will have it so; the fact that the victim has no heart must not be taken as a bad omen."

[78.1] But it was the following conduct especially that gave rise to the hatred that proved fatal to him: when the entire senate approached bearing a large number of proclamations that conferred wide-ranging honors on him, he received it while remaining seated before the temple of Venus Genetrix. Some think that Cornelius Balbus held him down when he tried to rise, others that he did not even try but glared at Gaius Trebatius,[133] who was suggesting that he get up. [78.2] This display of rudeness seemed even more insufferable because he had been so angry with Pontius Aquila, one of the tribunes,[134] who had not stood for him when he passed the tribunes' benches during his triumph, that he shouted, "You, tribune Aquila! Take the Republic from me!" For several days he never promised anyone anything without adding the condition ". . . if Pontius Aquila will allow it."

[79.1] Something even more insolent than this insult to the senate demonstrated his overt contempt. When he was enjoying the extravagant and unprecedented cheering of the populace on his way back to the city from the Latin festival,[135] someone in the crowd placed on his statue a laurel crown with a white ribbon tied in front.[136] The tribunes Epidius Marullus and Caesetius Flavus ordered the ribbon stripped from the crown and the man taken away in chains. Caesar was displeased—either because this suggestion of

132. A Pompeian who was a contemporary historian or biographer.

133. Lucius Cornelius Balbus, consul in 40 BCE, political agent, and close friend of Caesar; see 81.2. Gaius Trebatius Testa, legal expert on Caesar's staff in Gaul.

134. Titus Pontius Aquila, one of the conspirators. His confiscated property had been sold to Servilia; see 50.2.

135. January of 44 BCE. The Latin festival took place on the Alban Mount, not far from Rome.

136. The white ribbon was a symbol of royalty.

royal power had been introduced with too little success or (as he
would have it) because he had been deprived of the credit of refusing
it—and he reprimanded the tribunes severely and removed them
from office. [79.2] But from that time on, Caesar could not avoid the
opprobrium of desiring the royal title, even though he replied to the
populace when it greeted him as king, "I am Caesar, not king." At
the Lupercalia he pushed away the diadem that the consul Antony
kept putting on his head as he presided before the rostra, and he
sent it to the temple of Jupiter Optimus Maximus on the Capitoline.
[79.3] The final straw was a rumor that made the rounds: Caesar
intended to move his place of residence to Alexandria or Troy, taking with him all the assets of the state after having weakened Italy
by his levies of troops, and to put his friends in charge of the city.
Furthermore, at the next meeting of the senate Lucius Cotta[137]
was scheduled to announce the findings of the Board of Fifteen,[138]
who had determined that Caesar should be called king since it was
recorded in the sacred books that only a king could conquer the
Parthians. [80] The conspirators advanced their timetable so that
they would not have to assent to this.

And so all of the men who were devising plots separately, often in
small groups of two or three, combined their designs into a single
strategy. By now, even ordinary citizens were unhappy with the way
things were. Behind closed doors and in the open, they criticized
Caesar's arbitrary rule and demanded leaders to take up their cause.
[80.2] In regard to the foreign born who had been given seats in the
senate, a pamphlet put it this way: "For the good of Rome! Let no
one offer to show the new senator the way to the senate house!" And
these verses made the rounds:

> Caesar led the Gauls in triumph—and into the senate house as well.
> The Gauls have removed their trousers and put on the wide-striped
> tunic.

[80.3] When Quintus Maximus, suffect consul for three months,
entered the theater and a lictor ordered his arrival marked as usual,

---

137. Lucius Aurelius Cotta, consul in 65 BCE, related to Caesar on his
mother's side. On his brother, see 1.2.
138. A board of fifteen priests in charge of the Sibylline books; see *Gal.*
8.1.

everyone shouted, "He's not consul!"[139] At the first voting assembly after the tribunes Caesetius and Marullus had been removed from office, their names were found on a number of ballots for consul.[140] On the base of the statue of Lucius Brutus, someone wrote, "If only you were alive."[141] And on the base of Caesar's statue,

> Brutus, because he got rid of the kings, became the first consul.
> This man, because he got rid of the consuls, has finally become
> king.

[80.4] More than sixty individuals took part in the conspiracy against Caesar. Gaius Cassius and Marcus and Decimus Brutus were the leaders. At first they could not decide whether to divide into two groups and throw him from the gangway[142] when he was summoning the tribes for the voting in the Campus Martius and then grab him and murder him, or alternatively to attack him in the Sacred Way or at the entrance to the theater. When a meeting of the senate was announced for the Ides of March in the arcade adjacent to Pompey's theater, they chose this as the opportune time and place.

[81.1] But clear omens made Caesar aware of impending assassination: a few months earlier, when settlers were being assigned to a colony near Capua under the Julian law,[143] they disturbed some ancient graves in order to build their houses. They were all the more eager to proceed when their searching unearthed a quantity of small pots of earlier workmanship and there was found in the tomb in which Capys, the founder of Capua, was said to be buried a bronze tablet with this message inscribed in Greek and in Greek letters: "When the bones of Capys have been uncovered, his descendant will be killed by the hand of a kinsman and soon thereafter avenged in great disaster for Italy." [81.2] No one should think this a dubious

---

139. Quintus Fabius Maximus. Suffect consuls became the norm in the empire, but they were a new idea at this point. The objection was to his appointment; see 76.2.

140. See 79.1. As write-in candidates, they were not even eligible.

141. According to tradition, Lucius Junius Brutus drove the last king from Rome and became the first consul in 509 BCE.

142. A temporary bridge of planks over which voters passed to cast their ballots.

143. A colony founded under a law carried in Caesar's consulship.

fabrication, for the story comes from Cornelius Balbus, Caesar's intimate friend. A few days before Caesar was murdered, he learned that the herds of horses he had declared sacred to the river Rubicon when he crossed it and had let roam wild were stubbornly refusing to graze and were weeping profusely. Also, when he was performing a sacrifice the soothsayer Spurinna warned him:

> Beware of danger that will not come later than the Ides of March.

[81.3] On the day before the Ides in question, a flock of different kinds of birds flew from a nearby grove and chased a little bird called a king's bird that was winging toward Pompey's arcade with a laurel twig in its beak; there they tore it to pieces. And on the night before the dawn of the day of his murder, Caesar dreamed that he was sometimes flying over the clouds, at other times holding the right hand of Jupiter with his own. His wife Calpurnia envisioned the pediment[144] of their house crashing down and her husband stabbed as she embraced him. The door of the bedchamber suddenly flew open on its own.

[81.4] Because of these warnings and also because he was not feeling well, Caesar was unsure for a time whether he should stay home and postpone the business he planned to do in the senate. But Decimus Brutus urged him not to disappoint the large number of senators who had been waiting for him a long time, and he finally set out at about the fifth hour. Along the way someone handed him a note that revealed the plot. He put it in his left hand with the other notes he was holding, apparently intending to read them later. Then, after a large number of victims had been sacrificed, despite the fact that he had been unable to obtain favorable omens, he entered the senate, ignoring any need for divine approval and laughing at Spurinna and accusing him of lying, because the Ides of March had come without harm. Spurinna replied that they had indeed come— but not yet gone.

[82.1] The conspirators stood around Caesar as he sat, and made a show of paying their respects. At that moment, Tillius Cimber, who had taken the lead role for himself, approached him on the pretext of requesting a favor. When Caesar turned away and made a

---

144. An architectural feature of a temple; Caesar had been voted one for his house.

gesture that deferred his petition to another time, Cimber grabbed Caesar's toga at both shoulders. Then as Caesar shouted, "This is real violence!" one of the Casca brothers[145] stabbed him from behind just below the throat. [82.2] Caesar grabbed Casca's arm and pierced it with a stylus and tried to rush forward but was stopped by another stab wound. When he saw that he was set about on all sides by drawn daggers, he covered his head with his toga and with his left hand drew its folds down to his ankles so that he would fall more decently with the lower part of his body concealed. And so he was stabbed twenty-three times. He uttered merely a single inarticulate groan at the first cut, although some have reported that he said to Marcus Brutus when he struck him, "You go to hell, boy!"[146] [82.3] Everyone fled and Caesar lay there lifeless for a time until three young slaves of his put him on a litter and carried him home, his arm hanging off the side. According to the doctor, Antistius, none of the many wounds was found fatal except for the second one in his chest.

[82.4] The conspirators had intended to drag Caesar's dead body to the Tiber, appropriate his property, and repeal his decrees, but fear of the consul Mark Antony and Lepidus,[147] master of the horse, prevented them. [83.1] As a consequence his will was opened at the demand of Caesar's father-in-law Lucius Piso and read in Antony's house. Caesar had written it on the previous Ides of September[148] at his estate at Lavicum[149] and entrusted it to the head priestess of the Vestal Virgins. Quintus Tubero[150] writes that from the time of his first consulship to the beginning of the civil war he had always named Gnaeus Pompey his heir and had read the document aloud to his soldiers in assembly. [83.2] But in his last will, he created three heirs, his sister's grandsons. Gaius Octavius would receive three-quarters of his estate and Lucius Pinarius and Quintus Pedius would

---

145. Gaius and Publius Servilius Casca.

146. Caesar spoke in Greek. His first two words (literally, "and you") were a curse to ward off evil. His third word, "boy" or "child," was a deprecating form of address. See also *Cl.* 15.4.

147. Marcus Aemilius Lepidus; he would join Mark Antony and Augustus to form the Second Triumvirate; see *Aug.* 13.1.

148. September 13, 45 BCE.

149. Not far from Rome, to the south.

150. Quintus Aelius Tubero, a historian.

share the remaining quarter. At the end of the document, he adopted Gaius Octavius into his family and gave him his name.[151] He named a number of the assassins among the guardians for any son who might be born to him and made Decimus Brutus an heir in the second degree. He left his gardens on the Tiber to the people for their use, and to each individual he gave 300 sesterces.

[84.1] Caesar's funeral was announced, a pyre was built in the Campus Martius next to the tomb of Julia,[152] and a golden shrine that was a replica of the temple of Venus Genetrix was placed upon the rostra. Inside it was an ivory couch with gold and purple coverings and at its head a pillar with the clothing in which he had been killed. It was clear that a single day would be inadequate for those who wanted to bring offerings, so they were instructed not to form a procession but to carry their gifts to the Campus Martius by any route they chose. [84.2] The verses that were recited at his funeral games were suitable for expressing compassion and outrage at his death. From Pacuvius' *Contest of Arms* came, "Did I save them so that they could destroy me?" and there was a similar thought from Atilius' *Electra*.[153] Instead of delivering a eulogy, Antony employed a public crier to recite the senate's resolution in which all honors divine and human had been voted him at one time and also the oath with which all had pledged to keep this one man from harm. He added to this a very few words of his own. [84.3] Magistrates and former magistrates carried the funeral couch down from the rostra into the Forum. Some were determined to cremate him in the sanctuary of Jupiter on the Capitol, others in Pompey's arcade. But two figures armed with swords, and each carrying two javelins, suddenly set the pyre on fire with flaming wax torches; the crowd of onlookers piled on dry wood and wood from the judges' platform along with its benches and whatever else they could find to add as an offering. [84.4] Then the musicians and actors ripped off the clothing they had taken from the triumphal equipage and put on for this occasion, tore it to pieces, and threw it into the flames. Discharged legionary soldiers hurled in the arms with which they had adorned themselves to attend the funeral. Even respectable married women threw in the

---

151. He became Gaius Julius Caesar Octavianus but never used Octavianus. He later became the emperor Augustus; see *Aug.* 7.2

152. His daughter; see 1.1, 21, and 26.1.

153. Pacuvius and Atilius were early Roman playwrights.

jewelry that they were wearing and their children's good luck charms and bordered togas.

[84.5] While the public display of grief was at its height, large numbers of foreigners gathered and lamented, each in their own way, especially the Jews who, night after night, crowded the spot where Caesar had been cremated. [85] Immediately after the funeral the common people made for the houses of Brutus and Cassius carrying torches. Driven off with difficulty, they happened on Helvius Cinna and killed him because they were mistaken about his name. They thought he was Cornelius Cinna,[154] for whom they were looking because on the preceding day he had given a speech to the assembly denouncing Caesar. They stuck his head on a spear and paraded it about the city. Later on they erected a solid column of Numidian stone almost twenty feet high in the Forum and inscribed it, "To the Father of His Country." They continued to sacrifice before it for a long time and to make vows and settle some of their disputes with the oath "by Caesar."

[86.1] Caesar had made some of his close friends suspect that he no longer wanted to live and that he had not taken precautions for his safety because he was in poor health and consequently had ignored the portents and their warnings. Some think he had divested himself of his Spanish bodyguards and their swords because he trusted in the senate's most recent resolution and in the oath.[155] [86.2] But others think he preferred to be caught, once and for all, in the traps that were being set all about him rather than to be always on his guard. And some recount that he often said, "My own safety is not so important as that of the state. I have long since obtained power and glory to spare. If anything should happen to me, the state will be in turmoil, the situation will deteriorate, and there will be civil wars." [87] But almost everyone agrees about this: he died the death he did almost by design. Once when he was reading in Xenophon[156] that Cyrus had given instructions about his funeral during his last

---

154. Helvius Cinna was a tribune ally of Caesar; see 52.3. Cornelius Cinna may or may not be the Cinna who was Caesar's former brother-in-law; see 5.

155. The resolution and oath that Mark Antony read at Caesar's funeral. See 84.2.

156. Late fifth- and early fourth-century BCE Greek writer whose work includes a life of the Persian king Cyrus.

illness, he rejected the idea of such a slow death and hoped that his own would be sudden and quick. And on the day before he was killed, in a conversation that took place after dinner at the house of Marcus Lepidus, the question arose as to the most desirable end of life. Caesar said it would be one that was sudden and unexpected.

[88] He died in his fifty-sixth year and was entered into the roster of the gods, not only in the words of the official proclamation but in popular belief as well. In fact, at the first games that his heir Augustus staged for him after he had been declared divine, a comet rose at about the eleventh hour and shone for seven days in a row, and it was believed that it was Caesar's soul taken up into the sky. This is why a star is placed on the head of his statue. It was decided that the meeting place of the senate where he was killed be walled up and that the Ides of March be called Parricidium, "Day of Assassination." This meant that the senate would never be convened on that day.

[89] Almost none of the assassins survived him more than three years, nor did they die of natural causes. All were condemned on one charge or another and perished, some by shipwreck, others in battle. Some killed themselves with the same dagger that they had used to stab Caesar.

THE DIVINE AUGUSTUS

63 BCE–14 CE
Emperor 31 BCE–14 CE

Rome's first emperor was born Gaius Octavius into a family of modest political achievement. But his grandmother was the sister of Julius Caesar, and Caesar's will made Octavius his heir and gave him his valuable name. The young man found himself in a maelstrom of conflicting interests after the assassination of Caesar in 44 BCE, and it took brash self-confidence for the eighteen-year-old to accept the role bequeathed him and the resources that came with it. The next years saw a nasty struggle that ended when his forces defeated those of Mark Antony in 31 BCE.

In 27 BCE, Octavius received the honorific name by which he came to be known, Augustus or "revered," when he had become the single dominant personality in Rome. The emperors who followed used it as a title. Augustus gathered to himself powers and offices that had in the Republic been shared among various persons and for limited periods, and he kept some of them indefinitely or for a long time. This concentration of powers gave new shape to the Roman government. In many respects it resembled that of the Republic, thanks to the nominal survival of traditional institutions, but in reality government during the empire was characterized by significant centralization. Augustus lived until 14 CE, forty-four years after the defeat of Antony, sufficient time for his changes to become permanent. His reign was a model for those that followed.

Of all of the Caesars, this one has the clearest organization. Suetonius begins with Augustus' ancestry and early years (as is always his pattern), but he soon announces that he will cover Augustus' adult history not chronologically but by topics or rubrics (chapter 9). The first rubrics are those of Augustus' ugly crawl to uncontested power, followed by his more positive contributions to public life, and finally a glorious climax of the honors he received. Then, with a change of direction (chapter 61), Suetonius describes the man and his private and domestic life, also arranged by topic. Portents provide a transition back to chronological structure, and the account ends, rather abruptly, with Augustus' death and his will.

49

[1] A number of indications point to the past preeminence of the Octavian family at Velitrae.[1] A neighborhood in the busiest part of the town had long been called Octavian, and an altar set aside for an Octavius was pointed out there. This Octavius was a general in a war against a nearby town, and he happened to be making a sacrifice to Mars when news came of a sudden invasion by the enemy. He seized the half-cooked entrails from the altar, cut off the portion intended for the god, and offered it up. He advanced into battle after this and returned victorious. There was also on record a decree of the people that stipulated that in the future entrails be rendered to Mars in just this way and that the remaining parts of the victims be given to the Octavii. [2.1] King Tarquinius Priscus admitted the family to the senate as one of the "lesser families," and Servillius Tullius later transferred it to the patricians. As time passed, it reverted to plebeian status and then, after a long time, returned again to patrician status through the agency of the Divine Julius.[2] [2.2] Gaius Rufus was the first member of the family elected to magisterial office by the people, and he reached the rank of quaestor.[3] He fathered Gnaeus and Gaius, and from them the two branches of the Octavian family descended in different circumstances: Gnaeus and all his progeny held the highest elected offices, but Gaius and his progeny, whether by chance or by choice, remained equestrians down to Augustus' father. An ancestor of Augustus served as a military tribune in Sicily during the Second Punic War under the general Aemilius Papus.[4] Augustus' grandfather was content to hold local office and live quietly to an old age while enjoying his considerable wealth. [2.3] But it is others who report these things. Augustus himself writes merely that he was descended from a venerable and rich equestrian family and that his father was its first senator. Mark Antony makes fun of Augustus' great-grandfather, calling him a freedman and a rope maker from the district of Thurii,[5] and he calls his grandfather a

---

1. About twenty miles southeast of Rome.

2. The early kings of Rome are credited with determining patrician or plebeian status. "Lesser families" seem to be those added to the patricians and thus to the senate in a second round of adlection.

3. Probably 230 BCE.

4. 205 BCE.

5. A town on the coast in the south of Italy.

money changer. This is all I have learned about Augustus' paternal ancestry.

[3.1] Augustus' father, Gaius Octavius, was all his life a wealthy and much-respected man, so I find it odd that some have charged that he too was a money changer and even one of the men who arrange for the bridges[6] or perform other functions in the Campus Martius at election time. Following his praetorship, Macedonia fell to him by lot, and on his way there he got rid of the runaway slaves who controlled the land around Thurii, a remnant band of those collected by Spartacus and Catiline.[7] This was an additional task given to him by the senate. [3.2] He governed his province with equal fairness and courage. After he had routed the Bessi[8] and the Thracians in a major battle, he dealt with allied states in such a way that Marcus Cicero, in letters that are still extant, strongly advises his brother Quintus to imitate Octavius in gaining the support of allies. Quintus was at that time a proconsul administering the neighboring province of Asia using methods that reflected badly on his good name. [4.1] Octavius died suddenly, shortly after he left Macedonia, before he could stand for the consulship. Surviving him were his children, Octavia Major, whose mother was Ancharia, and Octavia Minor and Augustus, whose mother was Atia. Atia was the daughter of Marcus Atius Balbus and Julia, the sister of Gaius Caesar. On his father's side Balbus had roots in Aricia[9] and a family that could boast the portraits of many senators, and on his mother's side he was closely related to Pompey the Great. After his praetorship he apportioned the Campanian territory to the plebs under the terms of the Julian law as a member of the Board of Twenty.[10] [4.2] But Mark Antony again, expressing his contempt for Augustus' mother's lineage too, charges that his great-grandfather was of African birth and had operated a perfume shop and then a bakery at Aricia. In a letter Cassius of Parma censures Augustus as the grandson of not only a baker

---

6. The planks over which people walked to cast their votes in elections.

7. 60 BCE. The gladiator Spartacus had led a slave rebellion in 73–71 BCE; Catiline led an uprising in 63 BCE; see *Jul.* 14.1.

8. A tribe in Thrace.

9. About fifteen miles south of Rome.

10. A distribution of public land when Julius Caesar was consul in 59 BCE; see *Jul.* 20.3.

but also a money changer: "Your mother is a lump of dough from
the cheapest bakery in Aricia. The money changer from Nerulum[11]
kneaded her with hands stained by dirty coins."

[5] Augustus was born just before sunrise on the ninth day before
the Kalends of October during the consulship of Marcus Tullius
Cicero and Gaius Antonius[12] at the Oxheads in the Palatine district
of Rome, where there now stands a shrine that was dedicated shortly
after he died. As can be seen in the senate record, Gaius Laetorius,
a young man from a patrician family, when he was using the excuses
of youth and good birth to reduce the heavy penalty imposed on him
for adultery, also put it before the senators that he was the owner and
in a manner of speaking the custodian of the ground first touched
by the Divine Augustus at his birth. He asked pardon for his own
sake and for the sake of the god to whom he was intimately connected, and it was decreed that that part of his house be declared
holy. [6] The place where Augustus was reared can still be seen in
his grandfather's country house near Velitrae. It is very modest, like
a small storeroom, and neighborhood tradition holds that he was
born there. Religious scruple prevents anyone from entering except
those who have been ritually cleansed and then only out of necessity.
Ancient belief maintains that a kind of shivering and dread awaits
anyone who enters casually, and this has been recently confirmed:
A new owner of the villa, either by chance or to test the story, went
there to sleep, and as it happened, a very short time after nightfall
a sudden force of some kind drove him out, and he was found half
dead outside the door together with his bedclothes.

[7.1] Augustus was given the cognomen Thurinus as a small child,
either in recollection of his ancestors' origin or because his father
Octavius had conducted his successful campaign against the runaway
slaves in the region of Thurii[13] shortly after his son was born. I am
able to offer quite certain proof of the cognomen Thurinus because
I found a statuette of him as a child; it was made of antique bronze
and inscribed with this name in iron letters that had almost faded
away. I gave it to the emperor,[14] and he keeps it among the *Lares* in his

---

11. An insignificant town in the south of Italy.
12. September 23, 63 BCE.
13. See 3.1.
14. Hadrian, emperor from 117 to 138 CE.

private chamber. But Mark Antony also addresses him as Thurinus as a mark of contempt in his letters, and Augustus merely writes back that he can only marvel that this early name is being hurled at him as an insult. [7.2] Later on he took the name Gaius Caesar and then the cognomen Augustus; the first he got from the will of his great-uncle, the second after a motion of Munatius Plancus carried the vote that he be called Augustus. Some had proposed that he be called Romulus[15] because he too was a founder of the city. Augustus was not only a new cognomen but a more significant one as well, because places of religious awe are called august as are places consecrated by augury. The word comes from "increase" or from the movement and eating of birds, as Ennius[16] also informs us when he writes:

> After famed Rome was founded with augury august . . .

[8.1] Augustus lost his father when he was four. In his twelfth year he delivered the funeral oration for his grandmother Julia before the assembled populace. Within four years after receiving the toga of manhood, he was awarded military decorations in Caesar's African triumph, despite the fact that he had had no fighting experience because of his age. He was scarcely recovered from a serious illness when he followed his uncle who was setting out for the Spanish provinces in pursuit of the sons of Gnaeus Pompey. Traveling with only a very few companions on roads that were unsafe because of enemy presence, and suffering a shipwreck as well, he quickly gained Caesar's approval because he displayed excellence of character in addition to enduring the hardship of the journey.

[8.2] After Caesar recovered the Spanish provinces and was planning an expedition against the Dacians and then against the Parthians, Augustus was sent ahead to Apollonia,[17] where he devoted himself to his education. As soon as Augustus learned that Caesar had been killed and that he was Caesar's heir, he thought for a time of calling for the help of the legions that were closest, but he abandoned the plan as rash and premature. Instead he returned to Rome and accepted his inheritance, although his mother had doubts and his

---

15. Augustus would appoint Lucius Munatius Plancus censor in 27 BCE. Romulus was the legendary founder of Rome.

16. An epic poet of the third and second centuries BCE.

17. A city on the Adriatic, north of Greece, opposite Brundisium in Italy.

stepfather, the consular Marcius Philippus, strongly advised against it. [8.3] He enlisted armies and then ruled the state, first with Mark Antony and Marcus Lepidus, then with Antony alone for almost twelve years, and finally by himself for forty-four years.

[9] Having set forth, as it were, this summary of his life, I shall go through the details of it, not according to chronology but by topic, so that they can be more clearly brought to light and understood.

He fought five civil wars, the wars of Mutina, Philippi, Perusia, Sicily, and Actium. The first and last of these were against Mark Antony; the second was against Brutus and Cassius;[18] the third against Lucius Antonius, the triumvir's brother; and the fourth against Sextus Pompey, the son of Gnaeus.[19] [10.1] All of these wars had their origin in this: since he thought no course more proper for him than to avenge the death of his uncle and preserve his achievements, as soon as he returned from Apollonia he determined to use force against Brutus and Cassius. They were not expecting this, but when they saw danger coming and fled, he resorted to the law and charged them with murder in absentia. When those who were responsible for presenting games in honor of Caesar's victory did not have the courage to put them on, he gave them himself. [10.2] And to pursue his other objectives more consistently, he stood as a candidate to take the place of a tribune of the people who had chanced to die. He did this despite his being a patrician and not yet a senator.

He had hoped that the consul Mark Antony would be his principal ally, but when Antony got in the way of his ambition and was unwilling to allow him even the ordinary justice available to all in any matter unless an onerous bribe had been arranged beforehand, he went over to the party of the *optimates*. He knew that they were hostile to Antony, especially because Antony was trying to use armed force to drive Decimus Brutus from Mutina, where he had him under siege. (Caesar had awarded Brutus the province, and the senate had confirmed the appointment.)[20] [10.3] And so when some urged him to kill Antony, he recruited assassins, but when the plot was detected

---

18. Leaders of the conspirators against Julius Caesar; see *Jul.* 80.4.

19. Pompey the Great.

20. Decimus Junius Brutus, one of Caesar's assassins, had command of Cisalpine Gaul (northern Italy). After Caesar's death, Antony transferred this command to himself and was attempting to assert his right to it (44–43 BCE). Mutina is in Cisalpine Gaul.

and he feared that he would be in danger in turn, he gathered experienced soldiers to protect both himself and the state, paying them as much as he could. He was put in command of this army that he had created with the rank of propraetor and directed to relieve Decimus Brutus with the help of Hirtius and Pansa, who had become consuls.[21] With two battles in three months, he brought an end to this war that had been assigned to him.

[10.4] Mark Antony writes that in the first of these battles Augustus fled and finally turned up two days later without his military cloak or his horse. But there is general agreement that in the second battle he performed the duty not only of a general but of an ordinary soldier as well. When his legion's eagle-bearer was seriously wounded in the middle of battle, Augustus took the eagle on his shoulder and carried it for a long time. [11] Since Hirtius was killed in battle in this war, and Pansa died shortly thereafter from a wound, the rumor spread that Augustus had been responsible for killing them both; with Antony routed and the state without consuls, he would have sole possession of the victorious armies. Pansa's death especially was so suspect that the doctor, Glyco, was arrested on the charge that he had applied poison to his wound. Aquilius Niger adds to the rumor that Augustus killed the other consul, Hirtius, in the confusion of battle.

[12] But when Augustus learned that Marcus Lepidus had welcomed Antony after he fled and that the other military commanders and their armies were joining his party, he did not hesitate to abandon the *optimates*. He accused the party of things said and done by some of them, and he made this his pretext for changing his allegiance. He charged that some had put it out that he was a boy, and that others said that he should be honored and then gotten rid of[22] so that proper gratitude would not have to be shown to either him or his veterans. And to make it absolutely clear that he regretted having belonged to this party that he had previously allied himself with, he placed a heavy fine on the citizens of Nursia,[23] which they could not

---

21. Aulus Hirtius and Gaius Vibius Pansa were the consuls of 43 BCE. Both had served with Caesar in Gaul.

22. Cicero is supposed to have said this. It involves a pun in the verb *tollo*, which means "raise up" but also "do away with." The pun appears also at *Ner.* 39.2.

23. A town in north central Italy.

pay, and then drove them from their town. He did this because they had erected at public expense a monument to their citizens who had been killed in battle at Mutina and had inscribed on it, "They fell for freedom."

[13.1] After he joined forces with Antony and Lepidus, he brought the war at Philippi to an end, again in two battles, although he was weak and sick. In the first battle he was driven from his camp and barely escaped by fleeing to the wing of the army that Antony commanded. He did not exercise restraint after the victory but sent Brutus' head to Rome to be cast at the foot of Caesar's statue, and he raged against all of the most distinguished captives and insulted them verbally. [13.2] He is said, for instance, to have replied to a man who pleaded humbly for burial, "The birds will decide that when the time comes," and to have ordered another pair, a father and son who begged for their lives, to draw lots or play *mora*[24] so that one or the other would have his prayer answered. Then he watched both of them die; the father was executed because he had volunteered his life for his son, and then the son killed himself as well. And so others—among them Marcus Favonius, the notorious imitator of Cato[25]—when they were being brought out in chains, honored Antony by saluting him as *imperator* but castigated Augustus to his face with the foulest of insults. [13.3] After the victory responsibilities were divided: Antony was given the task of establishing order in the East, and Augustus was to take the veterans back to Italy and settle them on land that belonged to the municipal towns. He earned thanks neither from the veterans nor from the landowners for this; the one group complained that they were being forced out, the other that they were not being treated as they had been led to hope that their merit deserved.

[14] At that point in time, Lucius Antonius,[26] trusting in the authority of his consulship and in his brother's influence, began a revolution. Augustus forced him to retreat to Perusia[27] and starved him into surrender but not without putting himself in great danger

---

24. A game in which one player tries to guess how many fingers the other is holding up.

25. The extreme republican who was Caesar's enemy; see *Jul.* 14.2.

26. 41 BCE. Mark Antony's brother.

27. Modern Perugia.

both before the war and during its course. For when he ordered a
lictor to dislodge an ordinary soldier who was sitting in the fourteen
reserved rows[28] in the seating area at the games, his enemies started
the rumor that he had afterward tortured the man and killed him.
He almost perished when an angry mob of soldiers rushed him, but
he was saved when the missing man suddenly appeared safe and unin-
jured. And when he was sacrificing outside the city wall of Perusia,
he was almost killed by a company of gladiators who had sallied out
from the town. [15] After the capture of Perusia, he punished many,
and to those who tried to beg for mercy or make excuses for themselves he always responded, "You must die." Some write that three
hundred of the men of the two highest orders who had surrendered
were selected for slaughter like sacrificial animals on the Ides of
March at the altar built for the Divine Julius. Some have written that
Augustus took up arms with the specific intention of flushing out his
hidden enemies and those who were loyal to him out of fear rather
than by choice by allowing them to follow Lucius Antonius. Then,
after they had been decisively defeated and their property had been
seized, he paid the rewards promised his veterans.

[16.1] The Sicilian war was among the first to begin, but it dragged
on with frequent interruptions, once for the rebuilding of the fleet
that had been wrecked twice in storms, unusual in summer, and
again when the populace demanded peace because trade had been
interrupted and famine was growing more serious; this cessation
lasted until the ships had been completely repaired and twenty thousand slaves freed and assigned to the oars and he had created the
Julian harbor near Baiae by bringing the sea into Lake Lucrinus and
Lake Avernus.[29] He trained his force there throughout the winter
and then defeated Pompey between Mylae and Naulochus.[30] As the
time of battle approached, Augustus suddenly fell into a sleep so
deep that his companions had to wake him so that he could give the
signal. [16.2] It was this, I imagine, that provided Antony with the
opportunity to reproach him: "He could not even look squarely at
the force drawn up for battle but lay dazed on his back, looking at
the sky, and he did not get up and show himself to the soldiers until

28. The first fourteen rows reserved for knights.
29. He made a canal that connected these lakes near the Bay of Naples
with the sea.
30. Towns on the north coast of Sicily, 36 BCE.

after Marcus Agrippa[31] had routed the enemy's ships." Others find fault with what Augustus said and did when his fleets were lost in the storm; they say that he shouted, "I shall gain victory—even if Neptune is unwilling," and that he left the god's statue out of the traditional parade the next time that circus games were held.

[16.3] Clearly in no other conflict did he encounter more frequent and more serious dangers. After he had crossed his army over to Sicily and was on his way back to rejoin the rest of his forces on the mainland, he was surprised by Pompey's prefects, Demochares and Apollophanes. He had great difficulty escaping but finally got away in a single vessel. A second close call came when he was going to Regium on foot by way of Locri[32] and saw Pompey's biremes skirting the coast. Thinking that they were his own ships, he went down to the shore and was almost captured. On that occasion, even as he was fleeing to safety along remote tracks, a slave who belonged to his companion Aemilius Paulus and was bitter because Augustus had earlier proscribed Paulus' father[33] seized the opportunity for vengeance and tried to kill him.

[16.4] After Pompey fled, Marcus Lepidus, the other member of the triumvirate, whom Augustus had summoned from Africa to help him, boasted of the loyalty of his twenty legions and used terror and threats to claim the best rewards for himself. Augustus relieved him of his army, and although he granted him his life when he begged for it, he banished him permanently to Cerceii.[34]

[17.1] The bond between Augustus and Mark Antony had always been uncertain and in doubt and was barely kept alive with an assortment of reconciliations. Augustus finally broke it completely, and to make it obvious how Antony's behavior had lapsed from normal Roman behavior, he saw to it that Antony's will, which had been left in Rome and named Cleopatra's children among his heirs, be opened and read in public assembly. [17.2] But when Antony was declared a

---

31. Marcus Vipsanius Agrippa would become Augustus' most trusted aide and later his son-in-law; see 63.1.

32. On the toe of Italy's boot.

33. Lucius Aemilius Paulus (*Jul.* 29.1) was proscribed by his own brother, the triumvir Lepidus, not by Augustus. Augustus would later (22 BCE) appoint his son, his supporter Paulus Aemilius Lepidus, mentioned here, censor; see *Cl.* 16.1.

34. On the coast south of Rome.

public enemy, Augustus nonetheless sent all of his relatives and friends to him, among them Gaius Sosius and Gnaeus Domitius, who were still the consuls at the time.[35] Because the citizens of Bononia[36] had long been clients of the Antonii, he exempted them from swearing allegiance to his party when the rest of Italy did. Shortly thereafter he won a naval battle off Actium[37] in a fight that went on so long that he, the victor, had to spend the night on his ship. [17.3] When he left Actium and had withdrawn to winter quarters on Samos,[38] he received alarming news of an uprising among the soldiers, who were demanding bonuses and discharge. These were men who had been selected from all sections of Augustus' army and sent ahead to Brundisium after his victory. Twice he was battered by storms on his crossing back to Italy, first between the promontory of the Peloponnesus and Aetolia and a second time off the Ceraunian Mountains.[39] On both occasions a number of his galleys sank, and the one in which he was traveling had its rigging blown away and its tiller broken. He stayed only twenty-seven days at Brundisium, only until the demands of his soldiers were settled, and then he sailed for Egypt by way of Asia and Syria. He laid siege to Alexandria, where Antony had sought refuge with Cleopatra, and took the city quickly.

[17.4] Although Antony tried to sue for peace at the last minute, Augustus forced him to suicide and viewed his dead body. Very eager to keep Cleopatra alive for his triumph, he brought in Psylli[40] to suck out the poisonous venom because it was believed that she had died from the bite of an asp. He allowed the two the dignity of a shared burial and ordered the common tomb that they had begun to be completed. [17.5] Young Antonius, who was the elder of Antony's two sons born to Fulvia,[41] he had dragged from the statue of the Divine Julius where he had taken refuge after his many appeals had failed,

---

35. 33 BCE.

36. Modern Bologna.

37. A promontory on the northwest coast of Greece.

38. An island off the coast of the province of Asia.

39. Aetolia is northwestern Greece; the mountains are on the eastern side of the Peloponnesus.

40. An African tribe of snake handlers thought to be immune to snake venom.

41. Antony's wife.

and he had him killed. Caesarion, too, whom Cleopatra claimed Julius Caesar had fathered, he caught when he tried to escape and put to death. He protected the other children of Antony and the queen and later cared for them and nurtured them as the needs of each required, just as if they were his own family.

[18.1] At the sarcophagus and the body of Alexander the Great, which had been brought out from the inner shrine and put before him, Augustus paid his respects by placing a golden crown on the head of the corpse and scattering flowers about. And when asked if he wanted to view the tomb of the Ptolemies, he said, "I wanted to see a king, not dead men." [18.2] He reduced Egypt to the form of a province, and to make it a more productive and convenient source of Rome's grain supply, he used military labor to clean out all of the canals that the Nile floods, which had long been filled with mud. And to make the memory of his Actian victory more celebrated and have it continue into future generations, he founded a city at Actium and called it Nicopolis, and he established quinquennial games to be held on the site. He enlarged the temple of Apollo and decorated the place where his camp had been with spoils of the naval battle and consecrated it to Neptune and Mars.

[19.1] After this, he suppressed uprisings and incipient revolutions as each arose, and he put a stop to a number of conspiracies that were betrayed before they could develop fully. The leaders of these were the young Lepidus,[42] and then Varro Murena and Fannius Caepio, then Marcus Egnatius, then Plautius Rufus and Lucius Paulus, the husband of Augustus' granddaughter.[43] In addition there were Lucius Audasius, a frail old man on trial for forgery; Asinius Epicadus, a half-breed of Parthian descent; and finally Telephus, a slave employed by a woman to remind her of the names of the people she encountered. These last names show that dangerous conspiracies arose even with the lowest class of men. [19.2] Audasius and Epicadus had planned to spirit away to the army Augustus' daughter Julia and grandson Agrippa[44] from the islands on which they were being

---

42. Marcus Aemilius Lepidus, the son of the triumvir.

43. Julia the Younger, a daughter of Julia and Agrippa. Lucius Aemilius Paulus was the son of the censor, Paulus Aemilius Lepidus; see 16.3, *Cl.* 16.1.

44. Meant here is probably his granddaughter Julia, who was exiled along with her brother Agrippa Postumus; see 65.1.

held. Telephus was planning to attack both Augustus and the senate under the delusion that it was his fate to rule. And once even a camp follower with the Illyrican army tricked his way past the guards at the door and was caught near Augustus' bedchamber at night armed with a hunting knife; it is unclear whether he was actually demented or just pretending to be mad, for nothing could be gotten out of him under torture.

[20] Augustus fought a total of two foreign wars under his personal leadership, the Dalmatian war when he was still a young man, and the Cantabrian war after the defeat of Antony. He was wounded in the Dalmatian conflict, once when a stone struck his right knee in battle and a second time when a leg and both arms were injured in a bridge collapse. Other wars he directed through appointed legates, although with some of the wars in Pannonia and Germany he was either on hand or not far away, advancing from the city as far as Ravenna or Mediolanum or Aquileia.[45] [21.1] Sometimes by his leadership, sometimes through commanders acting under his authority, he subdued Cantabria, Aquitania, Pannonia, and Dalmatia together with the rest of Illyricum, and also Raetia and the alpine tribes, the Vindelici and the Salassi. He stopped incursions of the Dacians, killing three of their chieftains and a large number of their men, and he pushed the Germans beyond the Elbe River, except for the Suebi and Sigambri. These tribes surrendered to him and he relocated them to Gaul and settled them in land near the Rhine. He brought other restive tribes into submission. [21.2] He did not make war on any nation unless it was just and unavoidable. He so lacked any desire to increase the boundaries of the empire or acquire military glory that he made some of the barbarian chieftains swear in the temple of Mars the Avenger that they would remain loyal and respect the peace that they were seeking. From some of them he even tried to exact a new kind of hostage, unknown up to that time, namely women; he did this because he knew that barbarians ignored the guarantees that male hostages provided. But he always gave all of them the power to take back their hostages whenever they wished. Upon those who rebelled too often or proved too untrustworthy, he never inflicted any punishment harsher than selling them as prisoners with the condition that they not be slaves in a region near their homelands or be

---

45. Mediolanum was modern Milan; Aquileia was at the head of the Adriatic.

freed in less than thirty years. [21.3] This reputation for fairness and moderation won over even the Indians and the Scythians, nations that the Romans knew only by report, and they took the initiative of sending emissaries to seek pledges of friendship with him and with the Roman people. The Parthians also surrendered easily after he laid claim to Armenia, and when he asked them to return the military standards taken from Marcus Crassus and Mark Antony, they gave them back and provided hostages as well. And once, when they had many candidates contending for their throne, they accepted the one that Augustus endorsed.

[22] Before Augustus' lifetime the temple of Janus Quirinus had been closed only twice since the city was founded.[46] With peace secured on land and sea, he closed it three times in a much shorter period of time. He entered the city twice with ovations, once after the war at Philippi and a second time after the war in Sicily. He celebrated three proper triumphs—for Dalmatia, Actium, and Alexandria—all in the course of three days.

[23.1] He suffered only two disgraceful military disasters, those of Lollius and Varus,[47] both in Germany. The Lollian defeat inflicted more shame than it did damage, but that of Varus proved almost fatal, with three legions, their general and his lieutenants, and all the auxiliary forces butchered. When news of this calamity reached Augustus, he set a watch throughout the city to prevent disturbances, and he lengthened the terms of provincial governors so that allies would be kept loyal by being familiar with experienced leaders. [23.2] He promised Great Games to Jupiter Optimus Maximus if the situation of the state improved; this had been done in the Cimbric and Marsic wars.[48] And they say that he was so beside himself that for months on end he let his hair and beard grow and sometimes hit his head against the doors, crying out, "Quintilius Varus! Give me back my legions!" He kept the anniversary of the disaster as an annual day of sadness and mourning.

[24.1] Augustus made many changes in military affairs. He introduced new practices and even revived some from former times. He maintained rigorous discipline. He was reluctant to allow even his

---

46. The doors of the temple were closed only in time of peace.

47. The first in 15 BCE, the second in 9 CE.

48. In 105–101 BCE in Gaul and in 90–88 in the Social (Marsic) War against the Italian allies.

commanders to visit their wives and permitted it only during the winter months. When a Roman knight cut off the thumbs of his two sons of military age so that they would evade military service, he had both the man and his property auctioned off, but when he saw that some tax contractors were on the verge of buying him, he had him knocked down to his own freedman so that he could be banished to the country but live as a free man. [24.2] He gave dishonorable discharge to the entire insubordinate Tenth Legion, and when others arrogantly demanded dismissal, he let them go without benefit of the rewards they had earned in full. He decimated cohorts if they fell back in battle and fed the ones who were left with barley.[49] If centurions left their posts, he put them to death, exactly as if they were common soldiers. He imposed various forms of disgrace for other kinds of infractions. He made centurions, for instance, stand the whole day in front of the general's tent, sometimes wearing only a beltless tunic, on occasion holding ten-foot measuring rods, or he even made them carry sod.[50]

[25.1] After the civil wars he never called any of his men comrades-in-arms,[51] either in assembly or in an edict. He called them soldiers, and he did not allow his sons to address them in any other way when they held command. He thought that "comrades-in-arms" pandered more than was appropriate for either military discipline or the current state of peace or the respect due him or his family. [25.2] Only twice did he make use of freedman soldiers, not counting the times when he used them to fight fires in Rome or when there was fear of riots because grain was in short supply; he used them once to protect the colonies adjacent to Illyricum and a second time to guard the bank of the Rhine. These were still the slaves of wealthy men and women whom he quickly freed, but he kept them with their original unit and did not mix them with the freeborn troops or arm them in the same way.

[25.3] In the matter of military decorations, Augustus granted ornaments for horses and elaborate collars made of gold and silver rather more liberally than he did the crowns awarded for scaling a rampart or climbing a city wall, prizes that brought more honor.

---

49. Usually eaten only by slaves and animals.
50. Tasks for the ordinary soldiers, not centurions.
51. Julius Caesar had used the term with his men; see *Jul.* 67.2.

These last he distributed as sparingly as he could and without partiality, often even to ordinary soldiers. He presented Marcus Agrippa with a blue banner in Sicily after his naval victory.[52] The only men that he thought should never be given decorations were those who celebrated triumphs, even though they had been his companions on expeditions and had shared in his victories. He reasoned that they too had the right to give awards to whomever they wished. [25.4] He also thought that there was nothing that suited the accomplished general less than haste and impetuosity and so he often exclaimed, "Make haste slowly," "A careful general is better than a bold one,"[53] and "Whatever is done well enough is done quickly enough." Indeed, he refused to enter into battle or start any war at all unless it was obvious that the hope of benefit was greater than the fear of loss. He said that those who took great risk in pursuit of small rewards were like those fishing with a golden hook, the loss of which, if it broke off, no catch could equal.

[26.1] Augustus held offices and received honors, some before the prescribed age and some of a new kind to be held permanently. He became consul in his twentieth year[54] when his legions marched on Rome as though on an enemy city and soldiers were sent to demand the consulship for him in the name of the army. When the senate hesitated, a centurion named Cornelius, head of the delegation, threw back his cloak and displayed the hilt of his sword and did not hesitate to say in the senate house, "This will do it, if you will not." [26.2] He held a second consulship after an interval of nine years, a third after an interval of one year, and then consulships in successive years until he reached his eleventh. After that he refused the consulship many times when it was offered, but after a long break of seventeen years, he asked for a twelfth and again two years later for a thirteenth, so that he would be holding the highest office when he introduced his sons, Gaius and Lucius, to public life.[55] [26.3] He held the five middle consulships (the sixth to the tenth) for the entire year, the remainder for either nine or six or four or three months, except the second,

52. 16.2.

53. Euripides, *Phoenician Women* 599.

54. 43 BCE, the year after Julius Caesar was assassinated.

55. His adopted sons; see 64.1. He was consul in 43, 33, 31–23, 5, and 2 BCE.

which he held for just a few hours; on that occasion he presided for a short time in the curule chair before the temple of the Capitoline Jupiter on the Kalends of January, resigned his office, and appointed someone else in his place. And he did not enter all of the consulships at Rome but commenced the fourth in Asia, the fifth on the island of Samos, and the eighth and ninth at Tarraco.[56]

[27.1] For ten years Augustus was a member of the triumvirate established to bring order to the state. For a time, to be sure, he held his ground against his partners and tried to keep the proscriptions from taking place, but once they had begun, he implemented them more aggressively than did the other two. They could often be moved by special considerations and by petitions on behalf of many individuals, while he alone insisted that no one be spared. He proscribed even his tutor, Gaius Toranius, who had been a colleague of his father, Octavius, when he was aedile. [27.2] Junius Saturninus bears further witness: he reports that when the proscriptions stopped, Marcus Lepidus justified what had taken place in the senate and offered hope for mercy in the future, inasmuch as punishment enough had been meted out. But he writes that Augustus announced the opposite: "I put an end to the proscriptions so as to leave all my options open." But later on he regretted this inflexibility and awarded Titus Vinius Philopoemen[57] equestrian status because he was said to have once hidden his patron who had been proscribed.

[27.3] There were many reasons why Augustus was intensely hated as a member of the triumvirate: When he was speaking before a military assembly with a mob of locals mixed in among the soldiers, he noticed Pinarius, a Roman knight, taking notes, and thinking that he was a spy nosing about, he ordered him stabbed while he watched. His threats so terrified Tedius Afer, consul elect, who had maliciously criticized something that he had done, that he threw himself to his death. [27.4] And the praetor Quintus Gallius, who was paying his respects while holding some double tablets under his clothing, he suspected of hiding a sword, but he did not dare investigate immediately for fear that that was not what he would find. Instead, shortly thereafter he had centurions and soldiers seize Gallius and drag him from the tribunal, and he had him tortured like a slave. When Gallius did not confess, Augustus ordered him

---

56. On the northeast coast of Spain.
57. Philopoemen was a freedman.

killed—after gouging out his eyes with his own hand. Augustus, on the other hand, writes that Gallius attacked him treacherously after asking for an audience and that he imprisoned him but then let him go and banished him from Rome, and that after that he died in a shipwreck or at the hands of brigands.

[27.5] Augustus was given permanent tribunician power and twice chose colleagues to serve with him for five-year terms. He was also given permanent authority to regulate customs and laws, and by that right, without actually holding the office of censor, he nonetheless held a census of the populace three times, the first and third times with colleagues, the middle time by himself.

[28.1] He twice thought about restoring the Republic. The first time was immediately after Antony was crushed, because he remembered that Antony had often challenged him, saying that it was his fault that it had not been restored. The second time, exhausted by a long illness, he summoned the magistrates and senate to his home and shared with them an account of the affairs of state. But he had second thoughts and retained control, reflecting that he would be in danger if he became a private citizen and that it was rash to entrust Rome to the government of the many. It is difficult to say which was better, the result of this decision or his intentions. [28.2] Although he prided himself on his intentions from time to time, he also gave witness of them in an edict with these words:

> May it be granted me to make the state stand safe and unharmed and to see the fruition of this goal that I seek, so that I may be called the author of the very best form of government and so that when I die I may bear with me the hope that the foundations that I shall have laid will remain in place.

He himself made his prayer come true by striving in every way to have no one disappointed with the new form of government.

[28.3] Augustus so much improved the city whose modest appearance was inconsistent with the grandness of empire and was at the mercy of floods and fires that he could legitimately boast, "I have left marble what I found brick." He also made the city secure, even for the future, to the extent that human planning could provide. [29.1] He built many structures at public expense, in particular, a forum with its temple of Mars the Avenger, a temple of Apollo on the Palatine, and a shrine of Jupiter the Thunderer on the Capitoline. He built the forum because the population and the large number of court proceedings seemed to require a third,[58] since two were inadequate. For this reason he opened it to the public quickly, before the temple of Mars was finished, with the stipulation that criminal trials be held only there and the selection of jurors be by lot.

[29.2] He had vowed to build the temple of Mars the Avenger during the war at Philippi, which he had undertaken to avenge his father, and this was why he decreed that the senate deliberate there about wars and triumphs, that those about to leave for their provinces with the right of command be sent off from there, and that those who returned victorious bring the trophies of their triumphs there. [29.3] He raised a temple to Apollo in that part of his house on the Palatine where the *haruspices* had pronounced that the god desired it after it had been struck by lightning. He added a portico with a library of Greek and Latin books, and it was there that as an old man he often convened the senate and reviewed the jury panels. He dedicated the shrine to Jupiter the Thunderer because he had been spared when lightning grazed his litter and killed the slave carrying the torch in front of him. This had happened when he was traveling at night on his Cantabrian expedition. [29.4] He also built works in the names of others, such as his grandsons and heirs and his wife and sister, the portico and basilica of Gaius and Lucius and the porticoes of Livia and Octavia, and the theater of Marcellus. He often urged other prominent men to make the city beautiful with monuments, new or restored or newly decorated, as each could afford. [29.5] As a result, many men built many buildings at that time: Marcius Philippus contributed the temple of Hercules and the Muses; Lucius Cornificius, the temple of Diana; Asinius Pollio, the atrium of Liberty; Munatius Plancus, the temple of Saturn; Cornelius Balbus, a theater; Statilius Taurus, an amphitheater; and Marcus Agrippa, a number of important buildings.

[30.1] Augustus divided the city into regions and wards and arranged for magistrates chosen annually by lot to be responsible for the safety of the former and for officers chosen by the people of each neighborhood to be responsible for the latter. To fight fires he created night watches and guards. To control floods he widened and cleaned the channel of the Tiber; it had been choked with rubble and narrowed by the buildings pushing into it. And to improve access to the city from all directions, he assumed responsibility for repairing

---

58. A forum was a convenient place in which to hold court.

the Flaminian Way clear to Ariminum[59] and assigned to men who
had earned triumphs the responsibility of paving the other roads
with the money from their booty.

[30.2] He repaired the temples that had collapsed from age or
burned down, and he adorned the rest with the most magnificent
offerings, making a single deposit in the inner chamber of the
temple of the Capitoline Jupiter of 16,000 pounds of gold and precious stones and pearls worth 50 million sesterces. [31.1] After he
became *pontifex maximus* (he had never been willing to take that
priesthood from Lepidus while he was alive but finally did so after
he died), he collected more than two thousand prophetic books in
Greek and Latin that were in circulation everywhere and were of
either unknown or unreliable authorship, and he burned them. He
kept only the Sibylline books,[60] making a selection even from these,
and he placed them in two golden cases under the base of the statue
of Apollo on the Palatine. [31.2] Since the calendar put in order
by the Divine Julius had been neglected and become disturbed and
confused, Augustus returned it to its earlier condition. In the process
of setting it right, he gave his cognomen to the month of Sextilis
instead of to the month of September, in which he had been born,
because Sextilis was the month of both his first consulship and his
most important victories.[61]

[31.3] He added to the number and prestige of the priesthoods
and increased their privileges, especially those of the Vestal Virgins.
And when a new one had to be chosen to take the place of one who
had died and many fathers worked hard to see that their daughters
were not subject to the lot, Augustus said under oath that if any of
his granddaughters had been of the appropriate age, he would have
put her forward. [31.4] He also revived some ancient rituals that
had disappeared over time, the Augury of Safety,[62] for instance, the
office of the *flamen dialis*, the Lupercalia, the Secular Games, and

---

59. On the Adriatic coast.

60. The most important of the prophetic books; of mythic origin, they were
consulted in times of crisis.

61. Sextilis, the sixth month, became August. September, the seventh, kept
its original name. See 100.3.

62. A ceremony to determine whether to offer a prayer for the safety of
the state.

the Compitalia.[63] At the Lupercalia he forbade breadless youths to participate in the running about, and at the Secular Games he did not allow young people of either sex to attend the entertainment at night without an older relative. He started the practice of having the *Lares Compitales*[64] decked with flowers twice a year, spring and summer.

[31.5] Augustus honored the memory of military leaders almost as much as he honored the immortal gods. These were generals who had advanced the empire of the Roman people from its smallest beginnings to its greatest power. And so he restored the public buildings that each had sponsored, keeping their original names on them, and he dedicated statues of them all in triumphal dress, placing one in each portal of his forum. An edict stated:

> I have created this so that the citizens may call on me, while I live, and on the leaders of future ages to follow in the footsteps of these men who serve as examples.

He also removed the statue of Pompey from the site where the senate was meeting when Gaius Caesar was killed and put it on a marble archway opposite the central door of Pompey's theater.

[32.1] Either the persistent lack of discipline during the civil wars had left a legacy of dreadful criminal activity that was harmful to the populace, or the dangerous situation had developed even in a time of peace. A large number of highway robbers went about openly armed on the excuse that they were protecting themselves, and they seized travelers in the countryside, free and slave indiscriminately, and locked them up in the slave barracks of large landowners.[65] Many gangs calling themselves "new associations"[66] were organized for the sole purpose of crime. Augustus stationed detachments of soldiers where they would do the most good, inspected the slave barracks, dissolved the associations that were not of ancient origin and legitimate, and so put an end to highway robbery.

[32.2] He burned the records of old debts owed the state treasury if they offered particular opportunity for false accusations. He

---

63. A festival celebrated in the individual wards.

64. The tutelary divinities of the individual districts.

65. Slave prisons also appear at *Tib.* 8.

66. Counterfeiting associations of people involved in legitimate trade.

decided questions about city land to which the state had dubious claim in favor of the owners. He cleared the names of people who had been awaiting trial for a long time and whose unkempt appearance[67] did nothing but give their enemies pleasure. He added the condition that if a plaintiff wanted to renew the charges, he would find himself in danger of suffering the penalty he was seeking. So that no crime would escape punishment or any private suit be lost because of delay, he added an additional thirty days to the court calendar, days that had been devoted to discretionary games. [32.3] He added to the existing three jury panels a fourth whose members were recruited from a lower census. It was called the panel of *ducenarii,*[68] and it handled cases that involved small amounts of money. He added jury-men thirty years old and older, that is, five years younger than usual. And he reluctantly made concessions to the many who complained about the burden of jury service; he gave a year's recess to the individual panels in turn, and the usual court sessions in the months of November and December were canceled.

[33.1] He himself administered justice diligently, sometimes continuing even into the night, and if he was feeling weak he presided from a litter placed on the tribunal or even heard cases lying down at home. Furthermore, he administered justice not only with the utmost care but also with compassion as is illustrated in the case of a defendant clearly guilty of parricide; to keep him from being sewn into the sack[69] (only those who confessed suffered this punishment), Augustus reportedly asked, "Surely you did not kill your father?" [33.2] And in a case dealing with a forged will in which all the witnesses who had signed were subject to the Cornelian law,[70] he gave his fellow inquisitors not only two tablets for their decisions, one for condemnation and the other for acquittal, but a third as well, for the pardon of those whom he determined had been induced to sign by false representation or from confusion. [33.3] Every year he referred appeals from litigants living in Rome to the urban praetor

---

67. People awaiting trial dressed shabbily in order to elicit pity.

68. People whose wealth was 200,000 sesterces.

69. The "sack" was the archaic punishment for parricides. The guilty man was tied in a sack and thrown into the sea or river; later, animals were added to the sack: a dog, a cock, a snake, and a monkey. See *Cl.* 34.1; *Ner.* 45.2.

70. Witnesses to a forged will were subject to the same penalty as the forger himself.

and from those in the provinces to former consuls whom he had
made responsible for the business of each province.

[34.1] He revisited laws and made fresh ones, laws about excessive spending, for instance, and about adultery and sexual behavior,
electoral bribery, and marriage regulations. His changes to the last
of these were more significant than to the others, but he would not
have been able to see them become law because of the stir made by
those who objected, if some of the penalties had not been eliminated or made less severe, a three-year grace period granted,[71] and
the rewards increased. [34.2] When at a public entertainment the
knights kept up a persistent demand for the regulations to be done
away with, Augustus called for the children of Germanicus and put
them on display, setting one on his lap, another on their father's,
and with his gestures and expression he indicated that they should
not be reluctant to emulate the young man's example.[72] And when
he realized that the spirit of the law was being evaded because fian-
cées were not yet of marriageable age and wives were frequently
changed, he shortened the time allowed for engagements and limited divorce.

[35.1] The senate was filled to overflowing with a disreputable and
ill-disciplined mob and numbered more than a thousand, some of
whom were totally unworthy. They had been added after the death
of Caesar with the help of personal favor and bribes. The common
people called them Orcini.[73] Augustus reduced the senate to its
original number and its earlier glory with two processes for select-
ing senators. The first was at the discretion of its members with
each man choosing a man; in the second he and Agrippa made the
decision. It is thought that when he presided in this second selection
process, he was protected by a breastplate under his clothing and had
a sword at his side and that ten of his most robust friends in the senatorial order stood around his chair. [35.2] Cordus Cremutius writes
that not even then was any senator admitted to his presence unless
he came alone and had had the fold of his toga searched. Augustus

---

71. Prompt remarriage was required for widows, widowers, and divorced
persons.
72. 9 CE; Germanicus was below the age required by law for marriage and
fatherhood. He would eventually have nine children; see *Cal.* 7.
73. Slaves set free by their masters' wills; Orcus was god of the
underworld.

made some senators resign in shame but allowed even these to keep
the distinction of their special clothing and the right to sit in the
orchestra and attend public banquets. [35.3] And to make those who
had been selected and whose status was confirmed perform their
senatorial duties more seriously and more easily, he directed that
each, before taking his seat, make an offering of incense and wine at
the altar of the god in whose temple the senate was being convened.
And he directed that regular sessions of the senate be held no more
than twice a month, on the Kalends and the Ides, and that in the
months of September and October only those who had been chosen
by lot needed to be present to constitute a quorum able to issue
decrees. To advise him, he provided for councils chosen by lot to
serve for six months with whom he would explore issues before they
were brought to the full senate. [35.4] He solicited opinions about
important matters not by the customary roll call but in whatever
order he chose to call on members. Each senator had to give his
attention to the problem since he might have to present a proposal
rather than give his assent.

[36] Augustus was responsible for other changes as well, among
them these: that the records of the senate not be made public;[74] that
magistrates not be dispatched to their provinces as soon as they left
office; that a fixed sum be allowed proconsuls for the mules and tents
they had customarily hired at public expense; that responsibility for
the *aerarium* pass from the urban quaestors to former praetors or
to praetors currently serving; and that the *decemviri* convene the
centumviral court, which prior to that time had been convened by
former quaestors.[75] [37] To allow a larger number of citizens a share
in running the state, he created new positions: he appointed people
to be responsible for public works, roads, aqueducts, the channel of
the Tiber, and the distribution of grain to the populace; he created
an urban prefect and appointed a triumvirate to revise the senate roll
and another to review the squadrons of knights whenever necessary;
he appointed censors, positions that had not been filled for a long
time; and he increased the number of praetors. He also insisted that
whenever he was consul, he have two colleagues instead of one. But
he did not carry this point. Everyone protested that his majesty was

---

74. Julius Caesar had had them published. See *Jul.* 20.1.

75. The *decemviri*, or Board of Ten, served as presidents of the Court of a
Hundred (*centumviri*) that heard civil disputes.

sufficiently diminished when he did not hold office alone but shared it with another. [38.1] And he was equally generous in rewarding courage shown in war, for he saw to it that more than thirty generals were voted proper triumphs and that a somewhat larger number received triumphal regalia.

[38.2] To permit senators' sons to become familiar with affairs of state more quickly, he let them wear the broad stripe when they put on the adult toga and attend meetings of the senate. When they were introduced to military life, he not only made them legionary tribunes but put them in charge of cavalry squadrons. And to allow all of them to gain military experience, he usually put two senators' sons in command of each squadron.

[38.3] He frequently reviewed the companies of knights, reviving after a long interval the tradition that had them parade on horseback. But he did not allow a person questioning their status to make any of them dismount as they rode past, something that had formerly taken place. And he permitted those who were obviously elderly or had bodily defects to send their horses on ahead in the line and to report on foot when they were summoned to present themselves. Then he offered those older than thirty-five the privilege of returning their horses if they did not want to keep them.[76] [39] With the help of ten men enlisted from the senate, he obliged each and every knight to render an account of his life. Of those whose behavior was reprehensible, he punished some and marked others for disgrace;[77] to most he issued warnings of various kinds. The least serious reprimand was the public delivery of written tablets to be read silently on the spot. He degraded some because they had borrowed money at low interest and invested it at a higher rate. [40.1] If candidates with senatorial status were unavailable to stand for election as tribunes, he appointed them from the ranks of Roman knights, with the stipulation that when their terms were finished, they would remain members of whichever order they chose. And when a number of the knights whose wealth had been reduced during the civil wars did not have the courage to watch the games from the fourteen rows[78] because they were afraid that they would be punished according to theater regulations, he

---

76. A knight had originally kept a "public horse" at state expense so as to serve as a member of the armed cavalry.

77. He placed a mark next to their names on a list.

78. The first fourteen rows in the theater were reserved for equestrians.

announced that this rule did not apply if they or their ancestors had ever been counted in the equestrian census.

[40.2] He conducted a census of the populace, neighborhood by neighborhood, and so that the distribution of grain would not take ordinary citizens from their work too often, he decided to give out vouchers for a four-month supply three times a year. But at their request, he returned to the earlier practice whereby a man received a voucher for himself every month. He restored traditional election procedures. He put in place numerous penalties for bribery, and on the day of the voting he distributed a thousand sesterces to each member of his own tribes (the Fabian and the Scaptian) so that they would not look for anything from any of the candidates.[79]

[40.3] He thought it especially important to keep the population pure and completely untainted by contamination from foreign and servile blood. As a consequence he awarded Roman citizenship quite sparingly and limited the freeing of slaves. When Tiberius petitioned him on behalf of a Greek client, he wrote back that he would not grant him citizenship unless the man put his case before him in person and convinced him that he had a legitimate basis for his request. And when Livia asked for citizenship for a taxpaying Gaul, he refused her but offered tax exemption, saying that it was easier for him to have the imperial purse deprived of revenue than the privilege of Roman citizenship cheapened. [40.4] He was not satisfied with putting obstacles in the way of freedom for slaves and, even more so, full citizenship rights by carefully spelling out details about the number and status and distinctions among those who were manumitted. He added a provision that none who had ever been held in chains or tortured would acquire citizenship under any terms of freedom.

[40.5] Augustus was very interested in reviving traditional habits of dress, and once when he saw a crowd dressed in dark and dingy clothing at a public assembly, he was outraged and shouted, "Behold! The Romans, masters of the world, the people of the toga!"[80] He gave the aediles the task of keeping anyone from appearing thereafter in the Forum or nearby except in a toga and without an outer cloak.

---

79. It was the practice for candidates to distribute favors to members of their own tribes. Augustus belonged to the first of these because of his adoption by Julius Caesar, to the second because he was an Octavius.

80. Virgil, *Aeneid* 1.282.

[41.1] He was frequently generous with all the orders when the occasion offered. When royal treasure was brought into the city for his triumph over Alexandria, he made so much money available that interest rates were lowered and the price of land increased. Later on, whenever there was a surplus from the property confiscated from condemned people, he lent it interest free for a set period to those who could provide collateral for twice the amount. He increased the financial qualification for senators; instead of an assessment of 800,000 sesterces, he required 1,200,000 and made good the deficiency for those who were short. [41.2] He gave the populace cash gifts but in varying amounts; one time it was 400 sesterces, another time 300, sometimes 250. He did not exclude even young boys, although they had usually not received a share until they were eleven. And when the grain supply met with difficulty, he would distribute a ration to each man at a very cheap price or sometimes for nothing at all, and he doubled the number of vouchers used to pay for it.

[42.1] But to impress on you that Augustus was an emperor more eager to serve the people than to win favor for himself, he chastised them sternly when they complained about the shortage of wine and its high price: "By bringing a large number of aqueducts into the city, my son-in-law Agrippa has taken sufficient care that men do not go thirsty." [42.2] And when the people clamored after a money gift that had been promised them, he replied, "I am a man of my word." But he rebuked them in an edict for their disgraceful insolence when they demanded money that had not been promised, and he declared firmly, "I will not give it to you although I was intending to." His reasoning was just as studied and consistent when he learned that a large number of slaves had been freed and been put on the citizen roll after a money gift had been announced. He said that those to whom he had not made the promise would receive nothing, and he gave less than promised to the others so that the money that had been set aside would be sufficient. [42.3] Once when there was a massive crop failure and the shortages were difficult to make up, he expelled from the city the slaves that were for sale, the gangs of gladiators, and all noncitizens except for doctors, teachers, and some slaves. He writes (when the grain supply had eventually been recovered), "I was inclined to get rid of the public grain ration for good because reliance on it has discouraged the cultivation of land. But I did not persist in this course because I was sure that at some point a desire for popular favor would bring it back." After that he changed the way he handled the program in order to address the concerns of farmers and businessmen as well as those of the urban populace.

[43.1] Augustus surpassed all rivals in the frequency, variety, and magnificence of the entertainments he put on. He says that he presented games four times in his own name and twenty-three times for other elected officials[81] who were either away from Rome or could not afford the expense. He sometimes gave them in the neighborhoods and on many stages with actors speaking all manner of languages. He organized races and gladiatorial combats not only in the Forum and the amphitheater but in the Circus and the Saepta as well, and sometimes he produced a beast hunt by itself. He gave athletic contests in the Campus Martius where wooden seats had been built, and he put on a naval battle in a lake dug near the Tiber where the grove of the Caesars now stands. On the days when entertainments were taking place, he stationed guards around the city so that it would not be open to gangs of thieves with so few people remaining at home. [43.2] In the Circus he introduced charioteers, runners, and men to dispatch the wild animals, sometimes young men with high social standing. He sponsored frequent exhibitions of the Game of Troy with troops of older and younger boys because he thought this noble tradition showed off the best of upper-class youth. He awarded Nonius Asprenas a golden torque[82] when he fell from his horse in the pageant and was disabled, and Augustus allowed him and his descendants to use the cognomen Torquatus. Later on he stopped these displays because the orator Asinius Pollio angrily entered a serious complaint in the senate about the fall his grandson Aeserninus took; he too broke his leg.

[43.3] At one point Augustus used Roman knights in his theatrical productions and his gladiatorial shows, but that was before a decree of the senate stopped the practice. After that he put no one of respectable family on the stage except for a young man named Lycius, and that was only for display: Lycius was less than two feet tall, weighed seventeen pounds, and had a very loud voice. [43.4] But on the day of one gladiatorial show, Augustus led Parthian hostages, the first ever sent to Rome, across the middle of the arena to the seating area and sat them above him on the second bench. If ever anything unusual

---

81. Suetonius copies directly from Augustus' *Res gestae*.

82. A close friend of Augustus; see 56.3. A torque was a military decoration in the form of a metal collar.

or worth looking at came to his attention on days when there were no shows, he made a special exhibit of them anywhere he could—a rhinoceros, for instance, in the Saepta, a tiger in the theater, a snake fifty cubits long in front of the Comitium.

[43.5] It chanced that Augustus was sick at the time of circus games that he had vowed, and he reclined in a litter when he headed the parade of carts carrying statues of the gods. At the opening of the games for the dedication of the theater of Marcellus, the joints of the curule chair happened to give way, and he fell over backward. At the gladiatorial show in honor of his grandsons, when the crowd was worried because it feared that the structure where they were sitting was about to collapse and he was unable to keep them from leaving or reassure them by any means, he left his place and took a seat in the section that seemed especially insecure.

[44.1] He remedied the extremely confused and disorganized manner in which spectators watched the shows. He was motivated to put order into the arrangements when a senator was injured because no one gave him a seat in the packed audience at heavily attended games at Puteoli. As a consequence, the senate decreed that whenever games were put on anywhere, the first row of benches be reserved for senators. In Rome, Augustus prohibited envoys who arrived from free and allied nations from sitting in the orchestra after he learned that some of them came from the freedman class. [44.2] He separated soldiers from the populace. He assigned married men from the general population to rows of their own, gave boys who had not yet put on the adult toga their own section and put their tutors next to them, and decreed that no one wearing dark and dingy clothing could sit in the middle section. He did not allow women to watch even the gladiators except from the topmost seats, although it had formerly been customary for them to watch from whatever seats they wished. [44.3] In the theater the only women to whom he assigned special seats were the Vestal Virgins; he placed them opposite the praetor's platform. At the athletic shows he shut out the entire female sex so effectively that at the games in honor of his becoming *pontifex maximus* he postponed a fight scheduled for a pair of boxers until the morning of the following day and issued an edict to the effect that women were not to come to the theater before the fifth hour.

[45.1] Augustus usually watched the races from the top-floor apartments that belonged to his friends and freedmen, but he sometimes sat on the *pulvinar* together with his wife and children. He would absent himself from a show for several hours, sometimes for whole days, asking to be excused and relying on others to preside in his place. But whenever he was present, he gave the action his total attention. He either did this to avoid the widespread criticism that he remembered about his father Caesar, who had used the time to read letters and petitions and reply to them while he watched, or he paid attention because he was interested and found pleasure in watching; he never denied his fascination but often confessed it openly. [45.2] This is why he also frequently offered generous prizes and cash rewards from his own purse at gladiatorial combats and games that were sponsored by others, and he never attended Greek games without rewarding each contestant as he deserved. He was especially enthusiastic about watching boxers, Latin ones in particular, and not just the usual professionals, whom he would match against Greek opponents, but also local gangs who fought recklessly and without training in the narrow streets of the neighborhoods. [45.3] Finally, he thought worthy of his protection every category of people who offered professional skills of any kind for the entertainment of the public. He continued privileges for athletes and added to them. He did not permit gladiators to be matched in the arena without the possibility of appeal.[83] He took from magistrates their right (long allowed by law) to punish actors any time or place and permitted it only at the games and in the theater. [45.4] Despite these protections, he strictly regulated the contests in the wrestling halls and the fights of the gladiators. He was so determined to rein in the free behavior of actors that he flogged Stephanio, an actor in Roman dramas, through three theaters and then banished him because he found out that he had been served by a married woman whose hair was cut short like a boy's. The pantomime actor Hylas he whipped before onlookers in the atrium of his own house after the praetor had complained about him. And Pylas he banished from Rome and Italy because he pointed his middle finger at a spectator who was hissing at him and made everyone look at him.

[46] With the city and city affairs thus put in order, he increased the population of Italy by founding colonies, twenty-eight in number, and provided many parts of it with public works and tax revenues. And he made Italy the equal (to some degree and in part) of Rome in its rights and influence by devising a new way of voting: the members of

---

83. A defeated gladiator could usually ask to have his life spared.

the local senate cast their votes, each in his own colony, for the magistrates in the city, and as election day approached, they sent the votes sealed to Rome. So that there could be found everywhere in Italy a sufficient number of respectable citizens or an ample population of children born to the common people, he appointed to the equestrian military service those who wanted to serve if they had official recommendation from their town, and to the commoners who presented him with proof of sons and daughters he distributed 1,000 sesterces for each child as he made the rounds of the various regions.

[47] Augustus took as his personal responsibility the more heavily garrisoned provinces, those that could not be governed easily or safely by magistrates who held power on an annual basis. The other provinces he entrusted to proconsuls assigned by lot. But he sometimes changed the arrangements for some of them and often made visits to many in both categories. Some cities bound to Rome by treaty he deprived of their freedom because lawlessness was leading them to ruin. For others struggling under debt, he lightened their burden. Those destroyed by earthquakes he rebuilt. To those who made a case for their services to the Roman people, he granted Latin rights[84] or full citizenship. I think that there was no province with the exception of Africa and Sardinia that he did not visit. He was preparing to cross over to these after Sextus Pompey had been routed, but severe storms that did not let up prevented him, and later on he had neither the opportunity nor a reason to go.

[48] The kingdoms that fell to him by right of war, except for a few, he returned to those from whom they had been taken, or he annexed them to other non-Roman states. He linked the kings with whom he had treaties to one another in reciprocal relationships, acting as a ready go-between and sponsor for their marriages and friendships. He treated them all as essential partners in the empire. It was his practice to set a mentor over young rulers and those who were of unsound mind until they grew up or recovered. And he reared many of their children together with his own and educated them.

[49.1] In regard to military resources, he distributed the legions and auxiliary units among the provinces and stationed one fleet at Misenum and the other at Ravenna to protect the Upper and Lower Seas.[85] He assigned some of the remaining units to guard

---

84. Limited citizenship; see *Jul.* 8; *Cl.* 19.
85. The Adriatic and the Tyrrhenian.

the city and others to protect himself, after he had let go the band of Calagurritani,[86] whom he had had in his bodyguard until the defeat of Antony, and the Germans, whom he had kept until disaster struck Varus. But he never allowed more than three cohorts within the city, and these had no camp. The rest he normally dispersed to winter and summer[87] camps in nearby towns. [49.2] He bound all soldiers everywhere to a fixed schedule of pay and bonuses with length of service and bounties on discharge dependent on rank. This was so that they could not be provoked to revolution by being discharged when they were still young and poor. He set up a military treasury funded by new taxes in order to have money readily available in the future to maintain the force and pay the bonuses.

[49.3] To make information about what was happening in any of the provinces more quickly available and more readily evaluated, he stationed young men short distances apart along the military roads. He did this in the beginning, but later on he posted means of transport there instead. This seemed a better policy because men bringing letters from any place can also be questioned if the situation requires. [50] When he put his seal on official documents and on replies to petitions and letters, he first used a sphinx, then an image of Alexander the Great, and finally his own image carved by Dioscurides.[88] All of the emperors who have followed have continued to make this their seal. On all of his letters he added the precise hour, not only of the day but of the night as well, to indicate when they were written.

[51.1] There are many persuasive examples of Augustus' mercy and unassuming behavior. Not to mention all of the men of various factions who received a pardon or immunity and were even allowed to hold important positions in the state, he was content with mild punishment for the plebeians Junius Novatus and Cassius Patuvinus, a fine for the one and light exile for the other. The former had made public a letter very critical of Augustus that was written in the name of young Agrippa;[89] the latter had announced to the guests at a dinner party that he lacked neither the desire nor the courage to stab

---

86. Spaniards.
87. Permanent and temporary camps.
88. A contemporary carver of gemstones.
89. Agrippa Postumus; see 64.1.

the emperor. [51.2] At a judicial inquiry involving Aemilius Aelianus of Corduba,[90] where the principal charge was that he frequently expressed a negative opinion of Caesar, Augustus turned to the accuser and said, pretending to be angry, "Please show me proof of that. I'll see to it that Aelianus knows that I have a tongue, too, for I'll have more to say about him." And he did not pursue the examination either then or later. [51.3] When Tiberius wrote him a letter also complaining about this case but in harsher language, he replied, "My dear Tiberius, do not surrender to the emotions of youth in this matter or be too angry that someone speaks ill of me. It is sufficient to ensure that no one can do us ill."

[52] Although Augustus knew that it was usual for temples to be voted even for the worship of proconsuls, he still did not allow one for himself, not even in a province, unless it was dedicated jointly to him and to the goddess Roma. In Rome he was absolutely determined to avoid this honor. He also melted down all the silver statues that had been set up for him earlier and used the money from these to dedicate golden tripods to the Palatine Apollo. When the people insisted that he accept the dictatorship, he got to his knees, tore the toga from his shoulders, and, with his chest bare, begged them not to compel him. [53.1] He always recoiled from the name *dominus* as insulting and shameful. When he was watching a production in the theater and these words were spoken in the mime, "O Lord and Master, just and good!" the entire audience was delighted and expressed its approval because it thought that the words were being spoken about Augustus. He immediately used a gesture and a look to stop the unseemly obsequiousness, and on the following day he rebuked them harshly in an edict. After that he did not allow even his children and grandchildren to call him *dominus* either in earnest or as a joke, and he forbade them to flatter him like this even among themselves. [53.2] He scarcely left or entered the city or any town except in the evening or at night so as not to inconvenience anyone with the required formalities. When he was consul, he usually went about in public on foot, and when he was not, often in a closed sedan chair. He let everyone attend his open morning receptions, even ordinary people, and he accepted requests from those who approached him with such courtesy that he jokingly criticized one of them who was hesitating, saying that he was handing him his petition "like a tiny

---

90. In southern Spain, modern Córdoba.

coin to an elephant." [53.3] On days of senate meetings he greeted the members only after they were in the senate house, and indeed, only after they were seated, and he addressed each by name without being prompted. And when he took his leave, he left them seated as before.⁹¹ He respected the obligations of friendship with many and did not stop attending their private celebrations until he was older and had once been jostled in a crowd on the day of a betrothal. Gallus Cerrinius, a senator whom he did not know well but who had suddenly gone blind and as a result had determined to starve himself to death, he personally consoled and encouraged to live.

[54] When he was speaking in the senate, someone said to him, "I did not understand," and someone else said, "I would oppose you, if I had the opportunity to speak." On several occasions when he rushed angrily out of the senate house because of the ceaseless bickering of opposing parties, some shouted at him, "Senators must be allowed to discuss public business." At the selection of senate members when each man was to choose a man,⁹² the senator Antistius Labeo chose Marcus Lepidus, who had been Augustus' enemy and was in exile at the time.⁹³ When Augustus asked him whether there were others who were more worthy, Labeo replied, "Each man has his own opinion." No one ran into trouble by expressing himself freely or by displaying a defiant attitude. [55] Augustus did not become alarmed at the defamatory pamphlets about him distributed in the senate. Instead, he refuted them carefully and, without even trying to find out who had written them, merely ruled that in the future inquiry must be directed toward those who were publishing such pamphlets and verses under someone else's name.

[56.1] When he was provoked by the offensive and insolent jokes that some men told, he responded by edict, but he vetoed any attempt to curtail freedom of speech in wills. Whenever he took part in the election of magistrates, he went around the tribes with the candidates whom he was recommending and begged for votes in the traditional way. And he cast his vote with his tribe, like one of the people. He graciously allowed himself to be called as a witness at trials and to be questioned and contradicted. [56.2] When he built his forum, he

---

91. Augustus did not require them to rise out of respect for him.
92. See 35.1.
93. See 16.4.

made it narrower than planned because he was reluctant to force out the owners of the nearby houses. He never recommended his sons to the people for election to public office without adding, "If they are worthy." He objected strongly when everyone in the theater rose for them and remained standing as they applauded them when they were still boys. He wanted his friends to be important and powerful in the state but still to be answerable to the same laws as others and equally subject to the jurisdiction of the courts. [56.3] When his close associate Asprenas Nonius was defending himself against a charge of poisoning brought by Cassius Severus,[94] he asked advice of the senate: "What am I to do? I find it difficult to decide. It may be thought that I am snatching a defendant from the grasp of the law, if I appear in his support, or if I do not, that I am deserting my friend and condemning him to defeat before the trial begins." With everyone's approval, he sat in court for several hours but did not speak, not even making a statement in praise of the defendant. [56.4] But he did appear in court in support of his clients, for one Scutarius, for instance, who had formerly been one of his praetorian officers and who was being prosecuted for defamation. Of all those on trial he saved only one man, and he did it by pleading, winning over the accuser in the presence of the jury; this man was Castricius, from whom he had learned about Murena's conspiracy.[95]

[57.1] It is easy to understand how very much Augustus was admired for these praiseworthy things that he did. (I do not mention the decrees of the senate since they can appear to have been issued out of necessity or deference.) The Roman knights on their own initiative and by consensus always held a two-day celebration of his birthday. Members of all the orders cast small coins into Lake Curtius[96] every year to fulfill a vow for his safety and brought New Year's gifts to the Capitol on the Kalends of January, even when he was not in Rome. He purchased expensive statues of the gods with this money and dedicated them in the neighborhoods, a statue of Apollo in the street of the sandal makers, for instance, and a statue of Jupiter in the tragic actors' district and others. [57.2] Veterans, guilds, tribes, and individuals with other occupations willingly

---

94. An outspoken orator.

95. See 19.1, 66.3.

96. A small pool in the Forum with sacred associations.

contributed money to rebuild his home on the Palatine after it had
been destroyed by fire, each as he could afford it. Augustus skimmed
only a small part of the money off the piles that were collected, taking no more than a denarius from each. They escorted him on his
return from the provinces, calling him names of good omen and
serenading him in song as well. And it was the practice that no one
was executed whenever he entered Rome. [58.1] In a strong and sudden show of unity, everyone tendered him the cognomen Father of
His Country: First the common people sent a delegation to Antium.
Next, when he did not accept it, a large crowd wearing laurel wreaths
offered it as he was entering the games at Rome. Then the senate
conferred it in the senate house, neither by decree nor acclamation
but with these words from Valerius Messalla.[97] [58.2] Messalla voiced
the feelings of all when he said, "May the blessings of good fortune
visit you and your household, Caesar Augustus! For in this way we
consider that we are praying for the everlasting success of the state
and for its happiness: the senate in accord with the Roman people
salutes you as 'Father of Your Country.'" Augustus wept when he
answered him like this (I have set down here his very words, just as
I did those of Messalla): "My desires are realized, senators. For what
else do I have to pray to the immortal gods than that I be allowed
to bear to the very end of my life this name that you have joined in
awarding me?"

[59] The people collected money and set up a statue of his doctor, Antonius Musa, next to the image of Aesculapius;[98] Augustus
had recovered from a life-threatening illness under his care. Some
heads of households wrote it into their wills that their heirs lead
sacrificial beasts to the Capitol and make satisfaction of their vows
because Augustus had outlived them and that they give notice of
their intentions with placards going before them. Some cities in Italy
made the day of his first visit to them the beginning of their year.
Many provinces established quinquennial games and also temples
and altars in almost all of their towns. [60] Kings that were friends
and allies of Rome founded cities named Caesarea, each in his own
kingdom, and together they determined to share the expense of finishing the temple of the Olympian Jupiter at Athens that had been

---

97. Marcus Valerius Messalla Corvinus, a senior senator and distinguished
orator and an important ally of Augustus.
98. The god of healing.

started long before and to dedicate it to his Genius.[99] And they often left their kingdoms, put on togas and removed their royal regalia, and attended him as if they were clients, not only at Rome but when he was traveling in the provinces.

[61.1] Since I have described what kind of man Augustus was when he was in power and served as a magistrate and when he directed war and peace throughout the world, I shall now give an account of his personal and domestic life, of how he behaved and how he fared at home and with his family from his youth until the last day of his life.

[61.2] Augustus lost his mother during his first consulship and his sister Octavia in his fifty-fourth year.[100] Although he had showed each singular respect when they were alive, he bestowed the highest honors on them after they were dead.

[62.1] As a young man he had been engaged to the daughter of Publius Servilius Isauricus,[101] but when he was reconciled with Antony after their first falling out and the soldiers of both armies demanded that they be connected by a family bond of some sort, Augustus married Antony's stepdaughter Claudia, the daughter of Fulvia and Publius Clodius.[102] Claudia was barely of marriageable age, and after a quarrel with his mother-in-law Fulvia, Augustus sent the girl back home, still an untouched virgin. [62.2] He then married Scribonia, who had been married twice previously to men of consular rank and had a child by one of them. He divorced her, too, "thoroughly weary," as he wrote, "of her intractable nature." He immediately took Livia Drusilla from her husband Tiberius Nero,[103] despite the fact that she was pregnant, and he loved her and her alone and held her in high regard all his life.

[63.1] From Scribonia he had a child, Julia, but he had no children from Livia although he wanted them badly; a baby was conceived but was born prematurely. He arranged a marriage for Julia first

---

99. The male spirit that resided in him. The temple was not completed until the second century CE.

100. In 43 and probably 9 BCE, respectively.

101. Consul with Julius Caesar in 48 BCE. This first betrothal was a political arrangement made shortly after the assassination of Caesar.

102. Fulvia's former husband was the notorious Publius Clodius Pulcher; see *Jul.* 6.2.

103. 38 BCE. Her husband was Tiberius Claudius Nero; see *Tib.* 4.3.

to Marcellus, his sister Octavia's son, who had only just reached adulthood, and then, when he died, to Marcus Agrippa, after he had persuaded his sister to let him have her son-in-law. (Agrippa was married to one of the Marcellas at that time and had children by her.)[104] [63.2] When Agrippa also died, Augustus searched a long time for a marriage partner for her, looking even among the ranks of the equestrians. He chose his stepson Tiberius and compelled him to divorce his wife, who was pregnant and with whom he had already fathered children.[105] Mark Antony writes that Augustus first betrothed Julia to his own son Antonius and then to Cotiso, king of the Getae,[106] at the very time when Augustus himself was trying to marry the king's daughter in exchange.

[64.1] Augustus had three grandsons, Gaius, Lucius, and Agrippa,[107] and two granddaughters, Julia and Agrippina, all the children of Agrippa and Julia. For Julia he arranged marriage to Lucius Paulus, the son of the censor, and for Agrippina marriage to Germanicus, his sister's grandson. He adopted Gaius and Lucius privately in a symbolic sale from their father Agrippa, and when they were still young he introduced them to affairs of state, and he sent them as consuls-designate to the provinces and the armies. [64.2] He reared his daughter and granddaughters to spend their time working with wool, and he forbade them to say or do anything that could not be reported in the household's daily dispatches for all to see. He was so strict about barring contact with outsiders that he once wrote to Lucius Vinicius, a respectable young man of the upper class, "You have not acted properly because you came to pay your respects to my daughter at Baiae." [64.3] He took a hand in teaching his grandsons how to read and how to swim along with other basic skills, and he worked especially hard at having them imitate his handwriting. He did not dine with them unless they sat at the foot of his couch, nor did he travel unless they went ahead of his conveyance or rode next to him on their horses.

---

104. In addition to her son Marcellus, Octavia had two daughters, both named Marcella.

105. Tiberius' love for his first wife appears at *Tib.* 7.2–3.

106. A tribe in Thrace.

107. Agrippa Postumus.

[65.1] But the goddess Fortune deserted him, content as he was and confident in his offspring and in the orderly conduct of his household. He banished the Julias, daughter and granddaughter, because they had been tainted by every kind of perversion. He lost Gaius and Lucius in the course of eighteen months, Gaius dead in Lycia and Lucius at Massilia. He adopted his third grandson Agrippa Postumus and at the same time his stepson Tiberius in the Forum under the terms of a law passed by the popular assembly.[108] But he soon disinherited Agrippa on account of his mean and violent temper and banished him to Surrentum.[109]

[65.2] But he endured the deaths of family members with greater fortitude than he did their bad behavior. He was not broken by the disaster that befell Gaius and Lucius, but he stayed away from the senate when he informed it about his daughter in a communication read aloud by his quaestor. Shame kept him from human company for a long time, and he even thought of killing her. In any case, when Phoebe, a freedwoman who was one of Julia's confidantes, hanged herself, he said, "I would rather have been Phoebe's father." [65.3] After Julia was banished,[110] he denied her the right to enjoy wine and every nicety that society provides, and he allowed no man, free or slave, to go near her without his permission and without being told how old the man was or how tall or of what complexion, and even what marks and scars he had on his body. Finally, after five years, he moved her from the island to the mainland, where he kept her in somewhat less restrictive confinement. But in no way could he be prevailed upon to recall her altogether. And when the Roman populace kept interceding on her behalf and tenaciously pressed their message, he cursed them in a public assembly with such daughters and such wives as these. [65.4] When his granddaughter Julia gave birth after she had been condemned, he did not allow the child to be acknowledged or reared. Agrippa became in no way more manageable but indeed grew wilder with each passing day, and so Augustus transferred him to an island[111] and surrounded him with a military

---

108. 4 CE. Neither had a living father, and so the kind of transfer made with Gaius and Lucius was not possible; see 64.1.
109. Modern Sorrento, on the coast near Naples.
110. To the island of Pandataria off the coast of Campania, 2 BCE.
111. Agrippa was disinherited in 6 CE and later sent into exile.

guard as well. He also used a decree of the senate to make sure that he would be confined there forever. And whenever Agrippa and the Julias were mentioned, he would groan and proclaim, "Would that I had remained unmarried and died childless,"[112] and he never called them anything except his "three boils" and his "three malignant growths."

[66.1] Augustus did not form friendships easily, but those that he had he preserved with unwavering loyalty. He not only valued appropriately the excellence and good qualities that each possessed but put up with their faults and misdeeds, provided they were not excessive. Scarcely any whom he counted among his friends will be found coming to ruin with the exception of Salvidienus Rufus, whom he had advanced to the consulship, and Cornelius Gallus, whom he had advanced to the prefecture of Egypt, both from undistinguished families. [66.2] The former he handed over to the senate to be convicted of plotting revolution; the latter he barred from his home as well as from the provinces that he controlled because he was ungrateful and mean-spirited. But when Gallus was also driven to suicide by the denunciations of his accusers and by the senate's decrees, Augustus, although he had great praise, it is true, for the loyalty of those who had supported his position, wept, and bemoaned his lot. He complained that it was he alone who was not permitted to limit anger toward his friends as he chose. [66.3] His other friends thrived in power and wealth all of their lives, each a leading member in his order, although there were difficulties along the way. To name only a few of them, he sometimes found Marcus Agrippa lacking in patience and Maecenas[113] unable to keep silent. Agrippa abandoned everything and went to Mytilene because of a slight suspicion that Augustus was cool toward him and because Marcellus was being advanced ahead of him.[114] Maecenas revealed to his wife Terentia the confidential information that Murena's conspiracy had been discovered.[115]

---

112. Homer, *Iliad* 3.40.
113. Gaius Maecenas, a wealthy friend, never held office and remained an equestrian.
114. 23 BCE.
115. See 19.1.

[66.4] But he required his friends to be generous to him in turn, both when they were alive and after death. Although he did not seek out inheritances aggressively—he never consented to receive anything from the will of someone he did not know—he nonetheless brooded heavily over the final determinations of his friends. He did not try to hide his displeasure if they treated him shabbily or did not add compliments or to suppress his delight if someone rewarded him with gratitude and due respect. When anyone who had offspring left him legacies or portions of their estates, he either transferred their bequests to their children immediately or, if their children were still under the care of a guardian, returned it with interest on the day they received the adult toga or were married.

[67.1] As a patron and slave master he was as lenient and merciful as he was strict. He respected his freedmen and was familiar with them, with Licinus, for instance, and Celadus and others. When the slave Cosmus spoke disparagingly of him, the only thing Augustus did with him was put him in shackles. When he was walking with his steward Diomedes, and Diomedes panicked and got behind him when a wild boar suddenly charged, he chose to accuse him of cowardice rather than wrongdoing, and although the incident involved significant danger, he turned the matter into a joke since no harm was intended. [67.2] On the other hand, he forced Polus, one of his favorite freedmen, to kill himself when he was discovered having sex with married women, and he broke the legs of his secretary Thallus because he had taken 500 denarii to reveal the contents of a letter. As for his son Gaius' tutor and attendants, who had behaved arrogantly and greedily in the province when the young man was sick and dying, he put heavy weights on their necks and threw them headlong into the river.

[68] Augustus was vilified for a variety of indecent sexual acts when he was young. Sextus Pompey attacked him for being effeminate, Mark Antony for earning adoption with the sexual favors that he did for his uncle; Lucius, Antony's brother, charged that in Spain he had abandoned his sense of shame (such as he had left after Caesar) to Aulus Hirtius for 300,000 sesterces and that he customarily singed his legs with a hot nut to make the hair grow in softer. And once on a day when theatrical productions were being given, the entire populace interpreted a verse recited on the stage as an insult to him and showed their approval with loud applause. It was a verse about a

priest of the mother of the gods who was playing on his drum: "Do
you see how the pervert beats the drum with his finger?"[116]

[69.1] To be sure, not even his friends deny that he committed
adultery, but they offer the excuse that he clearly did not do this out
of lust but with the rational intent of making it easier to find out the
plans of his adversaries through their wives. Mark Antony found
fault with him not only for his hasty marriage to Livia but also for
taking a consul's wife to his chamber from the dining room where
her husband was a guest and bringing her back again to the dinner
party, blushing to her ears and with her hair in disarray. Antony also
accused him of divorcing Scribonia because she had been too uninhibited in expressing her unhappiness about the great power that
his mistress enjoyed. And Antony blamed him for the assignations
that were arranged by his friends, who stripped married women and
grown virgins and looked them over like the slave dealer Toranius
making a deal. [69.2] And Antony writes to him in this familiar fashion when he was not yet Augustus' enemy or an enemy of the state:
"Why have you changed your mind? Is it because I am humping the
queen?[117] Is she my wife? Did I just start this or did I begin nine
years ago? Is Drusilla[118] the only one you screw? I wish you luck if
when you read this letter you haven't screwed Tertulla or Terentilla
or Rufilla or Salvia Titisenia or all the others. Does it matter where
or with whom you get a hard-on?"

[70.1] Then there is the story about a secret dinner party generally
referred to as the "dinner of the twelve gods." It is not only letters of
Antony that scold the guests for reclining at table dressed like gods
and goddesses, with Augustus costumed as Apollo, and take malicious delight in identifying the participants. These notorious verses
of unknown authorship tell the same story:

> As soon as the table guests hired a costumer,
> Mallia[119] beheld six gods and six goddesses
> While Caesar as Phoebus acted out a sacrilegious lie,

---

116. The priests of the mother goddess Cybele were eunuchs and so could
be thought effeminate or passive homosexuals. Words meaning "beat the
drum" can also mean "rule the world."

117. Cleopatra. Antony uses the word for animals mating.

118. Augustus' wife, Livia Drusilla.

119. Perhaps the host of the dinner party.

While he dined amid fresh adulteries of gods.
Then all Divine Powers left the earth,
And Jupiter fled his golden throne.

[70.2] The scarcity of grain and hunger in the state at that time[120] fueled the rumors about the dinner party, and the next day there was shouting: "The gods have eaten up the grain supply, and Caesar really is Apollo—Apollo of the Torturers." (The god was worshiped under this cognomen in one section of the city.) Augustus was further stigmatized as greedy for expensive furnishings and Corinthian ware and given to playing dice. The following was written on his statue at the time of the proscriptions: "My father was a banker, a dealer in silver; I deal in Corinthian bronze," since it was thought that he had made sure that some people were put on the list for their Corinthian vases. Then during the Sicilian war[121] this epigram made the rounds:

After he has been beaten twice and has lost two fleets,
He plays dice constantly—hoping to win something.

[71.1] By the blameless conduct of his life at the time and later, Augustus had no trouble clearing his reputation of the charges (or slanders) of sexual perversion.[122] He also countered the disgust at his extravagant taste when even after the capture of Alexandria, he kept none of the royal furnishings for himself except for a single agate drinking cup, and he melted down all the golden vessels meant for everyday use. As for his sexual appetite, that continued, and later on (or so they say) he was quite prepared to deflower virgins who were acquired for him from all quarters—even by his wife.

He did not worry at all about the talk of his dicing, and he played for pleasure freely and openly, even when he was an old man, and not just during the December holidays[123] but also on other holidays and on ordinary days. [71.2] There is no question about this. He says in a letter written in his own handwriting: "I dined, my dear Tiberius,

---

120. Perhaps the winter of 39–38 BCE.
121. See chapter 16.
122. Allegations that he was a passive homosexual; see chapter 68.
123. Dicing was illegal, although the ban was not much enforced. Rules were relaxed during the Saturnalia in December.

with the same company; Vinicius and the elder Silius joined us as guests.[124] During dinner both yesterday and today we gambled like old men. When the dice were thrown, each one who rolled the 'dog' or a six contributed a denarius to the pot for each of the dice. Whoever threw Venus took it all."[125] [71.3] Again in another letter: "My dear Tiberius, we spent the Quinquatria[126] quite pleasantly, for we gambled the whole day and kept 'the dice players' forum'[127] warm. Your brother[128] complained loudly while he was playing but didn't lose much in the end; he was losing badly but gradually recovered from a hopeless position. Myself, I lost twenty thousand, but this happened because I had been carelessly generous in my play—as I often am. If I had made anyone repay any of the stakes that I let go, or if I had kept what I gave everyone, I would certainly have won fifty thousand. But this way is better; my openhandedness will see me out to heavenly glory." [71.4] He writes to his daughter: "I have sent you 250 denarii, the amount I gave each of my guests in case they wanted to play dice or 'even-odd'[129] during dinner."

[72.1] In other areas of his life, all agree that he practiced great restraint and was not suspected of any vice. At first he lived near the Roman Forum above the Steps of the Ringmakers in a house that had belonged to the orator Calvus.[130] Later on he lived on the Palatine but in the modest house that had belonged to Hortensius,[131] remarkable neither for its size nor its elegance. Its porticoes were short with columns of stone from the Alban Hills, and it had no rooms decorated with marble and no beautiful floors. He lived in the same room, winter and summer, for more than forty years, and although

---

124. Marcus Vinicius and Publius Silius Nerva, suffect consul in 19 BCE and consul in 20, respectively.

125. These were four-faced tokens made from the anklebones of sheep. The dog was the lowest throw and Venus the highest throw.

126. A festival in March honoring Minerva.

127. Augustus' joke for the gaming table.

128. Drusus the Elder; see *Cl.* 1.

129. A game in which one guessed how many small objects another was holding.

130. Licinius Calvus; see *Jul.* 49.1, 73. The steps and their location are unknown.

131. The orator; see *Tib.* 47.

he found the city not very good for his health in winter, he continued to spend his winters there. [72.2] Whenever he intended to do
anything in private without being interrupted, he had a special place
high up that he called his "Syracuse" or his "little workroom."[132] He
would retreat there or to the suburban house of one of his freedmen,
but when he was sick, he took to bed in the home of Maecenas. Of
his country retreats he most often visited those on the seaside and
on the islands off Campania or those in the towns closest to Rome,
Lanuvium, Praeneste, or Tibur, where he often dispensed justice in
the portico of the temple of Hercules. [72.3] He disliked large and
grandiose mansions so much that he even razed a house that his
granddaughter Julia had built at great expense. He decorated his own
houses, modest as they were, not so much with statues and paintings
as with walkways, groves, and objects that were interesting because
of their age or novelty. At Capri, for instance, he kept the limbs
of huge sea creatures and wild animals that he called the bones of
giants and the arms of heroes. [73] It can still be seen today from his
couches and tables that remain how homely his furniture and household articles were, many of a quality scarcely suitable for a private
individual. They say he did not sleep on a bed unless it was low and
spread with ordinary blankets. He rarely wore garments that were
not for home wear, and these were made by his sister, wife, daughter,
and granddaughters. He neither wrapped his togas too tightly nor
let them hang too loosely. His purple stripe was neither too broad
nor too narrow. His shoes were rather high so that he would appear
taller than he was. And he always kept clothing for public wear in
his bedchamber along with his shoes so that he would be ready for
sudden, unanticipated situations.

[74] Augustus gave dinner parties often, always with proper protocol and careful attention to social rank and to the choice of guests.
Valerius Messalla[133] writes that he never invited a freedman to his
table with the exception of Menas, but Menas was given freeborn
status after he betrayed Sextus Pompey's fleet.[134] Augustus himself
writes that he once invited a former bodyguard at whose villa he used
to stay. Sometimes he went to dinner late and left early; his guests

---

132. Perhaps because at the center of Syracuse was an island where limited
accessibility offered privacy.

133. See 58.1.

134. Menas had been one of Sextus Pompey's admirals.

would begin eating before he took his place on his couch and stayed behind after he had departed. He gave dinners of three courses or, when he was most extravagant, six, modestly presented but served with great good cheer. When guests were quiet or talked softly, he drew them into the general conversation. And he introduced entertainment, actors, and even street performers from the Circus neighborhood and often professional declaimers.

[75] He celebrated holidays and anniversaries with great enthusiasm—although sometimes only with jokes. He distributed gifts on the Saturnalia and whenever he pleased—clothing and gold and silver, sometimes all kinds of coins, even ancient royal coins and foreign coins, but at other times he gave out nothing but goat's-hair blankets, sponges, pokers, tongs, and other things of that kind accompanied by obscure descriptions that had double meanings. At dinner he would sell chances on objects of very disparate value or on pictures that faced away from the buyer, thus frustrating or satisfying expectations with the element of chance. He had the bidding take place by couches,[135] and the loss or gain was shared.

[76.1] He ate little food (I am unwilling to omit even this trivial information), and what he did eat was quite ordinary. He especially liked coarse bread and little fish and hand-pressed spongy cheese and twice-bearing green figs, and he ate before dinner whenever and wherever hunger struck. I quote from his letters: "We nibbled on bread and dates in our carriage," [76.2] and, "While I was on my way home from the *regia*[136] in my litter, I ate a bit of bread with a few grapes from a bunch that had firm skins." Again: "Not even a Jew, dear Tiberius, keeps the Sabbath fast so religiously as I did today. Finally after the first hour of the night, I chewed two mouthfuls before I began to be oiled."[137] Because his habits were so irregular, he sometimes dined alone before a dinner party began or after it was over but touched nothing in the company of his guests. [77] It was his nature to be very cautious about wine as well. Cornelius Nepos[138] reports that he usually did not drink more than three times

---

135. The guests who usually reclined three to a couch were evidently to place their bids as a unit.
136. A small structure in the Forum with religious associations.
137. The oil put on in the bath and then scraped off.
138. See *Jul.* 55.1.

at dinner when he was in his camp before Mutina.[139] Later on when he indulged more liberally, he did not drink more than a pint, and if he did, he vomited it. He particularly liked Raetian wine[140] and rarely drank during the day. When he wanted something to drink, he took bread soaked in cold water or a bit of cucumber or a lettuce leaf or an apple, fresh or dried, that tasted like wine.

[78.1] He would take a short nap after his midday meal, just as he was, with his clothes and shoes on, his feet uncovered, and his hand across his eyes. After dinner he would retire to a small couch suitable for working at night, and there he remained late into the night until he finished what remained of the day's work, either completely or for the most part. From there he went to bed where he slept not more than seven hours at the most, and not even these went without interruption since he would wake up three or four times during that stretch. [78.3] When it happened that he could not go back to sleep, he called for readers and good talkers and then went back to sleep again and often stayed asleep until after daybreak. He never lay awake after dark unless someone sat beside him. He hated to get up early in the morning, and if he was forced to in order to perform a duty or sacred office, he would spend the night in a room in the neighborhood belonging to one of his entourage so that it would be convenient. These habits often left him in need of sleep, and he would nod off when some delay or other caused his litter to be set down while he was being carried about the neighborhoods.

[79.1] Augustus was handsome and his appearance was pleasing throughout his life, although he paid no attention to things that added to his good looks. He was so remiss about taking care of his hair that he employed several barbers at the same time; one hurried to cut his hair and another to shave his beard while he either read something or wrote at the same time. Both when he spoke and when he was silent, his expression was so calm and composed that one of the leading men of the Gauls confessed to his countrymen that it was the look on his face that had weakened his resolve and kept him from throwing him over a cliff as he had planned. (This incident took place when they were crossing the Alps and the Gaul was allowed to approach him by pretending that he wanted to talk with him.) [79.2] Augustus had bright shining eyes, and he wanted it thought

---

139. See 10.2–4.
140. From the alpine region.

that they possessed a measure of divine strength. He was pleased when someone lowered his glance before him as before the radiance of the sun when he was staring at him intently. But when he was old, he saw less well with his left eye. His teeth were widely spaced, small, and decayed. His hair was slightly wavy and light yellow. His eyebrows met in the middle. His ears were of average size. His nose curved out somewhat at the top and in somewhat at the bottom. His complexion was between dark and pale. He was short (although Julius Marathus, the freedman who served as his record keeper, reports that he was five feet nine inches),[141] but the well-balanced proportions of his body obscured this so that it could not be noticed unless someone taller was standing next to him.

[80] It is said that his body was covered with spots. Birthmarks were scattered across his chest and abdomen like the stars of the heavenly bear[142] in their shape, arrangement, and number. And he was covered with tough calluses that had hardened into scaly patches; these were caused by the itching of his body and by the constant, vigorous use of strigils.[143] His left hip, thigh, and leg were weak, and he even limped sometimes, but he gained strength from a remedy of sand and reeds. He sometimes found the forefinger of his right hand so weak that when it was numb and cramped from the cold he had difficulty writing, even with the support of a horn circlet. He also complained about his bladder; the pain was relieved when he finally passed kidney stones in his urine.

[81.1] Augustus suffered serious life-threatening illnesses several times in his life. After the conquest of Cantabria in particular, when his liver had been damaged by inflammation and his case seemed hopeless, he had to undergo an unusual and risky treatment. Hot poultices had not been effective, and he was forced to take a cold cure at the advice of Antonius Musa.[144] He suffered from ailments that recurred at certain times every year. He generally fell sick around the time of his birthday, and at the beginning of the spring he suffered from distention of the abdomen, and when the wind was from the south, from a head cold. These illnesses compromised his health, and

---

141. In English feet, the equivalent of five feet seven inches.
142. The constellation Ursa Major, of which the Big Dipper is part.
143. Instruments for cleaning the body by scraping off oil and dirt.
144. His doctor; see chapter 59.

he had difficulty tolerating either cold or heat. [82.1] In the winter he protected himself with four tunics, a heavy toga, underwear, a woolen vest, and wrappings for his thighs and shins. In the summer he took his rest with the doors of his bedchamber open and often in the inner courtyard with water splashing and someone fanning him. He could not tolerate the sun even in the winter, and he did not go about outside without a broad-brimmed hat even while at home. He traveled in a litter, usually at night and by short and unhurried stages so that it took him two days to get to Praeneste or Tibur. And if it was possible to go by sea, that was how he made his journey. [82.2] But he tended to his frail health with great care, primarily by bathing only rarely. He was often scraped with oil or sweated near a fire and then had water poured over him, either tepid or warmed from standing in the sun for a long time. But whenever he took the seawater cure or the warm water cure at the Albula springs[145] to restore his muscles, he was content to sit in a wooden chair that he called by the Spanish word *dureta* and thrust in his hands and feet alternately.

[83] As soon as the civil war was over, Augustus gave up exercising on horseback and with arms in the Campus Martius and instead played first with a hard ball and then with a large inflated ball. After that he did nothing but ride and take walks; on his final laps he would run and jump wrapped in a cloak or a small blanket. To relax he would sometimes go fishing and other times play at dice or games with small stones and nuts. His companions were charming little boys with appealing looks who chattered delightfully. He had searched them out from all over, but principally from Mauretania and Syria, and he had chosen them because he detested dwarfs and misshapen people and all grotesques of that kind as freaks of nature and bearers of bad luck.

[84.1] From an early age Augustus studied oratory and the liberal curriculum eagerly and most conscientiously. It is reported that he read, wrote, and declaimed every day under the heavy burden of the war at Mutina.[146] This diligence had its use, for later on he never delivered a speech in the senate, before the people, or to the soldiers without composing it ahead of time and rehearsing it well, although he had the ability to speak without preparation on short notice. [84.2] So as not to risk forgetting or waste his time memorizing, he

---

145. Curative sulfur springs near Rome.
146. See 10.2–4.

made it a practice to read them all. He did not converse with anyone on serious matters, not even with his wife Livia, unless he wrote down his thoughts and had them in a notebook.[147] He did this so that he would not say too much or too little as he might if he spoke unprepared. He had a pleasing voice that was distinctly his own and studied regularly with a speech teacher. But sometimes when his throat was weak he addressed the people through a herald.

[85.1] He wrote a large number of prose works of various kinds and read some of them aloud in gatherings of his close friends as though in a public recital hall. One was his *Reply to Brutus on Cato*.[148] He had almost come to the end of the volumes containing it when he grew tired (he was quite old by then) and handed them over to Tiberius to finish reading. There were also *The Encouragement to Philosophy* and *On My Life*, which he set forth in thirteen volumes as far as the Cantabrian war but going no further. [85.2] He dabbled in poetry. A single book of his hexameters[149] survives with the subject matter and title *Sicily*, and there is another equally modest book of *Epigrams*, which he composed largely while in the bath. He began a tragedy with a great burst of energy, but his stylus failed him and he destroyed it. When his friends asked him what Ajax was doing, he replied, "Ajax has fallen on his sponge."[150]

[86.1] He practiced a speaking style that was exact and restrained and avoided the absurdity of epigrams and excessive refinement and (as he puts it) "the foul stench of obscure words." He took particular care to set forth his ideas as clearly as possible. To do this more effectively and so as never to confuse the reader or listener and make him pause, he did not hesitate to place prepositions before the names of cities[151] or repeat conjunctions several times. (When these are absent, obscurity increases, although their omission adds to a pleasing style.) [86.2] He shunned affected stylists and antiquarian

---

147. For his communication with Livia, see *Cl.* 4.1–6.

148. Marcus Junius Brutus, Caesar's assassin (see *Jul.* 80.4), in praise of Cato Uticensis (see *Jul.* 14.2, *Aug.* 13.2).

149. A line of verse made up of six metrical units, the meter in which epics were written.

150. Ajax was a Greek warrior in Homer's *Iliad*. Romans wrote on wax tablets with a stylus and rubbed words out with a sponge. Augustus played with the expression "fall on one's sword."

151. Latin normally does not use prepositions with the names of cities.

enthusiasts, whom he found equally distasteful, although bad for different reasons, and he sometimes attacked them. He never missed an occasion to go after his good friend Maecenas in particular and make fun of him by mimicking his "perfume-suffused ringlets," as he calls them. Nor does he spare Tiberius, who would sometimes hunt out obsolete and abstruse expressions. As for Mark Antony, he calls him a mad man for writing things that men stand in awe of rather than comprehend and then makes fun of his faulty and inconsistent ability to choose a speaking style. He adds, [86.3] "Are you hesitating as to whether you should imitate Annius Cimber or Veranius Flaccus so that you use words that Crispus Sallustius[152] stole from Cato's *Origines*?[153] Or do you think that the long-windedness of Asiatic orators[154] with their inane thoughts should be introduced into our speech instead?" In a letter to his granddaughter Agrippina, in which he praises her talent, he says, "But you must take care not to write and speak in a tiresome way."

[87.1] Letters in his own handwriting provide evidence that he used certain distinctive expressions often in his daily speech. For instance, when he wants to indicate people who will never pay their debts, he says, "They will pay on the Greek Kalends."[155] And when he advises that the present state of affairs be tolerated, whatever it may be, "Let us be content with this Cato";[156] and to describe the speed of a hasty action, "Faster than asparagus cooks." [87.2] For *stultus* [stupid] he always uses *baceolus*[157] [pea brain]; for *pullus* [chick], *pulleiaceus* [chickie]; for *cerritus* [demented], *vacerrosus* [fencepost]. He uses *vapide se habere* [feel poorly] for *male se habere* [feel bad] and *betizare* [be limp like a beet] for *languere* [be weak]. (In colloquial usage the word is *lachanizare* [be limp like a vegetable].) He uses

---

152. Titus Annius Cimber was an adherent of Antony. Gaius Sallustius Crispus was a well-known archaizing historian of the late Republic. Nothing is known of Veranius Flaccus.

153. The *Origines* of Marcus Porcius Cato Censorinus was a very early prose work, c. 160 BCE.

154. In the late Republic, two oratorical styles competed: the Asiatic, verbose and ornate, and the Attic, lean and direct.

155. There was no such date.

156. On the conservative Cato, see 13.2.

157. The meaning of this word and some of the others is uncertain.

simus for *sumus*[158] and *domos* for the genitive singular case instead of
domuos,[159] and he is consistent in the way he writes these two words
so that no one will think it an error rather than a habit.

[87.3] These are the unique features I have noticed in his handwriting: he does not put spaces between his words, and when there
are too many letters at the end of a line, he does not put them on the
next line but directly underneath and curls them around. [88] He
does not pay much attention to orthography (the proper rules for
spelling established by the grammarians) but seems instead to adhere
to the opinion of those who think the language should be written
exactly as it is spoken. He frequently transposes or omits not only
letters but also syllables, but these are mistakes that all men make. I
would not call attention to this issue if it did not seem odd to me that
some authors have reported that he replaced a governor of consular
rank on the grounds that he was ignorant and uneducated because
he noticed that he had written *ixi* instead of *ipsi*. And whenever he
writes in code, he substitutes B for A, C for B, and the rest of the
letters that follow in the same plan; for X, he uses a double A.

[89.1] He was just as interested in Greek learning as he was in Latin,
and he pursued it with great success. He employed Apollodorus of
Pergamum to teach him public speaking, and when he left Rome for
Apollonia as a young man he took the old man with him. Augustus
was later educated on various subjects from his close association with
the philosopher Areius and his sons Dionysius and Nicanor. Still, he
did not speak Greek fluently or dare to compose anything in it. If
the need arose, he wrote in Latin and gave his text to someone else
to translate. But he was clearly not unacquainted with Greek poetry.
He enjoyed "Old Comedy"[160] and often presented it at public entertainments. [89.2] When he read authors in both languages, there was
nothing that he looked for so carefully as teachings and exempla that
were helpful for the public in general and for individuals. These he
would often copy verbatim and send to the members of his household
or to the generals of his armies and to the governors of provinces
or to the magistrates in the city, as each needed guidance. He even
read entire books to the senate and often used edicts to call popular

---

158. Two forms of "we are." The words may have been pronounced very
similarly.

159. Augustus modified this older form of the word for "home."

160. Broad comedy that flourished in Athens in the fifth century BCE.

attention to them, for example, the speeches of Quintus Metellus, *On Increasing the Number of Children*, and Rutilius, *On Limiting the Height of Buildings.*[161] His purpose was to convince them that he was not the first to be aware of these two issues but that they had already been of concern to men of past ages.

[89.3] Augustus encouraged the talent of his own age in every way that he could. He listened considerately and patiently when writers read their work, not only their poems and histories but their speeches and dialogues as well. But he took offense when anything was written about him that was not in a serious vein and not the work of the best authors. And he warned the praetors not to allow his name to be cheapened in public speaking contests.

[90] This is what we have been told about his attitude to the divine: he was rather too afraid of thunder and lightning and always carried around a sealskin to protect himself from it. At the least sign of a serious storm he retreated into a vaulted hiding place. Once in the past, when he was traveling at night, he had been unnerved by a flash of lightning, an incident described earlier.[162]

[91.1] He paid attention to his dreams and to the dreams that others had about him. In the battle at Philippi,[163] although he had decided not to leave his tent because he was ill, he left nevertheless because he had been warned by the dream of a friend. And it was a good thing that he did because when the enemy attacked and took the camp, his bed was stabbed through and torn apart on the assumption that he was still lying in it. Every spring he had a large number of insignificant dreams that frightened him a great deal but meant nothing; the rest of the year his dreams were fewer but more substantive. [91.2] Since he often visited the temple of Jupiter the Thunderer that had been dedicated on the Capitoline, he dreamed that the Capitoline Jupiter complained that his worshipers were being drawn from him and that he replied that the Thunderer had been placed nearby to be his doorkeeper. In response to the dream he garlanded the temple's gable with bells because bells usually hung from doors. And it was because of a dream that he begged gifts from

161. Quintus Caecilius Metellus and Publius Rutilius Rufus, both political figures and orators of the late second century BCE.
162. See 29.3.
163. When Julius Caesar's assassins were defeated; see 13.1.

the people on a certain day every year, holding out a cupped hand as they offered their small coins.[164]

[92.1] He considered certain portents and omens totally reliable. If his shoes were put on wrong in the morning (the left one for the right one), he thought it ominous. If it happened to drizzle when he was setting out on a long journey on land or by sea, he thought it a good sign, a prediction that he would return soon with good fortune. But he was especially influenced by marvels. When a palm tree sprouted in the cracks between the stones in front of his house, he moved it to the inner court of the shrine that held Rome's *Penates*,[165] and he took great care of it so that it would grow. [92.2] When he arrived on the island of Capri and the branches of an ancient oak tree that were drooping and already touching the ground became strong again, he was so delighted that he arranged for the city of Naples to give him the island in exchange for Aenaria.[166] And he paid attention to certain days and did not set out on a journey on the day after a market day[167] or begin any important business on the Nones. The only thing that he was avoiding with the latter was, as he writes to Tiberius, the "evil sound" of the name.[168]

[93] He treated ancient and well-established foreign rites with great reverence but held the rest in contempt. He had been initiated into the mysteries at Athens, and sometime later when he was presiding in his official capacity over a hearing that involved special treatment for the priests of the Attic Ceres[169] and some of the cult's secrets were being revealed, he dismissed his advisory body and the crowd that was standing around and heard the arguments alone. On the other hand, he not only neglected to make the short detour to

---

164. Evidently a ritual of playing beggar for the day.

165. Just as each family had household gods, so did the city, and these had allegedly been brought from Troy. Alternatively these were the household gods in Augustus' own house, and he tended the tree in his own courtyard.

166. The nearby island that is now Ischia.

167. Market days took place every eight days.

168. The negative word *non* included in Nones was apparently sufficient to warn him off.

169. He had been initiated into the mystery cult at Eleusis, near Athens, where the Greek goddess Demeter was worshiped. The Roman goddess Ceres was identified with Demeter.

visit Apis[170] when he was traveling through Egypt, but he praised his grandson Gaius for not offering prayers at Jerusalem when he passed by Judaea.

[94.1] And since the subject of portents has arisen, it will not be inappropriate to append here those that occurred before he was born and on the day of his birth and afterward, portents that made it possible to anticipate and mark his future greatness and everlasting good fortune.

[94.2] When, a long time ago, a part of the city wall at Velitrae[171] was struck by lightning, the omen was interpreted to mean that a citizen of the town would one day hold supreme power. The citizens of Velitrae believed in this portent and immediately began to make war on the Roman people and fought with them often after that, almost to their own destruction. Finally, much later, events made it clear that the omen had predicted the power of Augustus.

[94.3] Julius Marathus[172] writes that a few months before Augustus was born a marvel occurred at Rome that warned that nature was giving birth to a king for the Roman people. The senate was terrified and voted that no one born that year be reared to adulthood. But men whose wives were pregnant made certain that the decree of the senate was not deposited in the *aerarium*,[173] since each of them had hopes for his own family.

[94.4] I read in the books of Asclepias of Mendes titled *Theologumena*[174] that when Atia[175] attended a sacred ceremony for Apollo that took place in the middle of the night and her litter was set down in the temple, she fell asleep along with the rest of the married women there. Without warning a snake slithered up to her and shortly thereafter slithered away again. When she woke up, she performed a purification ceremony as if she had had sex with her husband. Immediately there appeared on her body a stain colored

---

170. The sacred bull at Memphis that pronounced oracles; see *Tit.* 5.3.

171. Augustus' birthplace; see chapter 1.

172. See 79.2.

173. Decrees of the senate were not valid until they were deposited in the treasury.

174. Asclepias was Egyptian. *Theologumena* means "Conversations of the Gods."

175. Augustus' mother; see 4.1.

like a snake. She was never able to get rid of it and consequently avoided the public baths for the rest of her life. Augustus was born in the tenth month following and for that reason was thought to be the son of Apollo. Atia, before she gave birth, herself dreamed that her internal organs were being carried to the stars and spread out over the whole expanse of the earth and the heavens. And his father Octavius dreamed that the radiant sun arose from Atia's womb.

[94.5] On the day he was born, when the conspiracy of Catiline[176] was being discussed in the senate house and Octavius arrived late because his wife was delivering a child, Publius Nigidius[177] (as is widely known), after he learned why Octavius was late and the hour of the birth, declared that the master of the world had been born. Later, when Octavius was leading his army through little-known parts of Thrace and consulted non-Roman rites about the future of his son in a grove of Father Liber,[178] the priests confirmed the earlier prophecy. When they had poured undiluted wine on the altars, the flame that shot up was so huge that it rose higher than the temple roof and carried all the way to heaven. They said that a portent like this had occurred only once before when a man sacrificed at those altars—that man was Alexander the Great. [94.6] The very next night, Octavius dreamed that he saw his son larger than human size holding a thunderbolt and a scepter and the attributes of Jupiter Optimus Maximus and wearing a radiate crown and riding in a chariot decorated with laurel and drawn by twelve gleaming white horses. It is found in the writings of Gaius Drusus[179] that when Augustus was still a baby, his nurse put him in his cradle on the ground floor; the next morning he was not to be found but after a long search was finally discovered in the highest part of the house, basking in the rays of the rising sun.

[94.7] When Augustus first began to talk, he ordered the frogs at his grandfather's country house to be quiet when it happened that they were in noisy competition with him. And it is said that since then, the frogs there do not croak. When he was eating his lunch in a

176. 63 BCE; see *Jul.* 14.1.
177. Publius Nigidius Figulus, a learned man, who was a supporter of Pompey.
178. The god Bacchus. This omen is dated to the time when Octavius was propraetor in Macedonia; see chapter 3.
179. Unknown.

grove at the fourth milestone on the road to Campania, an eagle suddenly snatched bread from his hand, and after it had flown up high, it swooped gently down again and just as suddenly gave it back.

[94.8] Quintus Catulus[180] had dreams on two successive nights after the dedication of the temple of Jupiter on the Capitoline. In the first, Jupiter Optimus Maximus chose one boy from the number of boys of good birth who were playing around his altar and put into the fold of his toga an image of the state that he was holding in his hand. On the second night, he dreamed that he saw the same boy sitting on the lap of the Capitoline Jupiter, and when he ordered him removed, the god stopped him with a gesture. It was as if the boy were being reared to be the protector of the state. The following day, Catulus met Augustus, whom he had never seen before, and looked at him in amazement and said that he was very like the boy about whom he had had the dream. Some describe Catulus' first dream differently. They say that the throng of young boys demanded that Jupiter give them a guardian and Jupiter pointed out one of them to whom all were to address their needs. And he touched the boy's lips with his fingers and put them to his own mouth.

[94.9] When Marcus Cicero was escorting Gaius Caesar[181] to the Capitoline, he happened to describe to his companions a dream that he had had the previous night: a boy with noble features was let down from heaven by a golden chain and stood before the doors of the temple on the Capitoline, and Jupiter gave him a whip. Then Augustus unexpectedly appeared (many still did not know him, but his uncle Caesar had invited him to the sacrifice), and Cicero declared that it was he whom he had seen in his dream.

[94.10] When Augustus received the adult toga, his tunic with the broad stripe fell apart on both sides and dropped to his feet. Some who interpreted this omen said that it could only mean that the order designated by the broad stripe would one day be beneath his feet.

[94.11] At Munda[182] when the Divine Julius was cutting down forest to clear a site for his camp, he ordered a palm tree that he found to be preserved as a harbinger of victory. A shoot sprouted from it

---

180. Responsible for rebuilding the temple of Jupiter on the Capitoline; see *Jul.* 15.

181. Julius Caesar.

182. The site of Julius Caesar's final victory in the civil war in Spain, 45 BCE.

immediately and grew so fast that in a few days it not only was as tall
as the parent tree but even hid it from view. It was filled with the
nests of doves, although that species of bird particularly avoids stiff,
sharp foliage. And they say that this omen in particular influenced
Caesar to want no one to succeed him but his sister's grandson.

[94.12] When Augustus was at Apollonia and uninvolved in political life, he mounted to the quarters of the astrologer Theogenes
together with Agrippa. Agrippa consulted the sage first, and after
an almost unbelievably magnificent future was predicted for him,
Augustus determinedly kept quiet about the time of his birth and
was unwilling to divulge it. He was afraid that he would be humiliated by being found the lesser man. But when he did reveal it after
much coaxing and hesitation, Theogenes sprang up and venerated
him. After that, Augustus had such total confidence in his destiny
that he made his horoscope public and struck a silver coin with the
stamp of the constellation Capricorn, under whose influence he had
been born.

[95] As he was entering Rome on his return from Apollonia after
the death of Caesar, a halo like a rainbow suddenly formed around
the sun, and although the sky was clear and cloudless, lightning
immediately struck the tomb of Caesar's daughter Julia. Further,
when he was taking the auspices during his first consulship, twelve
vultures appeared to him as they had to Romulus. And when he was
sacrificing, the livers of all the victims appeared with the bottom
lobes folded back on themselves, and all of the men skilled in inter-
preting such signs judged that this portended great good fortune.

[96.1] Augustus undoubtedly knew beforehand how all of his
wars would end. When the forces of the triumvirs were collected at
Bononia, an eagle landed on his tent and attacked two ravens that
were harassing it, one on each side, and drove them to the ground.
The whole army understood that discord would one day arise among
the colleagues (it did indeed arise) and predicted the outcome. When
he was on his way to Philippi, he was told about his coming victory
by a Thessalian who had learned of it from the Divine Caesar, whose
ghost he had met on an isolated road. [96.2] When the sacrifices
that he was performing outside Perusia[183] did not produce favorable
omens and he ordered more victims brought out, the enemy suddenly
sallied forth and carried off everything that was prepared for the

---

183. See 14–15.

holy ceremony. The *haruspices* agreed that all the dangers and unfavorable occurrences that had been predicted at his sacrifice would fall instead on those who were now in possession of the entrails. And so it turned out. The day before he joined battle with his fleet off Sicily, a fish jumped from the sea and fell in front of him as he was walking on the shore. At Actium he met an ass and its driver as he was going into battle. The man's name was Eutychus and that of the animal, Nicon.[184] After Augustus' victory he set up a bronze statue of each of them in the sacred precinct that he had created on the site of his camp.

[97.1] His death, too, of which I shall speak next, and his divine status after death were foretold by very clear portents. When he was performing the ceremony for closing the period of the census in the Campus Martius, which was crowded with people, an eagle circled him several times, flew over to the nearby temple, and perched on the first letter of the name of Agrippa.[185] When Augustus saw this, he ordered his colleague, his son Tiberius, to pronounce the customary prayers for the next five-year census period, although they were already written out and ready for him; he said that he would not undertake vows that he would not pay. [97.2] At the same time lightning struck the first letter of his name and melted it off the inscription on his statue. This was interpreted to mean that he would live only a hundred days longer, the number that the letter C represented, and that he would be taken up among the gods because *aesar*, the part of the name Caesar that was left, meant "god" in the Etruscan language.

[97.3] And finally, Augustus was preparing to send Tiberius to Illyricum and was intending to go with him as far as Beneventum[186] when petitioners kept him holding court by presenting one case or another. He shouted, "I will not stay longer at Rome, whatever keeps me from leaving," and this too later found its place among the omens. And so he began his journey and got as far as Astura[187] and from there took a ship at night (something he did not usually do) to take advantage of a fair wind. This brought on an illness that began with

---

184. "Lucky" and "Victor."
185. Agrippa's name was on the building he had built.
186. Modern Benevento, northeast of Naples.
187. An island just off the coast south of Rome, near Antium.

diarrhea. [98.1] Then he cruised along the shore of Campania and around the nearby islands and spent four days relaxing completely in the seclusion of Capri, devoting himself to leisure and every civilized pleasure. [98.2] As he passed through the gulf of Puteoli, it chanced that a ship from Alexandria had just landed, and its passengers and sailors, dressed in white and garlanded and offering incense, greeted him with good wishes and showered him with extravagant praise: "We live under your protection, we sail under your protection, and it is under your protection that we enjoy our liberty and our good fortune." This made him very happy and he distributed forty gold pieces to each member of his party and exacted a solemn promise in writing from every one of them that they would use the money given them only to purchase goods from Alexandria. [98.3] In the following days he also gave togas and Greek cloaks along with small gifts of various kinds, and he made a rule that Romans wear Greek clothing and speak Greek and that Greeks do the same with Roman clothing and language. He regularly watched the exercises performed by Greek youths; there were still a number of them on Capri who trained according to the ancient tradition. He also gave them a banquet that he attended in person. And there joking was allowed—even required—and so was the grabbing of tokens to be redeemed for fruit and edible treats and other prizes. In sum, there was no sort of merriment in which he did not take part.

[98.4] He called an island off Capri Apragopolis[188] because the members of his entourage who went there did absolutely nothing. And he had been in the habit of calling Masgaba, one of his favored companions, Ktistes,[189] as if he were the founder of the island's society. When he observed from his dining room that the tomb of this Masgaba, who had died the year before, was surrounded by a large crowd carrying a great many torches, he recited aloud a verse that he composed on the spot: "I see the founder's tomb ablaze with fire." He turned to Tiberius' companion Thrasyllus, who was reclining opposite and unaware of what was going on, and asked him who he thought had written the verse. When Thrasyllus hesitated, Augustus added another line: "Do you see the torches in honor of Masgaba?" and asked him about this one, too. When Thrasyllus

---

188. The Greek means "town of doing nothing."
189. Greek for "founder."

merely responded that the verses were excellent, whoever had written them, Augustus laughed and started to joke about it.

[98.5] Augustus then crossed over to Naples, although he was still troubled intermittently by difficulties with his bowels. He nevertheless watched to the end the quinquennial gymnastic contest that had been established in his honor and started off to go with Tiberius to the agreed-upon point.[190] But on his way back his illness worsened and he finally collapsed at Nola.[191] He called back Tiberius, who was on his way, and kept him in private conversation for a long time. After that, he did not give his attention to any important business.

[99.1] On his last day he kept asking whether a commotion about him was going on outside. And asking for a mirror, he gave instructions that his hair be combed and his sagging jaw put right. He admitted some friends and questioned them as to whether they thought that he had acted the mime of his life well. He added these closing lines:

> Since our play has gone so very well, clap your hands.
> And may all of you see us off with your good wishes.

Then they were all sent away. As he was asking some who had just come from the city about the daughter of Drusus,[192] who was sick, he died suddenly as he kissed Livia and spoke these words: "Live mindful of our marriage, Livia—and farewell!" It was his fate to have an easy end, one such as he had always hoped for. [99.2] For almost always when he heard of someone who had died quickly and painlessly, he prayed for a similar *euthanasia*[193] (this was indeed the word that he used) for himself and for his family. He showed only one sign that his mind was drifting before he breathed his last; he all of a sudden grew frightened and complained that forty youths were carrying him off. And this was more intuition than a fading of his mental powers since that was the number of praetorians that carried him to his state funeral.

---

190. Beneventum; see 97.3.

191. East of Naples.

192. Livilla, the daughter of Drusus the Elder, married to Tiberius' son Drusus the Younger; see *Cl.* 1.6.

193. "Good death."

[100.1] Augustus died in the same bedchamber in which his father
Octavius had died, in the consulship of two men named Sextus,
Pompeius and Appuleius, nine days before the Kalends of September,
in the ninth hour of the day,[194] at the age of seventy-six, less thirty-
five days.

[100.2] The leading citizens of the municipalities and colonies
carried his body from Nola to Bovillae[195] at night because of the time
of year; during the day it was placed in the basilica of the town that it
had reached or in the largest of the temples. At Bovillae equestrians
took it up, brought it into the city, and set it in the forecourt of his
house. The senate was so eager to arrange a magnificent funeral for
him and honor his memory that its members competed in proposing a large number of ideas: Some recommended that the funeral
procession move through the triumphal gate led by the statue of
Victory which stands in the senate house and that the children of
the leading citizens of both sexes sing the funeral hymn. Others
proposed that on the day of the procession they remove their gold
rings and put on iron ones. Some suggested that the priests of the
most senior colleges collect his bones. [100.3] There was even one
senator who recommended that the name August be transferred from
the month of August to the month of September, because the latter
was the month in which Augustus had been born and the former
the month in which he had died, and someone else suggested that
the entire span of time from the day that he was born to his death
be called the Age of Augustus and so written into the calendars.
A limit was put on the honors, but his eulogy was spoken at two
sites. Tiberius delivered it before the temple of the Divine Julius, and
Tiberius' son Drusus, from the old rostra. Senators carried his body
into the Campus Martius on their shoulders where it was cremated.
[100.4] And there was a man, a former praetor, who swore that he
had seen the likeness of Augustus progressing to heaven after he had
been cremated. The leading men of the equestrian order collected his
remains and with tunics unbelted and feet bare placed them in the
Mausoleum, the structure that Augustus had built during his sixth
consulship between the Flaminian Way and the bank of the Tiber.[196]

---

194. August 19, 14 CE.
195. A town on the Appian Way not far from Rome.
196. The tomb for himself and his family, built in 28 BCE.

He had at that time opened to the public the wooded areas and surrounding walkways.

[101.1] Augustus wrote his will three days before the Nones of April in the consulship of Lucius Plancus and Gaius Silius,[197] a year and four months before he died. It was in two tablets, one written in his hand, the other in the hands of his freedmen Polybius and Hilarion. These were deposited with the Vestal Virgins, who brought them out along with three rolls that were sealed in the same way. All of these documents were opened and read aloud in the senate. [101.2] Augustus named as heirs of the first degree Tiberius for two-thirds of his estate and Livia for one-third, and he ordered them to bear his name. Heirs of the second degree[198] were Tiberius' son Drusus for a third part and for the remaining portion, Germanicus and his three male offspring. In the third degree were many family members and friends. To the Roman people he left 40,000,000 sesterces; to the tribes, 3,500,000; to the soldiers of the praetorian guard, 1,000 each; to the city watch, 500; and to the legionary soldiers, 300. This amount he ordered paid at once, for he had always set the money aside and kept it in the treasury. [101.3] He made other bequests to various people, some as large as 20,000 sesterces, and he arranged for these to be paid a year later. He gave the excuse that his personal resources were modest and declared that not more than 150 million would pass on to his heirs, although he had acquired 1,400 million from the wills of his friends over the past twenty years. He had spent almost all of it for the state, along with inheritances from his two fathers[199] and other legacies. He forbade burial in his tomb for the Julias, his daughter and granddaughter,[200] if anything were to happen to them. [101.4] In one of the three rolls he included instructions about his funeral, in the second, a summary of what he had accomplished that he wished to be inscribed on bronze tablets to be set up before the Mausoleum,[201] in the third, an accounting of the entire empire, how many soldiers were beneath the standards

---

197. April 3, 13 CE.

198. To inherit if the primary heirs could not; the second and third degrees were more or less honorary designations.

199. His biological father and Julius Caesar.

200. See 65.1.

201. A copy of this survives and is known as his *Res gestae*, his "deeds."

everywhere, how much money there was in the state treasury and under his personal control and in outstanding taxes. And he appended the names of freedmen and slaves from whom an explanation could be exacted.

TIBERIUS

42 BCE–37 CE
Emperor 14–37 CE

After Augustus had made several aborted attempts to arrange for the transfer to a successor the powers that he had accumulated, he chose his stepson Tiberius Claudius Nero. Tiberius was forty-five when Augustus adopted him as his son in 4 CE and his name became Tiberius Julius Caesar. They shared responsibility during the last ten years of Augustus' life.

Tiberius' accession marked the first transfer of power in the state that was developing into the Roman empire. Since what specifically was being handed down had not been formally defined, hesitation and confusion were perhaps inevitable. When Augustus died, Tiberius was in his mid-fifties, a competent and experienced general who had lived most of his life near the center of power. But he remained essentially a Roman noble, a member of one of Rome's most entitled families, a proud Claudian. Augustus had maintained a charade of the Republic while keeping everything under his own control. Tiberius, on the other hand, apparently did not have the personal skills to make the balance work nor did he expend the effort.

When things went badly or Tiberius was uncomfortable in his role, he retired from the scene, once while Augustus was alive, in 6 BCE, and a second time to the island of Capri, where he spent the last ten years of his life. Reclusive, arrogant, and insecure, he left behind a reputation as a bloody tyrant. The reigns of Augustus and Tiberius together lasted almost seventy years. There was no turning back to the Republic.

[1.1] The patrician branch of the Claudian family (there was a plebeian branch, too, and it was no less important or less revered) had its origin in the Sabine town of Regilli.[1] The clan and a large number of

---

1. The Sabine people lived in central Italy, northeast of Rome.

its dependents migrated from there to Rome soon after the city had
been founded under the sponsorship of Titus Tatius, the colleague of
Romulus.[2] Alternatively, according to a more widely accepted story,
they came with Atta Claudius as head of the family about six years
after the kings had been driven out. They were made patricians and
in addition acquired from the state land across the river Anio[3] for
their dependents and burial ground for themselves at the foot of the
Capitoline Hill. [1.2] As time went on they held twenty-eight consulships, five dictatorships, and seven censorships and celebrated six
triumphs and two ovations. The family had various first names and
cognomina, but it agreed not to use Lucius after two family members
with that name were found guilty of crimes, one of banditry and the
other of murder. Among its cognomina it took Nero, which means
"strong" and "spirited" in the Sabine language.

[2.1] Many Claudians performed many services of outstanding
merit for their country; on the other hand, many committed crimes
against it. To mention a few of the most important on both sides:
Appius Caecus advised against entering into agreement with King
Pyrrhus because he thought it of little benefit.[4] Claudius Caudex was
the first to take the fleet across the strait and drive the Carthaginians
from Sicily.[5] Tiberius Nero overwhelmed Hasdrubal when he came
from Spain with a huge force, before he could connect with his
brother Hannibal.[6]

[2.2] On the negative side, Claudius Regillianus, a member of the
Commission of Ten charged with codifying the laws, tried to use
force to enslave a freeborn young woman in order to satisfy his lust;
this was the reason that the plebeians seceded from the patricians
a second time.[7] Claudius Russus set up a statue of himself wearing
a diadem at Forum Appi and tried to use his dependents to gain

2. The legendary founder of Rome.

3. A tributary of the Tiber.

4. Appius Claudius Caecus advised against settlement after the victory
of King Pyrrhus of Epirus in southern Italy in 279 BCE.

5. In the First Punic War, 264 BCE.

6. Hannibal led the Carthaginian force in the Second Punic War, 207
BCE.

7. The story of Verginia whose father killed her to keep her from being
raped, 449 BCE.

control of Italy.[8] Claudius Pulcher began a naval battle off the coast of Sicily despite the fact that the chickens refused to eat when he was taking the auspices. He drowned the birds in the sea to show how little patience he had for religious scruple, saying, "They will drink since they are unwilling to eat."[9] He lost the battle. And when the senate ordered him to name a dictator, he named his errand boy Glycias. This made it appear that he was for a second time making light of the danger the state was facing.

[2.3] There are also examples of both kinds of behavior in the women just as there are in the men. Both Claudias belonged in the family. One was the Claudia who pulled free the ship carrying objects sacred to the Idean mother of the gods when it got stuck in the shallow water of the Tiber.[10] She had prayed for all to hear, "Let it yield when I pull—but only if my chastity is beyond question." The other was the Claudia who was tried by the people for treason, an unprecedented charge against a woman. When her carriage had difficulty making its way through large throngs of people, she had openly expressed the wish that her brother Pulcher would come back to life and lose his fleet a second time so that Rome would be less crowded.

[2.4] Furthermore, it is accepted without question that all the Claudians had always belonged to the party of the *optimates* and were the consummate defenders of patrician eminence and influence. The sole exception was Publius Claudius, who had had himself adopted by a member of the plebeian branch of the family, a man younger than himself, so that he could force Cicero from the city.[11] They were so hostile and defiant toward the plebeians that when any of them was on trial for his life in a public court, he would not even condescend to put on mourning or plead for clemency. Some of them assaulted the tribunes during quarrelsome disputes. A Vestal

---

8. Forum Appi was a town south of Rome on the Appian Way. This attempt to seize power may have taken place in the early third century BCE.

9. 249 BCE. If the sacred chickens ate before the start of a battle, victory would follow.

10. The cult of the Phrygian mother goddess Cybele was introduced to Rome in 204 BCE.

11. Publius Claudius Pulcher was adopted in 59 BCE and became Publius Clodius Pulcher; see *Jul.* 20.4. Only a plebeian could be a tribune, and it was as tribune that he could attack Cicero.

Virgin even got into her brother's chariot when he was celebrating a
triumph not authorized by the people and went with him all the way
to the Capitoline so that it would be sacrilege for any of the tribunes
to interfere or stop him.[12]

[3.1] It was through this line that Tiberius Caesar traced his
ancestry, on both sides, in fact. On his father's side, he was descended
from Tiberius Nero, on his mother's, from Appius Pulcher, both
of them sons of Appius Caecus.[13] He also belonged to the Livian
family because his maternal grandfather had been adopted into it.[14]
This family, although plebeian, had nonetheless enjoyed exceptional
success, for it was honored with eight consulships, two censorships,
three triumphs, and even the offices of dictator and master of the
horse, and it was famous for outstanding men, especially Salinator
and those named Drusus. [3.2] As censor, Salinator put the mark of
disgrace on all the tribes, charging them with inconsistency because
they had found him guilty after his first consulship and imposed a
penalty but then elected him consul a second time and made him
censor.[15] Drusus earned his cognomen for himself and his descendants when he killed an enemy chieftain named Drausus in hand-to-
hand combat. It is also said that as propraetor, he retrieved the gold
that had earlier been given to the Senones when they laid siege to
the Capitoline and that it was not, as the story has it, Camillus who
extracted it from them.[16] His great-great-grandson, who was named
Patron of the Senate because of his outstanding service against the
Gracchi, left a son who was tricked and murdered by his political
opponents when he was struggling with various problems of state in
a time of similar conflict.[17]

---

12. Another Appius Claudius Pulcher, who was consul in 143 BCE. It was
forbidden to touch a Vestal Virgin.

13. This Tiberius Claudius Nero only appears here. On Pulcher, see 2.2,
2.3; on Caecus, see 2.1.

14. Marcus Livius Drusus Claudianus; see 7.1.

15. Marcus Livius Salinator, consul in 219 and 210 or 207 BCE, censor in
204. He was charged with embezzlement.

16. This first Drusus disappears into legend. The Senones, a Gallic tribe,
besieged Rome in 390 BCE. Furius Camillus was dictator in 309.

17. Marcus Livius Drusus, tribune in 122 BCE, opposed the populist
politicians Gaius and Tiberius Sempronius Gracchus. His son of the same
name, also a tribune, was killed in 91.

[4.1] Nero, the father of Tiberius, was quaestor under Gaius Caesar and put in charge of the fleet during the Alexandrian war,[18] and he contributed greatly to success in that conflict. For this he was named to a priesthood in place of Publius Scipio[19] and was sent to Gaul to establish colonies, Narbo and Arelate among others.[20] But when Caesar was assassinated and everyone voted for amnesty out of fear of the Roman mob, Nero went further and proposed rewards for the tyrannicides. [4.2] Then when dissension arose among the triumvirs at the end of the year when he was praetor, he kept the regalia of his office beyond the allotted time and followed the consul Lucius Antonius, brother of the triumvir, to Perusia.[21] The rest surrendered, but he alone remained loyal to the cause and escaped first to Praeneste and then to Naples. He fled to Sicily after an offer of freedom to slaves failed.[22] [4.3] When he was not immediately admitted into the presence of Sextus Pompey there and was forbidden to use the *fasces*,[23] he felt insulted, and he crossed over to Achaia and transferred his allegiance to Mark Antony. Soon all of the parties made peace and he returned to Rome with Antony. Augustus asked Nero for his wife, and he gave her to him. This was Livia Drusilla, who was pregnant at the time and had already given birth to a son. Nero died shortly thereafter, survived by both of his children, Tiberius Nero and Drusus Nero.[24]

---

18. Tiberius Claudius Nero. The Alexandrian war was the last phase of the conflict between Julius Caesar and Pompey, 48–47 BCE; see *Jul.* 35.1, 64.

19. Quintus Caecilius Metellus Pius Scipio may be meant; see *Jul.* 35.2, 37.1, 59.

20. Modern Narbonne and Arles.

21. Praetor in 42 BCE. For Lucius Antonius, brother of Mark Antony, and the Perusine war, see *Aug.* 14–15. The second triumvirate was Octavius (Augustus), Mark Antony, and Marcus Lepidus; see *Aug.* 8.2, 13.1.

22. Offering slaves freedom to fight on one's side was a desperate measure.

23. Sextus Pompey was the son of Pompey the Great; for his conflict with Augustus (the Sicilian war), see *Aug.* 16. The *fasces* were part of praetorian regalia.

24. Tiberius Claudius Nero and Nero Claudius Drusus ("Drusus the Elder"); see 7.3, 50.1; *Cl.* 1.1–2.

[5] Some think that Tiberius was born at Fundi.²⁵ They are subscribing to the insubstantial speculation that his maternal grandmother was a native of Fundi and that the senate later erected a statue of good fortune there. But as many more reliable authors report, he was born in Rome on the Palatine Hill on the sixteenth day before the Kalends of December in the consulship of Marcus Aemilius Lepidus (his second) and Lucius Munatius Plancus while the war at Philippi was going on.²⁶ This is how his birth is recorded in the calendars and in the public record, but some still write that he was born in the preceding year, in the consulship of Hirtius and Pansa, and others that it was in the following year, in the consulship of Servilius Isauricus and Lucius Antonius.

[6] His infancy and boyhood were difficult and troubled since he went with his parents wherever they had to flee. His crying almost gave them away twice at Naples when enemies broke into the city as they were furtively seeking boat passage. Once he was removed from his nurse's breast, and a second time those trying to relieve the women of their burdens in this time of crisis took him abruptly out of his mother's arms. [6.2] After being taken all over Sicily and Achaia, he became an official ward of the Spartans because they were clients of the Claudians. His life came into danger when the family was leaving there at night; flames suddenly broke out on all sides of the forest and enveloped the whole company, and a part of Livia's clothing and her hair caught fire. [6.3] The gifts that Pompeia, the sister of Sextus Pompey, gave him in Sicily still exist and are on display at Baiae: a cloak, a clasp, and golden amulets. After he was back in Rome, he was adopted in the will of the senator Marcus Gallius and given an inheritance, but he soon stopped using his new name because Gallius belonged to the party that opposed Augustus. [6.4] Tiberius' father died when he was nine years old, and he delivered the funeral oration for him from the rostra. Then as a youth he escorted Augustus' chariot in his triumph after Actium, riding the left trace-horse while Octavia's son Marcellus²⁷ rode the one on the right. He presided over the Attic Games and as part of the circus entertainments led the troop of older boys in the Game of Troy.

---

25. A town halfway between Rome and Naples. See *Cal.* 23.2.

26. November 16, 42 BCE. For Philippi, see *Aug.* 13.1.

27. Octavia was Augustus' sister; see *Jul.* 27.1. Marcus Marcellus was Augustus' first choice as successor; see *Aug.* 63.1.

[7.1] After Tiberius received the adult toga, he passed the whole of his young manhood and the time before his principate more or less like this: He presented a gladiatorial combat in memory of his father and another in memory of his grandfather Drusus,[28] these at different times and in different places. The first was held in the Forum, the second in the amphitheater with retired gladiators brought back into the arena at compensation of 100,000 sesterces each. He gave other games, too, although he did not attend them. All were presented magnificently at the expense of his mother and stepfather.

[7.2] He married Agrippina, daughter of Marcus Agrippa and granddaughter of Caecilius Atticus, the Roman knight to whom Cicero had addressed his letters.[29] Tiberius acknowledged Drusus as his son from her but was forced to divorce her (despite the fact that they got along well and she was pregnant again) and to marry Augustus' daughter Julia hastily. This caused him no little pain since he was happily married to Agrippina and disapproved of Julia's character; he knew that Julia had desired him when she was still married to her former husband, something that was common knowledge. [7.3] After the divorce he was sorry that he had sent Agrippina away, and the one time that they chanced to meet, he gave her such a loving and tearful look that care was taken that she never again come into his sight. He lived with Julia in peace and mutual affection at first, but as time went on he grew so distant that he slept apart from her permanently. The bond formed by a son born to them at Aquileia was broken when the child died as an infant. Tiberius lost his brother Drusus[30] in Germany and brought his body back to Rome, going before it on foot for the entire journey.

[8] Tiberius' initiation into civil duties came when he pleaded before Augustus in defense of King Archelaus[31] and of the citizens of Tralles and Thessaly, each charged on different grounds. He intervened on behalf of the peoples of Laodicea, Thyatira, and Chios,[32]

28. His maternal grandfather, adopted into the Claudian family; see 3.1.
29. Vipsania Agrippina. Marcus Agrippa (Marcus Vipsanius Agrippa) was Augustus' right-hand man.
30. Nero Claudius Drusus; see 4.3, *Cl.* 1.1–2.
31. King of Cappadocia; see 37.4.
32. Tralles, Laodicea, and Thyatira were cities in the province of Asia; Chios was an island off the coast.

who had suffered from earthquakes and were begging the senate for relief. He entered a charge of treason against Fannius Caepio, who had conspired with Varro Murena against Augustus, and he convicted him.[33] During this time, he held responsibility in two areas, care for the grain supply that had fallen short and clearing the whole of Italy of the slave prisons on large estates;[34] the masters of these had made themselves hated because they seized and imprisoned not only travelers but also men whom the fear of military service had driven to hiding places of that sort.

[9.1] Tiberius earned his first military pay as a tribune on the Cantabrian campaign.[35] He next led an army to the East and restored the kingdom of Armenia to Tigranes, to whom he presented a crown in his official capacity. He retrieved the legionary standards that the Parthians had taken from Marcus Crassus.[36] Then for about a year he was governor of Gallia Comata,[37] which was in disarray because of barbarian incursions and discord among its leaders. After that he fought wars against the Raetians and the Vindelicians, then against the Pannonians, and next against the Germans. [9.2] In the Raetian and Vindelician wars he conquered the alpine nations; in the Pannonian, the Breuci and the Dalmatiae; in the German war he transferred forty thousand prisoners to Gaul and settled them in places allocated near the bank of the Rhine. In recognition of these achievements he entered Rome in a chariot with an ovation after first, according to some, being honored with triumphal regalia, a new distinction never before given to anyone. [9.3] He started on the course of magisterial offices before the usual age and moved through them with scarcely any intervals between the quaestorship, praetorship, and consulship. He was consul again later and received tribunician power for a period of five years.

[10.1] Enjoying such an abundance of success, in the prime of life and in good health, Tiberius suddenly decided to withdraw and

---

33. The conspiracy in 23 BCE; see *Aug.* 19.1.
34. On slave prisons, see also *Aug.* 32.1.
35. Cantabria, the northern part of Spain, 25 BCE.
36. The triumvir Crassus (*Jul.* 24.1) was defeated in Parthia in 53 BCE. The military standards were returned in 20 BCE; see *Aug.* 21.3.
37. For "Hairy Gaul," see *Jul.* 22.1.

to remove himself as far as possible from public life.³⁸ It is unclear whether he did this because he was disgusted with a wife whom he could no longer tolerate but dared neither denounce nor divorce, or because by eliminating the irritant of his constant presence, he would preserve his authority with his absence and even increase it if the state should need him one day. Some think that with Augustus' sons now grown,³⁹ Tiberius had of his own volition yielded position and abandoned the role of second place that he had long held. In so doing he was following the example set by Marcus Agrippa, who had gone to Mytilene when Marcus Marcellus was assigned official duties so that his presence would not appear to stand in the way or detract from that young man's importance. [10.2] This is the reason that Tiberius gave later, but at the time his excuse was that he was sated with honors and needed rest, and he asked for a leave of absence. He did not change his mind when his mother begged and pleaded or his stepfather went so far as to complain to the senate that he was being abandoned. He even fasted for four days when they persisted in trying to keep him from going. Finally given permission, he left his wife and son in Rome and quickly went down to Ostia. He said not a word to those who were escorting him and kissed only a few when he departed. [11.1] From Ostia he skirted the shore of Campania and stopped there briefly when he received word that Augustus was ill. But after the rumor spread that he was delaying in the expectation of something greater, he sailed on to Rhodes with the wind almost dead against him. He had been attracted by the charm and healthy climate of the island from the time when he had stopped there on his way back from Armenia. Content with a modest house in town and a country villa that was not much larger, he began living almost like a private citizen. He sometimes walked about in the gymnasium without a lictor or attendant and exchanged courtesies with ordinary Greeks more or less as an equal.

[11.2] One morning when he was setting his program for the day, he happened to announce that he wished to visit any in the community who were sick. His staff understood differently, and all the sick were ordered carried to the public colonnade and were arranged by type of sickness. Dismayed at this unexpected scene and for a long

---

38. 6 BCE.

39. Gaius Julius Caesar and Lucius Julius Caesar, Augustus' grandchildren, adopted as his sons; see *Aug.* 64.1.

time at a loss as to what to do, in the end he made the rounds of all, apologizing to them individually for what had happened, even to the most humble, nameless person. [11.3] There was one and only one instance when he was observed exercising the might of his tribunician power: he frequently visited the schools and the lecture halls where learned men gathered, and when he had joined in a heated dispute among the arguing scholars, someone abused him verbally, charging him with being too partisan in favoring the opposing side. Tiberius retreated slowly to his house and then reappeared suddenly with the full panoply of office, ordered the herald to summon the man who had insulted him before the tribunal, and had him carted off to prison.

[11.4] Tiberius soon learned that his wife Julia had been found guilty of sexual impropriety and acts of adultery and that notice of divorce had been sent to her in his name on the authority of Augustus. This news pleased him, but he nonetheless held it his duty to write a number of letters in which he did his best to plead with the father on behalf of his daughter. And he let her keep any gifts that he had given her, whether she deserved them or not. [11.5] When his tribunician power came to an end,[40] he finally admitted that his only motive for retirement had been to avoid any hint of rivalry with Gaius and Lucius Caesar, and he asked, now that he was no longer troubled about that issue (they were grown up and having no trouble maintaining their status as successors), that he be allowed to visit his relations, whom he very much wanted to see. But his request was denied. He was also warned: "Let him give up all thoughts of the family that he had been so eager to abandon."

[12.1] Tiberius therefore remained on Rhodes involuntarily, and it was only with difficulty and with his mother's help that he was able to conceal the shame of this fact with the pretense that he was away from Rome as a representative of Augustus. [12.2] And indeed, from that time on, he lived not only as a private citizen but as one who feared for his life. He hid himself away in the island's rural interior and avoided the delegations from passing ships that were constantly calling on him. (No one with a military command or a civil office failed to turn aside to Rhodes wherever he was headed.) He had still more reasons to worry: when he crossed over to Samos to see his

---

40. 1 BCE.

stepson Gaius,[41] who held command in the East, he felt that the
young man had become less friendly to him because of accusations
made by Marcus Lollius, his companion and guardian. [12.3] He was
also suspected of having used centurions who owed their appointments to him and were returning to Gaius' camp after military leave
to deliver his instructions to a number of people, instructions that
were ambiguous but appeared to incite revolution. When Augustus
informed Tiberius that he was under suspicion, Tiberius insistently
demanded that someone, of any rank whatsoever, be appointed to
monitor his actions and his words.

[13.1] He put an end to his usual exercise on horseback and with
arms, stopped dressing as a Roman, and restricted himself to a Greek
cloak and sandals. He lived like this for almost two years, becoming
more scorned and detested as each day passed. Antipathy toward him
was so strong that the citizens of Nemausus[42] went so far as to tear
down his images and statues. Once when his name was mentioned
at a private dinner, a man stood up and promised Gaius that, if he
ordered him, he would sail for Rhodes immediately and bring back
the exile's head—for exile was what they were calling him. [13.2] It
was this threat especially—he was no longer merely afraid but felt
rather that his life was in danger—that made him sue for his return
both with his own insistent appeals and with those of his mother.
He succeeded, although partly by chance. Augustus had determined
to make no decision about Tiberius' return without agreement from
his elder son,[43] who at that moment happened to be displeased with
Marcus Lollius but felt open and amenable toward his stepfather.
And so Tiberius was recalled with Gaius' sufferance but on condition
that he play no role in the state or assume any responsibility.

[14.1] Tiberius returned in the eighth year after he had left with
confidence and great hope for the future, hope planted by signs and
portents from his earliest years: [14.2] When Livia was pregnant
with him and was looking for omens of some kind or another to
learn whether she would give birth to a son, she took an egg out from
under the hen that was sitting on it. She and her maids took turns
holding it in their hands and keeping it warm until a chick with a

41. Samos was off the coast of Asia. Gaius Julius Caesar was Tiberius'
stepson because he was the son of his wife Julia.
42. A town in Gaul where Tiberius had been governor; modern Nîmes.
43. Gaius.

prominent crest hatched out. From the time when Tiberius was an infant, the astrologer Scribonius made solemn promises of wonderful things to come, even that he would rule one day, although without the trappings of royalty. (The power of the Caesars was obviously still unknown at that point in time.) [14.3] When he was leading his army through Macedonia into Syria on his first campaign, it happened that at Philippi the altars that had earlier been consecrated by victorious legions suddenly burst into flames on their own. And later on his way to Illyricum he approached the oracle of Geryon near Patavium[44] and drew a lot that advised him to cast golden dice into the spring of Aponus to find answers to his questions. When he did, they chanced to come up the highest number, and one can see those dice under the water today. [14.4] Just a few days before he was recalled, an eagle never before seen on Rhodes landed on the roof beam of his house. And on the day before he learned that he would return, his tunic appeared to be on fire as he was changing his clothing. It was also at that time that he obtained convincing proof that Thrasyllus, the astrologer whom he had introduced into his circle as a teacher of philosophy, was worthy of the trust placed in him: Thrasyllus stated with conviction that the ship he saw approaching was bringing good news. At that very moment they were strolling together, and Tiberius had decided to throw Thrasyllus headlong into the sea. Things had kept turning out badly and not as Thrasyllus predicted, so Tiberius had thought that he was unreliable and that he had been rash in making him privy to his inner thoughts.

[15.1] After Tiberius returned to Rome and his son Drusus had been presented in the Forum,[45] he moved from the Carinae and the house of Pompey to the gardens of Maecenas on the Esquiline[46] and devoted himself completely to a life of retirement; he fulfilled private obligations only and took no part in public duties.

[15.2] Gaius and Lucius were dead within three years, and Augustus adopted Tiberius along with their brother Marcus Agrippa,[47] and Tiberius was first required to adopt his brother's son Germanicus.

---

44. In Cisalpine Gaul; modern Padua.

45. The ceremony in which he received the toga of manhood.

46. A move from an exposed quarter to a quieter part of Rome.

47. Known as Agrippa Postumus, he was the youngest child of Marcus Agrippa and Julia, born after his father's death. All of these adoptions took place in 4 CE.

After that, Tiberius did not act as a head of household and kept none of the entitlements that he had lost with his adoption. He neither gave gifts nor freed slaves and did not even receive inheritances or legacies other than those that were allocated to his personal allowance.[48] From then on, no opportunity was missed to magnify his importance, especially after Agrippa was disowned and removed from the scene,[49] and it was clear that the hope of succession rested with one man alone.

[16.1] Tiberius received tribunician power a second time for a period of five years. He was assigned the task of pacifying Germany, and after the Parthian legation had laid their directives before Augustus in Rome, they were told to present them to him in his province as well. But when news came of the revolt in Illyricum, he took command in the new conflict and for three years fought this most serious of all foreign wars since those with Carthage.[50] He had fifteen legions and the same number of auxiliary units and campaigned under all kinds of extreme conditions with a profound shortage of provisions. [16.2] Although he was often ordered to fall back, he kept on fighting because he feared that such a very powerful enemy so close by would take the offensive against an army that gave ground of its own accord. His perseverance yielded important results, for he suppressed Illyricum totally and brought the whole of it—an area that lies between Italy, the kingdom of Noricum, Thrace, and Macedonia and between the Danube River and the Adriatic Sea—under Roman control.

[17.1] Circumstance added still more to the glory of this campaign: at about the same time Quinctilius Varus and his three legions were lost in Germany,[51] and no one doubted that the victorious Germans would have joined with the Pannonians if Illyricum had not been made to submit earlier. This is why Tiberius was voted a triumph and many significant honors. [17.2] Some also proposed that he be given the cognomen Pannonicus, others Invictus, still others Pius.[52] But

---

48. All property belonged to his father (now Augustus), but he had an account for personal use.

49. Agrippa Postumus was disinherited in about 6 CE; see *Aug.* 65.1, 65.4.

50. The three Punic wars in the third and second centuries BCE.

51. 9 CE; see *Aug.* 23.1–2.

52. Invictus = "unconquered"; Pius = "dutiful."

Augustus intervened about the cognomen, promising that Tiberius would be happy with the one that he would have after he himself was dead. He postponed his triumph because the city was in mourning for the disaster that had befallen Varus. He nonetheless entered the city wearing the *toga praetextata* and crowned with laurel. He ascended the tribunal setup in the Saepta as the senate stood watching, and he sat between the two consuls together with Augustus. From there he exchanged greetings with the people and was escorted on a round of the temples.

[18.1] Tiberius returned to Germany the next year. When he came to understand that Varus' disaster was the result of the general's own recklessness and lack of care, he did nothing without consultation. Before that time he had always kept his own counsel and had acted with total independence, but then, contrary to his usual habit, he discussed the conduct of the war with a large number of advisers, and he paid more attention to detail than usual. When he was about to cross the Rhine, he restricted all supplies to a fixed amount and did not send them over until he had stood on the bank and inspected the contents of the wagons to see that nothing was being transported that was not approved or necessary. [18.2] These are the practices that he maintained once over the Rhine: He ate sitting on bare grass, often spent the night outside his tent, and communicated in writing all his orders for the following day and any tasks that had to be assigned on the spur of the moment. He further instructed that if there was anything about which anyone was uncertain, he should bring the matter to him personally at any hour, day or night. [19] He imposed exceptionally stringent discipline, resurrecting methods of punishment and humiliation from the past, and he went so far as to degrade the commander of a legion who had sent a few soldiers across the river to go hunting with his freedman. Although he left little to luck and chance, he was nonetheless more confident entering battle whenever it happened that when he was working into the night, his light suddenly wavered and died with no one putting it out. He trusted, as he said, in this sign sent by his ancestors because it had proved astonishingly reliable in every test of leadership for him or for them. This German campaign was successful, but one of the Bructeri[53] almost killed him. The man had insinuated himself

---

53. A tribe in the north of Germany.

among his attendants, but his nervousness betrayed him, and he confessed under torture to the murder that he intended to commit.

[20] After two years Tiberius returned to Rome from Germany and celebrated the triumph that had been postponed. Joining him were his subordinate commanders for whom he had procured triumphal regalia. Before he turned aside to ascend the Capitoline, he climbed down from his chariot and knelt at the knees of his father who was presiding. He sent Bato, the Pannonian leader, to Ravenna and rewarded him generously for allowing him to escape the time when he and his army had been surrounded in difficult terrain.[54] Then he gave the people a banquet of a thousand tables and each man a money gift of 300 sesterces. From his spoils he dedicated a temple of Concord and in his own name and that of his brother, a temple of Pollux and Castor. [21.1] The consuls soon saw that a law was passed that gave him joint charge of the provinces with Augustus and also the mandate to conduct a census. After the purification ceremony that concluded the census, he set out for Illyricum but was quickly called back on his way. He found Augustus in a weakened condition but still breathing and was closeted with him for the entire day.[55]

[21.2] I know that it is generally believed that when Tiberius emerged from this private conversation, the chamber attendants heard Augustus' voice cry out, "The wretched Roman people! To be crushed by such slow jaws!" I know, too, that others have written that Augustus so disapproved of Tiberius' threatening presence that, openly and without pretense, he sometimes broke off pleasant and relaxed conversations when Tiberius arrived on the scene. They write further that his wife's pleas on behalf of her son kept him from repudiating the adoption. Or they suggest that he may have been influenced to look to his interest because with a successor like Tiberius, he would one day be more greatly missed. [21.3] But I cannot help thinking that so very thoughtful and careful an emperor as Augustus did anything without good cause, especially in so important a matter. Or rather I think that he put Tiberius' vices and virtues in a balance and found that the virtues had the greater weight. This seems most likely because he swore before the people that he was adopting him for the good of the state, and he describes him in a number of letters

---

54. Sending Bato to Ravenna kept him from being humiliated in the triumph.

55. Suetonius also describes their final meeting at *Aug.* 98.5.

as the most skilled of military men and the sole bulwark of the state.
I include below a few extracts from these as a sample:

[21.4] "Farewell, my dearest Tiberius, and good luck to you as you
play the role of general for me and for the Muses. Dearest and—bless
my soul—bravest of men and most loyal of generals, farewell."

[21.5] "I truly admire the way you have managed your campaigns,
my dear Tiberius. Considering all the difficulties you faced and the
lack of support from your men, I do not think that anyone could
have acted more sensibly than you. And all those who were with you
testify that this verse fits: 'The vigilance of one man has restored to
us our state.'"[56]

[21.6] "If something comes up that requires careful thought or if
something makes me angry, then, by Jupiter, I need my dear Tiberius
badly, and this Homeric verse comes to mind:

> If this man follows me, then even through the blazing flames
> May we both come home; for he has understanding and is wise."[57]

[21.7] "When I hear and read that you are exhausted from the
hard work that never lets up, I'll be damned if my own body does
not give a shudder along with yours. And I beg you to take care of
yourself so that news that you are unwell will not kill your mother
and me and that the whole of the empire that belongs to the Roman
people will not be in danger."

"It doesn't matter whether or not I am in good health, if you are
not."

"I beg the gods to keep you safe for us and grant you health, now
and always—if they do not hate the Roman people totally."

[22] Tiberius did not make Augustus' death public until after
young Agrippa[58] had been done away with. The military tribune
assigned to guard him killed him after he read instructions ordering
him to do so. It is unclear whether it was the dying Augustus who
left these instructions to eliminate a source of civil unrest after his
death or if Livia composed them in the name of Augustus together
with Tiberius, who was either complicit or not. When the tribune
reported to Tiberius that he had done what had been ordered,

---

56. Ennius, *Annales*.
57. Homer, *Iliad* 10.246–47.
58. Agrippa Postumus; see 15.2.

Tiberius replied, "I did not give the order, and you will make your report before the senate." This evidently fended off opprobrium for the moment. He later buried the matter in silence.

[23] When Tiberius had used his tribunician power to convene the senate and had begun to address them, he suddenly groaned as if overcome by grief. He said that he wished that it would be not only his voice that failed him but the breath of life as well, and he handed his speech to his son Drusus to finish reading. Then Augustus' will was brought in, and he had it read by a freedman.[59] Only signators of senatorial rank were admitted to the senate house; others validated their seals outside. The will began like this: "Since bitter fortune has stolen from me my sons, Gaius and Lucius, let Tiberius Caesar be heir to two-thirds of my estate." These words themselves encouraged the suspicions of those who thought that he had adopted Tiberius as his successor more out of necessity than as the result of considered judgment, since he had included this preface in his will.

[24.1] Tiberius did not hesitate to grasp the power of the principate immediately or to exercise it, and he enlisted a bodyguard in a show of force that suggested despotism. But for a long time he continued to play an insolent game by refusing the title. Sometimes he complained that the friends who were encouraging him did not know what a monstrous beast the empire was. At other times his vague replies and clever delaying tactics kept the senate guessing as they pleaded with him and fell at his knees. Some ran out of patience, and one shouted out in the noisy confusion, "Let him take it or leave it!" Another senator charged his fellows with being too slow to do what they had promised but Tiberius with being too slow to promise what he was actually doing. [24.2] Finally, as if he were forced and complaining that a wretched and burdensome servitude was being imposed on him, he accepted the empire—but only after creating the expectation that he would lay it aside someday. His words were "until I come to the time when it may seem proper to you to provide an old man some rest."

[25.1] His hesitation stemmed from his fear of the dangers that threatened on all sides, and he often said that he was "holding a wolf by the ears." A slave of Agrippa named Clemens had collected a force of no small size with which to avenge his master. A noble, Lucius Scribonius Libo, was inciting revolution on the sly. Two mutinies

---

59. On Augustus' will, see *Aug.* 101.

began in the armies in Illyricum and Germany. [25.2] Both armies were demanding a large number of special concessions, first and foremost that their pay be the same as that of the praetorians. The German legions were even refusing to accept an emperor whom they had not put into power themselves and were vigorously pressing Germanicus, their commander at that time, to assume governance of the state, although he steadfastly resisted their efforts.[60] This was the eventuality that Tiberius feared most, and he asked the senate to give him the portion of the government that they chose, protesting that no one person was adequate to manage the whole of it without a partner or even with several. [25.3] He also pretended to be ill so that Germanicus would wait more patiently for swift accession or at least a shared principate. After the military uprisings had been put down, he caught Clemens in a trap and kept him under guard. So that nothing too rancorous would disturb his reign still in its infancy, he waited until the second year to bring his case against Libo to the senate, content in the meantime merely to be on his guard. When Libo was performing a sacrifice with him and the other priests, Tiberius was careful to replace his sacrificial knife with a knife made of lead. When Libo asked for a private audience, he did not grant it except when his son Drusus was also present, and during the whole of their conversation, he held onto Libo's right arm as if leaning on him as they walked together.

[26.1] But after he stopped being afraid, he lived a modest life—at least at first—even somewhat more modest than that of a private citizen. Of the many important honors offered him, he accepted only a few commonplace ones. He permitted the celebration of his birthday that fell during the Plebeian Games[61] but with scarcely a single chariot added. He did not permit temples, *flamines*, or priests to be voted for him or statues and busts of him erected without his permission, and he allowed these only on condition that they not be put alongside representations of the gods but be part of the temple decorations. [26.2] He prohibited the swearing of oaths to uphold his official decrees and the renaming of September as Tiberius and October as Livius.[62] He refused to take *imperator* as a first name and

---

60. On the mutiny on the Rhine, see *Cal.* 1.1, 9.

61. The most ancient of religious games, days of entertainments that included races.

62. After his mother.

the cognomen Father of His Country, and he did not permit the civic crown to hang in his entrance hall. Despite the fact that he had inherited the name Augustus, he did not use it on letters, except those to kings and eastern princes. He held only three consulships when he was emperor, one for a few days, a second for three months, and the third until the Ides of May, although he was not in the city.[63]

[27] He hated flattery so much that he did not allow any of the senators to approach his litter either to pay his respects or to do business, and he was so anxious to get away from a man of consular rank who kept apologizing to him and trying to fall at his knees that he fell over backward. If something too obsequious was said about him in conversation or in the course of a speech, he did not hesitate to interrupt and rebuke the speaker and correct his language on the spot. When someone addressed him as *dominus*, he warned him not to insult him like that again.[64] When someone else spoke of his "sacred" attention to the affairs of state and another said that he had come before the senate on the emperor's "order," he made them change their words and use "recommendation" for "order" and "diligent" for "sacred." [28] He remained unmoved and tolerant even when confronted with abusive language and malicious rumors and notorious verses about him and his family. He was constantly letting it be known that thought and speech should be free in a free state. And once when the senate was demanding judicial inquiry into transgressions of this sort and the people charged with them, he said, "We do not have enough time to get involved in a large number of problems. If you open this window, you will not allow anything else to get done. It will be an excuse for everyone to bring his personal enmities to your attention." The following completely unassuming statement that he made to the senate has been preserved: "If someone speaks unfavorably of me, I shall take care to render an account of my words and deeds; if he persists, I shall reciprocate his hatred."

[29] The following behaviors made his self-effacement all the more obvious: When he addressed the senators and paid them his respects both as individuals and as a body, his civility went almost beyond good manners. When he disagreed with Quintus Haterius at

---

63. 18, 21, and 31 (until May 15) CE. He was also consul twice under Augustus; see 9.3.

64. Augustus made the same objection; see *Aug.* 53.1.

a meeting of the senate, he said, "Pray forgive me if I speak too freely in opposing you in my capacity as a senator." And then, addressing all of them,

> I say now, senators, and have often said on other occasions that a beneficent emperor, one who promotes the well-being of the people, one whom you have provided with so much and so wide-ranging power, ought to be the servant of the senate and often of all the citizenry and sometimes even of individuals. Nor do I regret having said this. I have thought of you as my good and just and indulgent masters and I think you so still.

[30] Indeed, he even introduced a semblance of freedom when he maintained the past grandeur and power of the senate and the magistrates. For there was no piece of public or private business so small or so large that he did not refer it to the senators: taxes, trade monopolies, the construction and repair of public works, even the enlistment and discharge of soldiers and the disposition of the legions and auxiliary units, and finally, decisions about whose command should be extended and to whom the conduct of unexpected wars should be entrusted and what should be the content and form of replies to letters from foreign kings. He compelled the commander of a cavalry unit who was charged with the unlawful use of force and plunder to plead his case before the senate. He always entered the senate house alone, and once when he was carried inside in a litter because he was sick, he dismissed his attendants. [31.1] He did not complain even when votes came down contrary to his wishes. Although he had made the rule that newly elected magistrates should remain in the city so as to grow familiar with their new duties, a praetor-designate was given permission to travel with ambassadorial privileges. Another time, when he recommended that the people of Trebiae[65] be allowed to transfer money left to them in a will for the building of a new theater to the improvement of a road, he could not keep the testator's intent from being followed. When a vote happened to be taken in the senate by the members moving apart and he joined the group in which there were fewer, no one followed him.

[31.2] Other business, too, was done only through elected officials and according to normal court procedures. The consuls had so much

---

65. A town in Italy northeast of Rome.

authority that a legation from Africa came to them complaining that they were making no progress with Caesar, to whom they had been sent. And no wonder, since everyone knew that he also rose to his feet in their presence and made way for them in the street. [32.1] He found fault with former consuls who commanded armies because they did not report their achievements to the senate in writing and because they deferred to him for the distribution of some military prizes, acting as if they did not have the right to make all the awards themselves. He praised a praetor for reviving the ancient custom of remembering his ancestors when he addressed the people on entering office. He followed the funeral processions of some distinguished men all the way to the pyre.

[32.2] Tiberius displayed this same self-effacement with less important people and in less pressing matters. When he summoned the magistrates from Rhodes because they had presented him with official letters that had not been signed according to the proper formula, he did not chastise them with so much as a word but merely sent them back with orders to sign them correctly. Diogenes, a grammarian who made it his practice to dispute on the Jewish Sabbath on Rhodes, had not let Tiberius enter when he came to hear him without prior arrangement, and he had had his young slave put him off for seven days. When Diogenes stood before the doors of the emperor's house in Rome, waiting to pay his respects, Tiberius merely advised him to come back in seven years. He wrote back to the governors who were urging a heavier tribute on the provinces, "A good shepherd shears his sheep; he does not fleece them."

[33] Gradually Tiberius unmasked the emperor that he was, and even though for a long time he showed himself a mix of good and bad, he was more often gracious and disposed to serve the welfare of the people. At first he meddled only to keep anything very bad from happening. That is why he annulled some decisions of the senate and often offered his services as an adviser to the magistrates when they were trying cases on the tribunal, sitting either next to them or facing them from the end of the platform.[66] At the barest suggestion that a defendant had been let off out of favoritism, he was immediately on the spot; and either standing below or on the tribunal of the investigator, he reminded the jurors of the laws and the moral principle involved and of the crime in regard to which they

---

66. He tactfully did not upstage the praetor who occupied the middle.

were judging. And if public morals deteriorated from laziness or bad habits, he took the correction of them on himself.

[34.1] Tiberius lowered the cost of games and gladiatorial contests by trimming the money spent on the actors and by cutting back the pairs of gladiatorial combatants to a prescribed number. He complained mightily that the price of Corinthian ware[67] had shot up to a huge figure and that three mullets were now 30,000 sesterces. He recommended that a limit be set on the cost of household furnishings and that the senate regulate the price of market provisions annually. He made the aediles responsible for cracking down on the cookshops and cheap restaurants so stringently that not even bakery products could be offered for sale. His own example supported this tightfisted public policy. At formal banquets he often served partially eaten dishes that were left over from the day before or half a boar, declaring, "The one half is just like the other."

[34.2] He issued edicts banning ordinary kissing and the exchange of New Year's gifts after the Kalends of January. It had been his custom to respond with a gift of fourfold value presented by his own hand, but annoyed at being disturbed the entire month by those who did not have access to him on the holiday, he stopped the practice.[68]

[35.1] He saw to it that married women who had lost their reputation for chaste behavior but had not been publicly accused were disciplined by family councils according to the traditional process. He released from his oath a Roman knight who had once sworn that he would never renounce his wife; he allowed him to divorce her because she had been caught having sex with her son-in-law.

[35.2] Women of loose sexual morals had begun to claim that they were prostitutes in order to be free from the rights and respect due married women and evade punishment under the law, and the most dissolute young men of the two upper classes voluntarily allowed the mark of disgrace to be placed next to their names so that they would not be bound by a senatorial decree preventing them from appearing on the stage or in the arena. He exiled all of these men and women so that none would take refuge in subterfuge of this sort. He took the privilege of the broad-striped tunic from a senator when he learned that he had moved into his country house close to the Kalends of July so that he could rent a house in the city more cheaply after

---

67. An alloy of gold, silver, and copper, luxury ware.
68. It had become customary to present gifts to the emperor on January 1.

that date.[69] He relieved another man of the quaestorship because he had married a wife the day before lots were drawn but divorced her the day after.[70] [36] He suppressed foreign ritual, the rites of the Egyptians and the Jews, for instance, and forced those who subscribed to these cults to burn their ceremonial clothing together with all their paraphernalia. He dispersed the young Jewish men to provinces with unhealthy climates, citing as the pretext that they were taking the oath of military service. He expelled from the city the rest of the Jews or those who adhered to Jewish customs, and he threatened them with a life of slavery if they did not comply. He also banished astrologers but pardoned those who asked for mercy and promised him that they would stop practicing their art.

[37.1] Tiberius was particularly concerned to maintain peace in the state, to keep it free from highway robbery and brigandage and the disorder of armed uprisings. He stationed military guard posts throughout Italy at closer intervals than usual. In Rome he created a camp to quarter the praetorian cohorts that had formerly been scattered and dispersed in temporary lodgings. [37.2] When unrest arose in the populace, he suppressed it with a very heavy hand, and he was vigilant in preventing its rise. When a riot in the theater led to bloodshed, he banished the heads of the factions[71] and the actors who were to blame for the disturbances, and no appeals of the people could ever induce him to recall them. [37.3] When the people of Pollentia[72] refused to let the dead body of a *primipilaris* be removed from the forum until they had forcibly extracted money from his heirs to pay for gladiatorial games, Tiberius sent one cohort from Rome and another from the kingdom of Cottius[73] to the town. He concealed the reason for their march, and so when they appeared at the different town gates, the noise of their arms and standards came as a surprise. He compelled most of the people and local magistrates

---

69. The date for rental contracts was July 1; see *Vit.* 7.2. A financial dealing of this sort was below the dignity of a senator.

70. Lots that would determine his assignment for the year. Married status was ostensibly an advantage.

71. Groups of fans.

72. In Cisalpine Gaul.

73. Marcus Julius Cottius was the native chieftain in the western Alps (the Cottian Alps) friendly to the Romans; a Roman detachment was based there. See *Ner.* 18.

to spend their lives in chains. He abolished the customary right of asylum wherever he encountered it. Because the people of Cyzicus[74] had dared do violence to Roman citizens, he took away the self-rule that they had won in the war against Mithridates.[75]

[37.4] Tiberius himself undertook no military campaigns after his accession but sent his generals to suppress insurrections, and not even then did he do this except reluctantly and when absolutely necessary. He used threats and complaints instead of force to restrain kings whom he suspected of hostile intentions. He used flattery and promises to entice some of them to come to him and did not let them return home again—for instance, Marobodus the German, Rhascuporis the Thracian, and Archelaus the Cappadocian—and he also turned the kingdom of the last into a province.

[38] After Tiberius became emperor, he did not set foot beyond the gate of Rome for two years. After that he left only to go to nearby towns, to Antium at the farthest,[76] and even then very infrequently and only for a few days. But he kept announcing that he would revisit the provinces and the army, and almost every year he prepared to set out. Wagons were collected, provisions were stockpiled in the free towns and colonies, and as a final note he allowed prayers to be offered for his departure and his return. This gave rise to a widely circulated joke that called him Callippides, known in Greek proverb as someone who ran and ran but did not move forward so much as a cubit.

[39] But when he lost both of his sons (Germanicus in Syria, Drusus in Rome), he sought seclusion in Campania. Almost everyone was firmly convinced and stated convincingly that he would never return and would soon die. Both eventualities came close to happening. He never did return to Rome again, and a few days after he left he was attending a banquet at a country estate near Tarracina[77] called the Grotto when a great many huge rocks chanced to fall from above. Many of the guests and servants were crushed, and Tiberius was lucky to escape. [40] After traveling all over Campania and dedicating a temple to Jupiter at Capua and a temple to Augustus at

74. A city in Asia, near the Hellespont.
75. See *Jul.* 4.2.
76. On the coast near Rome; a place of resort for the imperial family.
77. On the coast south of Rome.

Nola[78] (the reasons that he had given for his journey), he retreated to Capri, an island that he particularly liked because access was limited to a single small landing place and because it was closed in on all sides by steep rocks of enormous height and by the deep sea. Very soon the populace appealed to him to return because of a disaster that had taken place at Fidenae, where more than twenty thousand people were killed when the amphitheater collapsed during a gladiatorial show.[79] Tiberius crossed back over to the mainland and allowed everyone to approach him, making up for the fact that when he left Rome he had issued an edict that no one was to bother him, and all during his travels he had denied access to those who did approach.

[41] After he returned to the island, he neglected his responsibilities to the state so completely that never again after that time did he raise the equestrian jury rolls to their full number or make changes with the military tribunes or prefects or any of the provincial governors. He left Spain and Syria without governors of consular rank for a number of years and did nothing when the Parthians took over Armenia and when the Dacians and Sarmatians[80] ravaged Moesia and the Germans the Gallic provinces—a great disgrace to the empire and just as much a danger.

[42.1] But when his isolation afforded him license to act without restraint, out of sight of his countrymen as it were, he finally, all of a sudden, gave free play to every vice that he had concealed so poorly for so long. I shall describe these in detail from the beginning. Even as a newcomer in the army camp he was called Biberius instead of Tiberius, Caldius instead of Claudius, and Mero instead of Nero because of his inordinate love of wine.[81] Later on, when he was emperor, at the very time that he was correcting public morals, he spent a night and two days in a row eating and drinking with Pomponius Flaccus and Lucius Piso.[82] He awarded one the province

---

78. Augustus had died at Nola; see *Aug.* 98.5, 100.2.

79. Fidenae was a town very close to Rome. The collapse was a notorious disaster; see *Cal.* 31.

80. A nomadic tribe that came into the Danube region.

81. Nicknames derived from words that mean "drink," "hot," and "wine."

82. Lucius Pomponius Flaccus and Lucius Calpurnius Piso, both consuls early in Tiberius' reign.

of Syria on the spot and made the other the city prefect, and in
their documents of appointment he stated that they were his closest
friends all hours of the day and night. [42.2] He invited himself to
dinner at the home of Cestius Gallus, a lecherous old profligate, to
whom Augustus had given the mark of disgrace in the past and whom
he himself had chastised in the senate a few days earlier. He imposed
the condition that Cestius not change his routine or omit anything
he usually did and that naked girls serve the dinner. He endorsed
a very obscure candidate for the quaestorship ahead of those from
the most important families because when he proposed a drinking bout at a banquet, the man drank down an amphora of wine.
He gave Asellius Sabinus 200,000 sesterces for writing a dialogue
that described a competition between a mushroom and a figpecker
and an oyster and a thrush.[83] To cap it all off, he established a new
administrative responsibility, the Department of Pleasure, with the
Roman knight Titus Caesonius Priscus in charge.

[43.1] In the seclusion of Capri he created *sellaria*, out-of-the-
way places for sexual pursuits. Troops of girls and male prostitutes,
inventors of deviant sex acts, were brought there from all parts, and
these he called *spintriae*. Joined in threesomes, they took turns performing obscenities as he watched; the sight of them was intended
to excite his flagging libido. [43.2] He decorated a large number of
chambers that he made available with paintings and statues, utterly
uninhibited images and forms, and he furnished them with books by
Elephantis[84] so that all his guests would have illustrated for them a
prescribed position for their sexual performance. And he contrived
places for lovemaking everywhere in the woods and groves; young
boys and girls dressed as Pans and nymphs stood in front of the caves
and grottos and offered sexual services. The people made a joke on
the island's name[85] and openly called it the Old Goat's Playground.

[44.1] He earned an even worse and more disgusting reputation in
a way that is scarcely to be described or heard described—much less
believed. He trained little boys (he called them his little fishes) to
circle around between his thighs when he swam and to play with
their tongues and give gentle little bites. And he put infants, fairly

83. Delicacies for the table.
84. A Greek writer of erotica.
85. "Capri" is related to the word for "goat" (*caper*), and goats were considered lascivious animals.

sturdy but not yet weaned, to his penis as if to a breast. His predilec-
tion and age obviously rendered him more disposed to this kind of
sexual gratification. [44.2] This preference is also apparent from a
painting by Parrhasius[86] that depicted Atalanta satisfying Meleager[87]
with her mouth. It had been left to him on condition that, if he found
the subject matter offensive, he would receive a million sesterces in
its place. He not only preferred the painting; he hung it in his bedchamber. The story is also told that one time when he was presiding
at a sacrifice, he was captivated by the good looks of the incense
bearer. He could not restrain himself and took him off and raped him
at once, then and there, almost before the divine proceedings were
over—and his brother the flute player at the same time. And then he
broke the legs of both when they complained jointly of the outrage.
[45] Just how much he was in the habit of taking sexual pleasure
at the heads of women,[88] even well-born women, can be seen very
clearly with the death of a woman by the name of Mallonia whom
he had taken to his bed. When she persistently refused to endure
any further mortification, he turned her over to informers. And
even when she was on trial he did not stop interrupting her, saying,
"You're sorry, aren't you!" until she left the court, hurried home, and
ran herself through with a sword, excoriating the disgusting mouth
of the hairy and foul-smelling old man so that all could hear. This
was the source of a tag put on him in the Atellan farce at the next
games, a saying that met with great approval and circulated widely:
"The old billy goat is licking the sex of the does."

[46] Stingy and tight-fisted with money, Tiberius never supported
his companions on his journeys abroad and his military campaigns
with a salary but only with a travel allowance. The one time that he
rewarded them came through the generous openhandedness of his
stepfather. He divided them into three groups and made distributions
according to the rank of each, to the first group 600,000 sesterces,
to the second 400,000, and to the third 200,000; this last group he
called not his friends but his Greeks.[89] [47] He did not construct any

---

86. A well-known Greek painter.
87. Characters from Greek mythology. Meleager fell in love with the virgin huntress Atalanta at a celebrated boar hunt.
88. Oral sex; see *Jul.* 22.2.
89. See chapter 56.

important buildings as emperor, and the only projects that he began, the temple of Augustus and the restoration of Pompey's theater, he left unfinished even after so many years. He did not sponsor any entertainments at all and rarely attended those sponsored by another for fear that some request or other would be put to him. This was especially true after he was forced to give a comic actor named Actius his freedom. He helped a few impoverished senators, but so as not to help many, he said that he would not aid others unless they demonstrated to the senate legitimate reasons for the sad condition of their finances. Because of this requirement a sense of propriety and embarrassment discouraged many from applying, among them Hortalus, grandson of the orator Quintus Hortensius,[90] who despite very modest means had fathered four children in conformity with Augustan policy.

[48.1] Twice all told, Tiberius displayed generosity to the populace, once when he offered to lend 100 million sesterces interest-free for a term of three years, and again when he compensated the losses of some of the owners of the apartment blocks on the Caelian Hill, which had burned. He was under pressure to enact the first of these measures because the people were demanding help at a time of severe financial stress, and he had not resolved the problem with his effort to get a vote from the senate that required lenders to invest two-thirds of their resources in land and debtors to pay a like portion of their debt immediately. The second measure alleviated temporary hardship, but he thought it such a valuable instance of generosity that he directed a name change for the Caelian Hill and had it called the Augustan Hill. [48.2] He never gave anything to the military beyond the doubling of the legacies provided in Augustus' will; an exception was a thousand denarii given to each of the praetorians because they had not supported Sejanus[91] and some bequests to the legions stationed in Syria because they alone had not venerated the images of Sejanus on their standards. Very infrequently did he allow veteran soldiers to retire; he preferred to have them die of old age and then profit from their deaths. He did not even aid the provinces with the exception of Asia, after an earthquake had destroyed its cities.

---

90. Quintus Hortensius Hortalus, a famous orator in the time of Cicero.

91. Lucius Aelius Sejanus, Tiberius' very powerful praetorian prefect, who challenged him; see 55, 60, 65, and elsewhere.

[49.1] As time went on, Tiberius turned his attention to acquiring wealth through coercion. Everyone knows that he used fear and apprehension to drive Gnaeus Lentulus Augur, an extremely wealthy man, to take his life and to make the emperor his sole heir. As a favor to Quirinus, a very rich former consul with no children, he pronounced Lepida guilty. A woman with very distinguished family connections whom Quirinus had divorced, she was charged, twenty years later, with having tried to poison him in the distant past.[92] [49.2] In addition, he seized property from the leading men of the Gallic and Spanish provinces and of Syria and Greece on such blatantly trivial and fabricated grounds that some were charged with nothing more than hoarding a portion of their wealth in cash. He deprived states and private individuals of their ancient immunities and of the right to mine precious metals and collect taxes. He even cheated Vonones, king of the Parthians, out of his wealth and killed him. Vonones had been driven from his throne by his kinsmen and had withdrawn to Antioch with his immense treasure, and he had entered into a relationship of trust with the Roman people—or so he thought.

[50.1] Tiberius revealed his hatred for his family first with his brother Drusus when he produced a letter in which Drusus discussed the plans they were making together to force Augustus to restore the Republic. And then with the rest: In the case of his wife Julia, he was so far from granting her the least bit, the barest minimum, of respect and kindness when she was in exile that, going beyond the restrictions of her father who had confined her to a single town, he kept her from leaving her house and from having human contact. He also defrauded her of the spending money that her father had let her have and her annual allowance on the legal pretense that Augustus had not put anything about these provisions in his will. [50.2] Annoyed with his mother because she seemed to be arrogating to herself power equal to his own, he avoided frequent meetings with her and private conversations that went on too long so that he would not appear guided by her advice—although he had sometimes needed it and

---

92. This Aemilia Lepida had once been betrothed to Lucius Caesar. Publius Sulpicius Quirinus was consul under Augustus. The details of this high-profile case are unclear, but Suetonius assumes that Tiberius wanted to inherit from the childless Quirinus. His former wife may have interfered with this in some way, perhaps claiming that there was a child after all.

was in the habit of following it. He was extremely aggravated at the senate's action when it added "son of Livia" (like "son of Augustus") to his titles. [50.3] As a result, he did not permit her to be called Parent of Her Country or to receive any special public honor but cautioned her to keep out of important business inappropriate for a woman. He warned her specifically after he learned that she had gone to the scene of a fire adjacent to the temple of Vesta and was urging the people and the soldiers on to more energetic efforts, just as she had done when she was married to Augustus. [51.1] It was the following incident that pushed him to the point of quarreling openly with her—or so they say: when Livia urged him repeatedly to add to the jury rolls the name of a man who had been given citizenship, he said that he would but only on condition that the roll be allowed to read, "My mother forced me to do it." This made her angry, and she took from a storage place some old memoranda that Augustus had written to her about Tiberius' cruel and unrelenting character, and she read them aloud. Tiberius was so irate about these papers that had been kept so long and were being used to excoriate him so viciously that some think that of the reasons for his retirement to Capri, this was the most important.

[51.2] Indeed, during the whole of the three years that he was away from Rome when his mother was still alive, he saw her only once and then for no more than a very few hours on a single day, and later, when she was sick, he did not bother to visit. After she died, following a delay of several days during which he encouraged the hope that he would come, she was finally buried when her body was beginning to decompose. He forbade her deification, claiming that this was at her instruction, and he also treated her will as invalid and quickly brought to ruin all of her friends and intimates, even those to whom she had entrusted responsibility for her funeral as she lay dying. One of them, a man of equestrian rank, he condemned to the treadmill.

[52.1] Tiberius did not have a father's affection for either his biological son Drusus or his adopted son Germanicus. He found the moral failings of the former abhorrent, for Drusus led a fairly irresponsible and dissipated life. Not even when he died did Tiberius display strong emotion but quite quickly returned to his usual business after the funeral and forbade a longer period of mourning. [52.2] When envoys from Ilium offered their rather tardy condolences, he laughed and replied, as if his loss were a thing of the past, "I grieve for your misfortune as well, for you have lost your splendid countryman, Hector."[93] As for Germanicus, he was critical of him to the point that he disparaged his celebrated achievements as meaningless and inveighed against his magnificent victories as ruinous to the state. He complained in the senate that it was without his permission that Germanicus had gone to Alexandria on account of the sudden devastating famine there. [52.3] He is even believed to have used Gnaeus Piso,[94] the governor of Syria, as the agent of Germanicus' death. Some think that later, when Piso was on trial for this crime, he would have produced his orders from Tiberius if Tiberius had not had the papers that he was showing around in private taken from him and had him executed. This is why the slogan "Give us back Germanicus!" was written everywhere and shouted over and over again at night. Tiberius added to the suspicion when he later cruelly persecuted Germanicus' wife and children, too.

[53.1] When his daughter-in-law Agrippina[95] complained rather too freely after her husband died, he took her by the hand and said, quoting a line of Greek, "Do you think that you are being injured, my little daughter, if you do not rule?" And he did not condescend to speak to her again. After he offered her an apple at dinner and she did not dare taste it, he stopped inviting her to his table, making the excuse that he was being accused of poisoning. But the incident had been prearranged between the two; he, on the one hand, was to offer the fruit to test her, and she, on the other, would be wary, as if the apple meant absolutely certain death. [53.2] Finally, after he had made the false charge that she wanted to seek refuge, first at the statue of Augustus, then with the armies, he banished her to Pandataria.[96] When she reviled him, he had a centurion beat her until he put out an eye, and when she determined to starve herself to death, he ordered her mouth forcibly pried open and food crammed in. After she persisted and died as a result, he continued to heap abuse on her by proposing that the day of her birth be numbered among days of ill omen. He prided himself on not strangling her with a cord and

---

93. The Trojan hero in Homer's *Iliad*. Ilium = Troy.
94. Gnaeus Calpurnius Piso. For his role in Germanicus' death, see *Cal.* 2, 3.3.
95. The wife of Germanicus; see *Aug.* 64.1.
96. An island off the coast of Latium.

throwing her body on the Gemonian Steps, and in acknowledgment of such clemency he allowed a resolution of thanks to be voted to him and a gift of gold consecrated to the Capitoline Jupiter.

[54.1] From Germanicus, Tiberius had three grandsons, Nero, Drusus, and Gaius,[97] and from Drusus, one, Tiberius.[98] Left childless by the death of his sons, he recommended the two eldest sons of Germanicus, Nero and Drusus, to the protection of the senate and celebrated the day when each entered public life with a money gift to the people. But when he learned that formal prayers had been offered at the beginning of the year for their well-being as well as for his, he put the matter before the senate, saying, "Such honors should be awarded only to those who are experienced and advanced in age." [54.2] From then on, it was clear how he really felt about them. He left them open to accusations from all sides and used an assortment of tricks to make them angry enough to insult him. And then when they did become angry, he informed on them. He accused them ruthlessly in writing and piled on invective, and once they had been declared enemies of the state, he starved them to death, Nero on the island of Pontia,[99] Drusus in the deep recesses of the Palatine. It is thought that Nero was forced to take his own life when an executioner, pretending that he was sent by the senate, showed him a noose and hooks,[100] and that Drusus was deprived of food to the point that he tried to eat the stuffing of his mattress. The remains of both were scattered so widely that it was only with difficulty that they could ever be collected.

[55] In addition to his old friends and members of his household, Tiberius had asked twenty of the leading men of Rome to be his advisers on matters of state. There were only two or three of all these that he kept from harm; the rest he destroyed in one way or another, among them Aelius Sejanus, who brought down many with him. Tiberius had advanced Sejanus to the height of power not so much for the man's benefit as to make him the one whose support and guile would help him get the better of the children of Germanicus

---

97. See *Cal.* 7. Gaius (Caligula) would succeed Tiberius.
98. Tiberius Julius Caesar (Gemellus), the survivor of twins. Gaius had him killed; see *Cal.* 23.3.
99. Off the coast of Latium, not far from Pandataria.
100. Hooks dragged the bodies of criminals to the Tiber.

and strengthen the succession claim of his biological grandson, the
son of his son Drusus.

[56] Tiberius was not a bit more lenient with the Greek companions whose company he enjoyed a great deal. When one of
them named Xeno was holding forth in a rather affected manner,
Tiberius asked, "What is that dialect that is so annoying?" Xeno
replied, "Doric," and Tiberius banished him to Cinaria[101] because
he thought that he was disparaging the island to which he had earlier
withdrawn, since the people of Rhodes speak Doric. And when he
was as usual choosing the subjects for dinnertime discussion on the
basis of his reading of the day and he learned that the grammarian
Seleucus was pestering his attendants about the authors he was reading and was thus coming to dinner prepared, he first removed him
from his inner circle and then even forced him to suicide.

[57.1] Even when he was a boy, Tiberius' cruel and unrelenting
character did not lie hidden. Theodorus of Gadara, his teacher of
rhetoric, appears to have been the first to see his nature clearly and
describe it with accuracy. Sometimes when he disciplined him, he
would call him "mud mixed with blood." But his nature was considerably more exposed when he became emperor, even at the beginning when he was still trying to gain the good opinion of men by
affecting restraint. [57.2] When a funeral procession was passing
by, a jokester charged the dead man in a loud voice to tell Augustus
that the bequests that he had left the common people had not yet
been paid. Tiberius had the man dragged before him, ordered him
to take what was due him, then had him led off to execution and told
him to tell his father the truth. Shortly thereafter, when a Roman
knight named Pompeius persisted in opposing an action of the senate, Tiberius threatened to imprison him and declared that he would
be made Pompeianus instead of Pompeius, a cruel joke that attacked
both his name and the past bad luck of a political faction.[102]

[58] At about the same time, a praetor asked whether he should
initiate legal proceedings in cases of treason. Tiberius replied, "The
laws must be enforced," and enforce them he did with savage cruelty. Someone had removed the head from a statue of Augustus so
that it could be replaced with a different one. The case was tried in

---

101. An island in the Aegean.

102. The Pompeiani were followers of Pompey the Great, loser in the
power struggle with Julius Caesar.

the senate and since the evidence was in dispute, information was extracted by torture, and the defendant was condemned. Accusations of this kind gradually escalated to the point that infractions like the following were also capital offenses: beating a slave near a statue of Augustus or appearing there in mourning clothes; taking a coin or ring stamped with his image into a latrine or a brothel; passing negative judgment on any of the emperor's words or deeds. Finally, a man even lost his life when he allowed an honor to be voted to him in his own town on the same day that honors had once been voted to Augustus.

[59.1] Tiberius did many savage and cruel things that appeared to be earnest corrections for the improvement of morals, but in reality he conformed to his natural proclivities. As a consequence, some used satirical verses to reproach him for present evils and to warn of those to come:

> Harsh and unforgiving man! Do you want me to put it in a
> nutshell?
> I'll be damned if your mother can love you.

> You aren't a knight. Why? You don't have the hundred thousands.
> And if you want to know it all, Rhodes is a place of exile.[103]

> You have, Caesar, found a substitute for Saturn's golden age;
> For so long as you are alive, all ages will be iron.[104]

> He doesn't care for wine, since he drinks blood now;
> He drinks it as thirstily as he used to drink wine.

> [59.2] Look at "Lucky" Sulla, Romulus—lucky for himself, not
> for you.
> And look at Marius, if you wish—but after he returned.[105]

---

103. Because he had been adopted by Augustus, he did not have money of his own and so did not have the requisite 400,000 sesterces for the equestrian census. Besides, exiles lost their citizenship.

104. The ages of the world were thought to deteriorate from gold through silver to iron.

105. The dictator Lucius Cornelius Sulla and Gaius Marius were bitter opponents in the bloody political struggles early in the first century BCE; see *Jul.* 1.1. Sulla was given the name Felix, "lucky." The name of the legendary founder of Rome, Romulus, here means "Roman citizen."

And at Antony, setting civil wars in motion,
His hands stained with murder more than once,
And say: "Rome is dead!" Whoever comes to rule
From exile has had a bloody reign.

At first he wanted these verses to be understood as written by those who were prejudiced against his reforms, written not so much as the result of considered thought as the products of spleen and ill temper. He said repeatedly, "Let them hate me, provided they show me respect."[106] But he later proved their words true and totally accurate.

[60] A few days after Tiberius reached Capri, a fisherman found him alone and surprised him with the gift of a large mullet. He was terrified because the man had crept up to him through the rough on the inaccessible back side of the island, and so he ordered the fish scrubbed over his face.[107] When the fisherman was congratulating himself during his punishment because he had not offered the emperor the particularly large crab that he had caught, Tiberius ordered his face lacerated by the crab as well. He executed a member of the praetorian guard for the theft of a peacock from his garden. One time on a journey, when thornbushes blocked the passage of the litter in which he was being carried, he made his advance scout, a centurion in the praetorian guard who was searching out the way, lie on the ground, and he beat him almost to death. [61.1] He soon burst out in every kind of cruelty and never lacked a pretext. First he persecuted his mother's friends and even her mere acquaintances, then those of his grandsons and his daughter-in-law, and finally those of Sejanus. He grew even more brutal after Sejanus was dead, and this made it clear that he was usually not prodded by Sejanus so much as Sejanus provided him with opportunities when he wanted them. But he had the gall to write in the journal in which he gave an abbreviated account of his life, "I punished Sejanus because I learned that he was raging against the sons of my son Germanicus." Tiberius had killed one of them when Sejanus was already under suspicion and the other after he was finally destroyed.

---

106. From a play written in the time of Sulla. For another version of the line, see *Cal.* 30.1.
107. The fish had sharp spines.

[61.2] It would take too long to describe one by one the vicious things he did; it will be sufficient to list categories of cruelty. No day went by when men were not punished, not even holy days set aside for religious observance. Some were executed on New Year's Day. Many were accused and condemned together with their children—and even by their children. The relatives of the executed were forbidden to mourn. Special payments were voted for accusers, and sometimes for witnesses as well. The testimony of informers was never discredited. [61.3] Every crime was tried as a capital offense, even when it consisted of a few ingenuous words: a poet was cited because he had abused Agamemnon[108] in a tragedy, a historian because he had said Brutus and Cassius[109] were the last of the Romans. The authors were summarily punished and their writings destroyed, although their work had been received favorably a number of years earlier when it was read aloud in the presence of Augustus. [61.4] Some of those held in prison were denied not only the comfort of their books but also the solace of speech and conversation. Of those summoned to defend themselves in court, some opened their veins at home because they were sure they would be condemned and wanted to avoid trouble and disgrace; others swallowed poison in full view of the assembled senate. But their wounds were bound up and they were taken off to prison, half alive and still breathing. Everyone who was executed was thrown onto the Gemonian Steps and dragged to the Tiber with a hook, twenty of them (thrown and dragged like this) on a single day, some of them women and boys. [61.5] Since tradition held that it was despicable to strangle virgins, the executioner raped young girls before he killed them. Men who wanted to die were forced to live, for Tiberius thought death so mild a punishment that when he heard that Carnulus, one of those on trial, had anticipated his execution, he exclaimed, "Carnulus has slipped away from me!" And when he was inspecting prisoners and one of them begged for quick punishment, he replied, "I have not yet made you my friend." [61.6] A man of consular rank reported in his *Annals*[110] that once at a large banquet at which he was a guest, a dwarf standing with the court

---

108. The leader of the Greek forces in the Trojan War, presumably identified with the emperor.

109. Leaders of the conspiracy against Julius Caesar; see *Jul.* 80.4.

110. This may have been the historian Servilius Nonianus, whose work is lost.

jesters near Tiberius' table suddenly asked the emperor in a voice that all could hear why Paconius, who was on trial for treason, was still alive. Tiberius quickly told him to hold his impudent tongue, but a few days later he wrote to the senate telling them to decide on Paconius' punishment as soon as possible.

[62.1] Tiberius' cruelty intensified and found focus when he became infuriated at what he learned about the death of his son Drusus. He had thought that Drusus died from illness as a consequence of his dissolute life, but when he finally learned that his wife Livilla[111] and Sejanus had tricked him and poisoned him, no one escaped torture and punishment. He was so obsessively fixated on this investigation all day, every day, to the exclusion of all else that when he was told that a guest from Rhodes had arrived, someone to whom he had written a friendly letter inviting him to Rome, he ordered him tortured at once; he thought that someone had come with important information for the inquest. When he recognized his mistake, he had the man killed so that he would not make public the wrong done him.

[62.2] One can see the spot where executions took place on Capri, the spot from which those who were found guilty after long and thorough torture were hurled into the sea while he watched. A crew of marines met the bodies when they fell and smashed them with poles and oars until not a breath of life was left in any of them. Among other methods of torture he devised this one: he tricked men into drinking themselves full with a large measure of wine, and then he suddenly tied their penises tightly and made them suffer from both the cords and the retention of urine. [62.3] But if death had not prevented him and if Thrasyllus had not convinced him (on purpose, they say) to defer some murders because he expected to live for a long time, it is believed that he would have killed a great many more and not spared even the grandsons that he had left: he was suspicious of Gaius, and he rejected Tiberius on the assumption that he had been born from an adulterous union.[112] And he might have done it, for he repeatedly called Priam[113] lucky to have survived all his family.

---

111. Daughter of Drusus the Elder and sister of Germanicus and Claudius; see *Cl.* 1.6, 3.2.

112. From an alleged liaison between Livilla and Sejanus; for their collusion, see 62.1.

113. The legendary king of Troy.

[63.1] Given these actions, there are many indications not only of how hated and detested he was but also of how very frightened and even subject to abuse. He forbade anyone to consult *haruspices* in secret and without witnesses. He tried to break the influence of the oracles near Rome but he gave up, because he was fearful and in awe of the sacred lots from Praeneste. (He had had these sealed and brought to Rome but did not find them in the chest until after they were returned to the temple.)[114] [63.2] He did not dare let out of his sight one or two former consuls to whom he had assigned provinces, and so he kept them in Rome for several years until he appointed their successors. In the meantime they maintained their titles, and he kept them busy with numerous tasks they performed with the help of appointees and assistants. [64] He never transported his daughter-in-law and grandsons anywhere after they had been banished unless they were chained and in a litter with its side curtains closed; a military escort kept any travelers they met from looking at them or even stopping.

[65.1] It was with difficulty and after a long delay that Tiberius brought down Sejanus, who was plotting the takeover of Rome—despite the fact that he could see that Sejanus' birthday was already a public holiday and that his golden statues were being venerated throughout the city. And he did it more with cunning stratagem than by using his authority as emperor. First, so as to dispose of him while pretending to honor him, he took him as a colleague in his fifth consulship.[115] He had assumed the office after a long hiatus for this very purpose, even though he was not in Rome. Then, after leading Sejanus to anticipate a connection with him through marriage[116] and to expect the tribunician power, he denounced him without warning in a disgraceful, self-pitying speech that he sent to Rome. Among other requests, he begged the senators to send one of the consuls to bring him, a lonely old man, into their presence and to dispatch a military escort for his protection. [65.2] He was so distrusting and so afraid of civil unrest that he ordered his grandson Drusus, still in chains at Rome, to be freed if the situation required it and put in

---

114. The temple of Fortuna Primigenia was at Praeneste, about twenty miles southeast of Rome. The lots (oracular responses) were written on pieces of wood kept in a special box.

115. 31 CE.

116. Sejanus wanted to marry Drusus' daughter Julia.

command of the armies. He also had ships ready and contemplated an escape to some of the legions. He watched constantly from the highest cliff for signals that he had instructed be raised far off so that news of what was happening would arrive quickly. But even after Sejanus' conspiracy had been crushed, Tiberius felt in no way more secure or confident, and for the next nine months he did not leave the villa that he called Jupiter.

[66] Abuse of all kinds coming from all quarters further stirred deep anxiety in him. Everyone whom he had condemned piled on insults of every kind, either face to face or in notes left in the orchestra.[117] He reacted to these slurs in contradictory ways. Sometimes he wanted to keep everything hidden away out of sight because he felt ashamed; at other times he was contemptuous and took the lead in exposing the offensive notices and making them public. A letter from Artabanus, king of the Parthians, was especially devastating for him. It charged him with killing his family and other murders and with indolence and licentious behavior and advised him to take his own life as soon as he could to render satisfaction for the hatred, so intense and so justly earned, that the Roman citizenry felt for him. [67.1] Finally, disgusted with himself, he came close to showing the depth of his anguish in a letter that began like this: "If I know what to write you, senators, or how to write, or what not to write at all at this time, may the gods and goddesses bring me greater pain than I know that I suffer every day."

[67.2] Some think that his knowledge of the future had made him aware of this dreadful life and that he had long since foreseen how much suffering and disgrace were waiting for him. Consequently, they think that when he became emperor, he refused the title Father of His Country and did not permit his official acts to be affirmed by oath so that he would not suffer more disgrace later on when he was found undeserving of such high honors. [67.3] This can be deduced clearly from a speech of his that touched on both distinctions, first when he says, "I shall always be consistent and never change my character so long as I am of sound mind. But as a hypothetical case, the senate must take care not to bind itself to the acts of any one person, since some circumstance or other can cause that person to change." And then he says, [67.4] "But if ever you should be in doubt

---

117. The notes were for the senators who sat in the orchestra section in the theater.

about my character or about my sincere devotion for you (before this happens, would that the last day of my life be at hand and liberate me from this your changed appraisal of me!), the mere title Father of His Country will add no whit of honor to me but will be a reproach to you, either for your lack of consideration in giving me the title or for your inconstancy in changing your opinion about me."

[68.1] Tiberius was a big, strong man, above average in height. He was broad across the shoulders and chest, and the rest of his body was in balance and well proportioned from head to foot. His left hand was the more dexterous and stronger one; it had joints so tough that he would drill right through a whole fresh apple with his finger, and a quick flick of it would injure the head of a boy, or even a young man. [68.2] He was fair-skinned, and he allowed his hair to grow somewhat on the back of his head so that it covered his neck, evidently a style for his family. His face was handsome but erupted in great numbers of blemishes. He had very large eyes that (marvelously) saw at dusk and even at night but only briefly when he first opened them after sleep; then they grew weak again. [68.3] He walked with his neck bent sideways. He usually frowned. He was silent most of the time; never or very rarely did he converse, even with those closest to him, but when he did, it was with great deliberation and a kind of subtle gesturing of his fingers. Augustus was aware of all his unpleasant traits that were signs of arrogance and often tried to excuse them, telling the senate and the populace: "They are faults of nature, not of the will." [68.4] Tiberius enjoyed excellent health. Almost the entire time when he was emperor he was in good physical condition, despite the fact that from his thirtieth year on, he took care of himself without help or advice from doctors.

[69] He was quite remiss about the gods and inattentive to religious ritual, obsessed as he was with astrology and totally convinced that everything was determined by fate. But he was inordinately afraid of thunder and always wore a laurel wreath on his head when the weather was somewhat unsettled because it was said that lightning did not set its leaves on fire. [70.1] He applied himself diligently to liberal studies of both varieties.[118] In Latin oratory he followed the lead of Corvinus Messalla,[119] whom he had heard speak when

---

118. Greek and Latin.

119. Marcus Valerius Messalla Corvinus, proponent of the "plain style"; see *Aug.* 58.

he was a young man and the orator was old. But he obfuscated his style by straining too hard for effect and subtlety and as a result was sometimes thought a better extemporaneous speaker than when he had prepared. [70.2] He also composed a lyric poem titled *Lament on the Death of Lucius Caesar*, and he wrote poems in Greek in imitation of Euphorion, Rhianus, and Parthenius.[120] He enjoyed these poets so much that he put the writings of all of them in the public libraries and placed their busts beside those of the most important ancient authors. Because of his interest, a large number of scholars competed to publish commentaries on them and dedicate their work to him. [70.3] But first and foremost, he cultivated a knowledge of mythology that reached absurdity and made him the butt of jokes. He would test literary experts, the kind of men whom, as we have said, he was especially eager to have as his companions,[121] and ask them questions like these: "Who was Hecuba's mother? What was Achilles' name when he was among the young maidens? What song did the Sirens usually sing?"[122] And when he entered the senate house for the first time after the death of Augustus so as to satisfy the requisites of both family duty and religion together, he took Minos[123] as his model and made offerings of incense and wine but without a flute player; this is what Minos had done in the distant past when his son died. [71] Although Greek came easily to him and he spoke fluently, he did not use it in all situations and avoided it in the senate especially. He was so strict about this that before he said "monopolium," he begged forgiveness for having to use a foreign word. And when "emblema"[124] was read aloud in a senatorial decree, he recommended that the word be changed and a native word substituted for the foreign one, or if one was not found, that the object be identified by a phrase of several words. Also, when a soldier was asked in Greek to give testimony, Tiberius forbade him to reply if not in Latin.

[72.1] Only twice during the entire time when he was in seclusion on Capri did he try to return to Rome. Once a trireme took him as far as the gardens next to the lake that had been constructed for sea

---

120. Greek poets popular in the late Republic.
121. His "Greeks"; see chapters 46, 56.
122. Questions relating to Homer's *Iliad* and *Odyssey*.
123. The legendary king of Crete.
124. "Monopolium" = monopoly; "emblema" = metal inlay.

battles, and he set a guard along the banks of the Tiber to keep away those coming to meet him. Another time he got as far as the seventh milestone on the Appian Way but turned back; he merely viewed the city walls but did not approach them. It is uncertain why he retreated the first time, but the second time, a bad omen frightened him off: [72.2] when he was about to feed from his own hand (as he often did) the pet snake that he liked to play with, he found that it had been devoured by ants. He thought that he was being warned to beware the power of the masses.

And so he went back quickly to Campania, fell ill at Astura, and after recovering somewhat there, went on to Cerceii.[125] So that no one would know that he was ill, he not only attended the games held in the camp but threw javelins down from his high place of honor on a boar that had been let into the arena. He immediately suffered a sharp pain in his side, and when he was struck by a draft while he was burning with fever, his illness grew worse. [72.3] But he continued on for some time, and when he got to Misenum, he maintained his regular routine and did not even skip dinner parties or other pleasures, partly because he lacked discipline but partly to conceal his illness. When his physician Charicles grabbed his hand to kiss it as he left a banquet (he was going on leave from his duties), Tiberius thought that the doctor had taken his pulse and urged him to stay and take his place on his couch again, and he kept the feast going. Not even at that time did he curtail his practice of standing in the middle of the dining room with a lictor by his side and addressing his guests individually by name as they said good-bye.

[73.1] During this period he read in the proceedings of the senate that certain defendants had been released before their cases had been heard. He had written briefly about these defendants, stating only that they had been named by an informer. This made him rant about being held in disrespect, and he determined to return to Capri any way he could, since he would scarcely have the courage to do anything unless he felt secure. But bad weather and the increasing seriousness of his illness kept him where he was, and he soon died in the villa of Lucullus[126] in his seventy-eighth year, in the twenty-third year of his reign, on the seventeenth day before the Kalends of

---

125. On the coast between Rome and the Bay of Naples.

126. Lucius Licinius Lucullus was a contemporary of Julius Caesar known for luxurious living; see *Jul.* 20.4. He had a villa on the Bay of Naples.

April in the consulship of Gnaeus Acerronius Proculus and Gaius Pontius Nigrinus.[127]

[73.2] Some think that Gaius[128] gave him a slow and wasting poison, others that he was denied food when he asked for it after a passing fever had abated, still others that a pillow was put over his face when he recovered and asked for the ring that had been pulled from his finger when he was unconscious. Seneca[129] writes that when he became aware that he was dying, he took off his ring and held it for a short time as if about to give it to someone but then put it back on his finger again and lay motionless for a long time with it clenched in his left hand. After he had called for his attendants but none appeared, he suddenly rose from his bed, and when his strength failed, he fell, not far from his couch.

[74] On his last birthday he had dreamed about Apollo Temenites, a statue remarkable for its size and artistry that had been brought from Syracuse to be erected in the library of the new temple;[130] the statue declared that it could not be dedicated by Tiberius. A few days before he died, a lighthouse tower on Capri fell in an earthquake. And at Misenum, ashes from the burned wood and bits of charcoal that had been brought in to heat the dining room but had already died out and were long cold suddenly burst into flame at dusk and cast a steady light far into the night.

[75.1] The people were so overjoyed at his death that as soon as they heard the news, some of them ran about in all directions shouting, "Tiberius to the Tiber!" Others prayed to Mother Earth and the gods of the underworld to allow the dead man no resting place except among the impious. And others, enraged by a fresh atrocity in addition to their memory of earlier brutality, threatened his corpse with the hook and the Gemonian Steps: a decree of the senate had provided that execution of the condemned always be put off until the tenth day after the sentence. It happened that the day of punishment for some was the day that the news about Tiberius' death arrived.

---

127. March 16, 37 CE.

128. Gaius (Caligula), who would succeed him.

129. Perhaps Lucius Annaeus Seneca, father of the philosopher of the same name who served in Nero's court. The elder Seneca survived Tiberius for a short time and wrote a history.

130. The statue had been brought from Temenos outside Syracuse for the new temple of the Divine Augustus; see chapter 47.

These men appealed to the goodwill of the people, but since Gaius
was not yet in Rome, there was no one who could be approached or
asked to intervene. In order to do nothing contrary to the established order, the guards strangled them and threw them onto the
Gemonian Steps. [75.2] This made Tiberius hated all the more—as
if the tyrant's cruelty lingered even after death. When the procession
carrying his body left Misenum, the crowds shouted that it should be
taken to Atella instead and half-burned in the amphitheater there.[131]
A military escort conveyed it to Rome where it was cremated in a
state funeral.

[76] Tiberius had made two wills two years earlier, one written in
his own hand, the other in the hand of his freedman, but the contents
were identical. He had had them sealed with the signet marks of men
from the lowest class. The will made his grandsons, Gaius, the son of
Germanicus, and Tiberius, the son of Drusus, heirs to equal shares
with the right of mutual substitution. He made a large number of
bequests, to the Vestal Virgins among others, but also to the whole
of the military and to the ordinary people of Rome individually, and
there were separate bequests to the magistrates in charge of the city
neighborhoods.

---

131. Atella was evidently nearby. It was thought appropriate that the body
of a tyrant be only partially destroyed.

GAIUS (CALIGULA)

12–41 CE
Emperor 37–41 CE

The actual name of the emperor often known as Caligula was Gaius Julius Caesar Germanicus. Ancient texts uniformly refer to him as Gaius. As an adult, he thought it insulting if someone tried to call him by his childhood nickname.

Gaius' sanity has always been in question. Suetonius was the first to use the expression "mental illness" with regard to him, although earlier authors wrote about a "confused mind" or "mad inconsistency." It was convenient for his successor to attribute the aberrations of his unsuccessful reign to madness, and too much time has passed for a proper diagnosis in any case. Despite this caution, it seems clear that Gaius struck his contemporaries and near contemporaries as unpredictable. This biography is somewhat different from Suetonius' others because of the nature of his source material, which consisted, to a large degree, of hostile anecdotes. He observes the young emperor through this scrim.

Although Suetonius always begins his biographies with the emperor's ancestry, this one devotes seven chapters to Gaius' father, Germanicus Julius Caesar. Germanicus had been in line for the throne at the time of his early death and is sometimes thought of as a "thirteenth Caesar." He was a popular figure, especially with the military. His large family, his sons and daughters and even his grandson, were involved in the power struggles that plagued the imperial family for fifty years after he died, until the Julio-Claudian line came to an end with Nero. The memory of Germanicus continued to influence events, and his reputation remained untarnished because he never had a chance to fail as emperor.

[1.1] Germanicus, the father of Gaius Caesar, the son of Drusus and Antonia the Younger, was adopted by his uncle Tiberius. He served as quaestor five years before he was of legal age and then immediately became consul. He had been sent to command the army in Germany when the news arrived that Augustus had died[1] and that all of the legions were stubbornly refusing to accept Tiberius as their commander in chief. They pressed him to accept supreme power in the state, but he put an end to their unrest. It is uncertain whether he did this out of loyalty to family or a sense of greater obligation to the state. Later he defeated the enemy and celebrated a triumph.[2] [1.2] Made consul a second time, Germanicus was sent to settle affairs in the East before he entered office. After he had defeated the Armenian king and reduced Cappadocia to provincial status, he died following a long illness at Antioch in his thirty-fourth year. Poison was suspected, for in addition to the bruises that covered his body and the foam that came from his mouth, his heart was found undamaged among his cremated remains. (It is believed that the heart, by its very nature, cannot be consumed by fire if it has been contaminated by poison.) [2] Furthermore, he died (or so it was thought) because of the treachery of Tiberius and Tiberius' agent, Gnaeus Piso,[3] who had charge of the province of Syria at the time. Piso did not hide the fact that he would have to give offense to one or the other, to father or son[4] (as though this choice were an absolute necessity), and he attacked Germanicus incessantly with violent verbal abuse and actions even when he was ill. Because of this, when Piso returned to Rome, the populace almost tore him to pieces, and the senate condemned him to death.[5]

[3.1] It is agreed that Germanicus possessed all the blessings of body and mind to an extent that no one else ever had: he had extraordinary good looks and was exceptionally courageous; he was talented in both branches of eloquence and learning;[6] he was unusually gracious and remarkably successful in his desire to win men's devotion

---

1. August 19, 14 CE.
2. Germanicus campaigned for three seasons in Germany with indecisive results before he returned to Rome for a triumph in 17 CE.
3. Gnaeus Calpurnius Piso, consul in 7 BCE; see *Tib.* 52.3.
4. He thought that if he supported Tiberius, he would wrong Germanicus and if he supported Germanicus, he would wrong Tiberius.
5. Piso committed suicide before the verdict on treason was pronounced. He was cleared of complicity in the death of Germanicus.
6. Greek and Latin.

and elicit their affection. (His thin legs did not fit this handsome impression so well, but they gradually filled out because he rode his horse frequently after eating.) He often struck down enemies in hand-to-hand combat. [3.2] He pleaded cases in court even after his triumph, and when he died, he left behind Greek comedies among his other writings. He behaved like an ordinary citizen both at home and abroad and entered free or allied municipalities without lictors. Whenever he came upon the graves of famous men, he performed funeral rites for their spirits. Intent on burying in a single mound the remains of the soldiers who had been massacred in the Varine disaster,[7] he was the first to pick up with his own hands and collect the bones that had long lain scattered about. [3.3] Germanicus was so gentle and devoid of malice toward those who attacked him (whoever they were and whatever their motives) that it did not enter his mind to become incensed with Piso, who was rescinding his orders and harassing his dependents—until he learned that Piso was also attacking him with curses and poison. Even then he did nothing more than follow traditional practice; he renounced his bond of friendship with Piso and commissioned his household to avenge his death if anything should happen to him.

[4] Germanicus was very richly rewarded for his exemplary character. His family valued and loved him so that Augustus (not to mention his other relations), after hesitating for a long time about naming him his successor, gave him over to Tiberius by adoption. The common people held him in such favor that sometimes (as many writers report) whenever he came or went, his life was in danger because of the large number of people who crowded around him and followed him. For instance, all the cohorts of the praetorian guard came to meet him when he returned from Germany after suppressing the mutiny there, although only two had been ordered to leave the city. And men and women of every age and from every order of the Roman people poured out as far as the twentieth milestone.

[5] But much greater and more substantial evidence for the esteem in which he was held became apparent at his death and afterward. On the day he died,[8] temples were stoned and the altars of the gods

---

7. 9 CE. The three legions under Publius Quinctilius Varus; see *Aug.* 23.1–2, *Tib.* 17.1.

8. October 10, 19 CE.

were overturned. Some men cast their *Lares* into the streets and left
their legitimate infants to die. It is also reported that foreigners who
were at war, whether with one another or with us, agreed to a cessation of hostilities as though they shared a private grief. Some kings
of small principalities got rid of their beards and shaved their wives'
heads as a token of deep suffering; and even the King of Kings[9] left
off hunting and dining with his nobles, a custom of mourning for
Parthians. [6.1] Back at Rome, the citizenry was struck dumb with
grief at the first report of his illness and waited for further news.
Finally, in the evening, a rumor from an unknown source spread
suddenly through the city: he had recovered. People came running
to the Capitoline from every direction with torches and sacrificial
victims. They almost tore the doors off the temple so that nothing
would get in their way in their eagerness to fulfill the vows that
they had made for his safety. Tiberius was awakened by the voices
of the populace everywhere as they rejoiced and shouted together:
"Safe is Rome! Safe our homeland! Germanicus is safe!" [6.2] When
his death was finally confirmed, no comforting thoughts, no edicts
could check the grief of the people who continued to mourn even
through the December holidays.[10] The savagery that Rome experienced in the years that followed added further to the praise for the
dead Germanicus and to the love felt for him. Everyone who thought
seriously about the matter concluded that Tiberius' cruelty that soon
burst forth had been kept in check by his respect for Germanicus
and by his fear of him.

[7] Germanicus was married to Agrippina, the daughter of
Marcus Agrippa and Julia,[11] who bore him nine children. Two of
these were carried off while still infants, and another, an unusually
charming child, when he was a small boy. Livia dedicated a statue
of him dressed as Cupid in the temple of the Capitoline Venus, and
Augustus put another in his private chamber and kissed it whenever he entered. The other children survived their father. There
were three females, Agrippina, Drusilla, and Livilla, born within a
period of three years. There were also three males, Nero, Drusus,

---

9. A title often used for Eastern potentates. Here it refers to Artabanus
III of Parthia.

10. The Saturnalia.

11. Augustus' daughter. The marriage was arranged in 4 CE.

and Gaius Caesar. The senate declared Nero and Drusus enemies of the state on charges introduced by Tiberius.[12]

[8.1] Gaius Caesar was born on the day before the Kalends of September in the year when his father and Gaius Fonteius Capito were consuls.[13] Contradictory accounts make his birthplace uncertain: Gnaeus Lentulus Gaetulicus[14] writes that he was born at Tibur[15] and Pliny the Elder that it was at Ambitarium, a village that lies in the high ground above the junction of two rivers in the territory of the Treveri.[16] To support his argument, Pliny adds that altars can be seen there with the inscription *ob puerperium Agrippinae,* "For the childbirth of Agrippina." An epigram that circulated soon after he became emperor claimed that he was born in the winter quarters of the legions:

> Born in a military camp, reared amidst his country's arms;
> This was the sign of an emperor to be.

[8.2] I, however, find in the public record that he was born at Antium.[17] Pliny refutes Gaetulicus on the grounds that he was falsifying evidence in order to flatter the egotistical young emperor by appropriating to him merit that belonged to a city sacred to Hercules. Pliny further states that Gaetulicus advanced this falsehood with greater confidence because about a year earlier a son, also called Gaius Caesar, had indeed been born to Germanicus at Tibur. I have already noted this boy's childish charm and early death.[18] [8.3] Pliny is proved wrong by chronology, for those who have written about the reign of Augustus agree that Germanicus was dispatched to Gaul

---

12. The conflict between Tiberius and the two eldest sons of Germanicus is described at *Tib.* 54.2–55.

13. August 31, 12 CE.

14. Gnaeus Cornelius Lentulus Gaetulicus, a commander in Lower Germany whom Gaius would replace. See *Cl.* 9.1, *Gal.* 6.2.

15. A town in the hills east of Rome, the site of an important temple of Hercules.

16. A Gallic tribe whose territory centered on the modern city of Trier. The rivers were probably the Rhine and Mosel, which meet at the modern city of Koblenz.

17. A town on the coast south of Rome, a retreat for the imperial family.

18. See chapter 7.

after his consulship was over and after Gaius had already been born. Nor does the inscription on the altar give any support at all to Pliny's position, since Agrippina gave birth to daughters twice in that part of the world. Furthermore, any birth is called a *puerperium*, without distinction of gender, because in the past girls were often called *puerae*, just as boys were called *puelli*.[19] [8.4] There is also a letter Augustus wrote to his granddaughter Agrippina a few months before he died. It concerns the Gaius I am writing about, for at that time no other small child with the same name was still alive: "Yesterday I arranged for Talerius and Asillius[20] to serve as escorts for the boy Gaius on the fifteenth day before the Kalends of June[21]—if the gods be willing. Furthermore, I am sending with him a doctor from among my slaves, and I have written Germanicus that he may keep him if he wishes. Farewell, my Agrippina, and take care that you reach your Germanicus safe and sound." [8.5] I think that it is entirely clear that Gaius could not have been born in a place to which he was taken from the city for the first time when he was almost two years old. The same considerations of chronology destroy the reliability of the epigram, and they do so the more easily because it is anonymous. And so we must defer to the authority of the public record, which remains our only reliable witness. Its testimony is corroborated by the special delight that Gaius took in Antium; he always preferred that town to all other places of retreat, as if it were his native soil. It is alleged that when he grew tired of the city, he intended to transfer there the seat of empire itself.

[9] Gaius got the nickname Caligula[22] from banter that went around the camp where he was being reared with the troops and dressed in the clothes of an ordinary soldier. The depth of the devoted affection that this upbringing gained him became particularly clear when the army rioted after the death of Augustus. It was the sight of Gaius and Gaius alone that had influence on the soldiers who were fast careening out of control. They did not stop until they

---

19. Suetonius introduces linguistic evidence to argue that the word *puerperium* can refer to either male or female births by noting that girls could be called by the feminine form of the word for "boy" and boys could be called by the masculine form of the word for "girl."

20. Evidently members of Augustus' household staff, probably freedmen.

21. May 18, 14 CE.

22. A diminutive form of *caligae*, military boots.

realized that he was being removed from the danger of mutiny and trusted to the care of a nearby town. Then, finally, they were sorry for their actions. They took hold of the wagon carrying him to keep it from moving on and begged to be relieved of the disgrace that his departure would cause them.

[10.1] Gaius also accompanied his father on his Syrian assignment. When he returned to Rome, he lived first with his mother and then, when she was sent into exile, stayed on with his great-grandmother Livia Augusta. When Livia died, he delivered her eulogy from the rostra, at that time still wearing the *toga praetextata*. He then moved into his grandmother Antonia's household, and when he was in his nineteenth year, Tiberius summoned him to Capri.[23] There, he put on the adult toga and shaved for the first time, both on the same day, but without the ceremony that had attended the initiation of his brothers into public life. [10.2] On Capri there were those who used every kind of devious trick to coax him and put pressure on him to air his grievances, but he never rose to the bait. It was as if he had forgotten the disasters that had befallen his family, and he acted as if nothing had happened to any of them. His pretense was incredible when he also ignored the wrongs that he had suffered himself. He was so subservient to his grandfather Tiberius and to those in his court that it was said, quite rightly, "There has never been a better servant or a worse master."

[11] But not even during this period was Gaius able to control his cruel nature and disgraceful appetites. He attended the torture and execution of condemned people and spent his nights visiting cheap taverns and brothels disguised in a wig and women's clothing. He worked energetically to become proficient at the stage arts of dancing and singing. Tiberius quite willingly tolerated his acquiring these skills because he hoped that they would soften the rough edges of his character. The keen-witted old man had come to understand Gaius so thoroughly that he made these predictions on a number of occasions: "If Gaius lives, it will mean my own death and the end of everyone else." And: "I am nurturing a viper for the Roman people and a Phaethon[24] for the world."

Read f Ct(hd

---

23. Tiberius had retreated from Rome to the island of Capri in 27 CE; see *Tib.* 40–41.

24. Phaethon, the exemplar of a youth in over his head, drove the chariot of the sun too close to the earth and damaged the world.

[12.1] Gaius soon married Junia Claudilla, the daughter of Marcus Silanus,[25] a ranking member of the aristocracy. Next he was named *augur* to take the place of his brother Drusus, but before he assumed office, he was promoted to a senior priesthood on the strong recommendation of the loyalty he had shown his family and as its rising member. With the court totally devoid of anyone else to prop up the imperial house and Sejanus[26] even then under suspicion and soon to be destroyed, he was gradually led to hope for the principate. [12.2] To support this hope, Gaius seduced Ennia Naevia, the wife of Macro,[27] at that time in charge of the praetorian cohorts; Junia had died in childbirth. Gaius promised to marry Ennia should he become emperor, and he guaranteed this promise by sworn oath and in writing. He used her to work his way into a close relationship with Macro and then poisoned Tiberius (as some think) and ordered the signet ring to be pulled from the emperor's finger while he was still alive. When Tiberius gave a slight sign that he wanted to keep it, Gaius had a pillow put over his face and, for good measure, strangled him with his own hands.[28] (A freedman was immediately crucified when he protested that this was a wicked crime.) [12.3] And it may well be true (some writers record it) that Gaius later confessed, not to actual parricide but to parricide that he had on one occasion surely intended to carry out. For when he was calling attention to the dutifulness that he showed his family (something he did constantly), he boasted that he had entered the bedroom of the sleeping Tiberius, dagger in hand, intent on avenging the deaths of his mother and brothers, but that overcome by pity, he had thrown away his weapon and retreated. Although Tiberius was aware of what had happened, he dared neither to investigate nor pursue the matter.

[13] After Gaius had become emperor in this less than commendable way, he was the answer to the prayers of the Roman people, or should I say, of all humankind.[29] He was the prince that most

25. Marcus Junius Silanus, suffect consul in 15 CE; see 23.3.

26. Lucius Aelius Sejanus, Tiberius' powerful praetorian prefect who fell in 31 CE; see *Tib.* 65.

27. Lucius Naevius Sutorius Macro. Tiberius had used him to get rid of Sejanus.

28. See *Tib.* 73.2 for other versions of the death of Tiberius.

29. He became emperor on March 18, 37 CE.

provincials and most of the soldiers had longed for because many
had known him when he was a small child. But the entire population
of Rome also awaited him eagerly, for they remembered his father
Germanicus and pitied his family that had been almost completely
wiped out. And so when he left Misenum,[30] even though he was
escorting Tiberius' funeral train dressed as a mourner, his journey
took him past altars, sacrificial victims, and flaming torches, and
he was met by a dense crowd of happy well-wishers. They called
him "shining star," "chick," "little boy," and "dear child," as well as
names that promised good luck. [14.1] When Gaius entered Rome,
the senate validated the desires of the unruly mob that was breaking into the senate house by granting him all the powers of state
immediately. Tiberius' wishes were ignored; in his will he had made
his other grandson, still wearing the *toga praetextata*,[31] coheir with
Gaius. Gaius' assumption of power was greeted with public rejoicing
so widespread that within the next three months, or even less, more
than 160,000 animals are said to have been sacrificed for him.

[14.2] When Gaius crossed over to the islands lying off Campania[32]
a few days later, prayers were raised for his return, and no one let
pass even the slightest opportunity to display concern for his safety.
And then when Gaius fell ill and all-night vigils were being held
around the Palatine, some promised to fight as gladiators if the ailing
emperor recovered and others promised to exchange their lives for
his, and they posted notices to that effect. [14.3] Foreigners added
their own significant devotion to the great affection that the citizens
of Rome felt for him. Artabanus, king of the Parthians, for example,
who never made a secret of his hatred and contempt for Tiberius,
sought friendship with Gaius of his own accord, entered into discussion with the consular legate, and crossed the Euphrates to pay
homage to the Roman eagles and the military standards that carried
portraits of the Caesars.

[15.1] Gaius did his own share of stirring enthusiastic support in
the people by bidding for popularity in every way he could. His tears
flowed freely when he praised Tiberius before a public assembly.

---

30. Where Tiberius died.

31. Tiberius Gemellus, the survivor of the twins born to Tiberius' biological son Drusus in 20 CE.

32. More properly lying off Latium. His purpose was to bring back the
ashes of his mother and brother; see 15.1.

He buried him with impressive pomp and then hurried quickly to Pandataria and the Pontian islands to retrieve the ashes of his mother and brother. The wild storm raging at the time made this show of piety more conspicuous. He approached their remains with reverence and placed their ashes in urns with his own hands. With the same sense of theater, he sailed to Ostia in a bireme, a military banner flying from its stern, and from there up the Tiber to Rome. He had the most prominent members of the equestrian order carry the urns to the Mausoleum on separate stretchers, at midday when a large crowd was on hand. He provided for funeral sacrifices to be made for them every year with due ceremony. For his mother he was even more generous; there were chariot races and a ceremonial carriage to carry her image in the circus procession. [15.2] In memory of his father, he named the month of September "Germanicus." And then, for his grandmother Antonia, he gathered all the honors that Livia Augusta had ever received and had the senate award them to her by a single action. His uncle Claudius, still a Roman knight, he made his colleague in the consulship. His brother Tiberius Gemellus he adopted on the day that the young man received the toga of manhood, and he called him Prince of the Youth.[33] [15.3] As for his sisters, he saw to it that they were included in every oath of allegiance: "I shall hold neither myself nor my children more dear than I hold Gaius and his sisters." Similar words introduced the consuls' proposals to the senate: "May goodwill and good fortune attend Gaius Caesar and his sisters."

[15.4] Equally popular were Gaius' pardon of the condemned and his restoration of exiles. He dismissed all criminal charges pending from the preceding reign. He collected in the Forum the written documents that had to do with the cases against his mother and brothers, and he burned them so that no informer or witness would have reason to be afraid in the future. But first, in a loud voice, he called the gods to witness that he had neither read nor touched any of the documents. When a note warning him of danger was handed to him, he refused to take it, maintaining that he had done nothing to make anyone hate him. And he said that he would not give ear to informers.

---

33. Both were grandsons of Tiberius. Latin can use "brother" to mean "cousin." The choice of the word here is ironic in view of Gaius' later treatment of Gemellus. See *Cal.* 23.3, 29.1.

[16.1] Gaius removed the *spintriae*[34] from Rome; it was only with difficulty that he was persuaded not to drown these performers of obscene acts in the depths of the sea. He allowed the writings of Titus Labienus, Cordus Cremutius, and Cassius Severus,[35] banned by order of the senate, to be located, owned, and read. He said, "It is very much in my interest that what has happened be made known to future generations." He made available the state's financial records. Augustus had posted these routinely, but Tiberius had discontinued the practice. [16.2] He allowed magistrates to dispense justice free from interference and without appealing to him. He reviewed the order of Roman knights strictly and carefully but with restraint; he took away the horses of those tainted by scandal or disgrace in full view of the public, but the names of those guilty of lesser offenses were merely omitted when the roll was read. To lighten the workload of jurors, he added a fifth jury panel to the four that already existed. He tried to restore voting rights to the citizen body by reviving the traditional electoral assemblies.

[16.3] Even though Tiberius' will was suppressed, Gaius immediately paid its bequests in full, honestly and without quibbling. He also honored the bequests in Julia Augusta's[36] will that Tiberius had held back. He abolished the tax of half of one percent on auctioned property in Italy and compensated many for property that they had lost from fire. Whenever he returned a kingdom to its prince, Gaius awarded him both the income from taxes and the revenue collected in the intervening years. Antiochus of Commagene,[37] for instance, received 100 million sesterces. [16.4] So as to increase the belief that he was an advocate for every kind of good behavior, he gave 800,000 sesterces to a freedwoman because she had kept silent about a crime committed by her former master, despite the fact that she was subjected to relentless torture. In recognition of these measures, he was voted, among other honors, a golden shield that members of the important priesthoods were to carry to the Capitol on a specified day every year. The senate followed in procession, as did boys and

---

34. See *Tib.* 43.1.

35. Writers who wrote under Augustus and were critical of the principate.

36. Augustus' wife Livia.

37. Commagene was a Roman province from 18 CE until Gaius restored it to the status of client kingdom in 37.

girls of noble families singing a hymn in praise of his goodness. A further decree named the day on which he came to power "Parilia,"[38] in token, as it were, of the city's second founding.

[17.1] He was consul four times, the first time from the Kalends of July for two months, the second time for thirty days from the Kalends of January, the third until the Ides of January, and the fourth until the seventh day before the Ides of the same month. The last two consulships fell in sequential years.[39] He began the third by himself in Lugdunum,[40] not, as some think, because he was arrogant and failed to follow precedent but because he was not in Rome and could not know that his colleague had died just before the Kalends.

[17.2] Twice he made gifts of 300 sesterces to each citizen, and twice he gave lavish feasts for the senate and the equestrian order and for their wives and children as well. At the second of these banquets he also gave presents, togas to the men and bands of cloth dyed shades of purple to the women and young people. And to keep the public happy in the future, he added a day to the Saturnalia and called it the Day for Youth.

[18.1] Gaius produced a number of gladiatorial contests, sometimes in the amphitheater of Taurus, sometimes in the Saepta, and he included troops of African and Campanian boxers, the best available from each region. He did not always preside in person at these shows but sometimes gave the task to elected officials or to his friends. [18.2] He regularly presented theatrical productions of various kinds at a range of sites. They sometimes even took place at night with the whole city lit up. He tossed out tokens that could be redeemed for various prizes and distributed baskets of delicacies to individuals. At one feast he sent his own portion of food around to a Roman knight who was sitting opposite him and laughing and eating with great gusto. To a senator who was enjoying himself the same way, he sent a document in which he named him praetor out of the regular order.[41] [18.3] He produced a great many circus games as well, and these lasted from morning until evening. Sometimes

---

38. A spring agricultural festival celebrated as Rome's birthday.

39. Suetonius is in error. The last three fell in sequential years: July and August of 37 CE; January of 39; January 1–13, 40; January 1–7, 41.

40. Modern Lyon.

41. His name would be at the top of the list of candidates, and his election would be certain.

between races there were beast hunts featuring African cats and sometimes a performance of the Game of Troy. There were special races when red and green sand was spread over the racetrack[42] and all the chariot drivers were senators. Gaius also started unscheduled races when a few people in the nearby stands asked him for them while he was watching preparations for the Circus from the Gelotiana.[43]

[19.1] In addition to these spectacles, he invented a new kind, never heard of before. He bridged the distance between Baiae and the breakwater at Puteoli, a space of about 3,600 paces, by gathering merchant ships from everywhere and anchoring them in a double line. Earth was piled on top and a road like the Appian Way constructed. [19.2] Gaius traveled over the bridge and then back again on two consecutive days. On the first he rode a decorated warhorse and looked splendid with his crown of oak leaves,[44] his shield and sword, and a golden cloak; on the second, he was dressed as a race driver and drove a chariot drawn by a pair of his horses that everyone recognized. With him he had the boy Darius, one of the Parthian hostages, and he was escorted by a column of praetorians and a group of his friends in war chariots of their own. [19.3] I know that many have thought that Gaius got the idea for this bridge from a desire to rival Xerxes, who was admired for bridging the shorter span of the Hellespont. Others have thought that he was trying to frighten Germany and Britain, where he was contemplating conquest, with the report of some kind of massive building project. But when I was a boy, I used to hear my grandfather say that court insiders gave as the reason that the astrologer Thrasyllus had made this promise to Tiberius, who was worried about his successor and leaning toward his biological grandson:[45] "Gaius will no more become emperor than he will ride about over the bay of Baiae with his horses."

---

42. The racing teams were named by their colors: green, blue, red, and white. Gaius favored the Greens and the Reds, which were evidently subordinate to the Greens.

43. Apparently a building on the Palatine Hill, possibly part of the palace complex.

44. The oak leaf crown was an important reward for saving the life of a Roman citizen.

45. Tiberius Gemellus.

[20] Gaius also produced games abroad, Attic games at Syracuse in Sicily and an assortment at Lugdunum in Gaul. The latter included a competition of Greek and Latin oratory in which we are told that the losers were forced to award prizes to the winners and compose speeches praising them. But the contestants who had been received especially badly were ordered to erase what they had written using their tongues as a sponge—unless they preferred to be beaten by rods or plunged into the nearby river.

[21] Gaius completed work on some public buildings left unfinished by Tiberius, the temple of Augustus and the theater of Pompey. He also began work on an aqueduct that had its source in the region of Tibur and on an amphitheater next to the Saepta. His successor, Claudius, completed the first of these projects but stopped work on the second. At Syracuse, Gaius rebuilt the city wall that had collapsed from age and restored the temples of the gods. He had intended to restore the royal palace of Polycrates[46] on the island of Samos, finish the shrine to Apollo at Didyma near Miletus,[47] and found a city on an alpine ridge. But his most ambitious project was to dig through the isthmus in the province of Achaia,[48] and he had already sent a *primipilaris* to make a survey of the worksite.

[22.1] So far, this has been about an emperor—so to speak. What is left is about a monster.

Gaius had acquired a number of descriptive names (he was called "dutiful," "child of the camp," "father of the armies," and "best and greatest Caesar"[49]) by the time he chanced to hear kings who had come to Rome to pay him their respects arguing at dinner about their noble lineages. He shouted out, "Let there be one lord, one king!"[50] At that moment he came close to putting on the royal diadem and turning what had the appearance of a principate into the reality of a monarchy. [22.2] But assured that his eminence surpassed that of both emperors and kings, he began, from then on, to claim divine majesty for himself. Arrangements were made to bring statues of the gods from Greece, the statues most famous for the reverence

---

46. A tyrant of the sixth century BCE.
47. A city on the coast of Asia, opposite Samos.
48. The Isthmus of Corinth.
49. A play on Optimus Maximus Jupiter = "Best and Greatest Jupiter."
50. Homer, *Iliad* 2.204.

they inspired or for their artistic excellence, among them the Jupiter from Olympia.⁵¹ Gaius intended to remove their heads and replace them with his own. He extended a section of the palace complex on the Palatine into the Forum and remodeled the temple of Castor and Pollux as its entrance hall. He often stood motionless in the middle, between the statues of the divine brothers, and offered himself as an object for adoration to those who approached. Some greeted him as Jupiter Latiaris.⁵²

[22.3] Gaius set up a temple for the worship of his own divine essence; he gave it priests and authorized the sacrifice of unusual victims. The temple held a golden statue that looked just like him, and every day it was dressed in clothes like the ones he was wearing himself. All the richest men competed for the priesthoods by campaigning and running up the bidding. The victims were flamingos, peacocks, black grouse, two kinds of guinea fowl, and pheasants—a different species sacrificed on each successive day. [22.4] To cap this, at night when the moon was full and shining brightly, he would over and over again invite the goddess into his embrace and into his bed. But during the day he made a habit of speaking privately with Jupiter Capitolinus, sometimes whispering to him and listening to his reply, but sometimes speaking quite loudly in an angry voice; he could be heard threatening, "Either you lift me, or I'll lift you!"⁵³ The god on his own initiative invited the emperor to come live with him and finally convinced him to do so—as Gaius claimed, for he joined the Palatine and Capitoline hills with a bridge stretched across the roof of the temple of the Divine Augustus.⁵⁴ To be closer yet, he soon laid the foundations of a new house in front of the temple of Jupiter Capitolinus.

[23.1] Gaius did not want to be thought of as the grandson of Agrippa⁵⁵ or called by his name because of this ancestor's undistinguished origin; he became incensed if anyone inserted Agrippa into the genealogy of the Caesars in either a speech or a poem. He

---

51. It never arrived; see 57.1.

52. The temple of Jupiter Latiaris stood on the Alban Mount outside Rome; ovations, lesser triumphs, were celebrated there.

53. Homer, *Iliad* 23.724, where wrestling is the context.

54. The temple evidently stood in the low land between the two hills.

55. Marcus Agrippa.

even claimed that his mother had been conceived in an incestuous
coupling of Augustus with his daughter Julia. Not content with this
attack on Augustus, he forbade the victories at Actium and off the
coast of Sicily to be celebrated as formal holidays but declared them
terrible disasters for the Roman people. [23.2] His great-grandmother
Livia Augusta he often called a "Ulysses in matron's dress,"[56] and he
even had the nerve to write the senate a letter in which he alleged
that she came from an undistinguished family. He claimed that she
was descended from a maternal grandfather who had been a local
magistrate at Fundi,[57] although it is certain on the evidence of the
public record that Aufidius Lurco served as a magistrate at Rome.
When his grandmother Antonia asked for a private interview, he
refused to talk with her unless the praetorian prefect Macro was
present as well. Insults and unpleasant experiences like this caused
her death, but some think that he also gave her poison. He did not
honor her when she was dead but watched her funeral pyre burn
from his dining room.

[23.3] Gaius had his unwary brother Tiberius[58] killed by a military tribune sent to take him by surprise, and he forced his father-
in-law Silanus to kill himself by cutting his throat with a razor. He
made charges to explain both murders: Silanus had not gone with
him when he set out to sea in foul weather but had stayed behind
in hope of taking control of the city if something happened to him
in the storm. Tiberius smelled of an antidote to poison that he had
supposedly taken to protect himself from Gaius. But, in fact, Silanus
had avoided sea travel because it was unpleasant for him and caused
nausea, and Tiberius had taken medicine for a persistent and worsen-
ing cough. As for his uncle Claudius, Gaius only kept him alive to
make him the butt of his jokes.

[24.1] Gaius made a habit of having sex with all of his sisters,
and at a large banquet he placed each of them in turn on the couch
just below him, while his wife reclined on the couch above.[59] He is

56. Sly cunning was associated with Ulysses (Odysseus).
57. See *Tib.* 5.
58. Tiberius Gemellus; for "brother," see note on 15.2.
59. The host (in this case, the emperor) took the upper position on the
lowest couch. His wife lay below him on the same couch and the guest of
honor at the lowest place on the middle couch. Gaius rotated his sisters
through the wife's position and gave his wife the seat of honor.

thought to have violated the virginity of Drusilla before he came of age; his grandmother Antonia, in whose house they were being reared together, once caught him in bed with her. Gaius took Drusilla away from her husband, the consular Lucius Cassius Longinus, and installed her openly as his wife. When he fell ill, he named her heir to both his goods and to the empire. [24.2] And when she died,[60] he declared a period of mourning during which it was a capital offense to laugh, bathe, or dine with one's parents, wife, or children. Unable to bear his grief, he left the city suddenly at night and traveled quickly across Campania. He went to Syracuse and then returned again just as quickly after growing a beard and letting his hair grow long. And never afterward, however important the question at hand, not even when addressing the people or before the troops, did he swear an oath except by the godhead of Drusilla. [24.3] As for his other sisters, he desired them less intensely and accorded them less honor to the point that he often made them available to his stable of male prostitutes. He did this so that it would be easier to find them guilty at the trial of Marcus Lepidus when they were charged with adultery and complicity in the plot against him.[61] Gaius not only made public the documents that all of the conspirators had signed and that he had gotten hold of through ruse and sexual entrapment; he also dedicated to Mars the Avenger three swords that had been readied for his death and put with them an explanatory inscription.

[25.1] It is difficult to say whether Gaius' behavior was more disgusting when he married, when he divorced, or when he kept a wife. Livia Orestilla was being married to Gaius Piso when the emperor, who was himself attending the ceremony, ordered the bride brought to his own house. He divorced her within a few days and two years later sent her into exile because she had apparently resumed relations with her former husband in the interval. Others say that at the wedding feast he sent a message to Piso, who was reclining opposite him: "Don't have sex with my wife!" He immediately took her away from the banquet with him and the next day issued a proclamation declaring, "I have married after the example of Romulus and

60. June 10, 38 CE.
61. Gaius had Drusilla married to Marcus Aemilius Lepidus after taking her from her first husband. At first Lepidus supported Gaius, but in 39 CE he was condemned for treason and executed.

Augustus."[62] [25.2] Lollia Paulina was the wife of Gaius Memmius, a man of consular rank with a military command.[63] When Gaius heard that her grandmother had been very beautiful in her day, he all of a sudden summoned Lollia from the province, got her in his bed (her husband acted the pimp), then quickly sent her away and barred her from having sexual intercourse with anyone ever again. [25.3] Caesonia was not especially attractive nor was she young, and she was already the mother of three daughters by another man, but Gaius loved this woman of boundless sexual appetite more passionately and more faithfully than he did the others. He showed her off to the troops as she rode next to him dressed in a cloak and carrying an Amazon's shield and helmet; he even let his friends see her bare-breasted.[64] He did not honor her with the name of wife until after she had given birth but declared that he had become, on one and the same day, a husband and the father of a baby girl. [25.4] He paraded the child, whom he named Julia Drusilla, through the temples of all the goddesses and then placed her in the lap of Minerva and entrusted her to the goddess' care and instruction. He thought that there was no more convincing proof of his paternity than the fiercely aggressive behavior that she displayed, even at a young age, when she used her savage little fingers to go after the faces and eyes of the children she played with. [26.1] It would be pointless to add to this dreary list, to describe the way he treated his other relations and his friends, Ptolemy, for instance, the son of King Juba, who was his cousin (he too was a grandson of Mark Antony through his daughter Selene), and significantly, even Macro and Ennia, who had helped him become emperor. A bloody death awaited all of them, either recompense for the family connection or in payment for their good offices.

[26.2] Gaius was just as disrespectful and harsh toward the senate. He permitted some who had held the highest offices to run beside his war chariot for several miles dressed in their togas. Or he let them attend him when he ate; they stood, dressed as slaves, sometimes at the head of his dining couch, sometimes at the foot. Others he

---

62. Legend has it that the first Romans took wives from the Sabines by force. Augustus took Livia from her former husband; see *Aug.* 62.2.

63. Publius (Gaius is incorrect) Memmius Regulus commanded legions in Moesia, Macedonia, and Achaia.

64. Amazons had to be unencumbered in order to fight.

murdered in secret but continued to summon as if they were still living. A few days later he would lie, saying that they had killed themselves. [26.3] He removed the consuls from office when they forgot to give public notice of his birthday, and for a period of three days Rome had no government. When his quaestor was implicated in a conspiracy, he had him flogged. The clothes stripped from him were put under the feet of the soldiers so that they would have firmer footing when they beat him.

[26.4] He dealt with the other strata of Roman society with this same arrogance and inappropriate force. Once when he was disturbed during the night by the noise of the crowd filling up the free seats in the Circus, he had all of them driven out with clubs. More than twenty Roman knights were crushed to death in the panic as were an equal number of respectable women and countless others. He started a fight between the common people and equestrians at a theatrical performance when he opened up the section reserved for knights too early and the rabble took the places for themselves. [26.5] Sometimes at gladiatorial contests, when the sun was very hot, he pulled back the awning shading the spectators and refused to let anyone leave. He did away with the usual arrangements for the gladiatorial games and instead sent into the arena emaciated beasts, totally contempt-ible old gladiators, and in place of comic fighters, respectable heads of households who had noticeable disabilities of some sort. And he sometimes made the people starve by closing the granaries.

[27.1] Here are some of the things Gaius did that best illustrate his innate cruelty: Since the cattle purchased to feed the wild beasts being readied for the arena were quite expensive, he selected crimi-nals for the beasts to rip apart instead. Standing no closer than the middle of the colonnade, he examined a row of prisoners, ignored the charges against them, and ordered them to be led off "from baldhead to baldhead."[65] [27.2] He exacted payment of the vow made by the man who had promised to fight as a gladiator in return for his recovery. He watched him fight and did not let him leave the arena until he had won his contest and begged repeatedly to be let go. When a second man (the one who had promised to give his life for the same reason) hesitated, Gaius handed him over to his slaves, ordering them to demand fulfillment of the vow. Carrying a cer-emonial branch and wearing a sacred headband, the man was driven

---

65. The phrase illustrates Gaius' capricious cruelty.

through the neighborhoods of Rome until he was forced headlong from the rampart surrounding the city.⁶⁶ [27.3] Gaius condemned many men of the upper class to the mines or roadwork or to face the beasts in the arena, and he first disfigured them by branding them like criminals. Or he shut them up in cages on all fours like animals or cut them in two with a saw. Not all of these were punished for serious crimes but because they had criticized the games that he presented or because they had never taken an oath in the name of his Genius.⁶⁷ [27.4] He forced fathers to be present at the executions of their sons and sent a litter to fetch one who begged off because he was ill. Another father he invited to dinner immediately after he had witnessed his son's punishment and, all affability, tried to get him to laugh and joke. He had his curator of gladiatorial games and beast fights beaten with chains in his presence day after day, but he did not have him killed until he was disgusted by the smell of his decaying brain. He burned to death the author of an Atellan farce in the middle of the amphitheater because he had written a line with double meaning. When a Roman knight whom he had thrown to the beasts shouted out that he was innocent, Gaius retrieved him but then sent him back again with his tongue cut out.

[28] He asked a man recalled after a long exile how he had spent his time away. The man replied, trying to flatter, "I always prayed to the gods that Tiberius would die and that you would become emperor—and that's what happened." This made Gaius think that the people whom he had himself exiled were praying for his death in the same way, and he dispatched agents around the islands to kill them all. When he very much wanted to have a senator torn to pieces, he instructed other senators to attack him without warning as he was entering the senate house and to call him an enemy of the state, and then, once they had stabbed him with their styluses, to hand him over to others to be dismembered. He was not satisfied until he saw the man's body parts, legs, and entrails dragged through the neighborhoods of the city and piled up in front of him.

[29.1] Gaius' vicious words made his brutal deeds worse. He used to say that there was nothing he liked better or found more laudable in his own character than (I use his word) his *adiatrepsia*, that is,

66. Their vows are described at 14.2. The second man was made a sacrificial victim.
67. The divine spirit within him.

his "shamelessness."[68] When his grandmother Antonia gave him advice, he said to her—as if ignoring her were not enough—"Keep this in mind: I can do anything I want to anyone I want." About to kill his brother whom he suspected of taking medicine to make himself resistant to poison, he asked, "Is there an antidote for Caesar?" When he sent his sisters into exile, he threatened, "I not only have islands; I have swords as well." [29.2] A praetor who had retreated to Anticyra for his health petitioned once too often to extend his leave of absence from Rome. When Gaius ordered him killed, he added, "Bloodletting is necessary in a case where a course of hellebore as long as this has proved useless."[69] Whenever he signed execution orders for prisoners who were to be put to death on the tenth day after their convictions, he would say that he was "balancing the books." He boasted that he had "subdued Gallograecia"[70] when a number of Gauls and Greeks were found guilty at the same time. [30.1] He rarely allowed anyone to be executed other than by repeated small thrusts of the knife; his instruction never varied and became notorious: "Strike so that he can feel that he is dying!" When the wrong man was executed because of mistaken identity, he said that the dead man deserved to be punished, too. He was constantly shouting the proverbial line from tragedy: "Let them hate—provided they fear!"[71]

[30.2] Gaius would often lash out at the entire senate, calling them dependents of Sejanus and informants against his mother and his brothers. He produced the documents that he had pretended to burn[72] and defended Tiberius' cruelty to his family as necessary since there had been so many accusers that he had to believe them. He frequently castigated the equestrians, rebuking them for their devotion to the stage and arena. Furious with the crowd when it pre-

---

68. The Greek word may have been Gaius' coinage. If taken positively, it means "steadfastness" but spun negatively, "stubbornness." "Shamelessness" may be Suetonius' interpretation.

69. Anticyra was a spa in Greece known for a medicinal herb, hellebore, that was useful as a purgative, among other things. A praetor was allowed to be away from Rome for a total of only ten days during the year when he was in office.

70. Another name for Galatia.

71. Tiberius is alleged to have uttered a version of this line; see *Tib.* 59.2.

72. See 15.4.

ferred another gladiator to his favorite, he shouted, "Would that the Roman people had a single neck!" And when the people demanded that the bandit Tetrinius appear in the arena, he said that those who were demanding him were Tetriniuses themselves. [30.3] A group of five *retiarii* wearing tunics surrendered to five *secutores* without much of a struggle. They had been ordered killed when one of them picked up his trident and slaughtered all the winners.[73] Gaius deplored this and issued an edict in which he termed it a very savage brand of murder and expressed his disgust at those who had been able to endure the sight. [31] He even complained openly about the age in which he lived, because it had not been marked by disasters felt by the population as a whole: Augustus' principate had been memorable for the disaster of Varus, that of Tiberius by the collapse of the viewing stands at Fidenae. The prosperity of the present time threatened to cast his own reign into oblivion, and he repeatedly expressed a wish for military disaster, famine, plague, fires, or an earthquake somewhere.

[32.1] Gaius' actions and his speech were just as cruel when he was not attending to duty, when he was amusing himself and enjoying the pleasures of the table. Often when he was at lunch or a celebration, he would watch important investigations being carried out under torture or else a soldier expert at decapitation cutting off the heads of some of the prisoners. At the ceremony that opened the bridge at Puteoli (we have already mentioned this structure that he invented),[74] he invited a large number of people to leave the shore and join him but then suddenly threw them all overboard, and the ones who grabbed hold of the rudders he pushed into the water with poles and oars. [32.2] When a slave took a strip of silver from a dining couch at a public banquet in Rome, Gaius turned him over to an executioner on the spot, and he was paraded through the company of diners with his hands cut off and hung in front of him around his neck and with a placard going ahead that gave the reason for his punishment. Once when he and a novice training as a *murmillo* in the gladiatorial school were sparring with wooden swords, his opponent intentionally assumed the posture of surrender. Gaius stabbed him with a real dagger and ran about with a palm branch like a victorious

73. Those who surrendered were at the mercy of the crowd and the person presiding.
74. See chapter 19.

gladiator. [32.3] On another occasion, Gaius was waiting, dressed as the priest's assistant, when a sacrificial victim was being brought to the altar. He lifted his mallet high and made the assistant holding the knife his victim. And once he burst out laughing at an elaborate dinner party; when the consuls sitting next to him were curious and asked what he was laughing at, he said, "What? Only that a nod from me could have the throat of either of you slit instantly."

[33] Here are some witty things that he said: He stood next to a statue of Jupiter and asked the tragic actor Apelles which of them he thought was greater. When the actor hesitated, he had him cut to pieces with whips. When Apelles pleaded for mercy, Gaius praised his voice from time to time and said that it was very sweet, even when he groaned. Whenever he kissed the neck of his wife or a mistress, he added, "This neck, beautiful as it is, will be severed the minute I give the order." And finally, he sometimes bragged, "I will find out from my wife Caesonia why I love her so—even if it takes the rack."

[34.1] With envy and spite that equaled his arrogance and cruelty, Gaius assaulted virtually the whole of humankind—whenever they had lived. He toppled the statues of famous men that Augustus had removed from the crowded Capitoline precinct to the Campus Martius, and he scattered their pieces so thoroughly that they could not be set up again with the proper identifications. And he kept the statue or likeness of any living man from being raised anyplace ever again without his approval and sponsorship. [34.2] He even considered banishing the poems of Homer and asked, "Why can't I do what Plato did, when he banned him from the state that he invented?"[75] But he came close to removing the writings of both Virgil and Livy and their images from all the libraries. He criticized the first for lack of talent and insufficient learning, the second for wordiness and careless research. As for the jurists, in order to get rid of their expertise altogether, he would boast, "By god, I will see to it that they can offer no opinion that is not just."[76] [35.1] From individuals of high rank Gaius took honorific tokens that had belonged to their families for a long time: he took the torque from Torquatus, curls from Cincinnatus, and from Gnaeus Pompey, the nickname

---

75. Plato described his ideal state in the *Republic*.

76. Gaius was ostensibly the arbiter of what was "just."

The Great, which he had inherited from his ancestor.[77] Ptolemy, whom I mentioned earlier,[78] was summoned from his kingdom and received with honor. Then Gaius killed him without warning merely because he noticed that the splendid purple cloak Ptolemy was wearing had attracted the attention of the spectators when he took his seat at a gladiatorial contest at which Gaius himself was presiding. [35.2] Whenever he encountered men who were handsome and had generous heads of hair, he spoiled their good looks by having the backs of their heads shaved. There was a man named Aesius Proculus, the son of a *primipilaris*, who had the nickname Colosseros[79] because of his exceptional size and handsome appearance. Gaius dragged him precipitously from his seat at the games, forced him into the arena, and matched him first with a Thracian gladiator and then with a *hoplomachus*. He won both contests, but Gaius ordered him tied up at once and paraded through all the neighborhoods of the city dressed in rags and displayed to the women. Then he had his throat cut.

[35.3] In short, there was no one whose circumstances were so degraded, no one whose lot was so mean, that Gaius did not object to what advantages he had. Because the king of Nemi[80] had already held his priesthood for a number of years, Gaius found a stronger champion to depose him. Once at a gladiatorial show, when the crowd applauded an *essedarius* named Porius enthusiastically because he had set free the slave who was his driver after a successful fight, Gaius rushed from the stands so fast that he tripped on the hem of his toga and went headlong down the steps. Furious, he shouted, "A people that is the master of nations accords more honor to a gladiator on the cheapest of pretexts than to their deified emperors or to their present emperor—me!"

---

77. Decimus Junius Silanus Torquatus was descended from Augustus through Julia the Younger; the torque was a collar, a military decoration. Gnaeus Pompey was a descendant of Pompey the Great, distantly related to Gaius through Augustus' first wife. The legendary Cincinnatus got his nickname from his curly hair, but no obvious person is referred to here. This may be a joke referring to Gaius' thinning hair.

78. See 26.1.

79. "Large love."

80. A priest of the goddess Diana, normally a runaway slave, who was safe in his position until deposed by another slave.

[36.1] Gaius had no regard for decency in his own sexual behavior nor for that of anyone else. He is said to have had sex with Marcus Lepidus,[81] with Mnester the pantomimist, and with certain hostages, and to have traded off roles with them.[82] Valerius Catullus, a young man from a consular family, bragged to everyone that he had sodomized Gaius and that he was exhausted from sharing his bed. In addition to incest with his sisters and a notorious affair with the prostitute Pyrallis, Gaius had difficulty keeping his hands off any woman of good reputation. [36.2] He would invite them to dinner along with their husbands, look them over as they passed by the foot of his couch, and assess them with the deliberation of a slave trader. He even used his hand to lift the face of any who looked down out of shame. And then, whenever it suited him, he called aside one whom he found especially attractive and left the dining room. A little later he would return, still showing traces of recent sex, and either praise his partner to the general company or find fault with her, enumerating the good or bad features of her body and her performance in bed. He took the initiative of sending notices of divorce to some of them using their husbands' names,[83] and he had the proceedings recorded that way in the daily register.

[37.1] The ingenuity with which Gaius managed his extravagant lifestyle exceeded that of all other spendthrifts. He thought up a new way to enjoy the baths and contrived very strange kinds of food and feasts, for he wanted to bathe in hot and cold perfumed oils, taste the most expensive pearls dissolved in vinegar, and set before his guests bread and cooked foods made of gold. He said, "A man has a choice: he can be stingy or be a Caesar."[84] Several days in succession he threw a considerable amount of money to the crowd from the roof of the Basilica Julia. [37.2] He built large Liburnian galleys with ten banks of oars. They had decks studded with precious stones, awnings of different colors, spacious baths and colonnades and banquet rooms, and all sorts of vines and fruit trees. He spent the day lounging on these as he coasted the shores of Campania,

---

81. His brother-in-law; see 24.3.
82. They took turns with the male and female roles.
83. Husbands could initiate divorce on grounds of adultery.
84. A relative was named Licinius Crassus Frugi; a Latin word for stingy is *frugi*.

entertained by singing and instrumental music. When it came to building mansions and country houses, he threw restraint to the winds and wanted to do nothing more than what was said could not be done. [37.3] Piers were built out onto the deep and menacing sea, the toughest bedrock was tunneled, level fields were heaped up like mountains, and mountain ranges were leveled by digging trenches. All this was done with unbelievable speed, since delay was punished by death. Without belaboring the details: Gaius spent a very large amount of money in a single year, 2,700 million sesterces, the entire sum he had inherited from Tiberius Caesar.

[38.1] With his resources exhausted and himself in need, Gaius turned to all sorts of ingenious plunder: He raised false legal issues, auctioned off his property, and imposed taxes. He claimed that those whose ancestors had obtained Roman citizenship for themselves and their descendants did not rightly hold it unless they were the sons of those who had acquired it, for the idea of "descendant" should not be understood as extending beyond that relationship. He dismissed as old and out of date the military discharges issued by the Divine Julius or the Divine Augustus. [38.2] He argued that a census report was invalid if any addition at all was later made to it for any reason.[85] He declared "undutiful," and thus invalid, the wills that *primipilares* had made from the beginning of Tiberius' reign if they did not include either Tiberius or himself as heir. He did the same with the wills of other people, declaring them null and void if the testator said that he intended to make Caesar an heir when he died but did not follow through. Fearing this, strangers anticipated the outcome and named Gaius an heir among the people they knew well, and fathers included his name among those of their children. Gaius accused such people of mocking him if they kept on living after making their intention known and sent many of them sweets laced with poison. [38.3] He presided over court proceedings that involved cases of this sort. First he calculated how much money he would raise by taking a case to trial, and then, when he reached his goal, he dismissed court. He refused to put up with even the slightest delay and once condemned more than forty people accused of a variety of crimes in a single judgment. He woke up Caesonia, who was sleeping, and bragged, "How much I have accomplished while you were taking a nap!"

---

85. The census included financial information.

[38.4] He held an auction and put on the block what was left over
from all the entertainments that he had sponsored.[86] He bid the
prices up himself and got them so high that some buyers opened
their veins when they had been forced to exhaust their resources
making expensive purchases. A notorious incident involved Aponius
Saturninus, who dozed off while attending a sale. Gaius cautioned
the auctioneer not to overlook the man of praetorian rank whose head
kept nodding, and before the bidding was over, thirteen gladiators
had been knocked down to him for 9 million sesterces without his
knowing it. [39.1] After Gaius had held an auction in Gaul and sold
at a very high price the personal property, household furnishings,
slaves, and even the freedmen that belonged to his condemned sisters, his greed prompted him to bring from the city the contents of
the old palace of Augustus. Hired wagons and the mules that turned
millstones were pressed into service to transport the furniture. As
a result, bread was often scarce at Rome, and a large number of litigants lost their cases because they could not present themselves in
court in person on the appointed date. [39.2] When it came to selling
these furnishings, there was no limit to Gaius' guile and flattery.
First he accused individuals of being greedy and of not feeling shame
because they were richer than he; then he pretended that he was
embarrassed about making the property of the imperial house available to private individuals. When he learned that a wealthy provincial
had paid 200,000 sesterces to the stewards in charge of his invitation
list to slip him into one of his banquets, he was not unhappy that the
honor of his table carried so high a price. The next day, when the man
was attending an auction, Gaius sent someone to hand him a small
trinket with a price tag of 200,000 sesterces and to convey to him that
he would dine with Caesar at the emperor's invitation.

[40] Gaius levied new taxes that had never before been heard of.
At first he used tax farmers to collect them but later, because they
were bringing in so much money, centurions and tribunes of the
praetorian guard. No source of revenue or segment of the population
fell beneath his notice when he imposed some kind of tax. A specific
fixed amount was levied on cooked food everywhere in the city. On
lawsuits and court judgments, wherever they were initiated, the tax
was one-fortieth of the money at stake, and a penalty was attached
if it was shown that someone had settled out of court or dropped his

---

86. This included gladiators who had survived the arena.

suit. From porters he took one-eighth of their daily profits and from the wages of prostitutes, the amount earned from one customer. An addendum to the lead paragraph of the law stipulated that both those who had been prostitutes and those who had kept brothels were subject to the tax and that they remained liable even if they married. [41.1] Taxes like these were imposed but not posted, and there were many failures to pay, since no one knew what had been stipulated. Finally, in response to the angry demands of the people, Gaius posted the legislation but had it written in very small letters and hung in a place extremely difficult to access so that no one could transcribe it.

In order not to miss any opportunity for the spoils he thought his due, he established a brothel on the Palatine. He fitted out a large number of cubicles in an elegant style appropriate to the special location, and there respectable married women and freeborn young men were to be displayed. He sent representatives around the markets and assembly places to invite young and old alike to the pleasures of his establishment. When they arrived, money was made available to them (at interest), and scribes were on hand to record their names for all to see as contributors to Caesar's income. [41.2] There was no source of revenue that he thought unseemly, even dicing. But he found more profit in deception, not to mention outright lies. He once gave up his turn at a game of dice to the person sitting next to him and went into the courtyard of the house where they were playing. When he saw two wealthy knights passing by, he immediately ordered them arrested and their property seized, and then he returned to the game, gloating and boasting that he had never enjoyed a more profitable throw of the dice.

[42] But when his daughter was born, he complained that he was poor since the responsibilities of parenthood had now been added to those of empire, and he accepted contributions for the little girl's maintenance and dowry. He announced that he would receive New Year's gifts and stood on the porch of the temple of the Capitoline Jupiter on the Kalends of January to receive them. A crowd representative of every social class placed their small offerings before him, pouring them out from full hands and from the folds of their togas. He was eventually seized by a desire actually to touch his money, and he walked back and forth barefoot over the huge piles of gold coins spread out over a large area and rolled around on them for a long time.

[43] Only once was Gaius concerned with military affairs or involved in actual fighting and then it was by accident. When he had journeyed to Mevania[87] to visit the river Clitumnus and its sacred grove, he was advised by the oracle to fill out the ranks of his bodyguard of Batavians,[88] who were accompanying him, and he conceived the idea of mounting an expedition against the Germans. He did not delay but called in legions and auxiliary troops from all quarters, imposed a heavy draft of new forces everywhere, amassed supplies of all kinds in quantities never seen before, and set out on his march. He was sometimes in such a hurry that the praetorian cohorts had to load their standards on pack animals and follow along after them, contrary to their normal practice. But at other times his journey was so leisurely and comfortable that he traveled in a sedan chair carried by eight bearers, and he ordered the inhabitants of the municipalities through which they passed to sweep the roads and sprinkle them with water on account of the dust. [44.1] When he arrived at the camp,[89] he was eager to prove that he was a strict and energetic general. He dismissed in disgrace the officers who had not brought the auxiliary forces in from their various posts quickly enough. He reviewed the troops and got rid of senior centurions on the grounds that they were of advanced age and in poor physical condition, although many were in fact experienced veterans, some only a few days short of retirement. He complained that the rest were greedy, and he reduced retirement benefits to 6,000 sesterces for those eligible.

[44.2] But the only thing that came of all this was the surrender of Adminius, the son of the British king Cynobellinus. Adminius deserted to the Romans after he and a small band of followers had been banished by his father. Gaius claimed that the whole island had been handed over to him, sent a splendid victory announcement to Rome, and instructed the praetorians who carried it to continue in their carriage all the way to the Forum and the curia and not to deliver their message except to the consuls in the temple of Mars

---

87. About a hundred miles north of Rome, known for its temple and oracle.

88. From Batavia, at the mouth of the Rhine.

89. The headquarters of the army of Upper Germany at Mogontiacum (modern Mainz).

with the full senate present.[90] [45.1] Then, since no real opportunity
for war had presented itself, he ordered a small number of German
prisoners moved across the Rhine and concealed in ambush. He then
had it reported to him with as much show of panic as possible (after
he had finished lunch) that the enemy was close at hand. This was
done, and he rushed out into the adjacent forest with his companions and some of the mounted praetorians. They cut down trees,
arranged them into a trophy, and then returned by torchlight. He
censured those who had not followed him, calling them lazy cow-
ards, but rewarded those who had accompanied him and shared in his
victory. Their reward was a new kind of military crown, decorated
with images of the sun and moon and stars. He gave it a new name,
the "explorer's crown."[91]

[45.2] On a second occasion, a number of hostages were taken from
an elementary school and sent secretly on ahead. Gaius abruptly left
a banquet that he was attending, chased down the children with the
cavalry, and brought them back in chains, pretending that they were
prisoners who had been recaptured. Another piece of theater also
went beyond conventional decorum: when he returned to the dinner table and soldiers arrived to report that the last of the hostages
had been rounded up, he urged the soldiers to take places on the
dining couches, just as they were, still wearing their chain mail. He
reminded them of a familiar line from Virgil, admonishing them to
"bear up and save themselves for better times."[92] [45.3] And while he
was acting out these charades, he rebuked the senate and the people
left behind in Rome with a particularly stern edict: "While Caesar
is exposing himself to great danger in combat, you enjoy banquets
that last all day and races and the theater and your pleasant country
retreats."

[46] Lastly, on the pretense that he was going to bring his war to
an end, he drew up a battle line on the shore of the ocean and put
catapults and siege engines into position. No one knew or could even
guess what he had in mind when he suddenly ordered the soldiers to
pick up seashells and fill their helmets and the folds of their clothing.
He called these "the spoils of the ocean owed to the Capitoline and

---

90. Vehicular traffic was prohibited in Rome during daylight hours.
91. An "explorer" might only be one who cleared a path for the emperor.
92. Virgil, *Aeneid* 1.207.

the Palatine." To mark his victory, he built a high tower from which light would shine at night to guide ships on their way as if from a lighthouse. When he proclaimed that each man would receive a bonus of a hundred denarii, he acted as if his bounty surpassed every previous act of generosity. He said, "Depart happy! Depart rich!"

[47] Gaius turned his attention from these adventures to concentrate on his triumph. In addition to prisoners and barbarian renegades, he chose for his parade the tallest of the Gauls, those "worthy of a triumph" (as he often said), and some of the nation's prominent men. He not only made them grow their hair and dye it red but made them learn the German language and take foreign names as well. He ordered the triremes he had used for his excursion on the ocean transported to Rome, overland for the better part of the journey. He wrote to his agents and instructed them to arrange a triumph at the least possible outlay to himself but to make it the greatest ever held, since they had access to the wealth of all men.

[48.1] Before Gaius left the province, he devised an unspeakably cruel plan: he would butcher wholesale the legions that had mutinied after the death of Augustus long ago. He remembered that they had obstructed the passage of their general, his father Germanicus, and himself, who had been a small child at that time.[93] It was with difficulty that he was kept from executing this reckless scheme, but his determination to decimate the legions could not be stopped. And so he summoned the legions to assemble unarmed, without even their swords, and he surrounded them with armed cavalry. [48.2] But when he saw that they had gotten wind of what was in store for them and that a large number were slipping away to get their weapons in case violence erupted, he ran from the parade ground and headed for the city at once.

He turned all of his vindictive feelings against the senate, threatening them openly in order to deflect attention from the rumors of the devastating humiliations that he had suffered. He complained (among other things) that they had cheated him of a proper triumph, although only a short time earlier he had warned them to make no plans to honor him, under penalty of death. [49.1] And so, when representatives of that distinguished order came to meet him on his journey and begged him to hurry back, he shouted in the loudest voice he could, "I shall come! I shall come! And this will be with

---

93. The army of Lower Germany; see chapter 9.

me!" and he struck over and over again the hilt of the sword he was wearing. He issued an edict to this effect: "I am returning but only for those who want me, the equestrian order and the ordinary people. To the senate I will no longer be either fellow citizen or emperor." [49.2] He even barred any member of the senate from meeting him. Whether it was because he was abandoning the idea of a triumph or postponing it, he entered the city on his birthday with an ovation.[94]

Gaius was dead within four months. He had dared to commit serious crimes and was contemplating even worse, since he planned to kill the most important members of each order and then to go to live first at Antium and after that, at Alexandria. [49.3] So that no one may question this, two lists with different titles were found among his private papers. One was headed "sword," the other "dagger,"[95] and both contained the names of people marked for death. There was also discovered a large chest filled with various kinds of poison. Claudius would later sink this in the sea, and it is said that its contents tainted the water and killed fish that the tide washed up on the nearby shore.

[50.1] Gaius was tall in stature, pale in complexion, and ill proportioned of body with a very skinny neck and legs. He had hollows about his eyes and temples, a broad scowling forehead, and thin hair, with none at all on the top of his head. He was hairy everywhere else. It was therefore held a capital offense to look down on him from a higher vantage point as he passed by or to say the word "goat" for any reason whatsoever. His face was naturally forbidding and repulsive, and he gave it a terrifying expression on purpose by practicing all sorts of horrible, menacing looks in front of a mirror.

[50.2] He suffered from poor health, both in body and in mind. When he was a child, he was subject to epileptic seizures, and as a youth, although he possessed a degree of physical endurance, he would suddenly become so weak that he could scarcely walk, stand, collect his thoughts, or hold himself upright. He was aware of his mental disorder and sometimes considered withdrawing from the court and clearing his mind. His wife Caesonia allegedly gave him

---

94. August 31, 40 CE. An ovation was a lesser triumph awarded for minor military accomplishments.

95. Some to be executed openly by the sword and others assassinated with a dagger.

a drug meant to be a love potion, but it made him mad instead. [50.3] He was plagued by insomnia, for he did not sleep more than three hours a night and not even then was his rest quiet. His sleep was filled with terrors and strange imagining. Once, for instance, he dreamed that he saw the spirit of the sea speaking with him. And so, because he grew tired of lying awake in bed for much of the night, he sometimes sat on his couch, sometimes wandered through the long colonnades, and over and over again summoned forth daylight and waited for it to come.

[51.1] Quite correctly I think, I attribute his mental illness to the presence of two very different character flaws in a single person: overwhelming self-confidence and, conversely, excessive fear. For Gaius, despite the great contempt that he felt for the gods, routinely shut his eyes tight and covered his head at the least hint of thunder and lightning. If the storm grew worse, he jumped out from under the covers and hid under the bed.[96] When he was visiting Sicily, he made fun of the marvelous stories told about the place but fled from Messina suddenly in the middle of the night, because he was frightened by the smoke and rumblings coming from the summit of Mount Etna. [51.2] He made threats against the barbarians, but when he was riding in his war chariot on the far side of the Rhine, passing through narrow defiles and surrounded by a densely packed column of soldiers, he heard someone say that if the enemy should appear, their ranks would be thrown into great disorder. He instantly mounted a horse and rode quickly back to the bridge, which he found crowded with camp attendants and baggage. He was unwilling to wait and so was handed back across the river over the heads of the men. [51.3] When he heard about an uprising in Germany, he made preparations to leave Rome and arranged for a fleet in which he could escape. He took comfort in the fact that at least the provinces across the sea would be left for him if the German tribes were victorious and seized the alpine peaks as the Cimbri had once done, or even the city as had the Senones.[97] I think it was this fear that later gave Gaius' assassins the idea for the story that they fabricated for the benefit of the soldiers rampaging after his death, the story that

---

96. Augustus and Tiberius were also afraid of thunder; see *Aug.* 90, *Tib.* 69.

97. Gallic tribes. The Cimbri had crossed the Alps at the end of the second century BCE, and the Senones sacked Rome in 390 BCE.

he had killed himself because he was terrified when he heard about a battle that had gone bad.

[52] Gaius invariably furnished himself with clothing, footwear, and other articles that were neither traditional nor suitable for a Roman citizen—let alone for a man—or even for a human being. He went out in public in embroidered, gem-studded cloaks and wore bracelets and garments with sleeves. He sometimes dressed in women's clothing made of silk. On one occasion he would appear in Greek sandals or boots, on another, in the kind of boots worn by elite members of the praetorian guard, and sometimes in women's slippers. He was often seen sporting a golden beard and carrying in his hand an emblem of divinity: a lightning bolt, a trident, or a caduceus. He also appeared dressed as Venus. Even before his military campaign, he wore the regalia of a triumphing general and sometimes the breastplate of Alexander the Great, which he had removed from his tomb.

[53.1] He paid little attention to liberal studies but a great deal to rhetoric. He had eloquence enough and a ready tongue, particularly when he had to accuse someone. Words and thoughts came to him when he was angry as did the ability to enunciate clearly and to project his voice. This made him too excited to stand still and enabled people to hear him from a long way off. [53.2] When he began to argue a case, he would threaten to "draw the weapon honed by his nighttime labors." He was so contemptuous of writing that was too smooth and polished that he said of Seneca, then at the height of his popularity, that he composed "mere exercises" and that he was like "sand without lime." He would write rebuttals to successful legal arguments made by orators and compose accusations and defenses in important cases being tried before the senate. According to where his pen wandered, his opinion brought the weight of the law down on the defendant or relieved him of its burden. He also summoned the equestrian order by edict to come listen to him expound.

[54.1] But Gaius pursued all kinds of other studies with great enthusiasm. He trained as a Thracian gladiator, a chariot driver, and even a singer and a dancer. He sparred with real weapons, drove his chariot in the circuses that had been built in many parts of the city, and was so transported by the pleasure of singing and dancing that even at public entertainments he could not refrain from singing along with the tragic actor on the stage and imitating the gestures of the mime. It was as though he were approving or correcting the performance as everyone watched. [54.2] The only reason he proclaimed an all-night festival on the day he died seems to have been to create the opportunity for himself to make his stage debut under the license that that hour allowed. Sometimes he danced at night, too. He once summoned three men of consular rank to the Palatine in the second watch and positioned them where they could see the stage. They were terrified and expected the worst. Then, with a loud racket of flutes and clappers, out sprang Gaius, dressed in a cloak and a tunic that reached his ankles. He performed his dance and left the stage. But for all his mastery of other skills, he did not know how to swim.

[55.1] Gaius showed irrational preference toward all his favorites. He would kiss Mnester even during performances, and if anyone made even the least bit of noise when the mime was dancing, he ordered the offender dragged off and beat him personally. When a knight was causing trouble, Gaius had a centurion instruct him to go to Ostia at once and then deliver a written message from himself to King Ptolemy in Mauretania. This was the message: "If I have sent someone to you, do nothing to him either good or bad."[98] [55.2] He put Thracian gladiators in charge of his German bodyguards and reduced the armor of the *murmillones*. He put poison on the wound of a slightly injured gladiator whose name was Columbus, despite the fact that he had won his fight, and after that he called the poison columbinum. It was found, without question, among other poisons, so labeled in Gaius' own handwriting. Gaius was so slavishly devoted to the Green faction that he dined often in their clubhouse and then spent the night. At one wild victory party, he gave his driver Eutychus, among other gifts, 2 million sesterces. [55.3] As for his horse Incitatus, he routinely had soldiers enforce silence in the neighborhood the day before a race so that the animal would not be disturbed. In addition to a marble stable and an ivory stall, as well as purple saddlecloths and collars studded with precious stones, he gave the horse a house, slaves, and furniture so that guests invited in his name would be received more elegantly. And it is said that he intended to name him to the consulship.

[56.1] While Gaius was behaving in this wild and violent manner, a number of people found the courage to mount an attack against

---

98. A mean joke on the knight who assumed he was carrying his own death sentence.

him. But after one or two plots had been detected and others put on hold because opportunity had not presented itself, two men joined in a conspiracy that succeeded with the help of Gaius' most important freedmen and the praetorian prefects. The latter joined the plot because they knew that the emperor suspected and despised them. They had been accused, wrongly, of being party to a conspiracy, and Gaius had quickly singled them out and created a great deal of animosity toward them when he drew his sword and declared, "I will take my own life if you too think that I deserve to die." From then on, he never stopped accusing each of them to the other and pitting them against one another.

[56.2] When it was decided to strike Gaius at the Palatine Games[99] as he left his seat for the midday break, Cassius Chaerea, tribune of a praetorian cohort, insisted on the leading role for himself. Gaius had been in the habit of disparaging Chaerea with all sorts of insults, calling him a man too old for military service and weak and effeminate. Sometimes when Chaerea asked for the watchword of the day, the emperor gave him "Priapus" or "Venus." And sometimes when Chaerea was expressing his thanks for something, Gaius made his hand into an obscene gesture, waved it around, and offered it to be kissed.

[57.1] Many omens anticipated the coming murder. The statue of Jupiter at Olympia, which Gaius had decided to have disassembled and taken to Rome, suddenly laughed so loudly that the scaffolding collapsed and the workmen ran away. At that very moment, a man named Cassius arrived on the scene, claiming that he had been ordered in a dream to sacrifice a bull to Jupiter. [57.2] On the Ides of March lightning struck both the temple of Jupiter on the Capitol at Capua and the chamber of the palace steward on the Palatine. Some interpreted the second of these portents as a sign that danger would come to their master from those who protected him, and the first as indicating that the murder of another important person would take place like the one that had taken place on that day in the past. Also, when Gaius consulted the astrologer Sulla about his horoscope, he learned that certain death was imminent. [57.3] The oracle at the temple of Fortune at Antium warned him to beware of Cassius, and

---

99. Held on the Palatine Hill in honor of the Divine Augustus; they traditionally began on January 17 and lasted for five days; Gaius may have added three more.

so he had Cassius Longinus, the proconsul serving in Asia at that time, killed; he forgot that Chaerea was also named Cassius. On the day before he died, he dreamed that he stood in heaven next to the throne of Jupiter and that the god kicked him with the big toe of his right foot and he fell headlong to the earth. Things that had chanced to happen a little earlier on the day itself were also thought omens. [57.4] When Gaius was sacrificing he was sprayed with the blood of a flamingo. The mime Mnester danced the tragedy that the tragic actor Neoptolemus had acted long ago at the games when King Philip of Macedon was killed. At a performance of the pantomime "Laureolus," the lead actor fell and vomited blood as he rushed off the stage; many of the supporting actors competed to display their skill, and the stage was covered with blood. An entertainment was being made ready for that night, in which Egyptians and Ethiopians were to present the story of the gods of the lower world.

[58.1] On the ninth day before the Kalends of February, at about the seventh hour,[100] Gaius left the games. He had hesitated about getting up and going to lunch since his stomach remained unsettled from too much food the day before. But at last, at the urging of his friends, he left. In the covered way through which he had to pass, he encountered some boys of noble birth who had been brought from Asia to perform on the stage. They were getting ready to go on, and he stopped to watch them and to wish them well. If the leader of the troop had not said that he was feeling cold, Gaius would have gone back and had them presented on stage at once.

[58.2] From this point on, there are two versions of the story: some report that while Gaius was talking with the boys, Chaerea slashed his neck from behind with a violent blow of his sword, first shouting, "Do it!"[101] Then the tribune Cornelius Sabinus, the other conspirator, stabbed him in the chest from the front. Others report that Sabinus first got Gaius away from the crowd with the help of centurions who were in on the plot and then asked him for the watchword in conformance with military protocol. When Gaius gave "Jupiter," Chaerea shouted, "Take it back!"[102] The emperor looked

---

100. The early afternoon of January 24, 41 CE.

101. His words, *Hoc age*, were those of a priest ordering a sacrifice to begin; see *Gal.* 20.1.

102. *Accipe ratum!* Gaius will get his watchword back; Jupiter will punish him.

around, and Chaerea sliced through his jaw with a thrust of his sword. [58.3] The rest of the praetorians finished the job, inflicting thirty wounds on him as he lay on the ground with his limbs drawn up to protect himself as he cried out, "I am alive." The watchword for all of them was, "Again!" Some even drove their swords into his genitals. At the first sign of a disturbance, Gaius' litter-bearers came running, bringing their poles for weapons. Then came his German bodyguards, who killed some of the assassins and some innocent senators as well.

[59] Gaius lived twenty-nine years and was emperor for three years, ten months, and eight days. His body was taken secretly to the Lamian gardens, and it was partially burned on an improvised funeral pyre there and buried in a shallow grave. Later, when his sisters returned from exile, they had it dug up, cremated, and properly buried. All agree that before this took place, ghosts disturbed the sleep of the garden's guards, and in the house in which he had lain dead, no night passed without the appearance of something terrible until the house itself burned down. Gaius' wife Caesonia perished with him. She was stabbed by a centurion's sword, and their daughter was dashed against a wall.

[60] Events that followed may also be able to give an idea of the atmosphere in Rome at that time. When news of the murder circulated, it was not immediately believed, and a suspicion arose that Gaius himself had invented the rumor that he had been killed and had spread it abroad so as to learn by this ruse what people thought of him. The conspirators had not fixed on the principate for anyone, and the senate was so united in declaring its independence that when the consuls convened the first meeting, it was not in the senate house (the building was called the Curia Julia) but on the Capitoline. Some of the senators expressed the opinion that the memory of the Caesars should be erased and their temples destroyed. It was thought especially significant and so noted that all the Caesars who had the first name Gaius had perished by the sword, beginning with one killed in the time of Cinna.

THE DIVINE CLAUDIUS

10 BCE–54 CE
Emperor 41–54 CE

Tiberius Claudius Nero Germanicus was the only one of the early emperors who was not a member of the Julian family either by birth or by adoption. He remained a Claudian. The brother of Germanicus, he came to power unexpectedly and more or less by default after the death of his nephew Gaius (Caligula). From birth, Claudius had suffered from what was evidently a mild degree of cerebral palsy, permanent neurological damage, and as a consequence he was marginalized within his family. He was never intended to play an important role in the dynasty.

Although Claudius had been denied an opportunity to participate in important public affairs, he had observed the operation of Rome's government and taken a keen interest in history. He may indeed have thought a partnership between emperor and senate possible. But as it happened, during his reign power became centralized to the court by accretion through numerous individual measures. His reign of thirteen years began seventy years after the inception of single rule under his great-uncle Augustus. The length of time that he was emperor did much to confirm the principate as an established entity at this point. His single most notable achievement was the addition of a part of Britain to the empire.

A body of sober administration is reported for his reign, but Claudius' reputation was that of an ineffective and oddly detached fool, the instrument of his domineering wives and his powerful freedmen. He was also thought a bloodthirsty tyrant. Suetonius associates him with the qualities of stupidity and cruelty, a dangerous combination. Claudius' cruelty was no doubt related to the insecurity that lingered after his irregular accession to the principate. And since he was a relatively old man when he became emperor, the tension created by the never resolved problem of the succession plagued him from the beginning. After he died, he was declared a god. Claudius' legacy was mixed.

Suetonius opens his life of Claudius with a short biography of Claudius' father Drusus the Elder, just as he opened the life of Gaius with a short biography of Germanicus.

[1.1] The father of Claudius Caesar was Drusus, whose first name had originally been Decimus but later became Nero.[1] There was speculation that he had been conceived in adultery and that his stepfather was really his father, since Livia was married to Augustus when she was pregnant and gave birth less than three months later.[2] In any case, this verse soon made the rounds: "to the lucky are three-month children born."

[1.2] As quaestor and praetor, Drusus commanded the army in the war against Raetia and then against Germany, and he was the first of the Roman generals to sail out onto the northern ocean. He also built a canal (still called the Drusian canal today) on the far side of the Rhine, a project completed after a tremendous amount of hard work. He never stopped trying to hunt down the enemy, even after many of them had suffered heavy casualties and been driven deep into uninhabited wastes, not until the apparition of a barbarian woman, larger than life and speaking to him in Latin, stopped him from pushing conquest further. [1.3] These successes earned him the right to celebrate an ovation and to merit triumphal regalia. As soon as his praetorship had ended, he became consul and resumed military operations. He died in his legions' summer camp, a place that has been called "Accursed" ever since. His body was taken up by the leading men of the towns and colonies and then met by the guilds of public secretaries, carried on to Rome, and buried in the Campus Martius. But the army raised a cenotaph to him, around which the soldiers were to make a ceremonial run on a prescribed day every year thereafter and where the Gallic states were to offer formal sacrifices. The senate also voted to him a marble arch capped by trophies on the Appian Way, among many other honors, and the cognomen Germanicus for him and his descendants.

[1.4] It is believed that he was as eager for glory as he was to behave like an ordinary citizen. In addition to defeating the enemy, he tried to win the opposing commander's armor and often chased the German chieftains over the entire battlefield at great personal

---

1. Nero Claudius Drusus (Drusus the Elder).

2. Drusus was born in 38 BCE. His father was Livia's former husband, Tiberius Claudius Nero; Augustus was his stepfather. See *Aug.* 62.2, *Tib.* 4.3.

risk.³ At the same time, he never pretended to conceal the fact that
he would restore Rome's earlier constitution if ever he could. For
these reasons, I think, some have dared to write that Augustus was
suspicious of him and recalled him from his province and that when
Drusus hesitated, he had him poisoned. [1.5] But I take exception
to this explanation and have included it here more to be thorough
than because I think it true or plausible. Augustus was so fond of
Drusus when he was alive that he always named him in his wills as
co-heir along with his sons⁴ and declared this once in the senate.
After Drusus was dead, Augustus praised him so effusively before
the assembly that he prayed thus to the gods: "May you make my
young Caesars like him. And when my time comes, give me a death
as filled with honor as the one that you have given him." Not satisfied with inscribing on his tomb a verse epitaph that he had written
himself, he also wrote a prose remembrance of his life.

[1.6] Drusus had a number of children with Antonia Minor,
but only three survived him: Germanicus, Livilla, and Claudius.
[2.1] Claudius was born on the Kalends of August in the consulship of Iullus Antonius and Fabius Africanus at Lugdunum on the
very day that the altar to Augustus was dedicated there for the first
time.⁵ He was named Tiberius Claudius Drusus. Later, when his
elder brother was adopted into the Julian family,⁶ he took the cognomen Germanicus. He lost his father when he was an infant and
suffered from a variety of chronic illnesses throughout most of his
childhood and youth. As a result, both mind and body were weak,
and even when he reached the appropriate age he was thought unfit
for any kind of public or private service. [2.2] For a long time, even
after he had legally become an adult, he had a guardian and remained
in the care of a tutor. In one of his writings Claudius complained

3. The most significant trophy (*spolia opima*) was the armor of the opposing
general taken in hand-to-hand combat by the general in command. Drusus
was ineligible because he served at the pleasure of Augustus. Trying to win
the spoils labeled him ambitious.

4. His grandsons Gaius and Lucius Caesar, whom he adopted; see *Aug.*
64.1.

5. August 1, 10 BCE, at modern Lyon. The Altar of Rome and Augustus
became a cult center for Gauls in the area.

6. In 4 CE, Augustus adopted Tiberius and Tiberius adopted Germanicus.
See *Tib.* 15.2, *Cal.* 4.

that this man, a barbarian who had once supervised mule drivers, had been assigned to him on purpose to punish him as harshly as possible on any excuse. Because of his poor health (noted above), he presided at a gladiatorial contest that he was sponsoring with his brother wrapped in a cloak, an unheard-of manner of dress, and on the day that he received the toga of manhood he was taken to the Capitoline in a litter around midnight and without proper ceremony. [3.1] But he paid serious attention to liberal studies from an early age and frequently offered his accomplishments in each subject to the public. Not even this could gain him respect or make his hopes for the future more promising.

[3.2] Claudius' mother Antonia used to say that he was a "monster of a human being, not finished by nature, only just begun." And if she charged anyone with being slow-witted, she would say, "He is dumber than my son Claudius." His grandmother Augusta[7] always treated him as something wholly contemptible and was in the habit of speaking to him only infrequently and telling him what to do only in short, unpleasant written messages or through intermediaries. His sister Livilla, when she heard that he would someday rule, prayed loudly for all to hear that the Roman people would be spared a fate so unjust and so undeserved. As for his great-uncle Augustus, I have appended excerpts from his letters so that what he thought about Claudius, good or bad, is better understood:

> [4.1] I have spoken with Tiberius because you, my dear Livia, have asked me what we must do with your grandson Tiberius at the Games of Mars.[8] We both agree that we must settle once and for all what course to follow in his case. For if he is of sound mind (and in a manner of speaking, "completely whole"), why should we hesitate to advance him through the same steps and grades through which his brother has been advanced? [4.2] But if, on the other hand, we feel that he is impaired and lacks soundness in body and mind, we must not provide men who mock and sneer at such things with the chance to laugh at him and at us. For we shall always be in a stew if we make decisions about each individual case, if we do not decide beforehand whether we think him able to enter office or not. [4.3] But as to the matters of the moment about which you seek my opinion, it is accept-

---

7. Livia.

8. The first Tiberius named is the future emperor; the second is Claudius. The Games of Mars were celebrated in the spring of 12 CE.

able to us for him to preside over the priests' table at the Games of
Mars—provided he allows himself to be monitored by Silvanus' son,
who is related to him by marriage;[9] Silvanus will keep him from
doing anything that will be noticed and subject to laughter. It is not
acceptable to us for him to watch the Circus games from the *pulvinar*,
for he will be conspicuous and in plain sight in the very front of the
spectator seats. It is not acceptable to us for him to go to the Alban
Mount or to remain in Rome during the Latin festival.[10] For why is
he not city prefect if he can follow his brother to the Mount? [4.4] You
know our thinking, dear Livia; we want a decision about the entire
issue once and for all so that we are not always being tossed about
between hope and anxiety. You may, if you wish, give this portion of
the letter to our dear Antonia to read.

Again, in a second letter:[11]

[4.5] I shall certainly invite young Tiberius to dinner every day while
you are away to keep him from dining alone with his friends Sulpicius
and Athenodorus. I wish that he would use greater care and be less
thoughtless when he chooses a companion to imitate with his movement and carriage and gait. The poor little fellow is a sad case, for in
serious matters, when his concentration does not wander, the nobility
of his mind is clear enough.

And also in a third letter:

[4.6] I'll be damned, dear Livia, if I'm not amazed that I could enjoy
the declaiming of your grandson. I do not see how one who speaks
so incomprehensibly can say what has to be said so clearly when he
declaims.

[4.7] But there is no doubt what Augustus later decided. He presented Claudius with no distinction but that of an augural priesthood and named him an heir only of a sixth portion in the third

---

9. Claudius was married to Plautia Urgulanilla at that time; see 26.2. His
brother-in-law was Marcus Plautius Silvanus.

10. The annual festival included a procession to the highest summit of
the Alban Hills, not far from Rome. Because all of the magistrates took
part, someone had to be left in charge of the city. Claudius was the obvious choice, and so it would be an embarrassment if he remained in Rome
without the appointment.

11. The letter is evidently to Livia.

degree,[12] alongside those who were almost strangers, and he furnished him with a legacy of only 800,000 sesterces.

[5] Tiberius, Claudius' paternal uncle, gave him the consular regalia when he asked permission to stand for office. When Claudius pressed harder for real distinctions, Tiberius responded with an official communication that said merely, "I have sent you forty gold pieces for the Saturnalia and the Sigillaria." At that point Claudius finally abandoned all hope for the career due him and withdrew into private life. He hid himself away, sometimes in his gardens and his country house, other times in retreat to Campania. And because his friends were the lowest of reprobates, he was charged with drunkenness and dicing—in addition to his long-held reputation for uselessness. But during this period, even when he behaved like this, he always received proper courtesy from individuals and official respect.

[6.1] The equestrian order twice chose him to act as their patron and to present petitions on their behalf: first when they asked the consuls for permission to carry the body of Augustus to Rome on their shoulders, and a second time when they congratulated the consuls on the overthrow of Sejanus.[13] It was their practice to rise and remove their cloaks when Claudius entered the games.[14] [6.2] The senate too voted that he become a priest of Augustus by special appointment, although these priests were normally chosen by lot, and then, when his house burned, they voted that it be rebuilt for him at public expense and that he have the privilege of expressing his opinion among the senators who had served as consuls. This last vote was rescinded when Tiberius made Claudius' feeble mental capacity an excuse and promised that he would make good the loss of the house through his own generosity. When Tiberius died, he named Claudius among his heirs as the recipient of a third portion of his estate in the third degree,[15] but he did provide him with a legacy of about 2 million sesterces, and he recommended him to the attention of the armies and the senate and the Roman people, mentioning him by name among his other relatives.

---

12. A will named a second level of heirs in case the first were unable to inherit and a third level in case those in the second were disqualified.

13. Tiberius' powerful praetorian prefect; see *Tib.* 55.

14. This action left their togas uncovered.

15. Like Augustus; see 4.7.

[7] Under Gaius, his brother's son, Claudius finally entered political office and was consul with him for two months. (Gaius courted
favor in every way he could at the beginning of his reign so as to gain
a favorable reputation.) And it happened that when Claudius went
into the Forum with the *fasces* for the first time, an eagle flew past
and landed on his right shoulder. He drew by lot a second consulship
four years later. He sometimes took Gaius' place presiding at the
games, and some of the people shouted, "Good luck to the emperor's
uncle!" and others, "Good luck to Germanicus' brother!" [8] But he
still had to endure insults. If he turned up a little late for the time
set for dinner, he was grudgingly given a place at the table but only
after making a circuit of the dining room. And whenever he dozed
off after eating (it often happened), he was bombarded with olive and
date pits. Sometimes the jokesters in the court entertained themselves by waking him up with a rod or a whip, and they routinely put
slippers on his hands when he was snoring so that when he awoke
suddenly, he would rub his face with them.

[9.1] He also found himself in real danger. The first threat came
when he was consul and came close to being removed from office
because he had been too slow in contracting for statues of Caesar's
brothers Nero and Drusus and for having them set up. Then he had
to defend himself in legal proceedings initiated by a stranger, or
worse, by a member of his own household, in which he was repeatedly charged with a variety of offenses. And when the conspiracy
of Lepidus and Gaetulicus was uncovered,[16] he, along with other
envoys, was sent to Germany to congratulate the emperor; he faced a
life-threatening situation, for a furious Gaius took offense, contending that his uncle had been intentionally sent to keep him in line
as if he were a young boy. Some say that as a result he was thrown
headlong into the river, just as he was, fully clothed. [9.2] And from
that time on he was always the last of the consulars to speak in the
senate, insulted by being called on after everyone else. The court
agreed to hear a case that involved a forged will to which he was himself a signatory. And finally, after he had been forced to pay 8 million
sesterces for the right to be admitted into the new priesthood,[17] his
personal finances became so straitened that when he was unable to

16. See *Cal.* 24.3.
17. A priest of the cult that Gaius allegedly established for himself; see
Cal. 22.3.

discharge his debt to the state treasury, the prefects posted notice of his property for sale without condition under provision of the law governing the sale of state securities.[18] [10.1] After passing most of his life under these and similar conditions, Claudius acceded to the principate in his fiftieth year as the result of a truly remarkable circumstance:

After the assassins lying in wait for Gaius had shut out Claudius along with the others when they moved the crowd away,[19] claiming that the emperor wanted to be alone, Claudius withdrew to a place in the palace called the Hermaeum. He soon grew terrified by the report that people were being killed, and he crept away to a nearby balcony and concealed himself in the curtains covering the door. [10.2] An ordinary soldier who happened to run past his hiding place noticed his feet and wanted to find out who he was. He recognized him and pulled him out, and as Claudius fell to his knees before him in fear, he saluted him as *imperator*. Then he brought him to the other soldiers who were merely grumbling, at a loss as to what to do. They put Claudius in a litter, and since his own bearers had run off, they took turns carrying him to the camp[20] on their shoulders. He was wretched and afraid, and everyone in the crowd that they met on the way pitied him because they thought that an innocent man was being hurried off to execution.

[10.3] After reaching the camp, he spent the night under military guard with much less hope for the future than confidence in his present situation. This was because the consuls, together with the senate and the urban cohorts,[21] had taken possession of the Forum and the Capitoline and were at the point of proclaiming freedom for all. When the tribunes summoned Claudius to the senate meeting so that he could advise them of what seemed best, he replied, "I am being held under forcible constraint." [10.4] But the next day, since the senators were quarreling tediously and at loggerheads with one another and as a consequence moving too slowly to accomplish their

---

18. The state was a moneylender, and Claudius had pledged property. But it would have been praetors who posted the notice. For Claudius' rearrangement of this responsibility, see 24.2.

19. See *Cal.* 58.1.

20. The camp of the praetorian guard located just outside the wall of Rome. See *Tib.* 37.1.

21. A city police force first organized by Augustus.

goals, and since the large numbers of urban cohorts surrounding them were by now demanding a single ruler and calling for Claudius by name, he permitted the assembly of armed praetorians to swear their allegiance to him, and he promised each of them 15,000 sesterces. He was the first of the Caesars to cement the military's loyalty with the payment of money.

[11.1] Once Claudius' power was firmly established, he considered nothing more important than erasing from memory the two-day period of indecision about changing Rome's government. And so he ordered pardon for everything that had been said and done during that interval and amnesty for all time to come. And he kept his word; of the men who conspired against Gaius, he executed only the tribunes and a few of the centurions as an example, because he learned that they had insisted on killing him as well. [11.2] He then turned to obligations of family. There was no oath that he took more seriously or used more frequently than "by Augustus." With regard to his grandmother Livia, he made sure that divine honors were voted to her and that she had a chariot for the Circus procession, one drawn by elephants like the one Augustus had had. For his parents there were state-sponsored commemorative rites, and over and above these, for his father, games in the Circus every year on his birthday, and for his mother, a ceremonial carriage on which her image was paraded around the Circus and the cognomen Augusta, a name that she had refused when she was alive. In memory of his brother, whom he honored at every opportunity, he produced a Greek comedy at the competition at Naples[22] and awarded it the prize as the judges had determined proper. [11.3] Not even Mark Antony did he leave without honor or grateful mention; on one occasion he issued an edict stating that he was all the more eager to hold an extravagant celebration for his father's birthday because it was the same as that of his grandfather Antony. For Tiberius he completed work on the marble arch next to the theater of Pompey that was voted to him by the senate but left unfinished. And although he revoked all of Gaius' official acts, he nonetheless kept the day of his death from being listed among days of celebration, even though it marked the beginning of his own principate.

---

22. Greek games founded in honor of Augustus. Germanicus wrote Greek comedies; see *Cal.* 3.2.

[12.1] But when it came to increasing the respect due himself, Claudius was restrained and unassuming. He refrained from using *imperator* as his first name;[23] he refused excessive honors; he let pass in silence his daughter's betrothal and his grandson's birth, marking the events with family celebration only. He brought back none of the exiles without senate approval. He asked—as if for a favor—its consent in bringing the praetorian prefect and military tribunes into the senate house with him and its stamp of approval on judicial rulings made by his procurators. [12.2] He requested from the consuls the right to hold a market on his private estates. He was often present as an adviser when the magistrates held hearings, and when they sponsored games, he too rose to his feet and honored them with his shouts and applause together with the crowd. He apologized to the tribunes because he could not hear them in the crowded space unless they stood when they approached him on the tribunal. [12.3] By these actions he quickly acquired such devotion and goodwill that when the report came that he had been ambushed and killed on his way to Ostia, the populace was deeply distressed and did not stop abusing the soldiers, calling them traitors, and the senate, calling them murderers and threatening and cursing them, until the magistrates brought first one or two and later more men to the rostra to swear that he was safe and on his way back.

[13.1] Yet Claudius was never immune from plots. He was set upon by individuals and by a faction and most seriously in civil war. A man of the lower class was caught near his bedchamber with a dagger, and two equestrians were apprehended lying in wait for him in public. One of them planned to attack him with a stiletto when he left the theater and the other with a hunting knife when he was sacrificing at the temple of Mars. [13.2] Gallus Asinius and Statilius Corvinus, grandsons of the orators Pollio and Messalla,[24] plotted revolution with the complicity of a number of Claudius' own freedmen and slaves. Furius Camillus Scribonianus, commander in Dalmatia, started a civil war, but within five days the legions that had transferred their allegiance to him ended it after a divine warning made them change their minds. When they were ordered to march to the camp of their new commander in chief, by chance (that is, by

23. Julius Caesar had; see *Jul.* 76.1.
24. Gaius Asinius Pollio and Marcus Valerius Messalla Corvinus were orators in the late Republic and the early empire. See *Jul.* 30.4, *Aug.* 58.1–2.

a sign from heaven) the decorations fell from the legion's eagle and the standards could not be pulled from the ground and taken with them.

[14] Claudius held the consulship four times in addition to the earlier one he had held with Gaius. The first two were in sequential years, the following two after intervals of four years. The last he held for half a year, the others for periods of two months. With the third he set a precedent for an emperor, serving as suffect consul in place of a consul who died.

He was very energetic in administering justice both when he was consul and when he was not a magistrate. He presided even on private days of celebration for himself and his family and sometimes on long-established feast days and on days of ill omen as well. He did not always follow the provisions of the law but moderated the severity and leniency of many as he was influenced by what seemed right and just. He reopened the right to sue to those who had lost their cases in the civil courts because they had asked for too much,[25] and he handed down punishments that exceeded the customary when he condemned to the beasts people convicted of serious crime.[26]

[15.1] Claudius was strangely inconsistent when he heard cases and rendered judgments, now careful and incisive, sometimes thoughtless and hasty, on occasion silly and outlandish. A man presented himself to him when he was revising the jury rolls and pretended that he did not have the exemption that his children entitled him to;[27] Claudius dismissed him on the grounds that he was too eager to serve as a juror. Another man had initiated a lawsuit, and his adversaries had opened proceedings against him when he claimed that his case was not a matter for a special hearing but for the regular courts. Claudius made the man plead his case before him at once, saying, "In dealing with your own affair you will provide evidence of how fair a juror you will be with someone else's."[28]

---

25. In a civil case, judge, plaintiff, and defendant agreed to the amount claimed ahead of time. The plaintiff received that sum or nothing; if he lost, he could not continue to sue trying for a lower amount each time.

26. To be killed by wild animals in the arena.

27. The father of three legitimate children was exempt from jury duty.

28. The emperor could hold his own hearing outside of the regular courts. Claudius maneuvered this reluctant juror into a position of proving himself competent.

[15.2] There was a woman who was not acknowledging her son as her own. Since the testimony of neither seemed credible, Claudius forced her to confess by ordering her to marry the young man. When parties to suits did not appear in court, he decided quite arbitrarily in favor of those present, making no distinction as to whether their opponents had failed to appear on purpose or for some good reason. When someone shouted that a forger's hands should be cut off, Claudius insisted on sending immediately for the executioner with his cleaver and butcher's block. In a case involving a man accused of presuming Roman citizenship, a trivial argument arose among the advocates as to whether the defendant should make his case wearing a toga or a Greek cloak. To show that he was completely impartial, Claudius ordered him to change clothes frequently, accordingly as he was accused or defended. [15.3] And in one case he is thought to have read this pronouncement from a prepared tablet: "I vote in favor of those who have told the truth."

By these actions, Claudius' stature was diminished to the point that he was everywhere and openly an object of contempt. A man who was making excuses for the absence of a witness whom the emperor had summoned from a province said that the witness could not appear, but he hedged about the reason for a long time. Finally, after much questioning, he said, "He has died. That, I think, is allowed." Another man thanked him because he had permitted an accused man to be defended, and the man added, "But after all, that is the usual procedure." I used to hear from my elders that the courtroom lawyers were so in the habit of taking advantage of his tolerance that when he left the tribunal they not only called him back verbally but even detained him by holding on to the hem of his toga and sometimes grabbing hold of his foot. [15.4] And if anyone finds these stories unbelievable, an unimportant Greek litigant let this slip in an argument in court: "Go to hell! You are a foolish old man!"[29] Everyone knows about the Roman knight who was accused of obscene acts toward women, a false charge that his powerful enemies had invented. When the man saw that prostitutes were being called to witness against him and that the court was accepting their testimony, he threw the stylus and tablets that he was holding in Claudius' face so hard that they scraped his cheek badly. And he berated him in a loud voice for his stupidity and cruelty.

---

29. For the exclamation, see note on *Jul.* 82.2.

[16.1] Claudius also held the censorship, an office that had lapsed for a long time, ever since Plancus and Paulus had served.[30] But its duties he also performed erratically, inconsistent in both his guiding principles and specific judgments. When he was reviewing the equestrian order,[31] he dismissed without censure a deeply disgraced young man whose father insisted that he found him totally acceptable, saying, "He has his own censor." Another man, notorious for seducing unmarried and married women alike, he merely cautioned, "Indulge your youth less often or at least more carefully," and added, "Why, pray, should I know who your girlfriend is?" And when he removed the mark of disgrace next to a name at the request of the man's friends, he said, "But let the erasure stand." [16.2] He not only expunged from the juror list an eminent man, a leader from the province of Greece, who did not know Latin; he reduced him to alien status as well. Nor did he permit anyone to render an account of his own life except, as best he could, in his own words, without the help of an advocate. And he found new grounds on which to give marks of disgrace to many, to some who did not expect that treatment, men who had left Italy without his knowledge and without being granted a leave of absence. He degraded one man in particular because he had been companion to a king in his province, citing as precedent the charge of treason laid before the court in an earlier age against Rabirius Postumus, who had followed Ptolemy to Alexandria to keep an eye on a loan.[32]

[16.3] When he tried to demote more men than he legitimately could, he discovered that most were innocent; his investigators had done very careless work, but his own role was even more discreditable. Those whom he charged with bachelorhood, childlessness, and poverty proved that they were husbands, fathers, and wealthy men. And one man alleged to have done violence to himself with his sword took off his clothes and showed his unscathed body. [16.4] These other actions during his censorship are also worth remarking: He

---

30. Lucius Munatius Plancus and Lucius Aemilius Paulus were censors in 23 BCE; see *Aug.* 7.2, 16.3. Claudius was censor in 47 and 48 CE.

31. To determine if a man's wealth and character qualified him for equestrian rank; see *Aug.* 38.3–39, *Cal.* 16.2.

32. When Ptolemy Auletes returned to his throne in Egypt in 58 BCE, the banker Gaius Rabirius Postumus, who had lent him money, returned with him.

ordered a light carriage sumptuously decorated with silver and for sale in the Sigillaria to be purchased and destroyed in his presence. He published twenty edicts on a single day, these two among them: in one he advised that wine jars be well caulked with pitch in anticipation of a plentiful grape harvest, and in another he imparted the information that there was nothing more effective against snake bite than the sap of a yew tree.

[17.1] He undertook only one military operation and that was of limited scope. When the senate voted triumphal regalia to him,[33] he thought the honor unbefitting the grandeur of an emperor and wanted the glory of a true triumph. To win one, he chose Britain as his field of action because no one had tried to conquer it since the Divine Julius and because it was currently in turmoil over fugitives who had not been repatriated.[34] [17.2] When Claudius sailed for Britain from Ostia, fierce storms twice almost sank his ship; he met one storm off the coast of Liguria and a second near the Stoechades Islands. That was why he journeyed over land from Massilia to Gesoriacum and from there crossed the Channel.[35] A part of the island surrendered within a few days without any fighting or bloodshed, and he returned to Rome less than six months after he had left and celebrated an extravagant triumph. [17.3] He allowed not only the provincial governors but even some exiles to travel to the city for the celebration. And along with spoils taken from the enemy he affixed the naval crown next to the civic crown on the pediment of his house on the Palatine, a marker that he had crossed the ocean and (in a manner of speaking) conquered it. His wife Messallina followed his triumphal chariot in a ceremonial carriage, as did those who had received triumphal regalia for their participation in the war; others followed on foot in civilian dress. Marcus Crassus Frugi rode on a horse decked out with military trappings

---

33. For the Roman victory in Mauretania that probably took place at the end of Gaius' reign rather than at the beginning of Claudius'.

34. Caesar invaded Britain in 55 and 54 BCE; see *Jul.* 25.2. Troubles sometimes spilled across the Channel, and fugitives may have petitioned Rome for help; see *Cal.* 44.2. Claudius' invasion took place in 43 CE.

35. Liguria was northwest Italy. The Stoechades are off the coast of France, east of Massilia (modern Marseilles). Gesoriacum was on the Channel coast.

and wore a tunic embroidered with palm trees because he had this honor a second time.[36]

[18.1] Claudius was always painstaking in his care for the city and conscientious in the responsibility he took for the grain supply. When the quarter of the city called the Aemiliana burned in a stubborn fire, he spent two nights in the Diribitorium,[37] and when the numbers of soldiers and slaves proved insufficient to control the blaze, he asked the magistrates to summon ordinary citizens from all the neighborhoods. Setting baskets of money in front of himself, he urged them to help and paid each on the spot the money due for his labor. [18.2] Once when a succession of bad harvests made the grain supply inadequate, a mob trapped him in the middle of the Forum and threatened him, mocking him and throwing pieces of bread at him at the same time. It was only with difficulty that he could slip out the back way and escape to the Palatine. He devised every scheme he could to bring in provisions, even in wintertime,[38] and he went so far as to guarantee profits to traders, promising to indemnify their loss if storms wrecked any of their ships. He created important benefits for those who built merchant ships, benefits appropriate to the status of each: [19] for a citizen, exemption from the *lex Papia Poppaea*; for someone of Latin standing, full citizenship; for women, the rights of those with four children.[39] These provisions are still in effect today.

[20.1] Claudius completed public works that were important and necessary rather than numerous, in particular these: an aqueduct begun by Gaius, the draining of Lake Fucinus, and the construction of a harbor at Ostia. He took on these projects even though he knew that Augustus had refused to attempt the second one, despite the fact that the Marsi pleaded with him again and again to do it.[40] He knew, too, that the Divine Julius had quite often proposed the third but had abandoned the idea as too difficult. Claudius brought the

---

36. Marcus Licinius Crassus Frugi was the father of Claudius' son-in-law Pompeius Magnus; see 27.2. His first triumphal honors were probably in connection with the war in Mauretania; see note on 17.1.

37. The large building in which electoral votes were counted.

38. Bad weather normally precluded shipping in the winter.

39. Women with four children were released from guardianship and could dispose of their property as they chose.

40. See *Jul.* 44.3; also *Cl.* 21.6, 32. The Marsi lived near the lake.

abundant cold waters of the aqueduct called *aqua Claudia* (one of its
sources was the Caeruleus, the other the Curtius or Albudignus) into
the city across a stone structure and also the water of the aqueduct
called *novus Anio*, and he made them flow together into a large number of beautifully decorated basins.[41] [20.2] He undertook the Lake
Fucinus project in the hope of profit as much as praise, since there
were people who contracted to drain the lake at their own expense
if the exposed land were given to them. A canal three miles long was
partly tunneled and partly cut through a mountain. Even though
thirty thousand men worked on it continuously without stopping,
it took eleven years of great effort to finish it. [20.3] He built the
harbor at Ostia by extending breakwaters that curved around to the
right and left and by placing an obstacle across the entrance where
the deep water began. To anchor this structure more firmly, he first
sank the ship that had brought the huge obelisk from Egypt[42] and
then set up a very tall tower modeled on the Pharos at Alexandria on
piles driven close together. This was so that ships could direct their
course by its fires that shone at night.[43]

[21.1] Claudius distributed money gifts to the populace quite
often, and he produced a number of splendid entertainments as
well—not only those of the usual kind in the customary places but
also some invented for the occasion or revived from ancient times,
and, in addition, at sites where no one had staged them before. He
sat on a raised platform in the orchestra to open the games that
celebrated the dedication of the theater of Pompey, which he had
restored after it had burned. But first he made offerings to the gods
at the shrines at the top of the theater and came down through the
middle of the seats as everyone sat in silence. [21.2] He also produced
Secular Games[44] on the rationale that Augustus had given them
too early and had not waited for their proper time—this despite the

---

41. Their sources were in the hills east of the city.

42. Gaius brought an obelisk to Rome on an oversized ship built for the
purpose.

43. The Pharos was a lighthouse that guided ships into the harbor at
Alexandria. Its name almost came to mean "lighthouse," and it occurs with
that meaning at *Tib.* 74, *Cal.* 46.

44. Augustus held them in 17 BCE (*Aug.* 31.4) and Domitian in 88 CE
(*Dom.* 4.3).

The Divine Claudius

fact that he writes in his own *History*[45] that Augustus had calculated
the years very carefully and then restored them to their proper date
after a long hiatus. And so everyone laughed at the herald's words
when he issued the invitation to the games with the traditional formula: "Games that no one has ever seen or will see again!" There
were people still alive who had seen them, and some of the actors
who had been on stage at the earlier games were being introduced
again. He often held races in the Circus Vaticanus[46] and elsewhere,
too, and he sometimes incorporated a beast hunt after every fifth
one. [21.3] He moreover made the Circus Maximus beautiful with
marble starting gates and golden turning posts (both had previously
been soft stone and wood), and he assigned seats to the senators,
who had been used to watching with everyone else. At races for
four-horse chariots, he put on the Game of Troy and brought out
African cats to be killed by a squadron of praetorian horsemen that
the tribunes and the prefect himself led. He also brought in riders
from Thessaly to drive wild bulls around the circus track and then,
when the animals tired, jump on their backs and drag them to the
ground by the horns.

[21.4] The gladiatorial combats that Claudius sponsored were of
many kinds and presented in many places: every year on the anniversary of his principate he put on a show in the praetorian camp but
without beast fights or extra theatrics. He put on the usual proper
combats in the Saepta[47] and at the same place a special one announced
on short notice and lasting a few days. He began to call this kind of
entertainment a *sportula*, because when he was about to present it
for the first time, he proclaimed, "It is as if I am inviting the people
to a hastily arranged little meal."[48] [21.5] At no other kind of diver-
sion was he more genial or relaxed. He stretched out his left hand[49]
and counted along with the crowd, out loud and on his fingers, the

---

45. 41.2.

46. Built by Gaius as a practice course for himself. The Circus Maximus
was the more usual venue.

47. The voting enclosure on the Campus Martius; see *Aug.* 43.1, *Cal.* 18.1,
Ner. 12.4.

48. *sportula* = "little basket," an informal distribution of food by patrons
to their clients, here, by analogy, by the emperor to the populace.

49. Upper-class decorum required that the left hand be covered in the
toga.

gold pieces for the winning gladiators, and he often encouraged the spectators to enjoy themselves, urging them on and pleading with them, calling them *domini* from time to time, sometimes mixing in inane and far-fetched jokes like this one: when the crowd called for Palumbus, he promised that he would present him, "If he can be caught."[50] But something else that he did was appropriate and quite helpful: he made everyone happy when he presented a wooden sword to an *essedarius* whose four sons were interceding on his behalf,[51] and he immediately sent around a placard that offered advice to the people: "How eager you should be to have children when you see what a protection and benefit they are, even for a gladiator." [21.6] In the Campus Martius he staged the attack and pillaging of a town to reenact his war against the British kings and their surrender. He presided wearing a general's cloak. He arranged for a sea battle just before he had the water let out from Lake Fucinus. But when the captives who were to fight on the ships shouted, "Hail, *imperator!* Those who are about to die salute you," he replied, "Or not!" No one was willing to fight after he said that because they thought that they had been pardoned. He hesitated for a time as to whether he should simply slaughter them all, but at last he sprang from his seat, ran stumbling along the lakeshore in his awkward gait, and partly by threats, partly by exhortation, forced them to fight. This extravaganza was a clash between the navies of Sicily and Rhodes, twelve triremes on each side. A silver Triton rose up from the middle of the lake, hoisted by a mechanical device, and summoned the navies to battle with his trumpet.

[22] When it came to religious observations, civil and military institutions, and the setting in order of all the strata of society both at home and abroad, he reformed some practices, reinstated others that had fallen out of use, or even introduced new ones. In choosing new members for the priestly colleges, he never named anyone except under oath.[52] Whenever an earthquake struck Rome, he took pains to see that the praetor assembled the populace and proclaimed a holy day, and whenever a bird of ill omen appeared on the Capitoline, he made sure that prayers were offered to drive it out, prayers that

---

50. The gladiator's name means "dove."

51. Claudius made the gladiator an instructor in a gladiatorial training school where wooden swords were used for practice.

52. He swore that the person whom he named was worthy of the position.

he himself dictated to the people from the rostra in his capacity of *pontifex maximus* after the horde of laborers and slaves had been moved away.[53]

[23.1] He linked the court sessions that had formerly been separated into winter and summer terms. He assigned permanent jurisdiction in cases of *fidei commissum*[54] to elected officials and to the governors of the provinces; this had formerly been the responsibility of the elected officials on an annual basis and only in the city. He suppressed a section of the *lex Papia Poppaea* that had been added under Tiberius on the assumption that men over sixty could not father children.[55] [23.2] He stipulated that the consuls assign guardians to dependents even though it was not their stated responsibility. He required that those whom the magistrates had barred from a province be kept from the city and from Italy as well. He banished some under a novel condition that forbade them to go further from Rome than the third milestone. When there was important business to be done in the senate, Claudius sat on the tribunes' bench between the consuls' chairs. Leaves of absence customarily granted by the senate became dependent on his own favor.

[24.1] He gave consular regalia even to procurators with a salary of 200,000 sesterces. From those who refused senatorial rank he took equestrian rank as well.[56] Although he had affirmed at the beginning of his reign that he would not make anyone a senator unless he was the great-great-grandson of a Roman citizen, he gave the broad-striped tunic to a freedman's son but on condition that he first be adopted by a Roman knight. He was afraid that he would be censured for this, too, so he pointed to the example of Appius

---

53. Secrecy was necessary to protect the correctness of the religious formula.

54. The obligation of heirs to honor the wishes of a testator in regard to legatees not eligible to inherit.

55. The marriage law that privileged those with children had apparently been emended under Tiberius to make men over sixty who had married earlier but had not had children subject to penalty on the grounds that they had not done so when they could. This new change evidently meant that the penalty was done away with because it was thought that men still had the opportunity to father children after sixty.

56. A senator enjoyed prestige and privilege, but some did not choose to assume the responsibility of senate membership.

Caecus the censor, an early ancestor in his clan, who had appointed
the sons of freedmen to the senate. (What he did not know was that
in the time of Appius and for some time thereafter slaves who had
been given their freedom were not called freedmen but that that was
the name given to their freeborn sons.) [24.2] He imposed on the
board of quaestors the task of providing gladiatorial games in place
of the task of paving roads. And he took from them responsibility
for Ostia and Gaul but put them back in charge of the *aerarium*, a
responsibility that the praetors (or as now, former praetors) had had
charge of in the meantime.

[24.3] He gave triumphal regalia to his daughter's fiancé Silanus,[57]
who was not yet grown, and to many older men as well. He bestowed
this honor so indiscriminately that a letter was written in the name
of all the legions requesting that decorations be presented to field
commanders of consular rank at the time that they received their
armies to keep them from looking for an excuse to make war. He
also ordered an ovation for Aulus Plautius and went out to meet him
when he entered the city. He walked on his left when he went to the
Capitoline and again when he returned.[58] He allowed Gabinius
Secundus to use the cognomen Cauchus because he had suppressed
the Cauchi,[59] a German tribe.

[25.1] He reordered the equestrian military grades in order to
give the command of an auxiliary cavalry unit after the command
of an auxiliary infantry unit, and after the cavalry command, the
post of legionary tribune. And he arranged for paid military positions, a kind of fictive service (called supernumerary) that was filled
in absentia and in title only. He also had the senate vote to prohibit
soldiers[60] from going to the homes of senators for the morning audience. He confiscated the possessions of freedmen who were passing
themselves off as Roman knights and returned to slave condition
those who failed to respect their patrons and against whom their
patrons had lodged complaints; he informed those who pleaded on
behalf of these freedmen that he would not hear similar cases if they

57. Lucius Junius Silanus, betrothed to his daughter Octavia; see 27.2.
58. Plautius was commander of the British expedition. Walking on the left
showed respect.
59. Publius Gabinius Secundus was governor of Lower Germany. The
Cauchi are more often the Chauci.
60. In this case, officers of the praetorian guard.

brought them against their own freedmen. [25.2] When some owners grew tired of taking care of their sick and incapacitated slaves and exposed them on the island of Aesculapius,[61] he decreed that all who were left to die were free and that if they recovered, they did not return to their master's control again. But if someone chose to kill a slave rather than expose him, the law held him liable to a charge of murder. He issued an edict reminding travelers not to journey through the towns of Italy unless they were on foot or carried in a chair or litter. He stationed a cohort of the city watch at Puteoli and another at Ostia[62] to protect against disasters caused by fire.

[25.3] He forbade men of alien status to use Roman names, at least not clan names. He put to death in the Esquiline Field[63] those who improperly appropriated Roman citizenship. He returned Achaia and Macedonia, provinces that Tiberius had made his personal responsibility, to the control of the senate. The Lycians he deprived of self-rule because of a dispute with Rome that had turned deadly; he gave independence back to the Rhodians because they asked forgiveness for past offenses.[64] For the citizens of Ilium he waived payment of taxes for all time on the grounds that they were the ancestors of the Roman people.[65] To support this measure, he read aloud an ancient letter written in Greek from the senate and the Roman people; it promised friendship and alliance to King Seleucus but only if he kept their kinsmen, the citizens of Ilium, totally free from the burden of taxation.[66] [25.4] He expelled the Jews from Rome, because they were continually causing public disturbances at the instigation of Chrestus.[67] He permitted envoys from Germany to sit in the orchestra because he was struck by their simplicity and self-confidence; they had been shown to the seats for the general

---

61. A temple of the god of healing was on an island in the Tiber.

62. Ports through which Rome's grain supply was imported.

63. A cemetery that was a site for executions.

64. Roman citizens had been killed in both Lycia and Rhodes.

65. Ilium = Troy. Myth held that Romans were descended from Aeneas, who fled from Troy.

66. Seleucus II, king of neighboring Syria in the third century BCE.

67. Chrestus may be Christus (Christ), and this report may (or may not) refer to disorder in the Jewish community caused by the arrival of early Christians in Rome.

population but noticed that Parthians and Armenians were sitting in the seats reserved for senators and so crossed over into that area, making it known that their own worth and station were not inferior to theirs. [25.5] He abolished totally the Gauls' Druidic religion with its horrid, brutal rites; Augustus had forbidden it only to those with Roman citizenship. On the other hand, he tried to import the Eleusinian rituals from Attica[68] to Rome, and he supported rebuilding the temple of Venus of Eryx in Sicily with public funds after it had fallen into ruin from age. He struck treaties with kings by sacrificing a pig in the Forum and employing the ancient introductory formula of the *fetiales*.[69]

But even these measures and other things that he did—and in fact almost the whole administration of his reign—he accomplished not so much by his own direction as under the direction of his wives and freedmen, and he was, most of the time and in every respect, a man whom they found useful or pliant to their wishes.

[26.1] Claudius was engaged twice when he was still a young man, to Aemilia Lepida, the great-granddaughter of Augustus, and then to Livia Medullina, who also had the second cognomen Camilla, of the ancient line of the dictator Camillus.[70] He broke off his engagement to the first, still a young girl, because her parents had given offense to Augustus; the second he lost because she became ill and died on the very day of their wedding. [26.2] After that he had two wives, Plautia Urgulanilla, whose father had celebrated a triumph,[71] and Aelia Paetina, whose father had been consul. He divorced both, Paetina for minor wrongdoing but Urgulanilla because of scandalous sexual behavior and suspicion of murder. After these, he married Valeria Messallina, the daughter of his cousin Barbatus Messalla. When he learned that she had (among other shameful and disgraceful behaviors) entered into a legal marriage with Gaius Silius with the terms of her dowry recorded before witnesses, he put her to death and swore before an assembly of the praetorians: "Inasmuch as my marriages have turned out badly for me, I shall remain a bachelor.

---

68. The territory of Athens.

69. Priests responsible for making treaties.

70. Furius Camillus was the legendary dictator of the fourth century BCE.

71. Marcus Plautius Silvanus, friend of Augustus; his son appears at 4.3.

And if I don't, I will not object if you kill me with your own hands."
[26.3] However, he did not have the strength to keep from contemplating new marriage arrangements at once, even marriage to
Paetina, whom he had divorced earlier, or Lollia Paulina, who had
been married to Gaius Caesar. But he was seduced by the charms of
Agrippina, the daughter of his brother Germanicus, who had taken
advantage of her right to kiss him[72] and made use of opportunities to
flatter. At the next session of the senate, he had some members propose that he be compelled to marry her because their union would be
of great advantage to the state and that permission be given to others
for marriages of this sort that had been considered incestuous until
that time. Scarcely a day passed before he celebrated the wedding.
None were found to follow their example except a freedman and a
primipilaris, whose marriage ceremony the emperor attended along
with Agrippina.

[27.1] He had children by three of his wives: by Urgulanilla, he
had Drusus and Claudia; by Paetina, Antonia; by Messallina, Octavia
and the boy who first had the cognomen Germanicus but later
Britannicus. He lost Drusus shortly before the boy reached the age
of adulthood when he choked to death playing with a pear that he
threw up high and caught in his open mouth. It was just a few days
earlier that Claudius had arranged for him to marry the daughter of
Sejanus. (This makes me wonder even more why some have written
that the boy was murdered by the devious Sejanus.) Claudia, who
was fathered by his freedman Boter, he ordered exposed and left
to die on her mother's doorstep without identifying marks, despite
the fact that she had been born five months before their divorce[73]
and had been accepted into the family. [27.2] He married Antonia
to Gnaeus Pompeius Magnus and then to Faustus Sulla, both young
men of the best families,[74] Octavia to his stepson Nero, but she had
been betrothed to Silanus earlier.[75] Britannicus was born on the

---

72. Kissing was acceptable between close relatives.

73. His divorce of Urgulanilla; see 26.2.

74. Gnaeus Pompey also appears at *Cal.* 35.1. Faustus Cornelius Sulla Felix
was a half-brother of Messallina.

75. Silanus (see 24.3) was descended from Augustus and was a distant cousin
of Claudius.

twentieth day of his principate in his second consulship.[76] Claudius carried the child around in his arms even when he was very small and recommended him to the care of the assembled military and to the people at the games, where he always held him on his lap or out in front of him. And he joined the cheering crowd in blessing the child with good wishes. Of his sons-in-law, he adopted Nero; Pompeius and Silanus he not only repudiated but even killed.

[28] Of his freedmen, he valued the eunuch Posides especially and granted him an honorary spear at the British triumph, treating him like a man who had done military service. He valued Felix no less, and him he put in charge of auxiliary infantry and cavalry units and also of the province of Judaea. (Felix was married to three queens.) He also favored Harpocras, to whom he gave the right of being conveyed through Rome in a litter and the privilege of producing entertainments for the public, and even more than these he favored Polybius, his cultural adviser, who often walked between the two consuls, but above all, Narcissus, his secretary for correspondence, and Pallas, his minister for accounts. He willingly allowed the senate to honor them by decree, not only with large monetary awards but also with the regalia proper for quaestors and praetors. He also permitted them to misappropriate and accumulate so much wealth that once when he was complaining about the meager straits of his own resources, this clever remark made the rounds: "He would have plenty if the two freedmen had made him their partners."

[29.1] A slave, as I said,[77] to these men and to his wives, he played the role not of emperor but of factotum. He bestowed honors, armies, pardons, and punishments for the profit of each or as their favoritism and whim required and, indeed, he often did this in ignorance, not knowing what he was doing. And not to belabor small matters, let it suffice to say that his grants were rescinded, his judgments voided, the letters of appointment that he issued substituted or even openly altered. He killed Appius Silanus, his fellow father-in-law,[78] and the Julias (one

---

76. Incorrect. Britannicus was born in February of 41 CE; Claudius' second consulship was not until 42.

77. See 25.5.

78. It is unclear what Suetonius means by "fellow father-in-law"; since Gaius Appius Junius Silanus was married to Messallina's mother, he was Claudius' father-in-law.

the daughter of Drusus,[79] the other the daughter of Germanicus), both on unspecified charges and with no defense allowed. He also killed Gnaeus Pompeius, the husband of his elder daughter, and Lucius Silanus, the fiancé of his younger. [29.2] Pompeius was stabbed when he was in bed with a favorite young boy; Silanus was forced to resign from his praetorship on the fourth day before the Kalends of January[80] and made to kill himself at the beginning of the next year on the very day of Claudius and Agrippina's wedding.

Claudius executed thirty-five senators and more than three hundred knights so casually that when a centurion reported that he had done what the emperor ordered, Claudius denied that he had given any order. But he approved the act nonetheless when his freedmen pointed out that the soldiers had done their duty because they had been quick to avenge their emperor before they were asked. [29.3] But the following may well exceed all credibility: Claudius signed with his own hand the document that described Messallina's dowry for her marriage to her lover Silius. He had been made to believe that the wedding was a charade intentionally devised to avert from himself a threat of danger foretold by portents and deflect it onto another.[81]

[30] Command and distinction were not lacking in Claudius' appearance when he was standing or sitting and especially when he was lying down, for he was tall and well built and had a handsome face, a striking head of white hair, and a strong neck. But his weak knees did not support him when he walked, and many unattractive mannerisms made him look disreputable both when he was relaxed and when he was doing something important. His laugh was unpleasant and his anger all the more disgusting because of his drooling mouth and dripping nostrils. He also stuttered and his head shook continuously but especially with even the least bit of physical activity. [31] Although he had been sickly when he was young, as emperor he enjoyed good health except for stomach pains; he said that he had even thought of killing himself when he suffered an attack.

[32] Claudius often gave lavish banquets, as a rule in very large open places so that six hundred could recline together at table. He even gave a feast next to the outlet of Lake Fucinus and was almost

---

79. The son of Tiberius.

80. December 29, 48 CE. He was put out of the way so that Nero could marry Octavia.

81. Omens had predicted a threat to the "husband of Messallina."

drowned when the water was released in a rush and overflowed its banks.[82] He always invited his children to dine with him along with other boys and girls of good birth, and they ate sitting at the foot of the dining couches in the old-fashioned manner. When a dinner guest was thought to have stolen a golden goblet, Claudius invited him back again the next day and set a clay cup at his place. They say that he even considered issuing an edict in which he excused the release of noisy farts at the table because he had learned of a man who risked his health when he held back out of embarrassment.

[33.1] Claudius had an inordinate craving for food and wine, any time, any place. Once when he was presiding at a trial in the forum of Augustus, he became aware of the smell of the meal being prepared for the Salii[83] at the nearby temple of Mars. He left the tribunal, went up the steps to the priests, and reclined at their table. Rarely did he leave the dining room unless he was sated and drunk and in such a state that he fell asleep immediately, lying on his back with his mouth open so that a feather would be put in to unburden his stomach. [33.2] He slept very little and often woke before midnight. But during the day he would sometimes go to sleep while holding court, and he scarcely woke up when the litigators talked louder on purpose. He had prodigious desire for sex with women; with males, none at all. He played dice enthusiastically and published a book on its rules. It was his habit to play dice even while he was driving about; his carriage and game board were modified so that play would not be disturbed.

[34.1] Claudius' behavior in matters great and small made it clear that he was cruel and bloodthirsty by his very nature. He directed torture at his interrogations and executed parricides[84] on the spot and in his presence. When he was eager to witness an execution being performed at Tibur according to the ancient method[85] and there was no executioner on hand after the guilty men had been tied to the stake, he sent for one from the city and continued to wait for him until evening. Whenever gladiatorial combat was being held,

---

82. See 20.1

83. Priests of Mars, known for their rich feasts.

84. For the "sack," see *Aug.* 33.1.

85. The prisoner was tied naked to a stake, beaten, and then beheaded, a punishment considered exceptionally cruel; see *Ner.* 49.2, *Dom.* 11.2.

either under his own sponsorship or under that of someone else, he ordered even those who had slipped and fallen by accident to have their throats cut, especially the *retiarii*, so that he could watch their faces as they died.[86] [34.2] When a pair of gladiators killed each other, he quickly ordered their swords made into small knives for his use. He took such pleasure in those who contended with the beasts and those who fought during the noon intermission that he arrived at the arena at dawn and stayed seated at midday after the crowd had dispersed for its noon meal.[87] And in addition to those already selected for combat, he forced into the arena some of the carpenters or workmen or men of that sort if the stage machinery or scaffolding or any other small thing did not function properly. He even sent one of his personal attendants into the arena, just as he was, wearing a toga.

[35.1] But Claudius was nothing so much as fearful and suspicious. Although in the first days of his reign he boasted (as we have said)[88] that he was behaving like an ordinary citizen, he did not dare attend banquets unless the dining room was surrounded by the elite of the praetorian guard armed with spears and unless soldiers served as waiters. Nor did he visit anyone who was sick without the bedchamber being searched ahead of time and the mattresses and bedclothes first tested and shaken out. Later on he always assigned men to search those who attended his audiences, and to search everyone very aggressively. [35.2] It was only reluctantly and at a late date that he stopped having women and young boys and girls searched bodily and stopped confiscating styluses[89] and stylus cases from any scribe who accompanied his master. During the civil war, when Camillus,[90] certain that Claudius could be bullied without recourse to war, wrote him an insulting, threatening, defiant letter that ordered him to withdraw from the principate and retire to the life of a private citizen, Claudius wavered and sought the advice of leading men as to whether or not he should comply.

---

86. They fought without helmets.

87. Beast fights usually took place in the morning. The combat during the noon "intermission" was particularly bloody, fights to the death between criminals without protective armor.

88. See 12.1.

89. For the sharpened stylus as a weapon, see 15.4; *Jul.* 82.2.

90. Arruntius Camillus Scribonianus; see 13.2.

[36] Claudius was so afraid of some of the groundless reports of conspiracies that he actually tried to give up power. When (as I noted earlier)[91] a man with a sword was arrested nearby when he was making a sacrifice, Claudius had the heralds quickly call the senate into session, lamented his condition in a loud and tearful outburst, declaring that he was never safe, and kept out of sight for a long time. He rid himself of the burning passion he felt for Messallina, not so much because he was humiliated by her insults as that he was fearful of danger, since he had come to believe that the principate was being passed to her lover Silius.[92] He was frightened in that crisis and disgraced himself by fleeing to the praetorian camp; the only thing that he asked on the way was, "Is my principate still safe?"

[37.1] There was no rumor so insignificant, no rumormonger so inconsequential that it did not put him on his guard and make him take the offensive when he was the least bit uneasy. A man involved in a lawsuit took him aside at the morning audience and swore that he had dreamed that someone had killed him; a short time later, the man pretended that he recognized the assassin and pointed to his opponent in the lawsuit, who was just then handing in his petition. The accused man was immediately sent off to be punished—as if caught in the act. [37.2] Appius Silanus is said to have been destroyed the same way: when Messallina and Narcissus conspired to get rid of him, they took separate roles for themselves. Narcissus, pretending to be shocked, burst into his patron's chamber before dawn and said that he had dreamed that Appius had attacked him. Messallina acted surprised and said that she had had the same dream for the past several nights. A short time later, as they had planned, Appius was reported pushing his way in; he had been instructed the day before to come at that moment. He was ordered arrested at once and killed because the dream had obviously come true. Claudius did not hesitate to lay an account of what had happened before the senate the next day and render thanks to Narcissus because the freedman was keeping watch over the emperor's well-being, even as he slept.

[38.1] Claudius was mindful both of the anger that he displayed and of his propensity for anger. He justified both in an edict and drew a distinction, promising that the one was surely brief and harmless, the other excusable. He lashed out at the citizens of Ostia

91. 13.1.
92. For the marriage, see 26.2 and 29.3.

because they had not sent boats to meet him when he entered the
Tiber,[93] expressing himself with such malice that he wrote a letter
charging that they had cut him down to the level of a commoner.
Then suddenly he pardoned them, almost as if apologizing. [38.2] He
used his own hand to push away people who approached him in
public at inappropriate times. He barred two men from Rome, one
a quaestor's secretary, the other a senator of praetorian rank, both
without trial and, what is more, both innocent. The former had been
quite aggressive in opposing him in court when he was still a private
citizen; the latter as aedile had fined Claudius' tenants for selling
prepared food illegally and had beaten his property manager when
he intervened. This was why Claudius took the responsibility for
policing the cookshops away from the aediles.

[38.3] He did not even keep quiet about his stupidity but claimed in
some short speeches that it had been an intentional pretense adopted
during the reign of Gaius. He would not have survived otherwise
and attained his present station. But he did not convince, for there
soon appeared a book titled *The Elevation of Fools*, with the message
that no one pretends to be stupid.

[39.1] Men wondered especially at his forgetfulness and thought-
lessness (or as I would say in Greek, his *metioria* and *ablepsia*).[94] After
Messallina was killed, he took his place at the table and asked shortly
thereafter, "Why has our mistress not come?" Many of the men
whom he condemned to death he ordered summoned the very next
day so that they could advise him or play dice with him. Thinking
that they were dawdling, he had a messenger scold them for being
sleepyheads. [39.2] When he was getting ready to flout accepted
morality by marrying Agrippina, he continued to refer to her in all
his speeches as "daughter and ward, born and reared in the protection of my embrace." When he was about to give Nero his own
name through adoption (as if he had not been criticized enough for
adopting a stepson when he already had a grown son of his own),[95]
he repeatedly informed the public: "No one has ever been grafted
onto the Claudian family by adoption."

---

93. When he was going upstream from Ostia to Rome, plausibly on his
return from the British campaign.
94. His "being up in the air" (detached) and his blindness.
95. An exaggeration; Britannicus was only nine in 50 CE when Nero was
adopted.

[40.1] Claudius was often so very careless about what he said and about the circumstances in which he spoke that it was thought that he neither knew nor considered to whom he was speaking or in what company or at what time or place. When a question arose about butchers and vintners, he shouted in the senate, "I ask you! Who can live without a snack?" and he described the abundant provisions in the old taverns where he had been in the habit of getting his wine in an earlier time. [40.2] He gave this among his reasons for supporting a candidate for the quaestorship: "His father gave me a drink of cold water when I was sick and needed it." When a female witness was brought into the senate, he said, "This woman was my mother's freedwoman and her personal maid, but she has always considered me her patron. I have said this because there are still some in my own household who do not think that I am their patron." [40.3] And when the citizens of Ostia petitioned him on behalf of their city, he lost his temper right there on the tribunal and yelled in a loud voice, "There is no reason why I should oblige you! If anyone is free to act, it is I!" He said things like the following every day, indeed, every hour, every minute: "What? Do you think I am Telegenius?"[96] and "Talk but don't touch!" and many other things inappropriate for a private citizen to say, much less for an emperor who was neither inarticulate nor untutored but devoted himself to liberal studies with great determination.

[41.1] When Claudius was a young man, he started to write a history at the urging of Livy and with the particular help of Sulpicius Flavus.[97] The first time that he tried to read it in an assembly hall full of people, he had difficulty finishing because he kept undermining his own performance. As he was starting to recite, laughter erupted when a fat man broke a number of benches. Not even after the commotion had died down could he keep from recalling from time to time what had happened and from laughing all over again. [41.2] He continued to work on his history, even when he was emperor, and he wrote a good deal of it then and frequently shared it with the public with the help of a reader. He began it after the death of Caesar but moved on to a later period and started over again with the "civil peace" because he knew that he could not write freely or truthfully about the earlier time. His mother and his grandmother

---

96. Telegenius is unknown, perhaps someone with a reputation as a fool.
97. Livy was an important historian; Sulpicius Flavus is unknown.

had constantly showed their disapproval when he tried.[98] He left two books about the earlier period and forty-one of the later. [41.3] He also wrote an autobiography in eight books, more inappropriate in content than inelegant in style, and a learned-enough defense of Cicero against the written attack of Asinius Gallus.[99] He invented three new letters for the alphabet and added them to the standard ones because he thought they were very necessary. Although he had published a book about the rationale for these letters when he was still a private citizen, it was as emperor that he easily brought them into common use. They can be found in numerous books, in the daily record, and in inscriptions on public works.

[42.1] He pursued Greek studies just as diligently, declaring his love for the language and maintaining its primacy whenever he could. He said to a non-Roman who was speaking in both Greek and Latin, "Since you are fluent in both of our tongues . . ." And in recommending the interests of Achaia to the senate, he said, "I feel affection for the province because we share a common culture." In the senate he often replied to Greek legations in formal speech. In fact, he would recite Homeric verses in court: whenever he punished an enemy of the state or a conspirator, and the tribune from his bodyguard requested the customary watchword, he almost always gave,

Defend against the man who shows anger unprovoked.[100]

Finally, he wrote histories in Greek, twenty books on Etruscan affairs and eight on Carthaginian. It was because of these that a new building bearing his name was added to the ancient shrine of the Muses in Alexandria, and it was established that on certain days every year his books were to be recited there in full as if in a recital hall by readers taking turns, in one building the books about the Etruscans, in the other the books about the Carthaginians.

---

98. "Civil peace" (as opposed to civil war) probably refers to 27 BCE when Augustus nominally "restored the Republic." Neither his mother Antonia nor his grandmother Livia wanted the bloody period of Augustus' rise to power recalled.

99. Gaius Asinius Gallus was the son of Asinius Pollio and the father of the Asinius Gallus who plotted against him; see 13.2.

100. Homer, *Iliad* 24.369; *Odyssey* 16.72, 21.133.

[43] Near the end of Claudius' life, he gave clear signs that he was
sorry that he had married Agrippina and adopted Nero. When his
freedmen were talking about a case that had taken place the preceding day, a case in which he had found a woman guilty of adultery,
and they were praising his verdict, he said in a loud voice, "It is my
fate too that all of my wives are unchaste—but not unpunished!"
And shortly thereafter he happened on Britannicus, held him close,
and urged, "Grow up and receive my explanation for everything that
I have done." And he added in Greek, "The one who has done the
injury will effect the cure." When he declared his intention of giving
his son the toga of manhood, inasmuch as he was tall for his age (in
reality, he was not yet mature), he went on to say, "so that the Roman
people may have a true Caesar at last." [44.1] Soon thereafter he
wrote his will and sealed it with the seals of all the elected officials.
Then, before he did anything more, Agrippina stopped him. She
was aware of what Claudius was saying and doing and of her own
wrongdoing, and informers were bringing charges against her.

[44.2] All agree that poison killed Claudius, but opinion differs
as to where it was given and by whom. Some say that his taster, the
eunuch Halotus, gave it to him when he was dining with the priests
on the citadel.[101] Others say that Agrippina herself served it to him
at dinner at home; she offered him a poisoned mushroom, a food
of which he was exceedingly fond. There are also different versions
of what happened next. [44.3] Many write that he fell silent as soon
as he had ingested the poison and that after suffering severe pain
the whole night, he died near daybreak. But some report that in the
first stages he was unconscious, and then he vomited everything up
because he had too much food in his stomach and had to be given a
second dose. This may have been put into gruel with the idea that
nourishment would restore him in his weakened state, or it may have
been introduced by enema on the grounds that this kind of purging
would bring relief to the suffering of his overloaded bowels.

[45] His death was kept secret until everything was ready for his
successor. Vows were consequently made for his recovery as though
he were still ailing, and as a ruse comic actors were brought in for
his entertainment as if by his request. He died three days before
the Ides of October in the consulship of Asinius Marcellus and

---

101. A part of the Capitoline Hill where priests of Augustus were celebrating the Augustalia, a feast in honor of Augustus.

Acilius Aviolus, in his sixty-fourth year, in the fourteenth year of his reign.[102] He was buried with the ceremony due an emperor and was enrolled in the company of the gods. This last distinction Nero ignored and rescinded but Vespasian later restored.[103]

[46] These were the most important forewarnings of his death: A hairy star (they call it a comet) rose in the sky, and lightning struck the monument dedicated to his father Drusus. Many magistrates of every level had died in that same year. There are a number of indications that he did not himself appear unaware that his final days were at hand or that he pretended otherwise, for when he named consuls, he named none for any month beyond the month in which he died. The last time he attended the senate he strongly encouraged his sons to be at peace with one another and with humility commended the tender ages of both to the care of the senators. And at his final court session he announced once and then again, "I have come to the end of my mortal life." But those who heard him prayed that it was not so.

---

102. October 13, 54 CE.

103. A temple begun for him was abandoned by Nero. Vespasian completed it; see *Ves.* 9.1.

NERO

37–68 CE

Emperor 54–68 CE

Tiberius Claudius Nero Caesar (Lucius Domitius Ahenobarbus before his adoption by Claudius) became emperor at the age of sixteen. He succeeded to the throne by inheriting it, insofar as it was possible to inherit a role that lacked a definition, from his adoptive father. However, he was also a direct descendant of Augustus, his great-great-grandfather, through his mother Agrippina the Younger. Agrippina's marriage to Claudius had maneuvered Nero into a position that enabled him to accede to the principate.

During the first years of the young prince's reign, he was guided by the experience of his tutor Seneca and the praetorian praefect Burrus, and the business of the empire went forward. He did, however, eliminate Claudius' other son Britannicus and rid himself of what he considered his mother's overbearing influence. As time passed, he became even bolder in his role. He had his mother killed, divested himself of his mentors, and divorced his wife, Claudius' daughter Octavia, who had provided a link to the previous reign.

Nero was always interested in the arts broadly defined: lyre playing, singing, acting, chariot racing, architecture, spectacle, and even himself as an art object. This passion pleased those who enjoyed his lavish entertainments, but critics focused on his un-Roman self-indulgence and on the extravagance necessary to bring it about. His confidence as a performer grew, and these interests occupied him until his death. Additional charges of sexual ingenuity and cruelty brought the notoriety that came to be associated with his rule.

Distracted by such nongovernmental interests, Nero lacked the resolution to deal with the uncertain loyalty of his generals in the provinces, and he caved quickly when he was challenged. Suetonius presents a gripping narrative of his flight and suicide. But something of Nero's popular appeal survived. Ordinary people put flowers on his grave; two emperors, Otho and Vitellius, identified themselves with him; and three impersonators appeared in the course of the next twenty years.

[1.1] In the Domitian clan, there have been two important families, the Calvini and the Ahenobarbi. Lucius Domitius was the founder of the Ahenobarbi and was also responsible for the cognomen. Legend holds that once when he was returning from the country, he was met by twin youths of dazzling beauty and ordered to announce to the senate and the people a Roman victory in a battle in which the outcome was still uncertain.[1] To prove to him that they were divine, they rubbed his cheeks, and this turned his beard from black to red and made it the color of bronze. The special mark survived in his descendants, most of whom had red beards.[2] [1.2] All the Domitii kept this same cognomen while they held seven consulships, a triumph, and two censorships and were admitted to the body of patricians. The only first names they used were Gnaeus and Lucius, and these they allocated in a particular order: first one or the other was assigned to three individuals in succession, then the names alternated with each generation. For we know that the first, second, and third Ahenobarbi were named Lucius, and then the next three in order were Gnaeus, and after that it was always first Lucius, then Gnaeus, in turn.

I think it appropriate to introduce here a number of family members so that it can be more clearly seen that although Nero discarded the virtues of his forefathers, he nonetheless perpetuated the vices of each of them as if they were inherited and a part of him from birth. [2.1] And so to go back some distance, his great-great-great-grandfather Gnaeus Domitius, when he was tribune,[3] felt insulted when the priests chose someone other than himself to fill his father's place, and he reassigned the right of electing successor priests from the colleges to the people. And when in his consulship he had subdued the Allobroges and the Arverni,[4] he rode through the province on an elephant escorted by a throng of soldiers as if celebrating a proper triumph. [2.2] This was the man about whom the orator Licinius

---

1. The battle of Lake Regillus in the early fifth century BCE.
2. The youths were the twin demigods Castor and Pollux. Ahenobarbus means "bronze beard."
3. In 104 BCE. The Domitii Ahenobarbi clan was still plebeian at that time.
4. Tribes in southeastern Gaul.

Crassus said, "No wonder he has a bronze beard. His face is iron and his heart is lead."[5]

His son, when he was praetor, called Gaius Caesar to account before the senate as Caesar was leaving his consulship, because it was thought that he had executed the office contrary to his mandate and to the law. Then as consul, he tried to divest Caesar of his command over the armies in Gaul, and his party named him Caesar's successor.[6] He was captured at Corfinium at the beginning of the civil war. [2.3] Released, he went to Massilia where his arrival brought heart to the inhabitants who were suffering under siege, but he left them suddenly and finally fell at the battle of Pharsalus.[7] An irresolute man with a vicious temperament, he was so afraid to die that when fear and desperation almost drove him to suicide, he changed his mind and vomited up the poison that he had drunk and gave his doctor his freedom.[8] (The physician was a wary man who knew his master well and had intentionally mixed a less than lethal poison.) Also, when Pompey sought advice about what to do with those who had remained neutral and had not taken sides in the civil conflict, Ahenobarbus was the only one who took the position that they should be designated enemies of the state.

[3.1] He left a son[9] who was, beyond doubt, the best of all the rest of his family. Although innocent, he was condemned to death under the Pedian law[10] among the conspirators responsible for Caesar's death and joined the cause of his close relations Cassius and Brutus. After both of them were dead, he retained command of the fleet that had been entrusted to him earlier, increased its size, and, after his party had met total defeat, handed it over to Mark Antony. But he did this voluntarily, as if he were bestowing a significant favor. [3.2] Of all those found guilty under the Pedian law, he was the only one

---

5. Lucius Licinius Crassus and this Gnaeus Ahenobarbus shared the censorship in 95 BCE.

6. This Lucius Domitius Ahenobarbus, a staunch adversary of Julius Caesar, was praetor in 58 BCE and consul in 54.

7. Corfinium, in central Italy, and Massilia fell to Caesar in 49 BCE; see *Jul.* 34. Pompey's force was defeated at Pharsalus in 48.

8. Doctors were slaves or freedmen.

9. Gnaeus Domitius Ahenobarbus, consul in 32 BCE.

10. A law that required that the assassins of Julius Caesar be brought to trial.

who got back his rights as a Roman citizen, and he moved quickly through the highest offices. When civil conflict was renewed and he was serving as an officer under Antony, he was offered supreme command by those who were ashamed of their leader's association with Cleopatra. But he fell ill suddenly and for that reason lacked the confidence either to accept the assignment or reject it. He went over to Augustus and was dead within a few days. But even that Domitius Ahenobarbus had his reputation tarnished, for Antony clearly made it known that he had changed sides because he wanted to be with his mistress Servilia Nais.

[4] His son was the Domitius[11] who gained notoriety because Augustus named him executor in his will. He was as celebrated for his skill in racing chariots when he was young as he was later for the triumphal regalia that he earned in the war in Germany. But he was arrogant, extravagant, and pitiless. When he was aedile he forced the censor Lucius Plancus to step aside for him in the street. When he was praetor and consul he put Roman knights and respectable women on the stage to act in a mime. He sponsored beast hunts in the Circus and in all the city neighborhoods and also a gladiatorial show, but one so savage that Augustus had to issue an edict to keep him in line after private warnings did no good. [5.1] With Antonia Major he fathered the father of Nero,[12] who was a vile man in every respect. When he went to the East as a companion of young Gaius Caesar,[13] he killed his own freedman because he refused to drink as much as he was ordered. He was dismissed from Gaius' circle, but his behavior continued to be just as undisciplined. In a village on the Appian Way he suddenly whipped up his team and intentionally ran over a boy, and at Rome, in the middle of the Forum, he gouged out the eye of a Roman knight who was arguing with him too vigorously. [5.2] He was so very corrupt that he not only defrauded the bankers on the price of items he had purchased but also, as praetor,

---

11. Lucius Domitius Ahenobarbus, consul in 16 BCE, an important military commander under Augustus.

12. Antonia Major was the elder daughter of Mark Antony and Augustus' sister Octavia. The Gnaeus Domitius Ahenobarbus who was the emperor's father was consul in 32 CE.

13. Ostensibly Gaius Julius Caesar, the adopted son of Augustus; see *Aug.* 64.1. This is an error, however, since the Domitius in question would have been too young to accompany Gaius.

cheated the chariot drivers of their prize money. His sister[14] told a joke that made these actions notorious, and when the managers of the racing factions complained, he issued an edict that in the future the prizes should be paid on the spot. Just before Tiberius died, Domitius was put on trial for treason and also for adultery and incest with his sister Lepida, but with the change of regime he got off. He died from retention of fluid in his body at Pyrgi[15] after he had acknowledged his son Nero, to whom Agrippina, the daughter of Germanicus, gave birth.

[6.1] Nero was born at Antium nine months after Tiberius died, on the eighteenth day before the Kalends of January,[16] just as the sun rose, so that he was touched by its rays almost before he was touched by the earth. Many quickly conjectured about the quantity of frightening details in his horoscope, and the words of his father Domitius were ominous as well. When friends offered their congratulations, he said, "Nothing could be born of Agrippina and me that is not vile and a portent of evil for the state." [6.2] A clear sign of the boy's unhappy future was manifest on his naming day:[17] When Gaius Caesar was asked by his sister to give the baby any name he wished,[18] he looked at his uncle Claudius (who would later adopt Nero) and said he would give him his. He was not serious but said it as a joke, and Agrippina rejected the idea, because at that time Claudius was the laughingstock of the court.

[6.3] Nero lost his father when he was three. Heir to a third of his estate, he did not receive even the whole of that amount because all of his property was seized by his coheir Gaius. His mother was soon exiled, and he was left without resources and in need. He was reared in the home of his aunt Lepida under the care of two tutors, a dancer and a barber. But when Claudius became emperor, Nero not only received his father's estate but was also made rich by inheritance

---

14. Domitius had two sisters. The elder, Domitia, is plausibly meant here because her sister (Domitia) Lepida is named below. She was married to Passienus Crispus (6.3), who became Agrippina's second husband and Nero's stepfather. She reappears at 34.5. Lepida also appears at 6.3 and 7.1.

15. On the coast north of Rome.

16. December 15, 37 CE.

17. The ninth day after birth.

18. Gaius Caesar is the emperor sometimes known as Caligula. Nero's mother Agrippina the Younger was one of his sisters.

from his stepfather Crispus Passienus. [6.4] When his mother was recalled and restored to her former position, he flourished so well under her protection and power that the story spread among the populace that Claudius' wife Messallina had sent agents to strangle him when he was taking a nap because she thought he was a rival of Britannicus.[19] An addendum to the tale has the would-be assassins fleeing in terror when a snake crept out from under the boy's pillow; the origin of the story lay in snake skins that were found twined around the neck rest in his bed. Despite this scant evidence, his mother had them encased in a golden bracelet that he wore on his right arm for a long time. Finally, when he wanted to forget about his mother, he threw it away, but when his position became desperate, he looked for it again and could not find it.

[7.1] As a young boy, not yet grown, he took part with considerable poise in the Game of Troy held in the Circus, and his performance was favorably received. Claudius adopted him when he was eleven and entrusted his education to Annaeus Seneca,[20] who was already a senator at that time. They say that Seneca dreamed the very next night that he was teaching Gaius Caesar, and Nero quickly turned the dream into reality, revealing his monstrous character by providing examples of it as quickly as he could. Because his brother Britannicus reverted to habit and called him Ahenobarbus after his adoption, he tried to make the case to his father that Britannicus was not really his son. And when his aunt Lepida was on trial, he gave public testimony against her in order to please his mother, who was trying to have her convicted.

[7.2] When he was introduced in the Forum for the first time, he announced a money gift for the people and a bonus for the soldiers, and he arranged a military exercise for the praetorians and led it with a shield in his hand. He then offered thanks to his father in the senate. And when Claudius was consul, Nero spoke before him, in Latin on behalf of the citizens of Bononia,[21] in Greek on behalf of the citizens of Rhodes and Ilium. He heard his first legal cases when he served as city prefect during the Latin festival. At that time the most renowned of the court pleaders competed to put before him

---

19. The young son of Claudius and Messallina; see *Cl.* 27.1–2.

20. Lucius Annaeus Seneca, writer and philosopher.

21. Modern Bologna.

large numbers of very important petitions instead of the usual short, inconsequential ones, although Claudius had forbidden them to do this. Shortly thereafter he married Octavia[22] and sponsored circus games and a beast hunt dedicated to the well-being of Claudius.

[8] Nero was seventeen when Claudius' death was announced to the public. He appeared before the guards on duty between the sixth and seventh hours since that time had seemed best for a new beginning on a day filled with ill omens.[23] He was saluted as *imperator* on the steps of the Palatine and carried in a litter to the praetorian camp, and after addressing the soldiers there, he quickly went on to the senate house. It was already evening when he left there, and of the great number of honors heaped on him he refused only one, the title Father of His Country, and that because of his age.

[9] Beginning then with a show of piety, he buried Claudius with elaborate funeral arrangements, spoke his eulogy, and enrolled him among the gods. To the memory of his father Domitius he offered the highest honors. To his mother he allowed the running of his affairs, private and public; he gave the watchword, "Best of Mothers," to the tribune of his bodyguard on the first day of his principate, and later on he was often carried through the streets with her in her litter. He founded a colony at Antium for veterans of the praetorians and added the wealthiest of the *primipilares* to their number by making a change of their place of residence. He built a port there at great expense.

[10.1] So as to reveal still more clearly what sort of person he was, he declared that he would rule according to Augustan precedent, and he neglected no opportunity to display generosity, mercy, or even affability. The heavier taxes he either abolished or decreased. He reduced the rewards to a quarter of what they had been for those who gave evidence against people disobeying the *lex Papia Poppaea*.[24] He distributed 400 sesterces each to the populace and established an annual salary for distinguished senators who lacked financial resources, 500,000 sesterces for some of them. He provided

---

22. Daughter of Claudius and Messallina.

23. Since Claudius died on October 13, 54 CE, Nero would not be seventeen for two more months; see *Cl.* 45. Astrologers determined that the best time for announcing the change of regime was between twelve noon and one o'clock.

24. Augustus' law that encouraged marriage; see *Cl.* 19, 23.1.

the monthly grain supply free to the praetorian cohorts. [10.2] And when he was asked to sign, as was customary, the execution order for someone who had been condemned to death, he said, "How I wish that I didn't know how to write." He always greeted members of all of the orders immediately and by name. When the senate offered him thanks, he responded, "When I shall have deserved them." He invited even commoners to watch him exercise in the Campus Martius, and he declaimed in public often. He recited his poetry not only at home but in the theater, too, and this gave everyone so very much pleasure that a day of thanksgiving was decreed to honor his recitation, and the parts of the poems that he had read were inscribed in golden letters and dedicated to the Capitoline Jupiter.

[11.1] He gave many entertainments of various kinds: the Juvenalia,[25] circus games, theatrical productions, and a gladiatorial combat. He invited elderly men of consular rank and aging matrons to take part in the Juvenalia. In the Circus he assigned the knights seats separate from those of the other spectators and arranged for competitions of chariots drawn by four camels. [11.2] At the games that he wanted to be called *Ludi Maximi*,[26] staged for the "Eternity of the Empire," many of each class and gender took their places on the stage. A distinguished Roman knight rode an elephant making a circuit of the roped-off enclosure. In a comedy by Afranius[27] titled *The Fire*, the actors were allowed to carry furniture out of the burning house and keep it for themselves. Every day, tokens good for all kinds of prizes were showered on the people: there were daily tokens for a thousand birds of every kind, for all manner of food and vouchers for grain and tokens for clothing, gold, silver, precious stones, pearls, paintings, slaves, mules, and even for tamed beasts, and finally, for ships, apartment houses, and land.

[12.1] Nero watched these games from a post above the stage. He held a gladiatorial show in a wooden amphitheater that was built in the region of the Campus Martius during the course of a year,[28] but he killed no one, not even condemned criminals. He also exhib-

---

25. Private games that celebrated the rite of the first shaving of his beard, 59 CE.

26. "Greatest Games," 59 CE.

27. Lucius Afranius wrote comedies of domestic Roman life in the second century BCE.

28. 57 CE.

ited four hundred senators and six hundred Roman knights at the combats, some of them wealthy and with exemplary reputations. And those who fought the wild beasts and filled various jobs at the arena came from the same orders. He presented a naval battle in salt water with sea monsters swimming about and Pyrrhic dances[29] performed by young men from Greece, to all of whom he gave certificates of Roman citizenship at the end of their performance. [12.2] Among the subjects enacted in their dance was a bull mounting Pasiphae, who was hidden away in a wooden replica of a heifer[30]—or so many of those watching believed. As soon as Icarus tried to fly,[31] he fell and landed next to the emperor's private box and spattered him with blood, for Nero rarely presided but was in the habit of reclining while he watched. At first he peered out through small apertures but then had the entire wall surrounding his platform opened up.

[12.3] He was also the very first to establish quinquennial games at Rome; these had three divisions in accordance with Greek custom: musical, gymnastic, and equestrian events.[32] He called these games the Neronia. At the dedication of his baths and gymnasium he gave oil to the senators and the knights.[33] Instead of putting praetors in charge of the competition as a whole, he assigned men of consular rank who were chosen by lot. Then he went down into the orchestra where the senate was sitting and accepted the crown for Latin oratory and poetry; despite the fact that all of the most distinguished men had competed for it, it was granted him by common consent. But he treated with religious awe the crown that the judges awarded him as a citharode[34] and ordered it brought to the statue of Augustus. [12.4] At the gymnastic contest he gave in the Saepta, he trimmed his first beard while oxen were being sacrificed, placed it in a golden casket decorated with costly pearls, and dedicated it on the Capitoline. He invited even the Vestal Virgins to the athletic

---

29. Originally war dances but evidently evolved to include the enactment of myth; see *Jul.* 39.1.

30. The Minotaur was the issue of a bull and the woman Pasiphae.

31. When Icarus tried to escape Crete on wings attached by wax, he flew too near the sun, the wax melted, and he fell.

32. A Greek competition, to be held every five years, first in 60 CE.

33. In 60 or 61 CE. Evidently for the baths.

34. A performer who sang while accompanying himself on the lyre.

games because the priestesses of Ceres had been allowed to watch at Olympia.[35]

[13.1] My decision to report the entrance of Tiridates into the city as one of Nero's entertainments should not be thought ill advised. Tiridates was the king of Armenia whom Nero enticed to Rome with the promise that he would be received as an important personage. Bad weather caused him to postpone presenting Tiridates to the people on the day that had been announced by edict, but he brought him forward at the first good opportunity. Armed cohorts were stationed around the temples in the Forum, and he himself sat on the curule chair on the rostra, in the garments of a triumphing general, surrounded by military standards and flags. [13.2] Tiridates approached across an inclined platform, and when he fell at Nero's knees, the emperor received him and lifted him up with his right hand and kissed him. Then as Tiridates paid homage before him, Nero removed the king's headdress and exchanged it for a diadem, while a man of praetorian rank translated the suppliant's words and relayed them to the crowd. From there Tiridates was escorted to the theater, and after he had paid homage a second time, Nero seated him next to him on his right. As a result, Nero was saluted as *imperator*, and he took victory laurels to the Capitoline and closed the twin gates of the temple of Janus[36] since there was no more war.

[14] Nero held four consulships: the first for two months, the second and last for six, and the third for four.[37] The middle two came in sequence; the others were spaced with a year in between. [15.1] When he dispensed justice, he rarely handed down decisions to plaintiffs except on the following day and in writing. This was how he heard cases: he did away with arguments that proceeded from beginning to end and had each pleader argue his individual points in turn. Whenever he withdrew to deliberate, he did not consult with others as a body or consider the questions openly. He had each of his advisers submit written opinions, which he read quietly by himself, and then he ruled as he pleased, although he made it appear that a large number of them had concurred with his decision.

---

35. In the western Peloponnese, the site of a sanctuary to Jupiter and of games in which Nero was eager to compete; see 23.1, 24.2, 25.1, 53.

36. The gates were open when Rome was at war, closed when it was not.

37. 55, 57, 58, and 60 CE.

[15.2] For a long time he did not allow the sons of freedmen to enter the senate, nor could those whom earlier emperors had admitted hold elected office. When there were more candidates for an office than there were places, he put the extras in command of legions to compensate for postponement and delay. He usually awarded consulships for six-month periods. When one of the two consuls died just before the Kalends of January, he did not name a substitute, since he disapproved of the example of Caninius Rebilus, who had been consul for a single day.[38] He awarded triumphal regalia even to those with the rank of quaestor and to some equestrians, although not necessarily for military service. Often when he sent speeches to the senate on some subject or other, he had them read aloud by a consul, bypassing the services of his quaestor. [16.1] He devised a new type of building for the city; apartment blocks and houses were to have porticoes in front so that fires could be fought from their roofs, and these he built with his own money. He planned to extend the city walls as far as Ostia and bring the sea in from there to the old city through a canal.

[16.2] Many crimes were punished rigorously during his reign, many practices were restricted, and an equal number of new regulations were put in place: A limit was set on expenditures. Public banquets were reduced to handouts of food. Cooked food, except for legumes and vegetables, was prohibited in taverns, although every kind of delicacy had been available earlier. Punishment was inflicted on Christians, a class of persons who were following a pernicious new cult. Chariot drivers were forbidden to run wild, to roam about cheating and robbing for amusement, a freedom that they had long enjoyed. The fans of the pantomime actors were banished along with the actors themselves. [17] A defense against forgers was devised then for the first time: no documents were to have seals affixed unless they were punched through and a cord drawn through the holes three times. In the case of wills, a law provided that the first two pages be shown to the witnesses empty of everything but the name of the testator. And no one who wrote a will for someone else was to write in a bequest for himself. People involved in lawsuits were to pay a firm price that had been agreed on for their defense but nothing at all for court expenses; the state treasury covered these free of charge. Cases that involved the treasury were to be transferred to

---

38. In 45 BCE.

the Forum[39] and to a board of assessors, and all appeals from juries were to be made to the senate.

[18] Nero never had the least desire or intention to expand the empire and enlarge its boundaries. He even considered withdrawing the army from Britain and refrained only out of deference, not wanting to appear disparaging of his father's glory. The only exceptions were for the kingdom of Pontus, which he had made into a province when Polemon ceded it, and Cottius' territory in the Alps when the king died.[40] [19.1] He planned a total of two trips abroad, one to Alexandria and one to Achaia. But he canceled the trip to Alexandria on the very day on which he was to set out because he had been made uneasy by a sign from the heavens that foretold danger: after he had visited the other temples, he took his seat in the temple of Vesta, and when he stood up, first the border of his toga caught and then such a dark mist came over him that he was unable to see clearly. [19.2] In Achaia he attempted to dig through the Isthmus.[41] He assembled the praetorians and urged them to begin work, and when the trumpet sounded, he made the first dig into the earth with a pickax and carried off the dirt piled in a basket on his shoulders. He prepared to make an expedition to the Caspian Gates[42] with a new legion of recruits drafted from Italy; they were six feet tall, and he called it his Phalanx of Alexander the Great.

[19.3] I have collected here these actions of his, some of them irreproachable, others worthy of praise to some degree, in order to separate them from his disgusting acts and criminal deeds, which I shall relate from this point on.

[20.1] Music was one of the studies to which Nero was introduced when he was a boy, and as soon as he came to power, he summoned Terpnus, the preeminent citharode at that time, and for days on end sat next to him after dinner as he sang late into the night. And little by little he began to practice and rehearse, neglecting none of the things that artists of this sort usually do to care for the voice or to strengthen it. He even lay on his back with a sheet of lead on

---

39. That is, they were subject to normal judiciary procedure.

40. Pontus was on the Black Sea. Cottius governed a small territory in the Alps; see *Tib.* 37.3.

41. A canal through the Isthmus of Corinth.

42. A mountain pass in the Caucasus.

his chest, and he purged with enemas and vomiting and abstained from fruit and harmful foods. Delighted with his progress despite a voice that was thin and husky, he conceived the desire of appearing on stage, and he often tossed this Greek proverb around among his friends: "Hidden music earns no regard."

[20.2] He appeared for the first time in Naples,[43] and he did not stop singing until he finished the song he had begun, even when an earthquake suddenly shook the theater. He sang there often over a period of several days, and when he took a brief time off to revive his voice, he could not tolerate being out of the public eye but went from the baths to the theater and dined in the orchestra crowded with people; he promised in Greek, "Once I have drunk a bit, I will let something stirring ring out." [20.3] Much taken with the rhythmic applause of some Alexandrians, who had converged on Naples from a recently arrived fleet, he summoned more of them to come from Alexandria. He quickly chose young men of equestrian rank and more than five thousand vigorous young commoners from all over and divided them into claques to learn methods of clapping (their clapping had names like "bees," "tiles," and "bricks") and to use their skill energetically when he sang. They were conspicuous because of their thick hair and elegant dress, and their left hands were bare, without rings. Their leaders were each paid 400,000 sesterces.

[21.1] Once he had decided that it was important for him to sing in Rome as well, he revived the Neronia earlier than had been planned,[44] and when everyone clamored for his divine voice, he replied, "I will give everyone who wishes to hear me the opportunity to do so in my gardens." But when the detachment on guard duty added their appeals to those of the crowd, he happily promised that he would satisfy them on the spot. He ordered his name posted on the notice board where citharodes declared their readiness to compete and placed the token with his name on it in the urn with the others. When his turn came, he entered, followed by the praetorian prefects carrying his lyre, then the military tribunes, and after that his closest friends. [21.2] And when he took his place on stage and had finished his introduction, he had the consular Cluvius Rufus[45] announce that

---

43. His first performance before the public was in 64 CE.

44. 64 or 65 CE. The date of this revival is uncertain.

45. A member of Nero's court but also a historian whose work (now lost) Suetonius used as a source in some of his *Caesars*.

he would sing the role of Niobe. He kept on with it until almost the tenth hour and postponed the awarding of the crown for this and the rest of the competition until the following year so that he would have the opportunity to sing more often. When this seemed too long to wait, he continued to appear before the public at frequent intervals. He even considered taking part in private performances as an actor when one of the praetors offered him a million sesterces. [21.3] He wore the masks of heroes and gods and sang tragic roles—he even wore the masks of heroines and goddesses. These were made to look like him or like any woman with whom he happened to be enamored. Among other roles, he sang Canace giving birth, Orestes the matricide, Oedipus blinded, and Hercules insane. There is a story that when he sang the story of Hercules, a newly recruited soldier stationed as a guard at the theater entrance ran forward to help him when he saw him bound in chains as the plot required.

[22.1] Nero took a deep interest in horses from an early age and talked constantly about the races in the Circus, even though he had been instructed not to. Once when he was complaining with his fellow students about the driver of the Greens,[46] who had been dragged behind his chariot, his tutor objected, but he lied and said he was talking about Hector. At the beginning of his reign, he played with ivory chariots on a game board every day, and he came in from the country to attend all the racing events, even the least significant. He did this secretly at first but later openly so that everyone knew for certain that he would be in Rome that day. [22.2] Nor did he make any pretense about wanting the number of prizes increased. He added to the number of races and extended the entertainment until late in the day, and the faction managers did not think it worthwhile to bring out their horses unless there was to be a whole day's racing. Nero soon wanted to drive himself and to put himself often before the public. After a first experience in his gardens with slaves and the lower classes watching, he showed himself to the eyes of all in the Circus Maximus.[47] A freedman stood where a magistrate usually stood and dropped the handkerchief for the start of the race.

---

46. For the racing factions, see *Cal.* 18.3, 55.2; *Vit.* 7.1; *Dom.* 7.1. Nero, like Gaius, was a fan of the Greens.

47. 64 CE.

[22.3] Not satisfied with showing off these skills at Rome, Nero went to Achaia (as we said)[48] with the following in particular in mind: the cities that regularly held competitions in music had decided to award him all the prizes given to citharodes. He was so happy to be given these crowns that he not only welcomed like leading citizens the representatives who brought them but even seated them at the table among his closest friends. When some of them asked him to sing after dinner and he accepted enthusiastically, he said, "The Greeks alone know how to listen, and they alone are worthy of me and my skills." He left Rome at once and sang first on his arrival at Cassiope[49] before the altar of Jupiter Cassius and then proceeded to enter every one of the competitions. [23.1] He could do this because he had ordered all of the contests crowded into a single year, even when there were long intervals between their dates, and some of them were held twice. At Olympia he arranged for an additional competition in music, not normally part of the festival. So that nothing would distract him or divert him when he was busy with these pursuits, he made this reply to his freedman Helios, when Helios advised him that his presence was required to deal with affairs in the city: "Although you advise me to return now and wish me to do so quickly, you should instead urge and desire that I return in a way proper for Nero."

[23.2] No one was permitted to leave the theater while he was singing, not even out of necessity. And so it was said that some women gave birth during his performances and that many, when they grew tired of listening to him and applauding for him, slipped out over the wall since the entrances were closed. Or they pretended to be dead and were carried out in a funeral procession. It is almost beyond belief how very nervous and timid he was when he competed, how jealous he was of his rivals, how frightened of the judges. He pretended that he and his rivals were in a real competition, and he would observe them, try to ingratiate himself with them, defame them behind their backs, curse them sometimes if he encountered them, and if any were more accomplished than he, he would bribe them. [23.3] He would address the judges with the utmost respect before he began: "I have done all that had to be done, but the outcome is in the hands of Fortune. But you, wise and learned men that you are, ought to

48. See 19.1; the Greek trip was in 66 and 67 CE.
49. On the Greek island of Corfu.

disregard the vagaries of chance." They urged him to take heart, and he left them with peace of mind, but he still did not stop worrying. He maintained that the quiet demeanor and sense of propriety that some of them displayed was really ill humor and malice and that he did not trust them. [24.1] When he competed, he obeyed the rules so very carefully that he never dared spit or use his arm to wipe the sweat from his brow. Once when he was acting a tragic scene and dropped his scepter and quickly picked it up again, he was aghast and afraid that he would be eliminated from the competition. He got his courage back only when his fellow performer swore that this slip had not been noticed in all the shouting and acclamation from the audience. He himself made the announcement when he won and for this reason entered the competitions for heralds wherever they were held. So as to erase all remembrance of other winners without a trace, he ordered the statues and busts of all of them toppled and dragged away with hooks and thrown into latrines.

[24.2] He also drove his chariot at many sites, even a team of ten horses at the Olympic Games, although he had criticized King Mithridates[50] in one of his poems for doing this very thing. He was thrown from the chariot and put back in again but was unable to continue and stopped before the finish; he won the crown nonetheless. When he left, he awarded the entire province self-government and at the same time gave the judges Roman citizenship and a substantial amount of money. He announced these rewards himself, standing in the middle of the stadium at the Isthmian Games.

[25.1] On his way back from Greece, he went to Naples because it was there that he had first put his artistry on display.[51] As was usual for winners in Greek games, he entered the city in a chariot pulled by white horses through a section of the wall that had been broken down. He entered Antium in the same way and from there, his Alban villa and from there, Rome. But when he entered Rome it was in the same chariot with which Augustus had once staged his triumph, and he wore a purple robe and a cloak embroidered with gold stars. He wore the Olympian crown on his head and carried the Pythian crown in his right hand. In the parade that preceded him placards described his other crowns, where he had won them and over whom, and the content of his songs and performances.

---

50. See *Jul.* 4.2.
51. See 20.2.

His claque followed behind his chariot like attendants in a triumphant parade, shouting, "We are the Augustiani, the soldiers of his
triumph." [25.2] He circled the Circus Maximus (the entrance arch
had been torn down for him) and passed through the Velabrum[52]
and the Forum on his way to the Palatine and the temple of Apollo.
Everywhere he went, victims were slaughtered, saffron was repeatedly sprinkled on the streets, and birds and garlands and sweets were
showered on him. He placed the sacred crowns among the couches
in his private chambers along with statues of himself dressed as a
citharode. He also struck coinage that carried this image of himself.
[25.3] Following this triumphant entrance, his enthusiasm was so
little diminished and his attention to his craft so little lessened that
to preserve his voice he never addressed the soldiers except by written communication or with someone else speaking his words. Nor
did he deal with any matter either seriously or in jest without his
singing teacher by his side warning him to spare his vocal cords and
to put a handkerchief over his mouth. He was friendly to many or
quarreled with others accordingly, as each praised him generously
or sparingly.

[26.1] Insolence, lust, extravagance, greed, cruelty—these are the
qualities that he exhibited. In the beginning they emerged gradually
and furtively, as if derived from youthful error, but even then they
were such that no one doubted that they were failings of character, not of age. When it grew dark, Nero would immediately grab
a freedman's cap or a wig and go into cheap cookshops and wander
around the neighborhoods looking for amusement. But this was not
harmless fun, for he would beat men who were returning home after
dinner, injuring them if they fought back and pushing them into the
sewers. He even broke into shops and robbed them and then set up
a marketplace at home where he parceled out the booty, auctioned it
off, and squandered the proceeds. [26.2] He often risked having his
eyes gouged out in street brawls of this sort, and his life came into
danger when he was almost beaten to death by a man of senatorial
rank whose wife he had molested. After that he never went out in
public at that hour without tribunes of the guard following at a dis-
creet distance. In the daytime he was carried secretly into the theater
in a sedan chair, and from his place over the stage, he provoked the
riots that involved the pantomime actors and then watched them

---

52. A market area in Rome.

unfold. And when the disturbance escalated to a brawl and there was fighting with stones and fragments of benches, he threw things at the people himself and even injured a praetor on the head.

[27.1] As his vices gradually gained strength and he abandoned jokes and secrecy and stopped wanting to pretend, he broke out into the open with worse crimes. [27.2] He had his feasts last from midday to midnight, often reviving himself in hot pools or, in the summer, in pools cooled with snow. He sometimes dined where the populace could watch him, in the artificial lake that he drained or in the Campus Martius or in the Circus Maximus, and he was served by prostitutes, male and female, brought in from all over the city. [27.3] Whenever he drifted down the Tiber to Ostia or sailed around the bay at Baiae, arranged along the shores and banks were taverns with private chambers, notorious for dissipation and infamous for their proprietors, who were respectable women pretending to be dancing girls and who urged him to step ashore on one side or the other. He made his close friends give dinners for him. One of them provided a banquet at a cost of 4 million sesterces where the guests wore silk headdresses, and another a "rose banquet" that cost considerably more.

[28.1] In addition to corrupting freeborn boys and sleeping with young matrons, he assaulted Rubria, a Vestal Virgin. He came close to contracting a legal marriage with the freedwoman Acte[53] after some former consuls were found willing to perjure themselves by swearing that she was of royal lineage. He tried to turn the slave boy Sporus into a woman by cutting off his testicles, and he had him conducted to him before many witnesses as his wife in a proper ceremony with dowry and red veil. Someone told a clever joke that has persisted: "Things could have gone well in human affairs if his father Domitius had had a wife like that." [28.2] Nero was seen with this Sporus in the public places and markets of Greece and later on in the Sigillaria in Rome. Sporus wore the jewelry and clothing of the imperial women and was carried about in a litter; Nero kissed him constantly. Everyone knew that Nero wanted to sleep with his mother but that those who did not like her restrained him because they feared that a relationship of this sort would give the strong, aggressive woman the upper hand. They were especially alarmed after he introduced among his mistresses a prostitute who was said

---

53. His mistress early in his reign.

to look very much like Agrippina. Even before that, so they say, whenever he was carried about in a litter with his mother, he satisfied his lust incestuously, and this was manifest by the stains on his clothing.

[29] Indeed, he fouled any sense of sexual decency that he had, until finally, after he had contaminated just about the whole of his body, he thought up what might be called a new kind of game. Covered with a wild animal skin and let loose from a cage, he attacked the genitals of men and women bound to stakes, and when he had satisfied his frenzy sufficiently, his freedman Doryphorus finished him off. Nero was given in marriage to this freedman, just as Sporus had been married to him, and he imitated the cries and shrieks of virgins being raped. Some have told me that he was totally convinced that no part of any man's body was pure and chaste but that most men pretended that they were uncorrupted and cleverly concealed their vice. He was so sure of this that he forgave other misdeeds in those who confessed their obscene behavior to him.

[30.1] Nero thought that the only pleasure to be had from wealth and riches was extravagant spending. He thought that people who kept a reckoning of their expenses were vulgar and cheap but that those who exhausted their resources and frittered them away were wondrously generous and truly magnificent creatures. He praised his maternal uncle Gaius and stood in awe of him simply because he had squandered the huge resources left by Tiberius so very quickly. [30.2] He therefore put no limits on giving away his money or spending it. On Tiridates (this seems almost unbelievable) he spent 800,000 sesterces every day,[54] and when the king departed, he gave him more than 100 million. On Menecrates, a citharode, and on Spiculus, a *murmillo*, he conferred fortunes and houses appropriate for men who had earned triumphs. He made the monkeylike[55] moneylender Paneros rich with city and country properties and buried him with almost regal pomp. He never wore the same clothes twice. [30.3] He played dice for 400,000 sesterces a point. He fished with a golden net whose cords were braided with purple and red. It is said that he never made a journey with fewer than a thousand traveling vans and that his mules had silver shoes, his mule drivers were dressed in

54. On his visit to Rome; see 13.1.
55. "Monkey" was evidently a term of abuse.

wool from Canusium,[56] and his escort of cavalry and footmen were Mazaces,[57] who wore armbands and collars.

[31.1] But what damaged his finances most was the building of a house that extended from the Palatine to the Esquiline Hill. He first called it the Passageway House, but after it burned and he restored it, he named it the Golden House. The following facts will be sufficient to indicate its size and decoration: It had a vestibule large enough to contain a colossal statue of himself 120 feet tall. The house's proportions were so generous that its triple arcade was a mile long. It had a pond as big as a sea surrounded by buildings that seemed like cities, and it had a park with open fields, vineyards, pastures, woods, and a large number of animals of all sorts, domestic and wild. [31.2] In the rest of the house everything was covered with gold and decorated with gemstones and mother-of-pearl. The dining rooms had coffered ceilings with ivory panels that rotated so that flowers could be scattered down, and these were fitted with tubes through which perfumes showered from above. The most important of the dining rooms was round and rotated continuously all day and night in replication of the world. The baths held seawater and water from a spring near Tibur. After his house was finished in this manner and he was dedicating it, he expressed his approval only so far as to say, "I have finally begun to live like a human being."

[31.3] He also started to construct a pool from Misenum to Lake Avernus[58] to be roofed over and surrounded by colonnades, and into it he intended to divert the waters of all the hot springs near Baiae. He began a canal from Avernus all the way to Ostia so that travel could take place without ships venturing out onto the sea. It was to be 160 miles long and wide enough for large galleys going in opposite directions to pass. To complete these projects he ordered that all prisoners everywhere be brought to Italy and that criminals be sentenced to no labor force other than this.

[31.4] To support his mad extravagance—in addition to relying on the resources of the empire—he was unexpectedly driven to hope for immense hidden riches. He learned of their existence from a Roman knight who promised it as fact that an ancient treasure,

---

56. A town in northern Italy, famous for its wool.

57. Horsemen from Mauretania.

58. A lake near the Bay of Naples.

brought from Tyre by Queen Dido[59] when she fled, was hidden in
vast caverns in Africa and could be unearthed with very little effort.
[32.1] When this hope proved false and Nero was left desperate and
so lacking in resources that the soldiers' pay had to be parceled out
and the veterans' bonuses postponed, he turned to false accusations
and plunder. [32.2] First he directed that five-sixths instead of half
of the property of deceased freedmen fall to him if they carried
the name of a family to whom he himself was related but a name to
which they had no right; next, that the assets of men who showed
themselves ungrateful to the emperor[60] pass to the imperial purse
and that the legal experts who had written or dictated their wills
be punished; then, that deeds and words be liable to prosecution
under the treason law if there was an informer present as a witness.
[32.3] He took back the money that he had paid for the crowns that
any of the states had conferred on him in the competitions. After he
had outlawed the use of the color of amethysts and Tyrian purple,[61]
he sent someone on the sly to sell a few ounces of the dye on market
day and shut down all the traders. And even while he was singing, he
is said to have pointed out to his agents a woman who was wearing
the forbidden purple at the games. She was seized on the spot and
stripped not only of her clothing but of her property, too. [32.4] He
never charged anyone with a task without adding, "You know what
I need," and, "Let's manage this so that no one has anything left."
Finally, he removed offerings from a large number of temples and
melted down statues made of gold and silver, among them statues of
the *Penates*. Galba restored them later.

[33.1] Nero began the killings of family members and murders
with Claudius. Although he was not the one who planned his death,
he nonetheless knew about it and did not pretend otherwise. As time
went on, he made it his habit to praise mushrooms with a phrase
from a Greek proverb, calling them the "food of the gods." (The
poison that Claudius consumed was served him in mushrooms.)[62]
Without question he attacked him after he was dead with all manner of insult, actions and words. At one moment he would charge

59. The legendary queen of Tyre, a character in Virgil's *Aeneid*.
60. They did not name him in their wills or did so only sparingly.
61. The color purple was reserved largely for the emperor.
62. See *Cl.* 44.2

him with stupidity and at another with cruelty. He would joke that Claudius had stopped "lingering" among his fellow men, lengthening the first syllable of the verb.[63] He held that many of the things that Claudius had decreed or instituted were not binding because they had issued from a foolish and deranged man. As a final insult, he neglected to fence Claudius' grave mound with anything more substantial than a flimsy, low wall.

[33.2] Nero poisoned Britannicus as much because he envied his voice (it happened to be more pleasing than his own) as from the fear that the memory of his father Claudius would someday earn him greater favor in men's eyes. He got the poison from an expert poisoner named Lucusta, and when the process did not go forward as quickly as he thought it should (Britannicus merely suffered bowel problems), he summoned the woman and beat her with his own hand, charging that she had given him an antidote instead of a poison. When she made the excuse that she had given a less potent dose in order to conceal the criminality behind the action, he said, "Of course! I'm afraid of the Julian law."[64] And he compelled her to concoct, in his private quarters as he watched, the quickest-acting poison that she could. [33.3] He tried it on a kid, but when the kid lived for five hours, he had her mix the potion again and yet again, and he offered it to a suckling pig. When the pig expired on the spot, he ordered it brought into the dining room and given to Britannicus, who was dining with him. When the boy fell dead at the first taste, he lied to his table companions, telling them that Britannicus had suffered an epileptic seizure as he often did. He buried him quickly the next day during a heavy rainstorm with no more than ordinary ceremony. To Lucusta he gave immunity and a generous reward for her skilled services. He sent her pupils as well.

[34.1] He found his mother annoying when she pried too insistently into what he did and said and when she found fault with him. In the beginning his irritation was such that he did no more than make her unpopular by constantly threatening that he was going to give up the principate and go off to Rhodes.[65] Then he deprived

---

63. The Latin word for "linger" differs in sound from the Greek word for "play the fool" only in the length of its first vowel.

64. Evidently a law forbidding assassination.

65. A reference to Tiberius' retirement to Capri that was blamed on discord between him and his mother Livia; see *Tib.* 40, 51.1.

her of all her honors and her power, took away her guard detail of
praetorians and Germans, and forced her out of his private quarters
and off the Palatine as well. Nothing was too much bother when it
came to making things difficult for her. He enlisted people to harass
her with lawsuits while she remained in Rome, and when she retired
to the country, to badger her with insults and ridicule whenever they
were nearby on land and sea.

[34.2] But her violent threats frightened him, and he decided to
kill her. He tried poison three times but realized that she had protected herself with antidotes. He arranged for a mechanism to loosen
the ceiling panels in her bedchamber and make them fall on her at
night as she slept, but those who knew about the plan did not keep
it very secret. And so he engineered a ship that would fall apart and
cause her to die in a shipwreck or by the collapse of her cabin. He
pretended to be reconciled with her and wrote her an extremely
affectionate letter inviting her to celebrate the Quinquatria with
him. He gave his trireme commanders the task of staging a chance
collision and destroying the galley in which she had come. He made
the banquet last a long time, and when she wanted to return to
Bauli,[66] he offered her the tricked-out vessel instead of the one that
had been damaged. He escorted her to it in high spirits and kissed
her breasts when she left. [34.3] The rest of the night he lay awake
and worried while he waited to hear how his plan had turned out.
But when he learned that what had happened was not what had been
intended and that she had escaped by swimming, he did not know
what to do. When her freedman Lucius Agermus arrived and gave
the happy report that she was safe and unharmed, Nero ordered him
seized and bound. A dagger was surreptitiously thrown down next to
him so that it would appear that he had been enlisted to assassinate
the emperor, and Nero ordered his mother killed, making it look as if
she had anticipated her arrest for the crime by taking her own life.

[34.4] Reliable authors have added further disgusting details: they
say that Nero hurried to view the murdered woman's corpse, fondled
her limbs, disparaging some parts of her body and praising others,
and that while doing this, he had grown thirsty and taken a drink.
But he could not live with the bad conscience that this crime left
him, not at the time or ever in the future, despite the reassurance
given him by the soldiers' congratulations and those of the senate

---

66. A small town on the coast not far from Baiae.

and the people. He often let it be known that he was pursued by his mother's ghost and by the whips and burning torches of the Furies.[67] He even tried to summon forth the spirit of the dead and appease it in a sacred rite performed by the Magi.[68] He did not dare attend the Eleusinian mysteries on his Greek tour,[69] for a herald warned away all who were sacrilegious and criminal before the rites began.

[34.5] Nero added the death of his aunt[70] to the murder of his mother. When he went to see her while she was in bed suffering from constipation, she stroked his soft beard as she often did (he was now grown) and chanced to say in the course of their pleasant conversation, "As soon as I receive this, I am willing to die."[71] He turned to his companions and said with a laugh, "I'll shave it at once," and he told her doctors to purge the sick woman aggressively. He suppressed her will and raided her estate even before she was dead so as to lose nothing.

[35.1] After Octavia, he married two more wives: Poppaea Sabina, whose father reached the rank of quaestor and who had earlier been married to a Roman knight, and then Statilia Messallina, the great-great-granddaughter of Taurus, twice consul and a triumphing general.[72] In order to marry Statilia, he killed her husband Atticus Vestinus while he was consul. Nero had quickly grown tired of sleeping with Octavia and replied to his friends when they reproached him about this, "It ought to be enough for her that she has the trappings of a wife." [35.2] After a number of desultory attempts to strangle her, he divorced her on the grounds that she was sterile. But when the populace objected to the divorce and mounted an angry protest, he added banishment. In the end he killed her on a charge of adultery that was so barefaced and untrue that when everyone persistently denied the allegations during the inquiry, he had to produce his former tutor, Anicetus, as a witness and have him lie and confess that

---

67. Avenging spirits from Greek tragedy.

68. Learned men from Persia, sometimes magicians.

69. The cult of Ceres at Eleusis near Athens; see *Cl.* 25.5.

70. Domitia, not Domitia Lepida; see note on 5.2.

71. Shaving the first beard and preserving it was the rite of passage to full manhood.

72. Titus Statilius Taurus, general and supporter of Augustus; see *Aug.* 29.5.

he had tricked her and forced her to have sex with him. [35.3] Nero married Poppaea, his one true love, twelve days after he divorced Octavia, but he killed her, too. He kicked her because she scolded him for coming home late from the races when she was pregnant and ill. His daughter by her, Claudia Augusta, died as a baby.

[35.4] No relation of any remove escaped his villainy: Claudius' daughter Antonia,[73] when she refused to marry him after the death of Poppaea, he killed on the grounds that she was plotting revolution, and he did the same to others related to him by marriage or by blood. Among these was Aulus Plautius,[74] a young man whom he raped before his death; "Now let my mother come and kiss my successor," he said, charging that Plautius had been Agrippina's lover and had been seduced by a hope for power. [35.5] His stepson Rufrius Crispinus, Poppaea's young son, he had the boy's own slaves drown in the sea when he was fishing because of a report that he played a game in which he was a general and an emperor. His nurse's son Tuscus he banished because as procurator of Egypt he had bathed in the baths that had been built for the emperor's visit there. His teacher Seneca he forced to suicide, despite the fact that when Seneca asked permission to retire and offered to surrender his property, he had given his most solemn assurance that Seneca was wrong to distrust him and that he would perish before he would do him harm. To his praetorian prefect Burrus[75] he sent poison instead of the throat remedy that he had promised. Wealthy old freedmen who had once helped him, first with his adoption and later to come to rule, he killed with poison; he introduced it into the food of some, into the drink of others.

[36.1] Nero was just as brutal abroad, against those not of his household. A comet, a sign commonly thought to portend the downfall of mighty rulers, began to appear in the sky several nights in succession. This worried him, and when he learned from the astrologer Balbillus that it was the practice of kings to avert omens like this with the death of some important person, to remove them from their own heads onto the heads of nobles, he planned death for all of the most distinguished men in Rome. He did this with greater confidence and

<hr/>

73. By Aelia Paetina; see *Cl.* 27.1.
74. Perhaps related through Claudius' first wife, Plautia Urgulanilla; see *Cl.* 26.2.
75. Sextus Afranius Burrus, an influential adviser along with Seneca.

with apparent justification after the discovery of two conspiracies. The first and more serious, that of Piso, was planned and uncovered at Rome; the second, that of Vinicius, at Beneventum.[76] [36.2] The conspirators pleaded their case in chains bound around them three times. Some confessed their guilt unprompted while others even claimed it to their merit, as if death were the only way they could bring relief to this man who had disgraced himself by every kind of shameful deed. The children of the condemned were driven from the city and poisoned or starved to death. Some are known to have been killed together with their tutors and personal slaves at a single meal and others to have been kept from earning the necessities of daily life.

[37.1] After this, Nero's killing continued without discrimination or limit. He killed whomever he wanted for any reason whatsoever. To give only a few examples: Salvidianus Orfitus was charged because he had rented three shops that were part of his house near the Forum to foreign nations to use as their headquarters in Rome; Cassius Longinus, a blind jurist, because he had kept likenesses of Caesar's assassin Gaius Cassius within his ancient family tree; Paetus Thrasea, because of a gloomy expression that made him look like a disapproving mentor. [37.2] He gave those whom he ordered to kill themselves no more than an hour in which to do it, and to prevent delay, he prompted doctors immediately to "take care of" (his expression for slitting veins to cause death) those putting it off. It is believed that he even wanted to throw living men to a certain omnivorous fiend from Egypt who would chew on raw meat and anything that was given him, because he wanted them torn limb from limb and devoured. [37.3] He considered these heinous actions his successes. They gave him confidence and made him feel invincible, and he said that no previous emperor had known what he could get away with. He often gave clear signs that he would not spare even the senators who were left alive and that he would one day banish the order from the state and entrust the provinces and the armies to equestrians and freedmen. What is certain is that he did not exchange kisses with any senator, either on arrival or departure, or even return their greetings. And when he began work on the Isthmus,[77] he expressed

---

76. It was evidently the intention to make Gaius Calpurnius Piso emperor in 65 CE; see *Cal.* 25.1. Nothing more is known of the second conspiracy.
77. The Corinthian canal; see 19.2.

this wish, stating it in a loud voice before a large crowd: "I hope that this undertaking will be a success for me and for the Roman people." He made no mention of the senate.

[38.1] But Nero spared neither the people of his native city nor its walls. Someone quoted him this line in the course of a conversation: "When I am dead, let the earth be consumed by fire."[78] "On the contrary," said Nero, "while I'm alive." And he made it happen. On the excuse that he disliked the ugly old buildings and the narrow twisting streets of the city neighborhoods, he set fire to the city so brazenly that many men of consular rank did not arrest his house slaves when they were caught on their property with tinder and torches. And some granaries near the Golden House (he especially coveted the ground on which they stood) were knocked down by military devices and were burned because they had been built with stone walls. [38.2] For six days and seven nights the conflagration raged, and the common people were compelled to take shelter among monuments and tombs. There burned at that time, in addition to the huge number of apartment blocks, the homes of Rome's earliest generals, which were still decked with enemy spoils, and the temples of the gods that had been promised and dedicated by the kings and later on in the Punic and Gallic wars, and everything else worth seeing and remarkable that had endured from ancient times. Nero watched the fire from the tower of Maecenas,[79] taking pleasure in the "beauty of the flames," as he said, and he sang "The Fall of Troy" dressed in his stage costume. [38.3] To gain the added benefit of getting his hands on as much loot as he could from this disaster (his due as commander in chief), he promised to remove the bodies and clear the rubble at his own expense and allowed no one to approach the ruins on his own property. He came close to bankrupting provinces and private individuals with the contributions that he not only received but even demanded.

[39.1] Chance misfortunes were added to the dreadful evils and scandals for which the emperor was responsible: A plague caused thirty thousand deaths to be entered in the register of the temple of Libitina[80] in a single autumn. A disaster occurred in Britain

---

78. A well-known but anonymous line from Greek tragedy.
79. In the gardens of Maecenas, on the Esquiline Hill.
80. The goddess of corpses, 65 CE.

when two important towns were plundered with great loss of life to Romans and their allies. Humiliation met the legions stationed in the East when they were sent under the yoke[81] in Armenia, and Syria barely remained under Roman control. What is strange and worth pointing out is that in the midst of all this there was nothing he tolerated with greater patience than the curses and mockery directed against him, nor was he more forgiving to any than to those who abused him verbally and in verse. [39.2] Many verses (Greek and Latin) were posted and circulated widely, such as these:

> Nero Orestes Alcmeon, matricide.[82]

> A new calculation: Nero killed his mother.[83]

> Who says that Nero comes not from Aeneas' line?
> The one took his mother's life; the other took up his father.[84]

> Since our Roman tunes his lyre and the Parthian bends his bow,
> Ours will be Apollo Paean; theirs, Apollo Hecatebeletes.[85]

> Rome is turning into a house. Go live in Veii, Romans—
> If the house does not cover Veii, too![86]

But he did not go looking for the authors, nor did he allow too harsh a punishment to fall on those on whom a spy had informed to the senate. [39.3] When he passed by the Cynic philosopher Isidorus, the man taunted him in a loud voice so that all could hear: Nero had

---

81. Captured troops were forced to pass under a bridge of spears.

82. He is given the usual three-part Roman name, but the second and third names are those of figures from Greek mythology who killed their mothers.

83. In Greek, numbers were expressed by letters; the value of those in "Nero" are equal to those in the rest of the sentence.

84. Aeneas took his father on his shoulders when he escaped from Troy. The Latin verb allows a pun; it means both "get rid of" and "lift up." The same pun appears at *Aug.* 12.

85. The god Apollo, both a musician and an archer, had different names in his different aspects. The Parthians were known for their skill with bow and arrow.

86. A reference to Nero's huge Golden House encroaching on Rome; see 31.1–2. Veii was about ten miles north of the city.

sung the evil deeds of Nauplius[87] well but managed his own fortune badly. Datus, an actor in Atellan farces, chanted, "Farewell, Father. Farewell, Mother," as he mimed drinking and swimming, clearly indicating the deaths of Claudius and Agrippina. And with the last verse, "Orcus[88] guides your steps," he pointed to the senate. Nero merely banished the actor and philosopher from Rome and Italy. He either felt that all insults were beneath contempt or did not want to encourage their talents by confessing his hurt.

[40.1] After almost fourteen years of suffering, the world finally rid itself of such an emperor. It began with the Gallic leader Julius Vindex,[89] who was governing that province as a propraetor at the time.

[40.2] Astrologers had once predicted to Nero that he would one day be thrown aside, and this led to a saying that he repeated often: "Art earns us our keep." It gave him an excuse to practice the citharode's art that served as entertainment for the emperor but was a livelihood for a private citizen. Some astrologers, however, had promised him dominion over the East after his support disappeared in Rome and others kingship in Jerusalem specifically, and many promised the restoration of all his earlier fortunes. He relied on this hope, for once Britain and Armenia had been lost but were both recovered again, he thought himself immune to the evils that had been foretold. [40.3] And when he consulted the oracle of Apollo at Delphi[90] and learned that he must beware the seventy-third year, he thought it the year when he would finally die. He did not think about Galba's age. He was so sure not only that he would live to old age but also that he would enjoy remarkable and everlasting good fortune that when he lost possessions of great value in a shipwreck, he immediately said to his friends, "The fish will return them to me."

[40.4] He was in Naples when he learned that the Gallic provinces were in revolt. It was the anniversary of the day on which he had killed his mother. He received the news so calmly and with so little

---

87. Nauplius tried to destroy the Greek fleet returning from Troy. Nero had acted the role.
88. The lord of the underworld. He was suggesting that Nero murdered senators as well.
89. Gaius Julius Vindex, a Romanized Gaul; his family had been given citizenship either by Julius Caesar or by Augustus.
90. A well-known site of an oracle in Greece.

concern that he invited the suspicion that he was happy because the rules of war were presenting him with an opportunity to plunder the richest of the provinces. He immediately set out for the gymnasium and watched with particular enthusiasm as athletes competed. He received a more upsetting letter at dinner and grew angry but only to the point of threatening to harm the renegades. Then for the next eight days he made no attempt to reply to anyone or appoint any agents or give any command but ignored the crisis in silence.

[41.1] The insulting edicts that Vindex kept issuing at frequent intervals finally irritated him, and he wrote a letter to the senate urging them to avenge both himself and the state. He blamed his sluggish response on throat trouble that was keeping him away. But the insults that caused him the most distress were criticism of him as an incompetent citharode and being called Ahenobarbus instead of Nero. He announced that he would get rid of his adoptive name and retrieve the family name that was being used to humiliate him. He refuted the other deriding remarks, saying that they were incorrect, but he offered no evidence other than that he was being criticized for knowing nothing of an art that his hard work had refined and brought to perfection. He was constantly asking individuals, "Do you know anyone better than I?" [41.2] But when urgent messages followed one after another, he returned to Rome in a panic. An insignificant sign that he met on the way provided some slight encouragement: he noticed a monument with a carving of a Gallic soldier being overpowered by a Roman horseman and being dragged along by the hair, and he jumped for joy at the sight and blessed heaven. But not even then did he address the senate or the populace in person. Instead, he summoned some of the leading men to his house and after discussing the problem briefly, he spent the rest of the day showing them his water organs that had been manufactured with the most recent innovations, pointing out their features and explaining how each worked and the difficulties with each. He even promised, "I will soon demonstrate all of them in the theater—if Vindex lets me."

[42.1] After he learned that Galba[91] and the Spanish provinces were also in revolt, he collapsed in a faint and lay unconscious for a long time, unable to speak. When he came to his senses, he tore his

---

91. Servius Sulpicius Galba, the next emperor, was governor in Spain with a legion under his command in the spring of 68 CE.

clothing, battered his head, and declared, "I am finished." When his old nurse tried to comfort him by reminding him that things like this had happened to other emperors in the past, he replied, "My suffering outstrips theirs, since I endure things unheard of and never imagined. I am losing supreme power while I yet live." [42.2] But he did not abandon the extravagant and indolent life that he had always lived or retrench in any way. In fact, whenever good news arrived from the provinces, he gave banquets sumptuous in their excess and mimed obscene songs that mocked the leaders of the revolt, songs that became notorious. When he had been carried secretly into a theater, he sent this message to a popular actor: "You are taking advantage of me while I am busy with other concerns."

[43.1] It is believed that when the uprising first began, he made plans to do many things that were brutal but not inconsistent with his character: He planned to replace the commanders of the armies and the governors of the provinces on the assumption that they were all of one mind and conspiring against him, and he sent assassins to kill them. He planned to butcher all exiles everywhere and all of the Gauls in the city, the former so that they would not join the dissidents, the latter because he thought they were in league with their countrymen and supported their cause. And he planned to allow the armies to ravage the Gallic provinces, to poison the entire senate at banquets, and to set fire to the city after letting loose wild animals so that it would be more difficult for the people to protect themselves. [43.2] It was not so much a change of heart that deterred him from these actions as that he despaired of carrying them out. In the belief that a military operation was necessary, he relieved the consuls of office before their terms were up and entered the consulship alone, taking the places of both on the grounds that it was fated that only a consul could bring the Gallic provinces to total submission. He took office, and as he was leaving the dining room after a banquet, leaning on the shoulders of his close associates, he announced, "As soon as I have reached the province, I shall appear unarmed before the armies and do nothing but weep. And when I have made the rebels regret their action, I shall, the very next day, rejoice along with them as they rejoice, and I shall sing victory songs . . . I ought to be writing them this very moment!"

[44.1] His first concerns in readying his expedition were the choice of wagons to transport his stage machinery, masculine haircuts for the concubines he was taking with him, and the

Amazon[92] battle-axes and shields with which he was outfitting them. Then he summoned the city tribes to take the military oath, and when no suitable candidates appeared, he obliged each slave owner to make available a specified number of slaves, and he selected the very best from each household with no exceptions even for stewards and secretaries. [44.2] He ordered men of every rank to contribute a portion of their wealth and compelled tenants who lived in private houses and apartments to pay their annual rent to the imperial treasury at once. He insisted that payment be made in newly minted coins of pure silver and tested gold. This stipulation caused many to refuse openly to pay any part of their contribution, and they demanded that rewards for informers be revoked instead. [45.1] He was hated more and more because of the profit he made from the high price of grain. It happened that when the people were suffering from famine, a ship was reported on its way from Alexandria with sand for the court wrestlers.

[45.2] And so, as the loathing that everyone felt for him intensified, there was no humiliation that he did not endure: a lock of hair was placed on the head of his statue with a Greek legend, "Now, finally, you have competition, and you must concede at last."[93] Around the neck of another statue was tied a leather bag and with it a note: "What could I do?" "But you have earned the sack."[94] Graffiti scribbled on columns claimed that his singing had awakened even the Gauls. At night, many pretended to be fighting with their slaves and kept calling for a "defender."[95]

[46.1] Nero was also frightened by portents that came to him in dreams and by auguries and omens, some that had appeared long before, others more recently. He had never in the past been accustomed to dream, but after his mother had been killed, he saw himself in his sleep at the helm of a ship, and the tiller was wrenched from him, and his wife Octavia was dragging him into the confines of darkness. At one point he saw himself crawling with a great mass

---

92. Amazons were mythical female warriors.

93. Nero wore his hair long in back; see 51.

94. The meaning is uncertain. Nero may be imagined asking what choice he had about killing his mother. The answer is that he still deserves the sack, the archaic punishment for parricides; see *Aug.* 33.1.

95. A pun on the name of the leader of the uprising; *vindex* means "champion," "avenger."

of winged ants, another time surrounded by the statues of the conquered nations that had been dedicated at the theater of Pompey,
and they kept him from moving forward. And he dreamed that
the back quarters of his Asturian horse,[96] his great favorite, had
been transformed into those of a monkey and that only its head
was unchanged. But it whinnied in tune. [46.2] The doors of the
Mausoleum flew open on their own, and a voice was heard calling
his name. On the Kalends of January the *Lares*[97] that were decorated
in preparation for the sacrifice toppled to the ground. When he
was taking the auspices, Sporus offered him the gift of a ring that
had the rape of Proserpina carved in its gemstone.[98] At the solemn
proclamation of the vows,[99] when a large crowd of all classes had
already gathered, there was difficulty finding the keys to the temple
of Jupiter on the Capitoline. [46.3] When the speech in which he was
making his case against Vindex was being read aloud in the senate,
and these words came up, "The wicked will be punished and will
soon meet the death that they deserve," everyone shouted together,
"It will be you, Augustus, who does that!" And it was noticed that
the last narrative that he sang in public was "Oedipus, the Exile,"
and that he ended with this verse: "Wife, mother, father, drive me
to my death!"

[47.1] While these ominous signs were appearing, he learned that
the rest of his armies had also defected. He tore up a letter that was
given to him at his midday meal, overturned the table, and smashed
to the ground two large goblets that he particularly liked. (He called
them his Homeric goblets because they were incised with scenes
from the Homeric poems.) He got poison from Lucusta, put it in
a small golden box, and went to the Servilian gardens.[100] He sent
his most trusted freedmen ahead to Ostia to get the fleet ready, and
at the gardens he tried to persuade the tribunes and centurions of
the praetorian guard to go with him when he fled. [47.2] But when
some were reluctant and others openly refused, one of them even

---

96. From a region in Spain.

97. Presumably January 1, 68 CE. *Lares* were the city's protective
deities.

98. Proserpina (Persephone) was carried off into the underworld.

99. Prayers for the safety and preservation of the emperor on January 3.

100. An imperial property.

shouting, "Is it so very wretched a thing to die?"[101] he pondered
his options: Should he go begging to the Parthians or to Galba, or
should he appear to the public on the rostra dressed in mourning
and beg forgiveness for his past actions as piteously as he possibly
could? And if he failed to change their minds, should he ask that the
prefecture of Egypt be awarded him? There was found later in his
writing box the speech that had been written for this occasion, but
it is thought that he was afraid that he would be torn to pieces before
he reached the Forum.

[47.3] And so he put off his decision until the following day. But
at about midnight he awoke to learn that his military guard had
withdrawn. He jumped out of bed and sent for his friends, and when
they did not respond, he took a few attendants and went to their
quarters in the palace. But all of their doors were closed and no one
answered him, and so he went back to his chamber where he found
that his personal guards had by then fled as well, stealing even his
bedclothes and taking the small box of poison. He immediately tried
to find the *murmillo* Spiculus or any other executioner at whose hand
he might perish. And when he found no one, he said, "So. Have I
neither friend nor foe?" And he ran out as if to throw himself headlong into the Tiber.

[48.1] But again he changed his mind and looked for an obscure
hiding place of some sort where he could collect his thoughts. When
his freedman Phaon offered his suburban house, which was near the
fourth milestone from Rome between the Salarian and Nomentanan
roads, he mounted a horse, just as he was, barefoot and wearing a
tunic, throwing on top a dingy cloak with a hood and with his head
covered and a cloth held across his face.[102] He had only four companions, Sporus among them. [48.2] He was immediately terrified
by a shaking of the earth and a flash of lightning full in his face,
and he heard soldiers shouting from the nearby camp, foretelling
misfortune for himself and good prospects for Galba. He heard one
of the travelers that they met say, "These men are hunting for Nero,"
and another asked, "What news in the city about Nero?" His horse
was frightened by the smell of a corpse that had been left on the road,

---

101. Virgil, *Aeneid* 12.646.
102. His route led away from the coast. It passed near the praetorian camp
on the way out of the city.

his face came uncovered, and a discharged praetorian recognized him and saluted him.

[48.3] They reached a turning and let their horses go, and Nero made his way through thickets and thornbushes along a path in the reeds to the back wall of the villa. This was difficult for him, and he had to have a garment spread beneath his feet. When he got there, Phaon, who had offered him the house, urged him to hide in a hollowed-out place where sand had been dug, but Nero said that he would not go into the earth while he still lived. He waited for a time until a secret entrance was opened into the house, and he took water in his hand from a nearby pool and drank it, saying, "This is Nero's distillation."[103] [48.4] Then he pulled out the twigs stuck in his cloak, which had been torn by the thorns, and like an animal he inched through the narrow passage that had been dug into the first small room. There he lay down on a bed with an ordinary mattress and an old cloak spread on top. Suffering from hunger and also from thirst, he rejected a bit of coarse bread that was offered to him but drank a small amount of tepid water. [49.1] Then, as each and every one of his companions pressed him to save himself as soon as possible from the ill treatment that was waiting for him, he ordered a hole, measured to the dimensions of his body, to be dug while he watched. At the same time he ordered bits of marble to be collected, if there were any to be found, and water and wood brought for taking care of the corpse after the event. He wept as these things were being done and kept saying over and over, "What an artist dies with me!"

[49.2] As he hesitated, he grabbed a letter that a courier had brought to Phaon and read that he had been declared an enemy of the state by the senate and was being hunted down so that he could be punished in the traditional manner. When he asked what kind of punishment that was, he learned that a man was stripped naked and his neck put into a fork and that he was beaten to death with rods,[104] and he was horrified. He seized the two daggers that he had brought with him and tested the blade of each but put them away again with the excuse, "The fatal hour is not yet come." [49.3] At one moment he would encourage Sporus to grieve and mourn him; at another he would beg someone to help him take his life by setting an example. At the same time, he found fault with his own inaction in

---

103. He supposedly liked his water boiled and then cooled in snow.
104. See *Cl.* 34.1, *Dom.* 11.2.

these words: "I live hideously, shamefully—it is not right for Nero, not right—one must control oneself in matters like this—come, stir yourself!" Now the horsemen who had been commissioned to bring him back alive were drawing near. When he grasped this, he said in terror, "The thunder of swift-footed horses strikes upon my ear."[105] Epaphroditus, his secretary for petitions, helped him drive a dagger into his throat. [49.4] He was still half alive when a centurion burst in pretending that he had come to help and put a cloak over the wound. Nero said to him, "Too late," and, "This is loyalty." With those words, he died, his eyes protruding and fixed, to the horror and dread of those who saw him. The most important promises that he exacted from his companions were that they allow no one to get possession of his head and that they find some way for his body to be cremated intact. Icelus, a freedman of Galba,[106] gave permission for this soon after he was freed from the chains with which he had been bound at the beginning of the uprising.

[50] Nero was buried in the white robes interwoven with gold threads that he had worn on the Kalends of January[107] at a cost of 200,000 sesterces. His nurses Egloge and Alexandria, together with his mistress Acte, placed his remains in the tomb of the Domitian family that had been built on the Hill of the Gardens and was visible from the Campus Martius. His sarcophagus inside the tomb was of porphyry, the altar above it of marble from Luna, and it was fenced around with stone from Thasos.[108]

[51] Nero was of about average height. His body was covered with spots and smelled bad. He had light-brown hair and a face that was handsome rather than pleasant. His eyes were gray-blue and rather weak. He had a fat neck, a stomach that stuck out, and skinny legs. He enjoyed excellent health; this man whose profligacy knew no bounds was unwell only three times during his fourteen-year reign and even then not so ill as to forgo wine or alter his other habits. He was so inappropriately obsessed with his grooming and his clothes that he always piled his hair up in tiers, and on his journey around Greece he let it hang down the back of his head. On many occasions

---

105. Homer, *Iliad* 10.535.
106. See *Gal.* 14.2.
107. The New Year's Day holiday.
108. A town in northern Etruria and an island in the Aegean.

he appeared in public unbelted and shoeless, wearing a loose robe and a handkerchief tied around his neck.

[52] As a boy Nero touched on almost all of the liberal subjects, but his mother steered him away from philosophy, warning that it was an inappropriate discipline for someone meant to rule. His tutor Seneca steered him away from familiarity with the orators of the past so that he himself would continue to be the object of the boy's admiration. As a consequence, Nero turned to poetry and wrote poems effortlessly for his pleasure. But he did not, as some think,[109] pass off the work of others as his own. Writing tablets and notebooks have come into my hands that contain very well-known verses of his written in his own handwriting. These make it obvious that they were not copied or taken down from dictation but clearly penned by someone as he was thinking and composing; that is, they contain many erasures, insertions, and superscriptions. Nero also took serious interest in painting and sculpture.

[53] But he was totally infatuated with a desire to be famous, and he made himself the rival of anyone who caught the interest of the people for any reason at all. It was thought that, after winning crowns on the stage, he would compete with the athletes at the next Olympic Games. He was constantly practicing his wrestling, and he always viewed the gymnastic games given anywhere in Greece like an umpire sitting on the ground in the stadium. And if any of the pairs moved too far away, he pushed them into the middle with his hands. He had also decided, since he was considered the equal of Apollo in singing and of Apollo as the sun god when he drove his chariot, to emulate the deeds of Hercules as well. They say that a lion had been made ready for him to crush with a club or in the grip of his arms, naked, as the people watched in the arena of the amphitheater. [54] Near the time of his death he vowed publicly that if he remained emperor and was unharmed, he would perform at the games that celebrated his victory by playing the water organ, the reed pipe, and the bagpipes and that on the last day he would appear as an actor and dance the role of Virgil's Turnus. Some say that he killed the actor Paris because he was his serious competition. [55] He wanted to live forever and for his fame to be lasting, but his desire was not coherently conceived. It was for this reason that he took away the old names of many things and places and gave them new names

---

109. The historian Tacitus cast doubt on the originality of Nero's poetry.

derived from his own. He called the month of April Neroneus and had decided to name Rome Neropolis.

[56] He had no use whatsoever for religious practices, with a single exception: the worship of the Syrian goddess.[110] But later he rejected her so vehemently that he defiled her statue by urinating on it. He had been caught up in a different obsession, the only one to which he clung stubbornly. This was his trust in the statuette of a girl that had been given to him by an unidentified commoner to protect him against conspiracies. A plot was discovered soon after he received it, and so he continued to revere it as his supreme guardian and to sacrifice to it three times a day. He wanted it believed that her warnings gave him knowledge of the future. A few months before he died, he attended an examination of entrails but never obtained a favorable reading.

[57.1] Nero died in his thirty-second year on the anniversary of the day on which he had killed Octavia. His death gave everyone such joy that the people ran all about the city wearing freedom caps.[111] But there were those who continued for a long time to decorate his tomb with flowers in the spring and summer. They sometimes displayed statues of him on the rostra wearing the *toga praetextata*, and they produced edicts from him as though he were still alive and soon to return to do his enemies harm. [57.2] When Vologaesus, king of the Parthians, sent representatives to the senate to renew their alliance, he asked most earnestly that Nero's memory be cherished as well. And finally, twenty years later, when I was a young man, someone of obscure origin appeared and bragged that he was Nero. This name was in such favor with the Parthians that they welcomed the imposter enthusiastically and were reluctant to surrender him.

---

110. Cybele or the Magna Mater, worshiped in the eastern part of the empire. See note on *Tib.* 2.3.

111. Small caps worn by slaves who were newly freed.

GALBA

3 BCE–69 CE
Emperor June 68–January 69 CE

Servius Sulpicius Galba was emperor from June 9, 68 CE, the day Nero died, until January 15, 69, the day he was murdered. Galba was the first of four generals to fight for the throne after the Julio-Claudian dynasty came to an end. Their very struggle proves that the principate was now a fact—it had evolved beyond being the fiefdom of a single extended family, and could be contested by men who had armies at their command. As the historian Tacitus put it, the civil war that followed Nero's death uncovered "the secret" of the empire: "It was possible for an emperor to be created elsewhere than in Rome" (Histories 1.4). The army had brought Julius Caesar and Augustus to power; it was only their descendants who had had the benefit of family for support.

Galba came from a family with a long and distinguished history. He himself had long served Rome and had often been close to the imperial center. He was already an old man when he became emperor, a strict disciplinarian with old-fashioned ideas about military loyalty who was unwilling to pay bounties on his accession. More importantly, he seems to have had neither the energy nor the audacity to deal with a chaotic and unstable situation. Galba was more promising as a contender than effective as an emperor.

Suetonius opens his account of Galba's life by calling attention to the important break that followed the Julio-Claudian dynasty.

[1] The family line of the Caesars ended with Nero. Many portents made it clear that this would happen, but two were especially compelling. When Livia, long ago, was returning to her villa near Veii,[1] immediately after her marriage to Augustus, an eagle flew past and

---

1. A city north of Rome.

dropped a white hen into her lap. It was holding a laurel branch in its beak, just as it had been when the eagle carried it off. She decided to feed the bird and plant the branch. The brood of chicks that resulted was so large that the villa is called today the place of the hens, and the laurel grove grew so large that the Caesars cut their laurel fronds from it for their triumphs. It became the custom for those who triumphed to immediately plant other branches in the same spot, and it was observed that as the death of each man drew near, the tree that he had planted lost its vigor. And so in Nero's final year the entire grove perished to its roots, and all the hens there died. In addition, lightning struck the temple of the Caesars shortly after that, and the heads fell from all the statues at the same time, and the scepter was dashed from Augustus' hands.

[2] Galba, who succeeded Nero, had no connection with the house of the Caesars. He was, however, incontestably an aristocrat from an old and renowned family of such prominence that he always added to the inscriptions on his statues that he was the great-grandson of Quintus Catulus Capitolinus.[2] When Galba was emperor, he displayed in the atrium of his house a family tree that traced his father's origin back to Jupiter and his mother's to Pasiphae, the wife of Minos.[3] [3.1] It would take a long time to go though the personages and the life histories of the entire clan; I shall touch briefly on his more immediate family. It is unclear who was the first of the Sulpicii to bear the cognomen Galba and why or where he got it. Some think that when a town in Spain had been besieged for a long time with no success, he finally used torches smeared with *galbanum*[4] to set it on fire; others that he constantly applied a *galbeus* (medicines wrapped in a wool bandage) during a long illness; still others that he was apparently very fat, a person that the Gauls call *galba*; and others, on the contrary, that he was as slight as the insects called *galbae* that hatch in oak trees.

---

2. Prominent in the 70s and 60s BCE. He was responsible for rebuilding the temple on the Capitoline that had burned; see *Jul.* 15, *Aug.* 94.8.

3. Minos was the legendary king of Crete. Pasiphae was the mother of the Minotaur.

4. A plant resin.

[3.2] The consul Servius Galba,[5] quite the best orator of his day, brought distinction to his family. He is said to have caused the war against Viriatus when he was governor of Spain after his praetorship because he treacherously slaughtered thirty thousand Lusitanians.[6] His grandson[7] had been one of Julius Caesar's subordinate commanders in Gaul but became incensed at him when he failed to help him win the consulship. He joined the conspiracy headed by Cassius and Brutus and was in consequence condemned under the Pedian law.[8] [3.3] From him were descended the grandfather and father of the emperor Galba. Galba's grandfather,[9] better known for his intellectual pursuits than for the office he obtained (he did not go beyond the rank of praetor), published a carefully written history in many parts. Galba's father served as consul,[10] and although he was a short man with a hump on his back and modest speaking ability, he was always tireless in pleading cases. [3.4] His wives were Mummia Achaica, the granddaughter of Catulus and the great-granddaughter of Lucius Mummius, who destroyed Corinth, and then the very rich and beautiful Livia Ocellina. It was she, however, who is thought to have taken the initiative and approached him with a proposal of marriage because of his prominence. She pursued him even more eagerly after he took off his clothes for her in private and showed her his deformity so that he would not appear to have deceived her if he left her ignorant. With Achaica he fathered sons, Gaius and Servius. Gaius, the elder, wasted his property and left the city, and when Tiberius kept his name from being in the drawing for a proconsulship when it was his year,[11] he took his life.

---

5. This Servius Sulpicius Galba was prominent in the mid-second century BCE.

6. 150–140 BCE. Viriatus escaped from the slaughter and led a guerrilla war against Rome.

7. This Servius Sulpicius Galba, praetor in 54 BCE, was probably not the grandson of the one previously mentioned. A generation seems to be missing.

8. The law passed to punish Caesar's assassins; see *Ner.* 3.1.

9. Gaius Sulpicius Galba.

10. Another Gaius Sulpicius Galba, suffect consul in 5 BCE.

11. This Gaius Sulpicius Galba was consul in 22 CE. The provinces of Africa and Asia were assigned by lot to the most senior former consuls, but because of the large number of suffect consuls each year, a former consul

[4.1] The emperor Servius Galba was born on the ninth day before the Kalends of January in the consulship of Marcus Valerius Messalla and Gnaeus Lentulus,[12] in a villa on a hilltop near Tarracina, off to the left on the way to Fundi. Adopted by his stepmother Livia, he took her name and also her cognomen Ocella; he changed his first name as well and used Lucius instead of Servius from that time until he became emperor.[13] It is common knowledge that when he was still a boy and was paying his respects to the emperor along with others of his age, Augustus pinched his cheek and said, "You too, boy, will take a bite of my power." And Tiberius, when he learned that Galba would rule but as an old man, said, "Let him live, by all means, since it has nothing to do with me." [4.2] When his grandfather was performing rites to avert the evil portended by a lightning strike, an eagle snatched the entrails from his hands and carried them off to an acorn-bearing oak. This was interpreted to mean that his family would reach the summit of power but that it would come late. His grandfather laughed and said, "Of course! When a mule gives birth!"[14] Later on, when Galba was entertaining revolution, there was nothing that encouraged him more than the offspring of a mule. Others shied from it as an ill-omened portent, whereas he alone took it as a most propitious one because he remembered the sacrifice and his grandfather's words.

[4.3] When Galba received the toga of manhood, he had a dream about the goddess Fortune, who spoke to him. She said that she was standing weary before his door and that if she was not let in quickly, she would become the prize of anyone who came along. When he awoke, he found the door to the forecourt open and near the threshold a bronze statuette of the goddess that stood taller than a cubit. He carried it off in his arms to the villa at Tusculum[15] where he spent his summers and set it apart in the house as a sacred object.

---

had to wait his turn. Gaius had not behaved well while he waited and lost his chance.

12. December 24, 3 BCE.

13. Lucius Livius Ocella Sulpicius Galba. Livia Ocella probably gave him her names in her will.

14. Mules are sterile.

15. About fifteen miles south of Rome.

From then on he worshiped it with sacrifices every month and an all-night vigil every year.

[4.4] Even before he reached mature middle age, he resolutely maintained an ancient custom of the country, one that was being neglected and could be found only in his house. He had his freedmen and slaves present themselves before him in a group twice a day and had each greet him in the morning and in the evening say good night. [5.1] Along with his liberal studies he also gave his attention to the law. He married, as was expected, but when his wife Lepida died, as did the two sons he had had by her, he remained a bachelor and could no longer be tempted by any match, not even by marriage to Agrippina, who had been made a widow by the death of Domitius.[16] Agrippina had pursued Galba so very aggressively when he was still married and not yet free that Lepida's mother attacked her verbally and even slapped her in a gathering of women.

[5.2] Galba held Livia Augusta in greater regard than he did anyone else. While she lived, her favor provided him with great influence, and when she died, her will came close to making him a rich man. The largest amount that she gave to any of her legatees she gave to him, 50 million sesterces. However, the number was not written out but indicated by symbols, and her heir Tiberius reduced it to 500,000, and Galba did not receive even that.

[6.1] He embarked on the course of elected offices before the established age. When he was praetor he put on a new kind of show for the Floralia, elephants walking in ropes.[17] After that he was governor of Aquitania for almost a year, then he served for six months as the consul who gave his name to the year.[18] It chanced that he followed Lucius[19] Domitius, the father of Nero, in that office and that Salvius Otho, the father of Otho, followed him, foreshadowing what would come, when he was emperor between the reigns of the sons of these two men.

---

16. Agrippina the Younger, the mother of Nero, whose first husband was Gnaeus Domitius Ahenobarbus; see *Ner.* 5.

17. Games held in the spring in honor of the goddess Flora. Elephants and ropes also appear at *Ner.* 11.2.

18. 33 CE.

19. This is an error; he was Gnaeus, not Lucius; see note on 5.1.

[6.2] Gaius Caesar made Galba general of the army of Upper Germany to take the place of Gaetulicus.[20] On the day after he reached his legions, he issued written orders to stop the clapping at the games that happened to be going on at that time; he wanted the soldiers to keep their hands inside their cloaks. This immediately went around the camp: "Soldiers, learn to be soldiers! This is Galba, not Gaetulicus!"

[6.3] He was just as strict about putting an end to requests for leave time. He toughened up the veteran legionaries and new recruits with relentless training, and after he had quickly corralled the barbarians who had already burst far into Gaul, he showed both himself and his army in such a good light before Gaius, who was present, that of all the many troops assembled from all the provinces there was none that received greater commendation or richer rewards. He himself was singled out for special praise because, after he had used his shield to direct a military drill, he ran next to the chariot of his commander in chief for twenty miles.

[7.1] When the news arrived that Gaius had been murdered, Galba chose to remain quiet, although there were many who urged him to seize the opportunity. His disinclination put him in great favor with Claudius, and he was brought into his circle of close advisers and treated so deferentially that when he came down with a sudden but not serious illness, the date for the invasion of Britain was postponed. He served as proconsul in Africa for two years, chosen specially and not by lot, to bring order to a province in turmoil from internal dissension and disturbances from the outside. He settled affairs there by being firm and taking great care to be fair even in small matters. [7.2] A soldier was charged with having sold for a hundred denarii what was left of his measure of the wheat ration when provisions were in very short supply on campaign. Galba allowed no one to help the soldier when he began to need food, and he died from hunger. And in a court case that concerned the ownership of a draft animal, when the truth was difficult to come by because arguments were inconclusive and witnesses on both sides were undependable, he ruled thus: the animal was to be led with its head cloaked to the pond where it was usually watered and the wrappings taken off there; it would belong to the person to whom it went on its own after it had drunk.

---

20. Gnaeus Cornelius Lentulus Gaetulicus, considered a lax disciplinarian. See *Cal.* 8.1–2, *Cl.* 9.1.

[8.1] For his accomplishments at that time in Africa and earlier in Germany he received triumphal regalia and three priesthoods, being made a member of the Board of Fifteen and the colleges of Titius and Augustus.[21] From then until almost the middle of Nero's reign he lived largely in retirement, and he never set out on any kind of journey, not even to take a drive, without having a million sesterces in gold along in a nearby carriage.[22] His retirement ended when he was offered the province of Hispania Tarraconensis while he was living in the town of Fundi.[23] [8.2] When he entered his province, it happened that, as he was performing a sacrifice in a public temple, all the hair on the head of one of the temple attendants, a boy holding an incense box, suddenly turned white. Some interpreted this as signifying a change of regime with an old man succeeding a young one; that is, Galba would succeed Nero. Shortly after that, lightning struck a lake in Cantabria and twelve axes[24] were found, an unmistakable token of absolute power.

[9.1] Galba governed the province for eight years and was erratic and inconsistent in doing so. In the beginning he was aggressive, energetic, and truly excessive when he punished offenses. He cut off the hands of a money changer who was dishonest when he made his exchanges, and he nailed them to his table. He crucified a guardian because he had poisoned his ward for whom he was the alternate heir. When the man called on the protection of the law and provided evidence that he was a Roman citizen,[25] Galba pretended to alleviate the punishment as a consolation and in a gesture of respect. He ordered the cross changed and a new one set up, taller than the rest and painted white. This energy gradually gave way to idleness and inertia because he did not want to give Nero any reason to worry and, as he used to say, "because no one is compelled to render an account of his leisure."

---

21. The Board of Fifteen were in charge of the Sibylline books; see *Jul.* 79.3. The second appointment was to an ancient fraternity of unknown origin but evidently the model for the third that was established at the death of Augustus to serve his cult; see *Cl.* 6.2.

22. He was ready to flee on short notice.

23. 60 CE.

24. Cantabria was in the north of Spain. Twelve lictors with *fasces* containing axes escorted an emperor.

25. Crucifixion was not a punishment for Roman citizens.

[9.2] While holding circuit court at New Carthage,[26] Galba learned of the revolt going on in the Gallic provinces when the governor of Aquitania begged for his help. A letter arrived from Vindex,[27] urging him to "assume the role of protector and champion of the human race." He did not hesitate for long but accepted the role, partly out of fear, partly with hope. He was afraid because he had intercepted orders for his death that Nero had issued and sent secretly to his procurators. His hope grew when the predictions of a well-born young girl were added to extremely favorable portents and omens, and it grew even greater because a priest of Jupiter at Clunia[28] had followed directions given in a dream and had unearthed from the inner shrine these same prophecies delivered in the same way by a girl who had spoken oracles two hundred years earlier. The meaning of the verses was: "Someday there will arise from Spain a leader and master of the world."

[10.1] And so Galba mounted the tribunal on the pretense of freeing a slave. Displayed in front of him were as many likenesses as could be found of those whom Nero had condemned and executed, and standing next to him was a boy of high birth whom he had summoned for this very purpose from his place of exile in the nearby Balearic Islands. He deplored the state of the times, and when he was hailed *imperator* he professed that he was governor serving by the leave of the senate and the Roman people. [10.2] Then he declared a suspension of public business and raised legions and auxiliary forces from the inhabitants of the province to augment his original army of one legion, two cavalry units, and three cohorts. He enlisted the older and wiser leading citizens for a kind of senate to which matters of importance would be referred whenever there was need. [10.3] He chose young men of equestrian rank to serve as guards around his private quarters in place of soldiers. He called them his special military escort but allowed them to keep their gold rings. He also sent edicts throughout the provinces to urge everyone to join the uprising both as individuals and with their communities and for each to help the common cause in any way possible.

---

26. Modern Cartagena.
27. For the effect of Vindex's revolt on Nero, see *Ner.* 40–43.
28. A town in Hispania Tarraconensis.

[10.4] At just about that time, when the town that he had chosen for his headquarters was being fortified, there was found a ring of ancient workmanship with a carved gemstone depicting the goddess Victory with a trophy, and a ship from Alexandria immediately put in at Dertosa[29] carrying a cargo of arms but without helmsman, sailor, or passenger. These proved to everyone that the war being undertaken was just and righteous and had the approval of the gods. But then, suddenly and without warning, almost everything was upended. [10.5] One of Galba's two cavalry units had second thoughts about changing its allegiance and attempted to desert him as he approached the camp. It was kept in line with difficulty. Slaves who had been given to him by one of Nero's freedman, who had coached them in treachery, almost killed him as he went through a narrow passage on his way to the baths. They would have succeeded if they had not been heard urging one another not to lose the opportunity; they were asked what opportunity they were talking about and were tortured until they confessed. [11] The death of Vindex compounded the dangerous crisis. It greatly unsettled Galba, who felt that all was lost, and he came close to taking his life. But when messengers arrived from Rome reporting that Nero was dead and that everyone had sworn allegiance to himself, he dropped the name of governor, took the name of Caesar,[30] and began his journey to Rome. He wore a general's cloak and hung a dagger from his neck on his chest. He did not wear the toga again until those conspiring against him, the praetorian prefect Nymphidius Sabinus in Rome and the governors Fonteius Capito and Clodius Macro in Germany and Africa, had been crushed.

[12.1] Galba was preceded by his reputation for cruelty and greed: he had punished the cities of the Spanish and Gallic provinces that had been too slow to join his cause by increasing their taxes, even tearing down their walls in some cases, and executing their governors and imperial agents together with their wives and children. He had melted down a gold crown weighing fifteen pounds from the ancient temple of Jupiter; it had been presented to him by the citizens of Tarraconensis, and he ordered from them three ounces that were lacking. [12.2] This reputation was confirmed and added to as soon as

---

29. A town in Spain at the mouth of the river Ebro.

30. This Julian cognomen had become a title to be used by the non-Julian Galba.

he entered Rome. Nero had turned rowers from the fleet into proper soldiers. Galba forced these marines to resume their earlier status, and when they refused and insisted on demanding an eagle and standards as well, he had the cavalry charge them and disperse them, and he decimated them as well. He disbanded the German cohort that previous Caesars had organized into a bodyguard and whose unquestioned loyalty had been tested many times. He sent them back to their country with no discharge bonus because he thought they were partial to Gnaeus Dolabella,[31] near whose gardens they had their camp.

[12.3] The following stories, true or false, ridiculed him: He groaned after an unusually extravagant dinner had been served to him; when the steward whom he employed presented him with an account of his expenses, he handed him a platter of beans in compensation for his hard work and careful attention. He gave five denarii to Canus, a flute player whose performance he had enjoyed immensely, taking the money from his private cashbox with his own hand. [13] He therefore did not receive a very warm welcome when he arrived in Rome. This became obvious at the next games when the actors in the Atellan farce began the popular song,

Onesimus[32] is coming from his country house.

The whole audience chimed in together with the rest of it and acted it out, repeating the line a number of times.

[14.1] He was thus better liked and more respected when he took power than when he exercised it, although he did provide many instances of behavior worthy of an excellent emperor. But these by no means won him as much favor as actions of the opposite sort made him hated.

[14.2] Galba was governed and controlled by three men who were commonly called his tutors because they lived with him on the Palatine and were always by his side. They were Titus Vinius, his representative in Spain, an enormously greedy man; Cornelius Laco, promoted from assessor to praetorian prefect and unbearable because of his conceit and indolence; and his freedman Icelus, just recently

31. Probably Publius Cornelius Dolabella; Galba considered him for adoption but did not choose him.
32. Evidently a parsimonious old man from the countryside.

given the gold ring and the cognomen Marcianus but already looking for the highest equestrian position.[33] Putting himself in the hands of these men, Galba allowed them to abuse him as they skulked about, each practicing his own particular vice. This scarcely contributed to consistent behavior; at one point he would be more harsh and tight-fisted, at another more indulgent and negligent than became an emperor who had been chosen as he was or one of his age.

[14.3] Galba condemned distinguished men of both orders on minimal suspicion and without allowing them to defend themselves. He granted Roman citizenship rarely and scarcely ever the rights of three children, only to one or two and not even then except for a specified limited time. When jurors begged for a sixth jury panel, he not only refused them but even took away the benefit that Claudius had let them have, that of not being called to jury service in the winter and at the beginning of the year.[34] [15.1] It was thought that he planned to limit the duration of senatorial and equestrian appointments to two years and to grant them only to those who did not want them and accepted them under protest. He employed fifty Roman knights to help him reclaim all but a tenth part of Nero's gifts, which he collected by this arrangement: if the actors or athletes had already sold what was given to them and had already spent the money and could not pay, it was taken from their buyers. [15.2] At the other extreme, there was nothing he did not permit his cronies and freedmen to sell for a price or give away as a favor: immunity from taxes, punishment for the innocent, exoneration of the guilty. Indeed, when the Roman people demanded that Halotus and Tigellinus, the two most criminal of Nero's agents, be punished, he protected them and even made Halotus[35] a procurator of the highest standing, and in defense of Tigellinus he used an edict to charge the populace with cruelty.

[16.1] These actions made all the orders angry with him, and the soldiers especially hated him. Although their officers had announced a bonus larger than usual[36] for those who swore their allegiance to

---

33. Icelus is first mentioned at *Ner.* 49.4. The highest position to which he could aspire was praetorian prefect.

34. See *Cl.* 23.1 for Claudius' arrangements.

35. Claudius' taster; see *Cl.* 44.2.

36. Both Gaius and Claudius had given 15,000 sesterces on their accession; see *Cl.* 10.4.

Galba in his absence, he did not make good on this but kept repeating, "I am accustomed to choosing my soldiers, not buying them." In saying this, he enraged all of them, everywhere. But he offended the praetorians even more by making them fearful and by showing them disrespect when from time to time he dismissed a number of them on suspicion of collaborating with Nymphidius. [16.2] But it was the army of Upper Germany that grumbled loudest because it was being cheated of its reward for the great efforts it had made against the Gauls and Vindex. They were therefore the first who dared to defect, and they refused to take the oath on the Kalends of January unless it was an oath of loyalty to the senate. They immediately sent a delegation to the praetorians with this message: "We do not like this emperor made in Spain. You must choose one of whom all the armies approve." [17] When Galba heard about this, he reasoned that it was not so much his age that made him an object of their contempt but the fact that he had no children. He had long had deep respect for Piso Frugi Licinianus.[37] Piso was a fine young man of good family, and every time Galba wrote a will he had brought him into his family and had given him a share of his property and the use of his name. He suddenly picked him out from amid the crowd at his morning audience, called him his son, led him to the camp, and formally adopted him before the assembled praetorians. Not even then was there mention of a bonus. And this made it easier for Marcus Salvius Otho to do what he wanted to do within six days of the adoption.[38]

[18.1] From the very beginning significant portents had, one after another, foretold Galba's death as it actually came to pass. When victims were being sacrificed right and left in all the towns on his route to Rome, a bull driven mad by a blow from the ax broke its chains and rushed at the emperor's chariot, and when it lifted up its feet, it soaked the chariot completely with blood. As Galba was getting off, the crowd shoved his bodyguard, who almost injured him with his lance. And when he entered the city and later on the Palatine, he was greeted by an earthquake that sounded very much like bellowing. [18.2] Even more unmistakable portents followed: He had saved out from all his booty a necklace made from pearls and

---

37. Lucius Calpurnius Piso Frugi Licinianus.

38. The adoption took place on January 10, 69 CE; the coup that brought Otho to power was on January 15.

precious stones and intended it to decorate the statuette of Fortune in his villa at Tusculum.[39] In an abrupt change of plan, he bestowed it on the Venus on the Capitoline on the grounds that it was an offering appropriate to that more revered place. The following night he saw in his dream the specter of Fortune complaining that she had been cheated of the gift meant for her and threatening that it would be her turn to take away what she had given. He was terrified, and after sending others ahead to make preparations, he rushed to Tusculum at daybreak to avert the dream's curse with expiatory rites. When he arrived, he found nothing but warm ashes on the altar and nearby an old man dressed in black, holding incense in a glass bowl and wine in a clay cup. [18.3] It was also noticed that the wreath fell from his head when he was sacrificing on the Kalends of January and that when he was taking the auspices, the sacred chickens flew away. When he was about to address the praetorians on the day of Piso's adoption, his attendants forgot to place his camp chair on the tribunal as they usually did, and in the senate his curule chair was set backward. [19.1] When he was sacrificing the morning before he was killed, a *haruspex* repeatedly warned him to watch for danger, that assassins were not far off.

Galba soon learned that Otho had gained possession of the praetorian camp, and although many urged him to proceed there as soon as he could (it was possible that his distinction and presence would give him the upper hand), he decided merely to stay where he was and strengthen his position[40] with the protection of the legionary soldiers who were encamped throughout the city. He put on a linen corselet, although he did not pretend that it would be of much use against so many swords. [19.2] But false rumors spread intentionally by the conspirators to lure him into the open persuaded him to leave. When a few of them brazenly claimed that an agreement had been reached, that those involved in the revolt had been crushed, and that the rest were on their way in large numbers to congratulate him and were prepared to offer total obedience, he went out to meet them with such confidence that when a soldier bragged that he had killed Otho, he replied, "On whose authority?" He got as far as the Forum. The horsemen who had been ordered to kill him, urging

---

39. See 4.3.

40. The Palatine Hill was defensible. Another account of the coup appears at *Oth.* 5–6.

their horses through the city and moving aside the civilian crowds in their way, caught sight of him there in the distance and stopped for a moment. Then they came on fast and cut him down, abandoned by his friends.

[20.1] Some say that in the first confusion Galba shouted, "What are you doing, comrades-in-arms? I belong to you and you belong to me!" And the bonus was promised.[41] More have reported that he offered his neck unasked and urged his assailants, "Do it!"[42] and "Strike, since this seems right to you!" It seems very strange (it must be acknowledged) that none of those present tried to help their emperor and that of the help that was summoned all except for a detachment of Germans disregarded the message. Galba had recently earned their gratitude by comforting them when they were ill and weak, and so they rushed to his aid—but too late. They were slowed because they were unfamiliar with the streets and so took an out-of-the-way route.

[20.2] Galba was killed beside Lake Curtius and his body left just as he fell until a soldier of the ranks returning from the grain distribution threw down what he was carrying and cut off the emperor's head. Since he could not grasp it by the hair,[43] he hid it under his clothing and then stuck his thumb through its mouth and took it to Otho. Otho gave it to the camp helpers and hangers-on, who fastened it on a spear and carried it around the camp making fun of it and shouting repeatedly, "Galba, lover boy! Enjoy your salad days!" They were whipped up to this crude mockery because a few days earlier the story had circulated that when someone praised his good looks as still blooming and vigorous, he had replied,

> My strength is still unimpaired.[44]

A freedman belonging to Patrobius Neronianus bought the head from them for a hundred gold pieces and tossed it away on the spot where his patron had been executed on Galba's order.[45] Finally, at

---

41. The bonus he had earlier refused to pay; see 16.1, 17.
42. The command of the priest to sacrifice a victim; see *Cal.* 58.2.
43. Galba was bald; see 21.
44. Homer, *Iliad* 5.254, *Odyssey* 21.426.
45. Galba had executed Patrobius, a freedman of Nero.

last, Galba's steward Argivus buried both it and the rest of his body in Galba's private gardens on the Aurelian road.[46]

[21] Galba was of average height and quite bald, with blue eyes, a hooked nose, and hands and feet so very crippled by arthritis that he could not bear a shoe for long, nor could he unroll books or even hold them. And the flesh on his right side had grown and hung down so that it was difficult to keep it contained by a band.

[22] It is said that he ate a great deal, that in winter he took nourishment even before daybreak and at dinner he ate so very much that he ordered everyone's leftovers piled up in front of him and distributed to the attendants waiting on him. He preferred sex with men, but only with strong adult men. They say that when Icelus, one of his longtime bedmates, brought the news of Nero's death to Spain, Galba not only received him with passionate kisses witnessed by everyone but begged him to have his hairs plucked at once.[47] And he took him aside.

[23] Galba died in his seventy-third year of age, in his seventh month as emperor. The senate, as soon as it was permitted, voted a statue of him to be put on top of a column decorated with ships' beaks and erected in the part of the Forum where he was murdered. But Vespasian rescinded their decree because he believed that Galba had sent assassins from Spain to Judaea to kill him.

---

46. A road leading north from Rome along the coast.
47. Depilation was considered effeminate.

OTHO

32–69 CE
Emperor January 69–April 69 CE

Marcus Salvius Otho lacked the republican pedigree of the Claudii, Domitii, or Sulpicii. His family achieved senatorial status only in the early empire, under the patronage of Livia and Tiberius. Otho was an intimate of Nero and had the reputation of an irresponsible young rake, participating in the emperor's dissolute recreation and even sharing his wife. The association did not, however, operate totally to his detriment, for when he himself was emperor, he tried to tap into Nero's posthumous popularity.

When Otho made his move for the principate, he did not have legions under his command as did the rival generals in this period of civil war. Legions supported him later, but he became emperor in a palace coup staged with the help of the praetorian guard, an effective instrument for the takeover because of their presence in Rome. The oath of the guard had been decisive for the accessions of Gaius (Caligula), Claudius, and Nero.

Despite youthful extravagance and effeminate habits—not to mention responsibility for the violent murder of Galba—Otho redeemed himself with a noble death. For the Romans, the manner of dying weighed heavily in the assessment of a life.

[1.1] Otho's ancestors came from the town of Ferentium,[1] an ancient and honorable family that was among the most distinguished in Etruria. His grandfather Marcus Salvius Otho, whose father was a Roman knight and whose mother was of low origin (perhaps not free-born), became a senator through the kind offices of Livia Augusta, in whose house he had been reared. But he did not rise beyond the grade of praetor.

---

1. A town in Etruria, north of Rome.

[1.2] His father Lucius Otho had prominent family on his mother's side who provided many important connections. Tiberius valued him so highly and he looked so much like the emperor that many thought he had been fathered by him. He was extremely strict in fulfilling the obligations of his elected offices, his proconsulate in Africa, and the special commands to which he was appointed. In Illyricum he even had the courage to execute some soldiers who had reconsidered their disloyalty during the uprising started by Camillus[2] and had killed their officers because they thought that these officers were the ones who had instigated the defection from Claudius. He had them executed in front of his headquarters while he watched, even though he knew that Claudius had promoted them to higher rank for that very same action. [1.3] This made him admired but lessened his favor with the emperor. He recovered quickly, however, when he uncovered the treachery of a Roman knight, who he learned from the man's slaves was planning to kill Claudius. The senate distinguished him for this with the rarest of honors, a statue on the Palatine, and Claudius made him a patrician, praised him generously, and added, "I do not even hope to have sons better than this man." With Albia Terentia, his wife from a distinguished family, he had two sons, Lucius Titianus and a younger one, Marcus, who had the same cognomen that he did. He also had a daughter whom he betrothed to Drusus, the son of Germanicus, when she was barely grown.

[2.1] The emperor Otho was born on the fourth day before the Kalends of May in the consulship of Camillus Arruntius and Domitius Ahenobarbus.[3] From early youth he was so undisciplined and profligate that his father often applied the whip for punishment. It was said that he would wander about at night and lay hold of anyone he met who was weak or drunk and put him on a stretched-out cloak and throw him up in the air. [2.2] After his father died, he pretended to be in love with a freedwoman who was old and almost infirm but whose good connections at court enabled him to access her influence more effectively. It was through her favor that he insinuated himself with Nero. He had no trouble holding first place among the emperor's intimates because of their similar characters and, as some

---

2. The revolt in Dalmatia in 42 CE during the reign of Claudius; see *Cl.* 13.2.

3. April 28, 32 CE. This Gnaeus Domitius Ahenobarbus was Nero's father; see *Ner.* 5.

say, because of intimacy derived from shared sexual indecency. He enjoyed great power. For instance, after he had arranged to be paid handsomely to intercede on behalf of a man of consular rank who had been found guilty of extortion, he did not wait for the man's status to be totally restored before ushering him into the senate to render thanks to the emperor.

[3.1] As someone who shared all of Nero's plans and secrets, on the day the emperor decided to kill his mother, Otho gave an exquisitely appointed dinner for both of them in order to divert suspicion.[4] When Poppaea Sabina was still Nero's mistress, she was taken from her husband and assigned temporarily to Otho in a sham marriage. Not content with enticing her to sleep with him, he fell so passionately in love that it was difficult for him to put up with even Nero as a rival. [3.2] What is certain is that he not only forbade entrance to those who were sent to retrieve her, but on one occasion he shut Nero out and left him standing at the door alternately threatening and begging to no effect and demanding back the "property" that he had left with Otho for safekeeping. And so the marriage was dissolved, and Otho was removed from the scene with the excuse of a commission to Lusitania. This seemed sufficient because a harsher punishment would have made the whole farce common knowledge. But this couplet made the affair public nonetheless:

> Why, you ask, is Otho an exile with a pretense of honor?
> He had begun to commit adultery with his wife.

Otho administered this province for ten years with the rank of quaestor, displaying restraint and remarkable fiscal responsibility.

[4.1] When the opportunity to get even finally arrived, Otho was the first to join those who exerted themselves on behalf of Galba, and at the same time he began to hope for imperial power for himself. It was a serious hope to be sure, because of what was going on at the time, but a declaration by the astrologer Seleucus made it significantly greater. Although Seleucus had earlier given solemn assurance that Otho would survive Nero, he turned up unasked and unexpected at that moment with the additional promise that he would soon rule. [4.2] And so Otho made himself attentive to everyone and curried popularity with all. Whenever he entertained

---

4. See *Ner.* 34.2.

the emperor[5] at dinner, he distributed a gold piece to each member
of the praetorian detachment on guard and put all of the soldiers in
his debt in one way or another. When he was asked to judge a case
in which a man was in litigation with his neighbor about a portion
of his land, he bought the entire property and made it over to him.
After that there was scarcely anyone who did not both feel inwardly
and state openly that Otho alone was worthy to inherit the empire.

[5.1] Otho had also hoped that Galba would adopt him, and he
lived in anticipation of this day after day.[6] But when the emperor
chose Piso instead, he lost hope and resorted to force. His large debt
prodded him even more than did his disappointment, and he did not
pretend otherwise: "I cannot keep my feet unless I am emperor, and
it does not matter whether I fall in battle by the hands of my enemies
or in the Forum at the hands of my creditors." [5.2] A few days earlier
he had extracted a million sesterces from one of Caesar's slaves by
getting him the stewardship that he had wanted. This constituted
the whole of his financing for the great undertaking. In the beginning, plans for the coup were entrusted to five bodyguards, then to
ten more chosen by the first five, two each. Each was paid 10,000
sesterces on the spot with a promise of 50,000 more. These men
recruited others but not very many, because it seemed certain that
more would join once things were under way. [6.1] Immediately after
Piso's adoption, Otho thought of taking over the praetorian camp
and attacking Galba while he was at dinner on the Palatine, but he
held back out of consideration for the cohort guarding him at the
time. He did not want to bring opprobrium down on them since it
had been this same detachment that was on watch when Gaius was
assassinated and Nero was abandoned. Omens and warnings from
Seleucus ruled out the intervening time.[7]

[6.2] And so, on the day that had been chosen, Otho told his con-
federates to wait for him at the golden milestone[8] in the Forum near
the temple of Saturn, and he attended Galba's morning audience. He
was received there with the usual kiss, and he was also with Galba

---

5. Galba.

6. See *Gal.* 17, 19–20 for these events with Galba as the central figure.

7. Piso was adopted on January 10, 69 CE. Galba was killed on January
15.

8. It ostensibly marked the center of Rome where all roads terminated.

when he offered sacrifice and heard the prediction of the *haruspex*.
Then when his freedman came with the news that the builders had
arrived (this was the agreed-upon signal), he left, giving the excuse
that he was going to look at a house that was for sale. He rushed out
the back of the Palatine to the designated meeting place. Others say
that he pretended to have a fever and gave this as his excuse to those
standing next to him, in case he should be asked for. [6.3] Then hiding himself in a sedan chair, he hurried toward the camp. But when
the bearers grew tired, he got out and started running. When he had
stopped because his shoe became unfastened, he was quickly lifted
onto shoulders and hailed *imperator* by the company at hand. He
arrived at praetorian headquarters amid acclamations wishing him
well and drawn swords. Those whom they met on the way joined as
if they knew about the plot and were participating in it. In the camp
he dispatched soldiers to kill Galba and Piso, and when he addressed
the soldiers, he made a single promise to win their loyalty, that he
would possess only what they left him.[9]

[7.1] It was already late in the day when he met with the senate and
gave a brief explanation; he said that he had been snatched from the
streets of Rome and compelled to become emperor and that he would
rule with the common consent of all. Then he went to the Palatine. In
addition to the other flattery of congratulation and praise, the
dregs of the populace called him Nero, and he gave no indication
that he would reject the name. Indeed, as some have written, he even
added the cognomen Nero on travel documents that he issued and on
the first letters he wrote to some of the provincial governors. What is
certain is that he allowed Nero's busts and statues to be set up again,
and he reinstated his procurators and freedmen in the positions they
had formerly held. The first order that he signed as emperor was for
50 million sesterces to finish the Golden House.[10]

[7.2] It is said that that very night he was frightened by a dream
and groaned deeply, and that those who came running found him
lying on the ground beside his bed. He tried every kind of expiatory
rite to make atonement to Galba's ghost, who he had dreamed was
throwing him out, head over heels. And they say that the next day,
when he was taking the auspices, a heavy storm blew up and he took

---

9. He was willing to give them everything he had.
10. Nero's extravagant palace; see *Ner.* 31.1–2.

a bad fall and kept muttering, "What business do I have with long pipes?"[11]

[8.1] At about this time the armies stationed in Germany swore allegiance to Vitellius.[12] When Otho learned this, he had the senate send a legation to inform them that an emperor had already been chosen and to urge peace and unity, but he nonetheless sent messengers and written communications to offer to share power with Vitellius and become his son-in-law. When war proved inevitable, however, and the generals and forces that Vitellius had sent ahead were already drawing near, he received a demonstration of the praetorians' loyalty to him when they almost annihilated the senate. [8.2] It had been decided that the marines would transfer some weapons and send them back by ship, and when the arms were being brought out in the camp at nightfall, some of the praetorians suspected betrayal and started to riot. With no one in particular in charge, they all suddenly went running to the Palatine demanding death for the senate. They fought off their tribunes who were trying to stop them and killed some of them and, bloody as they were, forced their way into the dining room. They asked where the emperor was and did not leave off until they actually saw him.[13]

[8.3] Otho began operations energetically and in very great haste, not waiting even for the approval of the gods. The sacred shields had not yet been restored to their places; this was something considered inauspicious since ancient times.[14] And he set out on the day when the worshipers of the mother of the gods[15] started to lament and beat their breasts. The omens were also very bad. When he killed a victim for the lord of the underworld he obtained favorable omens, but in this sacrifice unfavorable omens are more desirable. When

---

11. Pipes blown to produce music; a proverb about taking on something for which one is ill equipped.

12. January 2, 69 CE; see *Vit.* 8 for the proclamation of Vitellius as emperor.

13. In face of the anticipated invasion, armaments were evidently removed from storage in the praetorian camp to be transferred to Ostia. This made the praetorians suspicious of the senate, whom Otho was entertaining when they found him.

14. The shields were carried through the city in sacred procession; they would be returned on March 24.

15. Cybele; see notes on *Aug.* 68, *Tib.* 2.3, *Ner.* 56.

he first left Rome, he was slowed by the flooding of the Tiber, and at the twentieth milestone the rubble of fallen buildings blocked his way. [9.1] No one doubted that it was a good idea to prolong the war, but Otho, with the same impetuous haste, decided to fight it out as soon as possible, since the enemy was hard pressed from lack of food and had no room to maneuver. Either he could no longer tolerate the anxiety and hoped to win a decisive victory before Vitellius arrived, or he was unequal to the demands of his soldiers who were eager to fight. He was not present for any of the fighting but remained at Brixellum.[16]

[9.2] He was indeed successful in three insignificant battles, in the Alps, near Placentia, and at Castor's (as the place is called).[17] But in the final and most important battle at Betriacum,[18] he was tricked into defeat. Hope for negotiation arose, and the soldiers had been brought out from camp to discuss terms of peace when they were unexpectedly forced into battle as they exchanged greetings. [9.3] Otho immediately resolved to die, as many rightly imagine, more from a sense of decency that kept him from continuing to secure power for himself at such great peril to property and human life than because he lost hope or lacked faith in his forces. Even then, the forces he had kept with him for a second attempt were still available and fresh, and others were arriving from Dalmatia, and from Pannonia and Moesia. Even those who had been beaten were not so shattered that they would not face any danger to redeem their disgrace, unasked and even alone.

[10.1] My father, Suetonius Laetus, took part in this war as an equestrian tribune with the Thirteenth Legion. He would later say repeatedly that even as a private citizen Otho detested civil war so much that he shuddered when someone said something at table about the deaths of Cassius and Brutus. And he said that Otho would not have challenged Galba if he had not been certain that what was between them could be settled short of war. He also said that the example of a soldier from the ranks had made Otho feel that his life

---

16. A town south of the Po. He had a large contingent of troops there with him in reserve.

17. Modern Piacenza, and a shrine dedicated to the twin divinities Castor and Pollux.

18. Between Cremona and Verona. A second battle took place there between Vitellius and Vespasian; see *Vit.* 10.1, 15.2.

was of little value. This soldier reported the disaster that had befallen the army, but no one believed him; when the other soldiers charged him first with lying and then with cowardice on the grounds that he had deserted from battle, he fell on his sword before the emperor. My father would say that when Otho saw this, he declared, "I will no longer put such men in danger, men who have deserved so much."

[10.2] And so Otho encouraged his brother, his brother's son, and each of his companions to take care of themselves as best they could, and he embraced them, kissed them, and sent them all away. He went off by himself and wrote two letters, one a letter of consolation to his sister and one to Nero's widow Messallina,[19] whom he had intended to marry, and he entrusted to her his remains and the preservation of his memory. Then he burned whatever correspondence he had with him so that it would not be dangerous or harmful to anyone if it fell into the hands of the victor. He divided the money that he had on hand among his household. [11.1] Ready thus to die and resolved to do so, he realized that a disturbance had arisen while he delayed and that those who were starting to depart were being arrested as deserters and detained. He said, in these exact words, "Let us add this night also to our life," and he forbade violence to be used on anyone. The door of his chamber stood open until late and if anyone wanted to approach, he allowed it. [11.2] After this, he satisfied his thirst with a drink of cold water and took two daggers and tested the point of each. When he had placed one of them under his pillow and the doors were closed, he fell into a very deep sleep. At last, about daybreak, he awoke and stabbed himself with a single thrust beneath his left nipple. He covered the wound, then uncovered it for those who came bursting in when they heard his first groan, and he died. He was buried quickly, for so he had directed, in his thirty-eighth year of age and on the ninety-fifth day of his imperial power.[20]

[12.1] Otho's physical appearance and style did not correspond well to this great courage. He is reported to have been of average height with bad feet and bowlegs. He groomed himself with almost feminine niceness; he had his body hairs plucked and, because his hair was thin, had a wig fitted to his head and glued on so that no one would know. They say he was in the habit of shaving every day and smearing his face with wet bread, a treatment he had started

---

19. Statilia Messallina, Nero's third wife; see *Ner.* 35.1.
20. April 16, 69 CE.

when his first down appeared so that he would never have a beard. He celebrated the rites of Isis often and openly, dressed in linen ritual robes.

[12.2] For these reasons I am inclined to think that his death, which was so inconsistent with his life, was the greatest wonder of all. Many of the soldiers who were there wept profusely and kissed his hands and feet as he lay before them, saying that he was the bravest of men and their one and only emperor. And immediately, then and there, they took their lives not far from his funeral pyre. Many who were not there also took up arms and killed one another in their grief when they heard the news. Finally, a large number of the men who had truly detested him when he was alive heaped praise on him after he was dead, and it was even common talk that he had killed Galba not so much in order to rule as to restore the Republic and bring back freedom.

VITELLIUS

15–69 CE

Emperor January 69–December 69 CE

The family of Aulus Vitellius, like that of Otho, first gained prominence in the early empire. His father Lucius Vitellius became known for flattering Gaius and Claudius and was the latter's most trusted ally within the upper class. Aulus Vitellius' attempt at the principate was opportunistic. Late in 68 CE, perhaps even before he had arrived in Rome, Galba appointed him to command the army of Lower Germany, four legions stationed in the northern region of the Rhine territory. These legions saluted him as emperor on January 2, 69, not long after he had reached their camp. Galba was still emperor in Rome, but by the time Vitellius had mobilized his forces and moved south, Otho had replaced Galba as emperor. Vitellius successfully confronted Otho but before long was bested by Vespasian's forces. Vitellius and the other emperors of the year and a half after the death of Nero can be thought of not so much as a sequence of rulers but as challengers jockeying for position in a fluid field.

The focus here is on the unsavory aspects of Vitellius' character: his cruelty, his lack of discipline, and most of all his insatiable appetite. At the end he dithered miserably and died a sordid death, and since Romans judged the manner of death indicative of character, Vitellius failed. Vespasian, the general left standing at the end of the difficult year 69, founded the Flavian dynasty, and the Flavians were the ones who influenced the writing of the history of the preceding years. There was no good word to be said about Vitellius.

[1.1] Some describe the origin of the Vitellii one way; others offer something quite different indeed. By one account, they were an old and distinguished family; by another they were newcomers, undistinguished, and even vulgar. I would assume that this difference arose from the flatterers and critics respectively of the emperor Vitellius if it were not for the fact that divergent accounts of the family's status already existed earlier.

[1.2] There is extant a memorandum that Quintus Elogius[1] wrote to Quintus Vitellius, special quaestor to the Divine Augustus. It reports that the Vitellii arose from Faunus, king of the Aborigines,[2] and from Vitellia, a divinity whose worship was widespread, and that the family ruled all of Italy. Their surviving stock relocated to Rome from Sabine territory and were made patricians. [1.3] Traces of the family remained for a long time in the name of the Vitellian road that led from the Janiculum[3] to the sea and in the colony of the same name that in the distant past the family had demanded the right to protect with its private army against the Aequiculi.[4] When a garrison was sent to Apulia at the time of the Samnite war,[5] some of the Vitellii settled at Nuceria;[6] after a long interval their descendants returned to Rome and rejoined the ranks of the senators.

[2.1] A number have presented an opposing thesis and written that the founder of the family was a freedman. Cassius Severus[7] and others as well add that this freedman was a mender of old shoes and that his son had amassed a rich fortune as a dealer in second-hand goods and as a stand-in for litigators. He also had a son with a woman from the lower class, the daughter of one Antiocus who ran a bakery, and that son became a Roman knight. But let these disagreements remain an open question.

[2.2] In any case, Publius Vitellius, who lived in Nuceria (whether descended from ancient stock or from parents and grandparents of whom he was ashamed), was without doubt a Roman knight and an agent of Augustus, and he administered his property. He left four sons who achieved great distinction. They had the same name

---

1. Unknown and perhaps nonexistent, possibly a mistake in the Latin text.

2. Faunus was a rustic deity. Aborigines were the pre-Roman inhabitants of Italy.

3. A hill along the Tiber outside Rome.

4. A warlike tribe in central Italy.

5. Late fourth century BCE.

6. An error: Luceria, not Nuceria, was an important city in Apulia.

7. A writer under Augustus who expressed strong views; see *Aug.* 56.3, *Cal.* 16.1.

and differed only in their first names: Aulus, Quintus, Publius, and Lucius. Aulus died in the consulship that he held with Domitius, the father of Nero Caesar.[8] Aulus was extravagant and known especially for the magnificence of his dinners. Quintus lost senatorial status when less financially able senators were disenfranchised and gotten rid of at the initiative of Tiberius. [2.3] Publius, who was a member of Germanicus' inner circle, accused Gnaeus Piso of being Germanicus' enemy and murderer and secured his condemnation.[9] After serving as praetor, he was arrested as a confederate of Sejanus and delivered into the custody of his brother. He slit his veins with a penknife but allowed himself to be bandaged and cared for, not so much because he had changed his mind about dying but because his friends and family pleaded with him. He died a natural death while still under detention.

[2.4] Lucius, governor of Syria following his consulship, enticed Artabanus, king of the Parthians, not merely to meet with him but even to venerate the legionary standards. Later with the emperor Claudius he held two consulships to which he gave his name; he was also censor and had charge of the empire while Claudius was away on his British expedition. Lucius was a good man and hardworking, but his passion for a freedwoman tarnished his reputation badly. He mixed her saliva with honey and used it as a medicine to soothe his windpipe and throat; he did this not just sometimes in private but openly, every day. [2.5] He had a remarkable talent for flattery and was the one who started the practice of paying homage to Gaius as a god. When he returned from Syria, he did not risk approaching the emperor unless he veiled his head, turned away from him, and finally prostrated himself. To gain credit in any way he could with Claudius, who was dependent on his wives and freedmen,[10] he asked Messallina[11] to do him great favor and allow him to take off her shoes. After he removed her right slipper, he always carried it between his toga and his tunics, and he sometimes kissed it. He also venerated golden images of Narcissus and Pallas[12] together with his

---

8. For half the year 32 CE; see *Oth.* 2.1.
9. See *Tib.* 52.3, *Cal.* 2.
10. See *Cl.* 25.5, 29.1.
11. Claudius' wife.
12. Claudius' two most influential freedmen; *Cl.* 28.

Lares. And when he congratulated Claudius on presenting Secular Games, he said, "May you do this often."[13] [3.1] He died from a stroke on the day after he was arrested.[14] He was survived by two sons whom he had by Sestilia, a fine woman of excellent family, and he saw them both become consuls, indeed, in the course of the same year when the younger succeeded the elder for a six-month term.[15] After he died, the senate honored him with a public funeral and with a statue on the rostra that had this inscription: "Staunch in his loyalty to the emperor."

[3.2] The emperor Aulus Vitellius, the son of Lucius, was born on the eighth day before the Kalends of October (or as some say, on the seventh before the Ides of September) in the consulships of Drusus Caesar and Norbanus Flaccus.[16] His parents were horrified when astronomers read his horoscope. His father, while he lived, always tried very hard to keep him from being assigned a province, and his mother mourned him as lost when he was posted to the legions and when he was saluted emperor. Vitellius spent his boyhood and early adulthood at Capri with Tiberius' stable of sex performers, and there he was dubbed permanently with the name *spintria*.[17] It was thought that he used his body to give his father's political career a start and to foster his advancement. [4] As time went on, tainted by perversion of every kind, he held center place at court. He was a close friend of Gaius because of his passion for chariot racing, of Claudius because of his enthusiasm for dicing, but he was still more popular with Nero, not only for these same shared interests but also because of a special service that he performed. When Vitellius was presiding at the Neronia,[18] Nero wanted to compete as a citharode[19] but did not dare commit himself despite the urging of the crowd; as a consequence, he left the theater. Vitellius called him back, pretending that he was

---

13. A critical remark, since the Games were meant to be held only once in anyone's lifetime.

14. For treason.

15. 48 CE.

16. September 24 or September 7 of 15 CE; Drusus the Younger.

17. Tiberius' playground at *Tib.* 42–45; on *spintriae*, see *Tib.* 43.1, *Cal.* 16.1.

18. Games that Nero established; see *Ner.* 12.3, 21.

19. A singer who accompanied himself on the lyre.

speaking as a representative of the people who were insisting on his presence, and he gave him the opportunity to be persuaded.

[5] And so with the indulgence of three emperors he advanced his career, not only by election to offices but also by appointment to the highest priesthoods. He was then proconsul in Africa, and he was responsible for public works, but his intentions varied in these duties, and the impact on his reputation was different in each case. In his province he exhibited remarkable integrity for two years in a row, since he stayed on as lieutenant to his brother, who succeeded him. But when he completed his tasks in the city, it was said that he stole the temple offerings and decorations and exchanged some of them, substituting tin and brass for gold and silver.

[6] His wife was Petronia, the daughter of a man of consular rank, and with her he had a son, Petronianus, who was blind in one eye. His mother made the boy her heir on condition that he not be kept under his father's power.[20] Vitellius emancipated him and soon thereafter (as was believed) killed him. In addition, the boy was charged with attempted parricide on the grounds that his guilty conscience had made him drink the poison that he had prepared for his crime. Vitellius then married Galeria Fundana, whose father had been a praetor, and he also had children with her, one of each sex, but the boy was almost mute and unable to speak because of stuttering.

[7.1] Galba appointed Vitellius to the command in Lower Germany, much to everyone's surprise. It is thought that he was helped to this appointment through the patronage of Titus Vinius, who was very influential at that time and with whom he had had a long and close relationship because of their shared devotion to the Blue faction.[21] That would be credible if not for the fact that Galba had made it clear that no men were less of a threat than those who thought about nothing but their dinner and that Vitellius' insatiable appetite could be satisfied by the resources of the province. This makes it obvious to everyone that he was chosen more out of contempt than out of respect for his worth. [7.2] It is common knowledge that when it came time for him to depart he had no travel money. His resources were in such straits that when he left his wife and children in Rome, he put them in hired lodgings and rented his

---

20. A father had absolute power over his children, especially in money matters.

21. One of the four teams in the chariot races; see *Cal.* 18.3.

house for the rest of the year,[22] and he took a large pearl from his
mother's ear and pawned it to cover the expenses of his journey. A
crowd of creditors was indeed waiting for him and kept him from
leaving, among them people from Sinuessa and Formiae[23] whose tax
revenues he had misappropriated for himself. The only way he got
rid of them was by making them afraid that they would be subjected
to false charges; he succeeded because he had instituted proceedings
for damages against a certain freedman who was quite insistently
demanding the repayment of money owed him. He alleged that the
freedman had kicked him, and he did not let the proceedings drop
until he had extorted 50,000 sesterces from him.

[7.3] When he reached his command, the army, ill disposed toward
the emperor and prepared to rebel, willingly and with hands lifted to
the heavens welcomed him as if he were a gift sent from the gods, the
son of a man who had been consul three times, in the prime of life,
and possessed of an easygoing and generous disposition. Vitellius
had reinforced this earlier reputation with new proofs: during the
whole of his journey he kissed the ordinary soldiers whom he met,
and in stables and taverns he was so very friendly with mule drivers
and travelers that he would ask each of them in the morning, "Have
you had breakfast?" And he would belch to show them that he had.
[8.1] When he entered the camp, he refused nothing that anyone
asked and on his own initiative removed citations from those who
had been disgraced, mourning clothes from those awaiting trial, and
punishments from those who had been found guilty.

And so with scarcely a month gone by and no account taken of the
day[24] or the time of day (it was already evening), the soldiers suddenly
seized him in his quarters and took him away, just as he was, in the
clothing he wore in private. And they saluted him as *imperator* and
carried him about through the most crowded parts of town[25] while
he held the drawn sword of the Divine Julius, which someone had
taken from the shrine of Mars and handed to him in the first wave
of congratulations. [8.2] After he had returned to his headquarters,

---

22. He left for the Rhine around November 1, 68 CE; the rental year was
from July to July. See *Tib.* 35.2.

23. Towns on the Appian Way, south of Rome.

24. January 2, 69 CE. The days after the Kalends, Nones, and Ides were
considered unlucky.

25. His headquarters were at Colonia Agrippinensis, modern Cologne.

the dining room caught fire from the chimney and burned, and when everyone was troubled and worried that this was a bad omen, he said, "Be of good spirits! It will light our way!" That was all he said that the soldiers could hear. Then when additional support came from the army of Upper Germany, which had earlier defected from Galba and sworn allegiance to the senate,[26] he eagerly took the cognomen Germanicus that everyone offered him, postponed taking the name of Augustus, and refused that of Caesar permanently.

[9] As soon as the news of Galba's murder arrived, Vitellius put affairs in Germany in order and divided his forces; one group he would send ahead to confront Otho and another he would command himself. As the column that was being sent ahead departed, it was met with a propitious omen. An eagle suddenly flew down on the right, circled the standards, and moved slowly ahead of the troops as they went forward. But when his own force departed, all of the equestrian statues of him that were being set up everywhere broke their legs in the same way and suddenly collapsed, and the laurel wreath that he put on for dutiful observance of religious ceremony fell into a stream. And then at Vienna[27] a cock lit on his shoulder and then on his head while he was rendering justice in his official capacity.[28] What happened later was consistent with these omens, for he could not by his efforts hold onto the power that his generals won for him.

[10.1] Vitellius was still in Gaul when he heard about the victory at Betriacum and the death of Otho.[29] Immediately, in a single edict, he dismissed all of the praetorian cohorts from service and ordered them to turn over their arms to their tribunes, citing them as bad examples. He furthermore ordered 120 of them hunted down and punished because he had found petitions to Otho in which they demanded reward for their services in the killing of Galba. These measures were truly good and commendable and would have offered hope of an excellent emperor if he had not done other things that were more consistent with his character and earlier life than

26. January 1, 69 CE; see *Gal.* 16.2.
27. Modern Vienne in France; Vitellius passed through on his way to Rome.
28. The omen predicted his defeat by Marcus Antonius Primus; see chapter 18.
29. See *Oth.* 9.2–3.

with the majesty of the principate. [10.2] For instance, when he had begun his journey to Rome, he rode through the center of cities like someone celebrating a triumph and was ferried over rivers on exquisitely luxurious boats decorated with all kinds of garlands and provided with elaborately prepared food. His entourage and his military forces were undisciplined, and Vitellius treated the pillage and insolent behavior of all of them as a joke. They were not content with the feasting available to them everywhere at state expense but set free whatever slaves they pleased and responded immediately to those who objected with whippings and blows that often left them wounded, sometimes dead.

[10.3] And when he arrived at the fields on which the fighting had taken place, he was brazen enough to encourage some who were appalled by the decaying corpses with this tasteless statement: "It's wonderful to smell a dead enemy and even better, a dead citizen." It was nevertheless observed that he drank a large dose of unmixed wine to alleviate the offensive smell, and he shared it around. With equal arrogance and lack of sympathy he looked at the stone inscribed to the memory of Otho and said, "This is the Mausoleum he deserves,"[30] and he sent the dagger with which Otho had killed himself to Colonia Agrippinensis to be dedicated to Mars. He also held an all-night festival on the ridge of the Apennines. [11.1] Finally, he entered Rome to the sound of a trumpet, wearing his general's cloak and his sword and surrounded by standards and flags. His companions were dressed as soldiers, and his troops had their weapons drawn.

[11.2] Then, showing increasing disregard for all laws, divine and human, he became *pontifex maximus* on the day of the Allia[31] and arranged the elections for the next ten years with himself consul in perpetuity. To eliminate doubt about the model that he was choosing to follow in regulating the state, he made funeral offerings for Nero in the middle of the Campus Martius with a large number of state priests present. At the banquet that marked the ceremony he requested in the hearing of all that a popular citharode "sing one of the emperor's compositions," and when the singer began Nero's songs, he was the first to applaud and even jumped to his feet.

---

30. Ironic; Otho was memorialized by a simple stone.

31. July 18, a day of ill omen that recalled the Roman defeat by the Gauls in 390 BCE on the river Allia, a tributary of the Tiber.

[12] After starting off this way, he directed most of the imperial business with the help and at the pleasure of the worst sort of actors and chariot drivers and especially his freedman Asiaticus. When Asiaticus was quite young, Vitellius raped him to their mutual satisfaction, but the boy ran off when he grew bored. When the emperor found him selling vinegar-water to the citizens of Puteoli, he put him in shackles but then immediately set him free and kept him as one of his pets again. Then once more exasperated with his insolence and his thievery, he sold him to an itinerant trainer of gladiators. But at a show at which Asiaticus was being held back for the final combat, he suddenly whisked him off. After Vitellius got his province,[32] he gave Asiaticus his freedom and on the first day of his principate presented him with gold rings during dinner—despite the fact that when everyone was asking that privilege for Asiaticus that very morning, he had vehemently expressed his distaste for such a contamination of the equestrian order.

[13.1] But Vitellius was especially given to extravagant living and cruel behavior. He always divided his daily feasting into three parts, sometimes into four: breakfast, lunch, dinner, and drinking bouts. He had no trouble finding capacity for all the meals because he made a habit of vomiting. Furthermore, for any given day he assigned the preparation of one meal to one person, another to another, and a single meal cost the host at least 400,000 sesterces. [13.2] The most notorious feast was a welcoming dinner that his brother gave for him on his entry into Rome; on the menu were said to be two thousand of the choicest fish and two thousand birds. But he topped this himself when he presented, as though it were a sacred object, a large dish that he called "the shield of Minerva, protectress of the city,"[33] because of its gigantic size. On this platter he mixed parrotfish livers, pheasant and peacock brains, flamingo tongues, and eel intestines that admirals had brought from Parthia and the Spanish straits[34] on their triremes. [13.3] And as a man who had an appetite that was both insatiable and inappropriately insistent at inappropriate times and who had disgusting tastes, he never restrained himself, not even

---

32. Africa; see chapter 5.
33. The Greek epithet for Athena (Minerva), "protectress," is similar to a word that means "holds a lot." In Athens, there was a large statue of Athena with a very large shield.
34. Gibraltar.

when he was offering sacrifices or traveling. Right there, among the
altars, on the spot, he would come close to grabbing meat and bits
of sacrificial cake from the hearth and chewing it down, and in the
cookshops along his route he would grab dishes that were steaming
hot or left over, half-eaten from the day before.

[14.1] Eager to punish and execute whomever he could for whatever reason, he put to death highborn men, accusing them on false
charges, men with whom he had been educated and who were his
social equals, and on whom he had used every flattery to entice them
almost to a sharing of power. He even gave poison by his own hand
to a man who was suffering from a fever, offering it in a drink of cold
water that the man had asked for. [14.2] He spared few, if any, of the
moneylenders, creditors, and tax collectors who had ever demanded
that he pay what he owed at Rome or a toll that was due on the road.
One of them he sent off to be executed directly from his morning
audience but then called him back immediately; while everyone was
praising his compassion, he ordered him killed as he watched, saying, "I want to feast my eyes." When the two sons of another man
tried to intercede on his behalf, he put them to death together with
their father. [14.3] A Roman knight who shouted as he was being
rushed off to execution, "You are my heir!" he forced to make public
the tablet that contained his will, and after he read that the man's
freedman was named his co-heir, he ordered him and the freedman
killed together. He also killed several ordinary citizens only because
they had openly spoken ill of the Blue faction; he thought they had
dared to do this to show disrespect for him and because they were
anticipating revolution. [14.4] But there was no one whom he hated
more than clever writers and astrologers. Whenever one of these was
accused, he executed him without allowing him to defend himself.
He was angry about this notice that was posted immediately after
his edict that ordered astrologers to leave Rome and Italy before
the Kalends of October: "The Chaldeans[35] proclaim—may all good
befall the state—that Vitellius Germanicus will not be anywhere on
those same Kalends."[36] [14.5] He was also suspected in the death of
his mother because he did not permit food to be given to her when

---

35. Astrologers were typically Chaldeans, a people who lived in Assyria.
36. Because he would be dead.

she was ill. A woman of the Chatti,[37] in whom he trusted as the mouthpiece of the divine, had predicted that his rule would finally be secure and would last for a very long time if he survived his parent. Others write that she was weary of present troubles and afraid of future threats and had asked her son for poison, easy enough to obtain.

[15.1] In the eighth month of his reign the armies stationed in the provinces of Moesia and Pannonia abandoned their allegiance to him. The armies in Judaea and Syria across the sea likewise swore to Vespasian, some when he was with them, others when he was not.[38] And so to maintain the support and goodwill of all the rest, there were no bounds on what Vitellius did publicly or privately. He levied troops in the city with the promise that after his victory he would discharge those who volunteered and would also give them the discharge benefits due veterans and regular soldiers. [15.2] Then with the enemy threatening on land and sea, he sent his brother into the field with the fleet and new recruits and a band of gladiators to face them on one front, and on another he put the forces and generals that had fought at Betriacum.[39] After he was defeated or betrayed everywhere, he negotiated with Flavius Sabinus, Vespasian's brother, for safe passage for himself and the payment of 100 million sesterces.

Standing on the steps leading to the Palatine, he immediately declared before a large assembly of soldiers that he was ceding the power he had taken up unwillingly. But he was faced with a general call of protest and put off his decision. The night passed, and at daybreak he went down to the rostra dressed in mourning clothes and crying profusely; he made the same declaration, but this time he read it from notes. [15.3] Again the soldiers and the people interrupted and urged him not to give up, and they competed in promising to use all of their resources to help him. His courage revived, and he mounted a sudden attack on Sabinus and the rest of the Flavian party, who felt that danger had passed by then, and he forced them onto the Capitoline. He set the temple of Jupiter Optimus Maximus on fire, destroyed them, and watched the battle and the fire while he

---

37. A German tribe; there was a tradition of female German oracles.

38. The legions in the east swore to Vespasian in early July of 69 CE. The major revolt came in August.

39. See 10.1 and *Oth.* 9.2–3.

ate his dinner in the house of Tiberius.⁴⁰ He soon regretted what he had done and blamed others for it. He called an assembly and swore and forced the rest to swear that nothing would have greater priority for him than the peace of the city. [15.4] Then he took the dagger from his side and extended it first to the consul, and then, when he refused it, to the magistrates, and then to the senators, one by one. When no one would take it, he left as if he were going to place it in the temple of Concord. But when some protested, "It is you who represent Concord," he returned and said that he would not only keep his weapon but take the cognomen Concordia.⁴¹ [16.1] He also persuaded the senate to send representatives together with the Vestal Virgins to seek peace or at least to set a time for discussing peace.

When he was waiting for a reply the next day, a scout reported that the enemy was approaching. And so he quickly hid himself in a sedan chair and was taken secretly to his family home on the Aventine with only two companions, a pastry cook and a chef, so that he could escape to Campania from there. Then on the basis of a vague and insubstantial rumor that the pact he had been seeking had been achieved, he let himself be taken back to the Palatine. When he discovered everything there deserted, and when even those who were with him were slipping away, he put on a belt filled with gold pieces and fled to the small apartment that belonged to the doorkeeper. He tied a dog in front and put a bed and mattress against the door.

[17.1] The vanguard of the approaching column had already burst in and, meeting no opposition, went searching through everything, which was the usual procedure. They pulled Vitellius from his hiding place, and when they asked him who he was (they did not know) and where Vitellius was, he lied to get away. After they did recognize him, he kept asking to be held under guard for a time or put in prison, submitting that he had something to tell them that concerned the well-being of Vespasian. He stopped when his hands were tied behind his back, a noose was thrown over his neck, his clothing was torn off, and he was dragged half-naked along the whole length of the Sacred Way⁴² into the Forum, derided physically and verbally. His head was pulled back by the hair as is done with convicted criminals,

---

40. By this time a section of the imperial palace.
41. "Peace," "harmony."
42. The road from the Palatine Hill down to the Forum.

and his chin was pushed up by a sword point so that his face would not be lowered but would be seen. [17.2] Some threw dung and mud at him; others shouted that he was an arsonist and a glutton, and a part of the crowd even made fun of his physical defects.

Vitellius was enormously tall; his face was unusually ruddy from excessive drinking and his belly was fat. One of his thighs was somewhat lame because a long time before he had been struck by a four-horse chariot as he was attending Gaius, who was practicing his driving. Finally, at the Gemonian Steps he was tortured with many little cuts and killed, and dragged from there by a hook to the Tiber.

[18] Vitellius died with his brother and his son in the fifty-seventh year of his life. Those were correct who interpreted the omen at Vienna (we have described it)[43] as a prediction that could only mean that he would come under the power of a man from Gaul. Vitellius was defeated by Antonius Primus, general of the opposing force, who was born at Tolosa[44] and whose boyhood nickname had been Becco, which means the beak of a cock.

---

43. See chapter 9; a cock stood on his head. The word for "Gaul" also means "cock."

44. Modern Toulouse.

THE DIVINE VESPASIAN

9–79 CE

Emperor July 69–79 CE

Titus Flavius Vespasianus was born into an equestrian family from the Sabine territory. He entered political life under Tiberius and Gaius (Caligula) but advanced when Claudius gave him command of a legion for the invasion of Britain. His career suffered for a time when Nero became emperor but recovered when he was sent to suppress rebellion in Judaea; his undistinguished background meant that Nero thought it safe to trust him with an army. The confusion following Nero's death found him positioned to make his move for the throne, and he was the contender left standing at the end of the civil wars of 69 CE.

Vespasian never completely left his modest background behind. He preferred simplicity to pomp and maintained his sense of humor. The Julio-Claudian dynasty had had a multigenerational heritage of power, and the terms of Galba, Otho, and Vitellius were short. As a consequence, Vespasian was the first outsider to become solidly established as emperor, and this accounts for the many reports of omens and miracles in his story. They served to show that he was worthy. Two grown sons as heirs to the throne promised stability after the recent chaos. His principate initiated the Flavian dynasty, and he was deified after he died. Suetonius acknowledges this new beginning in his first paragraph by making a statement about the dynasty as a whole. These last three lives function as a unit.

[1.1] Armed insurgency and the violent deaths of three emperors had left the empire long without direction and, so to speak, adrift. In the end, it was the Flavian family that undertook governance and brought the empire under control. This family lacked distinction and could boast no parade of ancestors, but it gave Rome no reason to regret that it had come to rule—despite the consensus that Domitian was rightly punished for his greed and cruelty.[1]

[1.2] Titus Flavius Petro, a native of Reate,[2] served Pompey's cause in the civil war as a centurion or as a reenlisted veteran. He deserted in the battle at Pharsalus[3] and returned home, where he sought pardon; he received it along with his discharge and became a money collector for bankers. His son (whose cognomen was Sabinus) did not serve in the military, although there are some who claim that he was a *primipilaris* and others that he was still in command of a cohort when he was released from his oath for health reasons. Instead, he collected the import tax in Asia, where there remained statues raised to him by the municipalities with the inscription, "To an honest tax collector." [1.3] Later, he was a moneylender in the Helvetian territory,[4] and he died there, leaving his wife Vespasia Polla and their two children. The elder of these, Sabinus, advanced to the prefecture of Rome, the younger, Vespasianus, all the way to the principate. Polla was born to a good family of Nursia.[5] Her father was Vespasius Pollio, military tribune three times and camp prefect. Her brother was a senator of praetorian rank. Six miles from Nursia on the way to Spoletium is a place on a hilltop called Vespasiae where numerous memorials to the Vespasii stand as unquestionable proof of the family's prominence and antiquity.

[1.4] I should not omit mention of the fact that some have claimed that Petro's father was from the Transpadane region[6] and had been a contractor for the laborers who used to go from Umbria to the Sabine district every year to work in the fields. The same sources have also claimed that he settled in the town of Reate and married a woman from there. I have not found the least evidence for this despite the fact I have investigated quite carefully.

[2.1] Vespasian was born in the Sabine district beyond Reate in a small village called Falacrina, in the evening of the fifteenth day before

---

1. See *Dom.* 9.1, 10.

2. A town in the Sabine territory, northeast of Rome.

3. The battle in which Caesar's forces defeated Pompey's; see *Jul.* 30.4, 35.1, 75.2.

4. In Gaul.

5. Another Sabine town.

6. The region north of the Po River.

the Kalends of December, during the consulship of Quintus Sulpicius Camerinus and Gaius Poppaeus Sabinus, five years before the death of Augustus.[7] He was reared by his paternal grandmother Tertulla on her estate at Cosa.[8] This is why, even when he was emperor, he often visited his childhood home where the house was kept just as it had been, so that nothing he was used to seeing disappeared. He so cherished his grandmother's memory that on anniversaries and feast days he always drank from a little silver cup that had belonged to her.

[2.2] For a long time after he had received the adult toga, he refused to try for the broad-striped tunic[9] despite the fact that his brother had gained it. Only his mother was finally able to force him to pursue it. She eventually hammered him into submission by ridicule rather than by appealing to him and using the weight of her authority. She mocked him repeatedly, saying that he was a menial clearing a path for his brother.

[2.3] Vespasian served as military tribune in Thrace. As quaestor, he received the province of Crete and Cyrene by lot. He was a candidate for the office of aedile and then of praetor. He was elected to the first after suffering an initial defeat and barely getting in on his second try in the sixth position; the second office he won right away, on his first try among the first contenders.[10] As praetor he was eager to win in every way he could the approval of Gaius, who was at odds with the senate. He called for special games to celebrate the emperor's victory over the Germans, and he proposed that the bodies of the conspirators be cast out unburied as an addition to their punishment.[11] He also tendered the emperor thanks before the illustrious order[12] because Gaius had honored him with the distinction of a dinner invitation.

[3] In the meantime, he married Flavia Domitilla, formerly the mistress of Statilius Capella, a Roman knight from Sabrata in the

---

7. November 17, 9 CE.

8. In Etruria (Tuscany).

9. Worn by the senatorial class.

10. He received the fewest votes of the six elected to the aedileship but was among the leading vote-getters when he stood for the praetorship.

11. On Gaius' negligible excursions against the Germans, see *Cal.* 45. For the alleged conspiracy, see *Cal.* 24.3.

12. The senate.

province of Africa. She originally had Latin status, but arbiters later declared her freeborn and a full Roman citizen.[13] The case was brought by her father Flavius Liberalis, born at Ferentium[14] and never more than a quaestor's secretary. Vespasian had children by her, Titus, Domitian, and Domitilla. He survived his wife and daughter, both of whom died before he became emperor. After his wife's death, he brought his former mistress Caenis back to live with him. She had been Antonia's[15] freedwoman and secretary, and even when he was emperor he treated her almost as if she were his lawful wife.

[4.1] Under Claudius, Vespasian, with the backing of Narcissus,[16] was sent to the province of Germany in command of a legion. From there he was transferred to Britain, where he engaged the enemy in thirty battles and brought under Roman control two of the strongest tribes along with more than twenty towns and the nearby island of Vectis.[17] This he accomplished partly under the consular commander Aulus Plautius and partly under Claudius himself. [4.2] For this service he received triumphal regalia and shortly thereafter two priesthoods and a consulship that he held for the last two months of the year.[18] He spent the time between then and his proconsulship in retirement, uninvolved in public life because he feared Agrippina,[19] who was still a powerful influence on her son and nursed an abiding hatred for the friends of Narcissus, even after the freedman was dead.

[4.3] The luck of the draw then gave him the province of Africa, where he governed with commendable honesty and earned a great deal of respect—except when turnips were thrown at him during an uprising at Hadrumetum.[20] He clearly came home no richer, since he had so little credit at that point that he had to mortgage all of his property to his brother and out of necessity stooped to earning

---

13. She had Junian Latin status, the half citizenship given to informally freed slaves. Claims of citizenship were adjudicated by a special board.
14. In Etruria, north of Rome.
15. Antonia Minor, the mother of Germanicus and Claudius.
16. Claudius' influential freedman; see *Cl.* 28.
17. The modern Isle of Wight.
18. 51 CE.
19. Agrippina the Younger, Nero's mother.
20. On the African coast not far from Carthage.

a living in common trade to maintain his senatorial status. For this reason the people called him muleteer.[21] He is also said to have been found guilty of extracting 200,000 sesterces from a young man for whom he had obtained the broad-striped tunic against the wishes of the man's father. For this he was severely reprimanded. [4.4] As one of Nero's companions on his tour of Greece, he gave serious offense, either because he left the theater too often while the emperor was singing or because he stayed but went to sleep. Nero banned him not only from his inner circle but from his public audiences as well. Vespasian retreated to a small town off the beaten track and there he remained, lying low and fearing the worst, until he was offered a province that had an army.

[4.5] There had spread everywhere throughout the East an ancient and persistent idea that fate would soon summon leaders from Judaea to power. Although events would make it clear that this prediction referred to the Roman emperor, the Jews interpreted it as referring to themselves and rebelled. They killed the legionary commander, repulsed the consular governor of Syria who was bringing reinforcements, and seized the eagle that belonged to his legion. A larger military force was necessary to put down the uprising, and there was need for a general who was energetic but still reliable when trusted with major responsibility. Vespasian was selected, primarily because of his reputation for hard work and because his inconsequential family name rendered him totally unthreatening. [4.6] Two legions were accordingly added to his command, along with eight cavalry detachments and ten cohorts, and his elder son was enrolled among his lieutenants. As soon as he arrived in his province, he attracted the attention of the neighboring provinces[22] because he had restored discipline in the camp quickly and had thrown himself into one battle and then a second with such passion that when he was attacking a fortress, a rock hit him on the knee and his shield took a number of arrows.

[5.1] When Nero and Galba were dead and Otho and Vitellius were contending for the principate, Vespasian began to hope that he might attain the power that the following omens had long intimated to him: [5.2] An ancient oak sacred to Mars on the suburban estate

---

21. His business was perhaps dealing in mules.
22. His command was in Judaea. Neighboring provinces were Egypt and Syria.

of the Flavians suddenly sprouted a branch when Vespasia gave birth to each one of her three children. These were clearly indicators of the fate in store for each: The first branch was stunted and dried up quickly; the girl who was born did not live even one year. The second branch flourished vigorously and portended great good fortune. The third was the size of a tree in and of itself. They say that when their father Sabinus observed this, he told his mother that the grandson born to her would be Caesar, a fate confirmed by the examination of entrails as well. She merely laughed and expressed astonishment that she was still in possession of her mental capacities—whereas her son was mad.

[5.3] Later, when Vespasian was aedile, Gaius Caesar was incensed because he thought that insufficient attention had been paid to the cleaning of the streets. He ordered soldiers to cover Vespasian with filth by loading it into the folds of his bordered toga. Some construed this as meaning that the crushed and leaderless state would come under his protection in some period of civil unrest and find refuge, so to speak, in the embrace of his arms. [5.4] Once when he was at lunch, a stray dog brought a human hand in from the rubbish and dropped it under the table.[23] Another time, when he was at dinner, an ox that was plowing threw off its yoke and burst into the dining room. It chased away the attendants and collapsed at the feet of the reclining Vespasian as if suddenly exhausted and bowed its neck. And a cypress tree on his grandfather's farm[24] was torn from its roots, even though there had been no wind, and lay on the ground; the next day it rose again, stronger and more vigorous.

[5.5] When Vespasian was in Achaia, he dreamed that his good fortune and that of his family would commence as soon as one of Nero's teeth was pulled. It chanced that the very next day a doctor came into the hall and showed him a tooth that had just been extracted. [5.6] In Judaea, when he was consulting the oracle of the god of Carmel, he received encouraging responses that assured him that whatever he conceived or desired, however grand, would come to pass. And Josephus, one of the captured nobles, while he was being cast into chains, persisted in stating that Vespasian would soon set him free—but as emperor. [5.7] Omens were reported from Rome, too: Nero, in his final days, was instructed in a dream to escort the

---

23. The Latin word for "hand" (*manus*) can mean "power."
24. At Cosa; see 2.1.

sacred chariot of Jupiter Optimus Maximus from its sanctuary to the house of Vespasian and from there to the Circus. A short time later, when Galba was drawing near to the voting assembly that would elect him to his second consulship,[25] the statue of Divine Julius, of its own accord, turned and faced the East. And before the armies closed with one another at the battle of Betriacum,[26] two eagles fought in plain view. After one had been vanquished, a third came on the scene from the direction of the rising sun and chased off the victor.

[6.1] But despite the fact that his own men were more than ready to follow him and were urging him on, Vespasian still did not make his move until he was encouraged by the fortuitous support of men whom he did not know and who were far away. [6.2] Two thousand men from the three legions of the army in Moesia had been sent to support Otho. After they had begun their march, they learned that Otho had been defeated and had taken his own life, but they went on as far as Aquileia because they were unsure that the report was true. There, as occasion offered and lack of discipline allowed, they pillaged the town, committing every kind of violence. They feared they would have to account for their actions when they returned and that punishment would inevitably follow, and so they decided to choose and invest an emperor. They rationalized that they were no worse than the Spanish army that had created Galba or the praetorian army that had created Otho or the German army that had created Vitellius. [6.3] And so they examined the names of the governors of consular rank, all those who were serving anywhere at that time. When they had rejected the rest for one reason or another and when some soldiers from the Third Legion that had been transferred from Syria to Moesia just before the death of Nero praised Vespasian and backed him, all agreed and quickly put his name on all their banners. Then, to be sure, their movement came to a halt, and the detachments returned to duty for a short while. But when what they had done became known, Tiberius Alexander, the prefect of Egypt, was the first to make his legions swear to Vespasian; this he did on the Kalends of July, the day later celebrated as the

---

25. 69 CE.

26. The armies of Otho and Vitellius in the first battle of Betriacum; see *Oth.* 9.2. The second battle between those of Vitellius and Vespasian appears at *Vit.* 10.1, 15.2.

day he became emperor. Then the army in Judaea swore to him in person on the fifth day before the Ides of July.[27] [6.4] A copy of a letter (genuine or forged) from Otho to Vespasian that circulated contributed a great deal to the undertaking. It contained a last appeal from the dead emperor for Vespasian to take on the burden of revenge and expressed the desire that he come to the support of the state. At the same time the rumor spread that after his victory, Vitellius had decided to exchange the permanent quarters of the legions and transfer the German legions to the East for less dangerous and demanding military service. Licinius Mucianus, one of the provincial governors,[28] and Vologaesus, the Parthian king, also contributed to Vespasian's success. The former put aside the quarrel that he was carrying on openly at the time, a quarrel that had its origin in his rivalry with Vespasian, and he promised him the Syrian army. Vologaesus promised forty thousand archers.

[7.1] And so with civil conflict under way and his generals and their forces dispatched ahead into Italy, Vespasian seized the opportunity to cross over to Alexandria to take strategic control of Egypt's resources. There he entered the temple of Serapis alone and shut out everyone else; he intended to seek a sign that would measure the strength of his power. After he had made many offerings to propitiate the god, he at last turned around, and his freedman Basilides stood before him, offering him fronds, wreaths, and sacrificial cakes as is customary at that sacred site.[29] It was clear that no one had let the freedman in, and furthermore, the man had for a long time had difficulty walking because of a nervous ailment and was far away. At that very moment a letter arrived with the news that Vitellius' forces had been routed at Cremona and that Vitellius himself had been killed in Rome.[30]

[7.2] Authority and a certain majesty (as one might call it) were lacking in this emperor who had come on the scene unlooked for and was still inexperienced. But he acquired these qualities, too. An ordinary citizen who was blind and a man with a weak leg approached

---

27. July 11, 69 CE.

28. Governor of Syria.

29. The offerings were symbols of kingship, and the freedman's name is related to the Greek word for king.

30. The second battle of Betriacum took place in late October of 69 CE. Vitellius was killed on December 20.

him together when he was sitting on the tribunal. They pleaded with him to cure their infirmities as Serapis had shown them in a dream. They said that Vespasian would heal the eyes of the one if he spat on them and that he would strengthen the leg of the other if he consented to touch it with his heel. [7.3] Although Vespasian had little faith that these actions would be effective and accordingly lacked the courage even to try, in the end, at the urging of his friends, he ventured both in full view of the assembled populace, and he was successful. At the very same time, divine guidance led to the excavation of vases of ancient workmanship at a sacred site in Tegea in Arcadia.[31] The vases had faces that were a close likeness of Vespasian.

[8.1] Vespasian returned to Rome with celebrity and as if touched by divinity. He celebrated a triumph over the Jews and added eight consulships to the one he had served earlier, and he assumed the censorship as well.[32] During the entirety of his reign he thought nothing more important than, first and foremost, setting a steady course for the state, which had been close to ruin and on the verge of collapse, and after that, making it beautiful.

[8.2] The soldiers, some of them confident because of victory and others wretched because they had suffered humiliating defeat, had turned to every kind of unrestrained violent conduct. The provinces and free states and even some of the client kingdoms were suffering internal disorder. He responded by discharging many of Vitellius' troops without honor and punishing them. And he avoided granting anything beyond the ordinary to those who had helped him win victory to the point that he was late with even the usual bonus. [8.3] Vespasian seized every opportunity to restore discipline. After he had used a dismissive nod to register his disgust for a young man who reeked of perfume when he was thanking him for the military command he had requested, he rebuked him in all seriousness, saying, "I would have preferred that you smelled of garlic." And he rescinded the man's commission. As for the marines who traveled back and forth from Ostia and Puteoli on foot,[33] when they asked

---

31. In the central Peloponnesus.

32. His triumph took place in June of 71 CE. He had been suffect consul under Claudius in 51; see 4.2. He and his son Titus were censors in 73 and 74.

33. They were stationed at these ports, possibly to guard against fire. See *Cl.* 25.2.

that a "shoe-money" account be set up for them, he ordered them to run barefoot in the future (he thought it unsatisfactory to send them away without a response), and they have run like that ever since. [8.4] He made Achaia, Lycia, Rhodes, Byzantium, and Samos into provinces, taking away their status as free states, and also Trachian Cilicia and Commagene, ruled by kings up to that time. He assigned legions to Cappadocia because of the frequent incursions of barbarians there and gave it to a governor of consular rank rather than to an equestrian.

[8.5] Past fires and collapse had made Rome an ugly sight. Vespasian allowed anyone who wished to take possession of vacant areas and build on them if they had been abandoned by their owners. When he began the reconstruction of the Capitol,[34] he was the first to put his hand to removing rubble, and he carried some of it off on his own back. He assumed responsibility for restoring three thousand bronze tablets that had burned in the same fire and hunted down copies of them in all quarters. These tablets constituted an ancient and deeply revered record of Rome's power inasmuch as they contained the decrees of the senate almost from the time when the city was founded, resolutions of the populace concerning alliances and treaties, and the special privileges granted individuals. [9.1] He constructed new public buildings as well, the Temple of Peace near the Forum and the temple for the Divine Claudius on the Caelian Hill, which Agrippina, it is true, had begun but Nero had torn down, almost to its foundations.[35] He also built an amphitheater in the center of the city when he learned that Augustus had had plans for one.[36]

[9.2] He purged and then replenished the illustrious orders that had been depleted by murders that had occurred at one time or another and were debased by long neglect. He reviewed the senate and the equestrian orders, expelled the least deserving members, and introduced the worthiest of the Italians and provincials. And since it was recognized that the two orders differed not so much in privileges as in the respect accorded them, he ruled like this in a dispute between a senator and a Roman knight: "It is not permissible

34. The temple of Jupiter on the Capitoline had burned in the fighting of December of 69 CE; see *Vit.* 15.3.
35. See note on *Cl.* 45.
36. This was the structure later called the Colosseum.

for senators to be insulted, but it is right and proper for the insult to be returned." [10] The number of lawsuits waiting to be resolved had increased greatly everywhere. Some cases of long standing remained because judicial proceedings had been interrupted, and the unsettled times had added new ones. Vespasian chose by lot people to restore property that had been seized in the war and to hear cases out of turn and thus reduce to a very small number those pending before the centumviral court. The lifetime of the litigants seemed scarcely sufficient to resolve all of them if they came up in their normal order.

[11] Sexual license and extravagant living had flourished with no one to rein them in. Vespasian brought to the senate a bill that provided that any woman who consorted with a slave belonging to someone else be considered a slave herself, and a second bill that made it never lawful for moneylenders to force repayment of a loan made to dependent sons, that is to say, even after the death of their fathers.

[12] In other matters Vespasian was unassuming and merciful from the beginning of his principate until the very end. He never pretended that his means had been anything other than modest earlier in his life, and he often even bragged of the fact. He broke into laughter at some who tried to assign the origin of the Flavian family to the founders of Reate and to a companion of Hercules whose tomb stands on the Salarian road. On the day of his triumph, weary because the parade was slow and tedious, he had so little interest in the decorations that others tendered him that he did not suffer in silence but said, "I deserve to be punished, an old man who stupidly wanted a triumph so very much—as if it were something owed my ancestors or I had sought out for myself!" He did not take the tribunician power immediately nor the title of Father of His Country until late in his reign. He ignored the customary practice of searching people who came to greet him, even when the civil war was still going on.

[13] He patiently endured the candor of his friends, the innuendos of lawyers, and the defiance of philosophers. Although Licinius Mucianus had a reputation for unacceptable sexual behavior and showed Vespasian little respect, relying on the favor that he enjoyed with him because of the services he had rendered, Vespasian could never bring himself to criticize him except once in private when he was complaining to a common acquaintance and added, "I, on the

other hand, am a man."[37] When Salvius Liberalis had the impudence to say while defending a rich client, "What does Caesar care if Hipparchus has a hundred million sesterces?" Vespasian applauded him.[38] When the banished Cynic philosopher Demetrius encountered the emperor on a journey, he did not bother to rise or greet him and even snarled something or other. Vespasian thought it sufficient to call him Dog.[39]

[14] He gave little thought to injuries done him and hostility shown him, nor did he seek to retaliate. He arranged an excellent match for the daughter of his enemy Vitellius and even provided her with a dowry and everything that she needed. When Nero's court became off limits to him, and he was frightened and kept asking what he should do or where he should go, one of the imperial doorkeepers threw him out and ordered him, "Go to Morbovia."[40] This man later begged forgiveness, and Vespasian became enraged at him, but his anger was restricted to words—of more or less the same number and content. Such restraint is not surprising, for the suspicion or fear that would make him harm someone was so alien to his character that when his friends warned him to be wary of Mettius Pompusianus because it was widely believed that the man had the horoscope of an emperor, he not only ignored the warning but made him consul, assuring that Pompusianus would one day remember the favor.

[15] Scarcely will there be found an innocent man who received punishment during his reign—unless Vespasian was away at the time and unaware that it was taking place or, at the very least, agreed to it reluctantly and was misled. Helvidius Priscus was the only one to address him by his private name Vespasian, when he came back from Syria, and as praetor he issued edicts that did not have the imperial titles or even the emperor's name. Vespasian did not grow angry until Helvidius' abusive insults came close to stripping him down to

---

37. Mucianus was allegedly a passive homosexual; see 6.4 for his services to Vespasian.

38. Vespasian had a reputation for being greedy and parsimonious. See chapter 16 and following.

39. "Cynic" is similar to the Greek word for "dog," and it was the nickname by which Cynic philosophers were traditionally called.

40. A coined word, ostensibly from "sickness" and "road." The phrase means "Go to hell."

the level of private citizen. And although he first banished Helvidius
and later ordered him killed, he thought it important to find some
way to save his adversary's life, and he sent agents to recall the assassins. And he would have saved him if it had not been reported incor-
rectly that he was already dead. But he never rejoiced at anyone's
death and even wept and grieved over the just punishments that he
meted out.

[16.1] The only fault of which Vespasian is rightly found guilty is
greed. It was not enough that he reinstated the taxes that Galba had
abolished, added heavy new ones, and increased the tribute paid by
the provinces, even doubling it in some cases. He openly carried on
business dealings that would be shameful even for a private citizen
to engage in, buying things only to dispose of them piecemeal at a
profit later.[41] [16.2] He did not hesitate to sell offices to candidates
or pardons to defendants, both innocent and guilty. And it is believed
that he routinely promoted his most predatory agents to important
posts on purpose so that he could find them guilty of extortion at a
later time when they had more money. Indeed, common talk had it
that he used them like sponges because he soaked them, in a manner
of speaking, when they were dry and squeezed them out when they
were wet.

[16.3] Some say that Vespasian's greed came naturally. When an
old herdsman had to pay for the freedom that he had humbly petitioned from his master at the time he became emperor, he declared,
"The fox changes its fur, not its nature." But others think that necessity drove him to plunder and theft because he found the state treasury and the imperial purse completely empty. He gave proof of this
when he said, at the very beginning of his principate, "Forty billion
sesterces are needed if the state is to stand firm." This explanation
for his greed seems plausible since he used well the wealth that was
gotten badly.

[17] He was exceedingly generous to people of every class: he
made good the property qualification required for senators, supported penniless former consuls with 500,000 sesterces a year,
and restored to better condition many cities throughout the world
after they had been damaged by earthquake or fire. He showed
particular favor to talent and acquired skill. [18] He was the first

---

41. The impropriety of business dealings for senators also appears at 4.3.
"Selling piecemeal" implies retail trade.

to use imperial funds to make an annual grant of 100,000 sesterces for teachers of Latin and Greek rhetoric. He gave large gifts and generous pay to outstanding poets and also to artists, to the sculptor who restored the Venus of Cos and the colossal statue of Nero, for instance. And to an engineer who promised to transport huge columns to the Capitol cheaply he offered a sizable reward for his invention but rejected the device itself, saying, "Let me feed ordinary folk."[42] [19.1] He brought back old-fashioned entertainments at the games celebrating the dedication of the new stage in the theater of Marcellus. To the tragic actor Apelles he gave 400,000 sesterces, 200,000 each to the lyre players Terpnus and Diodorus, to others 100,000, and to those who received the least, 40,000. He also awarded numerous gold crowns, and he gave dinner parties frequently, often consisting of several courses, and served large portions. In this way he provided business to the market vendors. He gave presents to the women on the Kalends of March just as he did to the men at the Saturnalia.[43]

Despite this generosity, he retained his reputation as a fundamentally greedy man. [19.2] The Alexandrians persisted in calling him Cybiosactes,[44] the nickname for one of their kings who was a very foul and nasty character. And at Vespasian's funeral, the lead mime, who was named Favor, wore a mask that looked like him and (as is customary) mimicked the things he did and said when he was alive. He asked the procurators, so that all could hear, how much the funeral and the funeral procession cost. When he heard the answer, "Ten million sesterces," he shouted, "Give me a hundred thousand and throw me into the Tiber!"

[20] Vespasian had a well-proportioned body. His limbs were solid and strong and his facial expression was that of someone straining. A court joker made an apt comment about this when the emperor asked him to tell a joke about himself as well: "I shall," he said, "when you have finished emptying your bowels." He enjoyed excellent health but did nothing to maintain it except massage his throat and other

---

42. He wanted to support his subjects by providing work for them, not giving it to a machine.
43. This Apelles may be the one named at *Cal.* 33. Juno, the goddess of marriage, was honored at the Matronalia on March 1.
44. "Dealer in salt fish."

parts of his body a set number of times in the ball court and fast one day a month.

[21] This is the routine that he generally followed: When he was emperor he always woke early, before daylight. He read through his correspondence and all of the official reports and then admitted his friends, and while they were paying their respects, he put his shoes on by himself and got dressed.[45] After taking care of any matters that had arisen, he had time to ride in his carriage and after that to rest, lying with one of his mistresses of whom he had a number to fill the place of Caenis, who had died. From his private quarters he went to the bath and the dining room. They say that at no time of the day was he more easily approachable or more generous, and his household staff took particular advantage of this moment when they wanted to ask for something.

[22] After dinner and at other times, too, Vespasian was always extremely sociable and resolved many problems with a joke. He had a very clever tongue, but his humor was offensive and tasteless to the point of including juvenile obscenities. Here are some of his most clever sayings that have been preserved: When Mestrius Florus recommended that he say *plaustra* instead of *plostra*, he addressed him the next day as Flaurus.[46] He was pursued aggressively by a woman who claimed that she was dying from love for him, and after he had taken her to his bed and given her 4,000 sesterces to pay for sex, his steward asked how he wanted the amount recorded in his accounts. He said, "Charge it to Vespasian, much beloved."

[23.1] He quoted Greek verses to good effect, like this one with which he described a tall man with enormous genitals: "Striding long, brandishing a spear that casts a long shadow."[47] And in the case of a very rich freedman named Cerylus, who had changed his name to Laches and had begun to pass himself off as freeborn in order to avoid paying what would be due the imperial purse in the future,[48] Vespasian remarked:

---

45. An emperor would normally be helped with these personal tasks.

46. Vespasian preferred the older pronunciation of the word for "wagons." Flaurus sounds like a Greek word meaning "useless."

47. Homer, *Iliad* 7.213.

48. The former master of an emancipated slave was heir to all or a portion of the latter's estate. Cerylus was evidently an imperial freedman.

O Laches, Laches,
When you die, just as you were in the beginning,
You will be Cerylus again.[49]

But most of the time he used his humor to dissipate the disgust provoked by his unseemly greed by laughing about it and turning it into a joke. [23.2] One of his favorite court attendants asked that a position as steward be given to a man he claimed was his brother. Vespasian put him off, summoned the applicant, took from him the amount that he had agreed to pay the attendant who was recommending him, and appointed him to the position at once. When the attendant inquired later about his petition, Vespasian said, "Find yourself another brother. The one you think is yours is mine." One time on a journey, when he suspected that the mule driver had gotten down to fix shoes on the animals in order to cause delay and to give a man involved in a lawsuit the opportunity to approach, he asked, "How much are you paid to shoe a mule?" Then he arranged to get part of the payment. [23.3] When his son Titus reproached him for devising a tax even on urine,[50] he put a coin from the first payment to the young man's nose and asked him whether the smell displeased him. When Titus said that it did not, he replied, "But it is made from urine." When a delegation announced that a colossal statue had been voted to him at significant public expense, he held out his empty hand and ordered them to set it up at once, saying that its base had been prepared.[51] [23.4] The jokes did not stop even when he was fearful of dying and his life was in mortal danger. When (among other portents) the doors of the Mausoleum suddenly flew open and a star with hair[52] appeared in the heavens, he said that the first omen pertained to Junia Calvina, who was descended from Augustus,[53] and the second to the king of the Parthians, who had a

---

49. Fragment from the Greek playwright Menander.

50. Fullers (cleaners) and tanners used urine.

51. He was holding out his hand to receive the money allocated for the statue. The empty hand was the base onto which the statue (or rather the money) should be placed.

52. The Romans called a comet a hairy star; see *Cl.* 46.

53. Junia Calvina was Augustus' great-great-granddaughter, descended through Julia the Younger.

full head of hair. And at the first sign of illness, he said, "Alas! I think I am becoming a god!"

[24] While he was in Campania during his ninth consulship, he was troubled by a slight fever. He immediately headed back to the city and went to Cutiliae[54] and the countryside near Reate where he spent the summer every year. Although his illness worsened and he had in addition done harm to his digestive system by drinking too much cold water, he still performed his duties as emperor as he always had while he was there, and he even received embassies while lying in bed. When a sudden attack of diarrhea made him weak, he said, "An emperor must die standing." And as he rose and struggled to stand, he died in the arms of those who were supporting him on the ninth day before the Kalends of July.[55] He lived sixty-nine years, seven months, and seven days.

[25] All agree that Vespasian always had such confidence in his horoscope and in the horoscopes of his sons that even after frequent plots had formed against him, he dared affirm to the senate that either his sons would succeed him or no one would. It is also said that he once dreamed about a scale resting in the center of the forecourt of his home on the Palatine. Its balance was level with Claudius and Nero standing on one pan, he and his sons on the other. And the dream proved correct, for each family ruled for the same number of years and for an equal length of time.

---

54. A town near Reate in the region where he was born; see 2.1.
55. June 23, 79 CE.

THE DIVINE TITUS

41–81 CE

Emperor 79–81 CE

The emperor Titus was the elder of Vespasian's two sons and had the same name as his father, Titus Flavius Vespasianus. He joined Vespasian in Judaea to assist in putting down the Jewish revolt, returned to Rome with him after the civil wars, and shared in his principate during the years that followed. Power passed smoothly to Titus in 79 CE. He died little more than two years later, seemingly remembered as the embodiment of all virtue.

Tradition assumed a process of deterioration for most of the early emperors; the promising prince or fledgling emperor turned bad with the passage of time. In Titus' case the reverse was true. Titus was a cruel, greedy, and dissolute prince, leading to the anticipation of a second Nero. His metamorphosis into a moderate, generous emperor is unexplained. Suetonius tapped into an encomiastic tradition about him when he wrote, but to his credit he also includes the unpleasant aspects of character shown by Titus during his early life. It would seem that Titus, like Germanicus, the father of Gaius (Caligula), had the good fortune to die before his reputation was tarnished.

[1] Titus, who carried his father's cognomen,[1] was the love and the light of humankind. Great were the resources—whether nature or skill or good fortune—that allowed him to earn the goodwill of all. And he did this as emperor, a thing that was very difficult, for as a private citizen and even during his father's principate he did not escape being an object of hatred, much less of public censure.

---

1. Vespasianus.

Titus was born on the third day before the Kalends of January in the notorious year of Gaius' murder,[2] in a squalid building near the Septizonium[3] in a small, dark chamber. It is still there to this day and can be visited. [2] He was reared in the court together with Britannicus[4] and instructed in the same subjects and by the same teachers. They say that at that time Claudius' freedman Narcissus brought in a *metoposcopus*[5] to examine Britannicus; the man declared unequivocally that it was impossible that the boy would rule but that Titus, who was standing nearby at the time, would do so for certain. The boys were furthermore such close friends that Titus, lying next to Britannicus, is thought to have sipped from the drink that killed him, because he was gravely ill for a long time. Titus remembered all of this later and erected a golden statue of Britannicus on the Palatine and dedicated a second equestrian statue made of ivory that is still displayed in the procession in the Circus today, and he escorted it at its dedication.

[3.1] Titus' gifts of mind and body were immediately conspicuous when he was a boy, and they grew stronger at every stage that followed. His handsome good looks gave evidence of leadership as much as they charmed. He was unusually strong although not tall, and his stomach protruded somewhat. His memory was exceptional, and he was a quick study with most of the skills necessary for both war and peace. [3.2] He was very adroit with arms and in horsemanship. A ready orator and poet in Latin and Greek, he was at ease with extemporaneous presentation also. Not even in music was he untutored, and he sang and plucked the lyre pleasantly and proficiently. Many have informed me that Titus would write shorthand very fast, competing in fun with his secretaries in sport, and would imitate any handwriting he saw and often say, "I could have been a truly excellent forger."

[4.1] Titus proved himself worthy when he served as military tribune in both Germany and Britain, earning the highest marks for his hard work and no less for his integrity. This is apparent from

---

2. December 30, 41 CE.

3. Evidently on the Quirinal Hill; his brother Domitian also seems to have been born in that section of the city; see *Dom.* 1.1.

4. The son of Claudius (*Cl.* 27.1) poisoned by Nero (*Ner.* 33.2–3).

5. A pseudoscientist who told fortunes based on head measurements.

the large number of statues and busts of him and from inscriptions throughout both provinces. [4.2] After he completed his military service he turned his attention to the Forum[6] in efforts that earned him more respect than they were frequent, and it was at that time that he married Arrecina Tertulla, whose father was a Roman knight but had been praetorian prefect. When she died he replaced her with Marcia Furnilla, a woman from a distinguished family, whom he divorced after acknowledging a daughter that she bore him. [4.3] Next, after his term as quaestor, he was given charge of a legion and brought Taricheae and Gamala, the strongest cities in Judaea, back under Roman control. In one of the battles his horse was killed under him, and he got on another whose rider had died fighting beside him.

[5.1] When Galba came to power, Titus was sent to congratulate him, and wherever he went he attracted the attention of men who assumed that he was being summoned to Rome for adoption. But when he realized that everything had once again become chaotic, he turned back and visited the oracle of Venus at Paphos.[7] In the course of consulting it about his voyage, he found his hope of imperial power confirmed as well. [5.2] That hope was soon fulfilled,[8] and when he was left behind to finish the conquest of Judaea, he killed twelve defenders with the shots of twelve arrows in the final assault on Jerusalem, and he took the city on his daughter's birthday. This delighted the soldiers and made them so pleased with him that when they congratulated him they saluted him as *imperator*, and they kept detaining him when he tried to leave the province, insisting with prayers and even threats that he either stay or take them all with him. [5.3] This gave rise to the suspicion that he had tried to desert his father and claim the rule of the East for himself. Suspicion grew when on his way to Alexandria he put on a diadem during the consecration of the bull Apis at Memphis, a practice that was in fact part of the traditional ritual of that ancient religion. But some interpreted the gesture for the worse. So he hurried to Italy, and after he had put in at Regium and then at Puteoli in a merchant ship, he rushed on to Rome very quickly and addressed his father, who was not expecting

---

6. That is, he pleaded cases before the courts.
7. On Cyprus.
8. His father had become emperor; he could expect to succeed him.

him, with, "I have come, Father, I have come," as if proving how baseless were the rumors about him.

[6.1] From then on Titus acted as his father's partner and even as the guardian of his power. He celebrated a triumph with him and was censor with him, and he was his father's colleague when Vespasian held tribunician power and in his seven consulships. He was given almost total responsibility since he dictated letters in his father's name, signed his edicts, and read speeches for him in the senate in place of his quaestor. He also became praetorian prefect, a position that had never before been held by anyone other than a Roman knight, and he exercised the office quite arrogantly and brutally. He did not postpone the ruin of anyone about whom he held deep suspicions but sent people around the theaters and the camp to demand their punishment, making it seem that he was punishing by consensus. [6.2] Among his victims was the consular Aulus Caecina,[9] whom he invited to dinner, but Caecina had scarcely left the dining room before Titus ordered him stabbed. Danger was really at issue, however, since Titus had seized papers in Caecina's handwriting containing a speech ready for delivery before a military assembly. Although these actions served his future security well, he was hated for them at the time. As a result there was scarcely any emperor who entered the principate with such a bad reputation and with so much hostility directed toward him.

[7.1] In addition to cruelty, Titus was suspected of undisciplined living because he kept drinking bouts with his most prodigal friends going until midnight, and also of promiscuity because of his large stable of male prostitutes and eunuchs and because of his signal passion for Queen Berenice,[10] to whom he was even said to have promised marriage. Greed was also suspected because everyone knew that he was in the habit of making deals and arranging rewards for himself at his father's private judicial hearings. In sum, people both thought privately and declared openly that he was another Nero. But this reputation gave way to a character that was good and turned into one deserving the greatest praise. No vice was found in him—on the contrary, the highest virtues.

---

9. Suffect consul in 69 CE.

10. Berenice was the daughter King Agrippa I of Judaea. After the defeat of the Jews in 70 CE, she came to Rome and lived with Titus.

[7.2] Titus held banquets that were enjoyable rather than extravagant. He chose for his circle of friends those whom even the emperors who came after him found satisfactory and particularly useful to themselves and to the state. He immediately sent Berenice from Rome, although both he and she were unwilling. He ended his generous support of some of his favorites whom he found especially delightful and even stopped watching them altogether when they performed in public, despite the fact that they were such skilled dancers that they later became popular artists on the stage.

[7.3] He took nothing from any citizen. He kept his hands off others' property as much as anyone ever had. And he did not accept gifts, not even the customary ones that were allowed. But he was nonetheless as generous as any of the emperors before him. At the dedication of the amphitheater[11] and the baths that had been built quickly next to it, he gave a gladiatorial show with extraordinarily elaborate effects and magnificence. He also put on a naval battle in the old basin constructed for the purpose,[12] and on the same site he presented both gladiators and, on a single day, five thousand wild beasts of every kind.

[8.1] Titus was by nature very accommodating. Whereas all of the Caesars after Tiberius had adhered to his precedent and did not hold the rights and privileges conferred by previous emperors valid unless they themselves granted the same benefits to the same people, he was the first to ratify all past favors by a single edict, and he did not permit recipients to beg for them. In the case of other petitions put before him, he was determined not to send anyone away without hope. Indeed, when his household advisers warned that he was promising more than he could deliver, he said, "No one should go away unhappy after talking with the emperor." And once when he recalled during dinner that he had done nothing to benefit anyone the entire day, he came out with this remark that has been remembered and praised deservedly: "Friends, I have lost a day."

[8.2] He was always so gracious, especially toward the populace as a whole, that when a gladiatorial show was announced, he declared, "I will arrange the entertainment not as I want it but as the spectators want it," and that was just what he did. For he agreed to everything

---

11. The Colosseum, begun by Vespasian (*Ves.* 9.1) and dedicated by Titus in 80 CE.

12. By Augustus; see *Aug.* 43.1.

that they asked and took the initiative in urging them to ask for what they wanted. He also made known his enthusiasm for the Thracian gladiators and behaved like a fan, joking with the people verbally and with gestures. But he maintained the dignity proper to his role and continued to be evenhanded in his judgments. So as not to forgo any opportunity to show himself the people's emperor, he sometimes bathed in the baths that he had built together with ordinary people who were allowed in.

[8.3] Some terrible disasters happened while he was emperor: the conflagration of Mount Vesuvius in Campania, for instance; a fire at Rome that lasted three days and three nights; and a plague that was worse than almost any that had ever occurred. In these many calamities he displayed not only the concern that was proper for an emperor but also the unique sympathy of a father, at times offering consolation by edict, at others bringing relief to the extent that resources made it possible. [8.4] He chose by lot supervisors for the reconstruction of Campania from any of the former consuls who were available. He allocated to the rebuilding of the afflicted cities the property of those who died in the Vesuvian disaster and whose heirs did not survive. The only public statement he made in regard to the fire at Rome was, "I am ruined"; he designated all the decorative objects in his country estates for public buildings and temples, and he put a number of men of equestrian rank in charge so that everything would be done more quickly. He overlooked no resource, divine or human, to cure the illness and lessen the effects of the plague but searched out every kind of divine sacrifice and every medicine.

[8.5] Among the evils of his time were informers and those from whom the informers got their information; these men had long had free rein. He regularly ordered them whipped and clubbed in the Forum and finally paraded across the sand of the amphitheater. Some of them he had put up for auction and sold as slaves; others were sent off to the least civilized of the islands. And to restrain in the future those who ventured to do things like this and to keep them from ever repeating such actions, he prohibited, among other measures, the same charges from being brought under different laws and inquiry being made about the status of anyone who had been deceased more than a certain number of years.[13]

---

13. The legality of wills depended on the status of the testator: freeborn, freedman, or slave.

[9.1] Stating that he was accepting the position of *pontifex maximus* in order to keep his hands uncontaminated,[14] he kept his word and afterward neither ordered anyone's death nor was an accessory to it. He sometimes had good reason to exact retribution but swore, "I will perish rather than put to death." When two men of patrician family were found guilty of aspiring to imperial power, he did no more than warn them to cease. He told them that the principate was a gift bestowed by fate but promised that if there was anything else that they wanted, he would confer it on them. [9.2] Then he quickly sent couriers to the mother of one of them, who lived some distance away, to tell the worried woman that her son was safe. The men themselves he not only invited to a private dinner but also, on the following day when they had been intentionally seated next to him at a gladiatorial contest, handed them for inspection the gladiators' weapons that had been brought to him.[15] And after he became familiar with their horoscopes, he is said to have declared, "They are both in danger but at another time and from another source." And that is how it turned out.

[9.3] His brother never stopped plotting against him.[16] He came close to overtly inciting the armies to revolt and planning to join them. But Titus could not bear to kill him or put him out of the way, or even hold him in less honor. As he had from the first day of his principate, he continued to declare that Domitian was his coregent and successor, although he sometimes begged him privately with prayers and tears to be willing to reciprocate the affection that he felt some day. [10.1] At that point, death intervened, bringing loss that was greater for humankind than for himself.

After the games were over[17] and he had wept copiously in full view of the people, he went to his estate in Sabine country. He felt some forebodings because the victim had run away when he was making sacrifice and because thunder was heard from a clear sky. Then at the very first stopping place on the way he contracted a fever, and when he was being moved from there in a litter, they say that he pulled

---

14. Free from blood; a priest could have no connection with death.

15. Whoever was presiding over the games examined the contestants' weapons to determine that they were sharp enough.

16. Domitian; see *Dom.* 2.3.

17. The games that celebrated the new amphitheater; see 7.3.

aside the curtains and looked up at the sky and complained bitterly: "I do not deserve to have my life snatched away, for with one single exception, there is nothing that I regret." [10.2] What that regret was he did not reveal at that time nor did it easily suggest itself to anyone. Some think that he had in mind the sexual liaison that he had had with his brother's wife, but Domitia swore on all that was sacred that it had not taken place. She would scarcely have denied it if there had been anything at all to the story. On the contrary, she would have bragged about it, as she was very ready to do with regard to all her sexual encounters.[18]

[11] Titus died in the same villa as his father on the Ides of September two years, two months, and twenty days after he had succeeded him, in the forty-second year of his life.[19] When his death became known, all grieved publicly just as if for a sorrow within the family, and the senate hurried to the senate house before they were convened by edict. With the doors still closed but later with them opened, they offered such thanks to him and showered him with such praise when he was dead as they had never given him, not even when he was alive and in their midst.

---

18. See *Dom.* 3.1.
19. September 13, 81 CE.

DOMITIAN

51–96 CE
Emperor 81–96 CE

Titus Flavius Domitianus, the second of the emperor Vespasian's two sons, was close to twelve years younger than his brother, the emperor Titus, and did not share in his father's and brother's triumphs against the Jews. Domitian became emperor in 81 CE when Titus died, and he spent much of his reign in the field with the army.

Sensible administrative measures and a genuine concern for Rome and its inhabitants can be laid to Domitian's credit, but his autocratic behavior made him unpopular with the upper classes. He ignored the idea that he was no more than "first" among his peers, and he seems to have enjoyed the trappings of monarchy. This attitude led to his assassination by court insiders in 96 CE.

Suetonius appends a coda to this last of his imperial biographies, a brief statement as his portrayals come to a close. Better times were ahead, he writes. He had little choice but to make this hopeful declaration about the twenty-five years or so between the death of Domitian and the time when he was writing. The reigns of Trajan and Hadrian were those in which he himself held major responsibility.

[1.1] Domitian was born on the ninth day before the Kalends of November in the year when his father Vespasian was consul designate and scheduled to enter office the next month.[1] He was born in the sixth region of the city on a street called Pomegranate, in a house that was later turned into a temple dedicated to the Flavian fami-

---

1. October 24, 51 CE. Vespasian was suffect consul in November and December of that year; see *Ves.* 4.2.

ly.² It is said that he spent his adolescence and young adulthood in poverty and disgraced by scandal; not a single silver pitcher could be found in his house. Everyone knows that Clodius Pollio (the man of praetorian rank whom Nero ridiculed in his poem "The One-Eyed Man") had kept a letter in Domitian's handwriting and sometimes showed it. It contained the emperor's promise to spend the night with him. Some confirm that Domitian was also seduced by Nerva, the emperor who would succeed him.

[1.2] In the struggle against Vitellius, Domitian retreated to the Capitoline with his father's brother Sabinus and some of the armed forces that he had with him.³ But when the enemy broke in and the temple caught on fire, he spent the night in the quarters that belonged to the temple attendant, and in the morning he disguised himself in the clothing worn by devotees of Isis⁴ and hid among the priests of that disreputable cult. He crossed the Tiber with a single companion and went to find the mother of one of his fellow students. He kept out of sight so successfully that he evaded capture even when the men looking for him were close on his heels. [1.3] Finally, after the Flavian victory, Domitian emerged from hiding and was greeted as Caesar. He assumed the office of urban praetor with consular power but in name only, for he ceded judicial responsibilities to his closest colleague.⁵ But he exercised the whole of the power that his authority made available to him with so little restraint that he revealed, even then, the kind of person that he would become. Not to go into detail, after having sex with a large number of married women he took Domitia Longina from her husband Aelius Lamia and married her. On a single day he appointed more than twenty men to official positions in the city and abroad, and this made Vespasian say on a number of occasions, "I marvel that he did not send me a successor, too!" [2.1] Domitian also launched a military operation to Gaul and the German provinces that was neither necessary nor

---

2. Evidently on the Quirinal Hill; see *Tit.* 1.

3. Titus Flavius Sabinus, Vespasian's brother, occupied the Capitoline Hill against the Vitellian forces at the end of December of 69 CE; see *Vit.* 15.3.

4. The followers of the Egyptian goddess Isis wore linen garments.

5. Domitian was representing his family in Rome. His father and brother did not arrive until the next year, 70 CE.

sanctioned by his father's advisers. His sole motive was to acquire wealth and a reputation equal to his brother's.

Domitian was reprimanded for this behavior and made to live with his father so that he would be reminded of his age and position. Whenever they went out in public, he trailed behind his father's and brother's sedan chairs in a litter, and he rode a white horse in their triumph over Judaea.[6] In fact, in only one of his six consulships did he give his name to the year, and that was the time when his brother yielded his place and suggested him as his replacement. [2.2] It was his idea to present himself as wonderfully modest and to pretend special enthusiasm for poetry, a subject as alien to him in this earlier period as it was later when he rejected and ignored it. He even recited in public. Despite this, when Vologaesus, king of the Parthians, requested auxiliary forces to use against the Alani[7] and asked for one of Vespasian's sons to be their commander, Domitian worked very hard to make sure that it was he who was sent. When this came to nothing, he used bribes and promises to try to persuade other eastern kings to make the same request.

[2.3] When Vespasian died, Domitian vacillated for a long time as to whether he should double his monetary gift to the soldiers.[8] He was never shy in claiming that he had been left a share in the principate and that his father's will had been forged. From then on, he never stopped devising plots against his brother, both secretly and in the open. At the end he ordered Titus left for dead when he was gravely ill but had clearly not yet breathed his last. Domitian saw him deified after he died but awarded him no other honors and criticized him indirectly in his speeches and edicts.

[3.1] At the beginning of his principate, it was Domitian's habit to spend hours by himself and do nothing but catch flies and stab them with a well-sharpened stylus. When someone asked who was inside with Caesar, Vibius Crispus gave the witty answer, "Not even a fly."[9] Domitian addressed his wife Domitia as Augusta. She had given birth to his son during his second consulship, but the child

---

6. Emperors were carried sitting in an upright position; a passenger in a litter reclined. He participated in the triumph but not as a general.

7. A tribe in southern Russia. For Vologaesus, see *Ves.* 6.4.

8. Whether he should give double what his brother gave.

9. This anecdote derives from a proverb that describes an empty place as inhabited by "not even a fly."

died the year after he became emperor. He sent her away in disgrace because she had had a liaison with the actor Paris, but he could not bear the separation and soon took her back, claiming that the populace demanded it.

[3.2] In administering the empire, Domitian showed himself an equal blend of vices and virtues—until he turned the virtues into vices as well. So far as one can guess, it was privation that made him greedy and fear that made him cruel—beyond his natural inclinations.

[4.1] He often put on magnificent and expensive shows, not only in the amphitheater[10] but in the Circus as well. There he staged (in addition to the customary races between two-horse and four-horse chariots) a battle in two parts, one a combat between cavalry units and the other between cohorts of foot soldiers. He also staged a naval battle in the amphitheater. Other innovations were beast hunts and gladiatorial games held by torchlight at night with both men and women as combatants. And his faithful attendance at the games sponsored by the quaestors (these he had reinstituted after they had been discontinued for a time) provided the people with the opportunity to demand two pairs of gladiators from his training school that he presented decked out in the grandeur of the court as the show's climax. [4.2] At every gladiatorial show there stood in front of him a small boy in red who had a misshapen little head. Domitian talked with him a great deal, sometimes seriously, and it is certain that he was heard asking him, "Do you know why I thought it a good idea to put Mettius Rufus in charge of Egypt when I made my most recent appointments?" He dug a lake near the Tiber, constructed seating around it, and pitted fleets against one another in naval battles that came close to being real warfare. He watched these combats to the end during torrential rains.

[4.3] Domitian put on Secular Games, calculating the date not from the year when they had recently been presented by Claudius but from the year when they had been presented by Augustus long before. On the day when the chariot racing took place during these games, he shortened individual races from seven laps to five so that it would be easier to hold a hundred races. [4.4] He established quinquennial games in honor of the Capitoline Jupiter with three

---

10. Built by the Flavians and later known as the Colosseum; see *Ves.* 9.1, *Tit.* 7.3.

divisions: musical, equestrian, and gymnastic. A considerably larger number of contestants won prizes then than do today, for they competed in prose declamation, both Greek and Latin, and in addition to singing to the accompaniment of the lyre, there was also lyre playing with a chorus and solo playing. Young women also raced in the stadium. Domitian presided over the competition wearing Greek sandals and a purple Greek robe, and on his head he wore a golden crown with images of Jupiter, Juno, and Minerva. Next to him sat the *flamen dialis* and the college of priests attached to the cult of the Flavian family. These were dressed similarly, except that their crowns carried his own image as well as the others. Every year he celebrated the Quinquatria of Minerva at his villa on the Alban Mount,[11] and he established a college of priests for the goddess. Its officers were chosen by lot from its members, and they sponsored excellent beast hunts and theatrical entertainments, as well as contests for orators and poets.

[4.5] Three times Domitian made gifts of 300 sesterces to the populace, and he provided a very generous feast during the gladiatorial games held in connection with the festival of the Seven Hills.[12] Large baskets of prepared food were distributed to the senate and the equestrian order and smaller baskets to the common people, and he himself was the first to start eating. The next day he scattered tokens good for all sorts of prizes into the crowd, and when most of these fell in the section where the common people sat, he announced that he would throw five hundred to each of the sections for the equestrian and senatorial orders.

[5] Domitian restored a number of very impressive structures that had been destroyed by fire, among them the temple of Jupiter on the Capitoline, which had burned a second time.[13] But on all of these he inscribed only his own name and gave no credit to the person originally responsible. He also built a new temple to Jupiter the Gatekeeper on the Capitoline and the forum that is now called the forum of Nerva, as well as a temple for the Flavian family, a stadium, a theater for musical performances, and a lake for mock sea

---

11. An annual festival celebrated on March 19. The Alban Mount was near Rome.

12. The festival on December 11 included a procession around Rome.

13. The fire in 80 CE when Titus was emperor; see *Tit.* 8.3.

battles. Stone from the last of these was later used to build the Circus Maximus after its two side sections had burned.

[6.1] Domitian initiated some wars because he wanted to, others because they were necessary. The campaign against the Chatti was his idea, whereas the one against the Sarmatians was forced on him when a legion was annihilated along with its commander.[14] He made two campaigns against the Dacians.[15] In the first the consular Oppius Sabinus was killed and in the second Cornelius Fuscus, prefect of the praetorian cohorts, to whom overall command of the war had been entrusted. After battles fought with varying success, Domitian celebrated a double triumph over the Chatti and the Dacians. To commemorate his victory over the Sarmatians, the only thing that he did was deposit a laurel wreath in the temple of the Capitoline Jupiter.

[6.2] Domitian suppressed a revolt that had been started by Lucius Antonius, commander in Upper Germany.[16] He accomplished this by a remarkable stroke of luck (he was not present) when the Rhine River unexpectedly thawed at the critical moment of the battle and prevented barbarian allies from crossing over to Antonius. Domitius learned of this victory from portents before he heard about it from messengers. On the very day the fighting took place, a magnificent eagle put its wings around his statue in Rome and gave exultant cries. A short time later, a rumor that Antonius had been killed circulated so widely that many swore they had seen his head being brought to Rome.

[7.1] Domitian also changed the way many things were done. He did away with the baskets of food that the state handed out and reestablished the practice of holding proper banquets. He added two circus factions to the four that already existed[17] and dressed their drivers in gold and purple. He banned actors from the stage but allowed them to practice their profession in private homes. He did not allow males to be castrated, and he held down the price of eunuchs who were still in the possession of slave traders. [7.2] Once

---

14. The first of these took place in Germany in 82 or 83 CE and the second in the Danube area in 92.

15. On the lower Danube in 85 and 86 CE.

16. Lucius Antonius Saturninus; the revolt took place in 89 CE.

17. See *Cal.* 18.3.

when a great abundance of wine was available but grain was in short supply, he decided that cropland was not being cultivated because there was too much interest in viniculture, and so he issued an edict stipulating that no one was to plant new vines in Italy and that the vineyards in the provinces were to be cut down so that no more than half were left standing. But he did not follow through with this plan. He divided positions that carried very important responsibilities between his freedmen and Roman knights. [7.3] He did not allow two legionary camps to be joined or anyone to deposit more than 1,000 sesterces with the standards,[18] for it appeared that Lucius Antonius had incited revolution in winter quarters shared by two legions and had been emboldened by the amount deposited there. And he added a fourth pay period to the soldiers' year to the amount of three aurei.[19]

[8.1] Domitian was conscientious and diligent when he dispensed justice, and he often presided on the tribunal over special courts in the Forum. He reversed judgments rendered by the centumviral court when their verdicts had been determined in their own interest. Again and again he warned assessors not to be taken in by unfounded claims of status.[20] He censured judges who had taken bribes and their advisers as well. [8.2] He was responsible for bringing a greedy aedile before the tribunes on a charge of extortion and for asking the senate to appoint judges for the case. He was so conscientious about reining in the magistrates in the city and the governors in the provinces that there have never been any who were better disciplined or more just than when he was emperor. Since the end of his reign, we have seen many men in these positions charged with all manner of crimes.

[8.3] When Domitian undertook the correction of morals,[21] he put an end to the disorder caused by spectators who took seats indiscriminately in the section of the theater reserved for equestrians. He destroyed widely circulated writings that libeled leading men and women, and he degraded their authors. He removed from the

---

18. The legion's insignia were kept in an inviolable shrine. Beneath it was a vault in which soldiers could deposit their money for safekeeping.

19. Since there had been three pay periods of 300 sesterces every year, the new annual wage was 1,200 sesterces. An aureus was equal to 100 sesterces.

20. The assessor decided whether a person was slave or free.

21. He became censor for life in 85 CE.

senate a man of quaestorial rank who was obsessed with gesturing and dancing like a mime. He took the privilege of a litter and
the right of receiving legacies and inheritances from women with
reputations for immorality. He erased the name of a knight from
the juror list because he remarried a wife whom he had divorced on
a charge of adultery. He found members of both orders guilty under
the Scantinian law.[22]

The unchaste behavior of the Vestal Virgins (wrongdoing that
even his father and brother had ignored) he punished severely in
two ways: in the first years of his reign by execution, in later years,
according to ancient custom. [8.4] Although he allowed sisters named
Oculata and another Vestal, Varronilla, to choose their manner of
death and relegated their seducers, he later ordered Cornelia, the
chief Vestal, buried alive. (She had originally been cleared but much
later was retried and found guilty.) And he ordered the men who had
had sex with her beaten to death with rods in the Comitium.[23] An
exception was a man of praetorian rank to whom Domitian granted
exile because he had confessed despite the fact that the outcome of
the case was uncertain and the information acquired from torture
was inconclusive. [8.5] And so that no disrespect for divine sanctity
would go unpunished, he had his soldiers destroy a funerary monument that one of his freedmen had built for his son with stone meant
for the temple of the Capitoline Jupiter, and he threw the bones and
whatever else was in the tomb into the sea.

[9.1] In the beginning, before his father had arrived in the city,
Domitian found all killing so repugnant that he planned to issue an
edict forbidding the sacrifice of cattle. He recalled a line written by
Virgil: "before the wicked race dined on butchered heifers . . . "[24]
And he gave scarcely any hint of greed and stinginess, never when
he was a private citizen or for a considerable time after he became
emperor. On the contrary, he often displayed both fiscal responsibility and generosity. [9.2] He was extremely openhanded with all his
friends and advised them that there was nothing more important or
that he could recommend more strongly than that they do nothing
on the cheap. He did not accept inheritances left him by men who

---

22. Both senators and knights. This was a law against the sexual predation
of freeborn boys.
23. The open area in the Forum that was the original place of assembly.
24. *Georgics* 2.538.

had children. He even invalidated a bequest in the will of Rustus Caepio, who provided that every year his heir pay a specified sum of money to each senator as he entered the senate house. He freed from prosecution all the defendants whose names had remained posted on the *aerarium* for more than five years, and he did not allow their cases to be reopened unless it was done within the year and with the stipulation that an accuser who did not win his case would be exiled.[25] He pardoned the past offenses of the secretaries for public accounts and records who had been in the habit of engaging in business, despite the fact that this was contrary to the Clodian law.[26] The discontinuous parcels of land left over after land had been divided up for veterans he assigned to the people who had farmed them for a long time, awarding them on the grounds of their continuous possession. He put an end to false claims that benefited the imperial treasury by punishing harshly those who fabricated them.[27] He was heard to say, "The emperor who does not punish informers encourages them."

[10.1] Domitian continued on a path neither of mercy nor of restraint in his financial dealings but plunged rather more quickly into cruelty than into greed. He killed a pupil of the pantomimist Paris, a boy still young and sick at the time, because he seemed not unlike his teacher in skill and appearance.[28] He also killed Hermogenes of Tarsus[29] because of certain innuendos included in the history he wrote, and he crucified the copyists who had transcribed it. He dragged a respectable head of household from the seats and threw him to dogs in the arena because he had said that a Thracian gladiator was a match for a *murmillo* but no match for the producer of the games.[30] Domitian hung a placard on him that read, "A fan of the Thracians, who spoke disrespectfully."

---

25. The state treasury (*aerarium*) was located in the temple of Saturn. Pending civil cases were dismissed except under the conditions stated. Clogged courts were a perennial problem.

26. Evidently a law that forbade their involvement in business.

27. That is, those whose charges resulted in property falling to the state.

28. Domitian's wife Domitia allegedly had an affair with Paris; see 3.1.

29. A city in Cilicia.

30. Domitian, the producer of these games, evidently favored the *murmillones*, and so a Thracian gladiator had no chance against the emperor's bias.

[10.2] He killed a number of senators, some of whom were former consuls. Among these were Civica Cerealis, put to death at the time when he was proconsul of Asia; Salvidienus Orfitus and Acilius Glabrio, when they were in exile, on the grounds that they were inciting revolution; and others, each of them for a trivial reason: He killed Aelius Lamia because of some jokes that were indeed suggestive, but they were also harmless and had been around for a long time. After Domitian made off with his wife, Lamia told someone who praised his singing voice, "I abstain from sex."[31] And when Titus urged Lamia to enter into a second marriage, Lamia replied, "Do you wish to marry also?" [10.3] Domitian did away with Salvius Cocceianus because he had celebrated the birthday of the emperor Otho, who was his uncle on his father's side; Mettius Pompusianus because it was widely acknowledged that his horoscope predicted that he would hold imperial power and because he carried around a map of the world drawn on parchment and copies of the speeches of kings and generals from the work of Titus Livy and because he had named his slaves Mago and Hannibal;[32] Sallustius Lucullus, his agent in Britain, because he had allowed a new kind of lance to be called a Lucullan lance; Junius Rusticus because he had published works that praised Paetus Thrasea and Helvidius Priscus and called them men greatly to be revered.[33] Domitian expelled all philosophers from Rome and Italy at the time of this accusation. [10.4] He also killed Helvidius' son, on the grounds that he had used the characters of Paris and Oenone in a farce to criticize his divorce of his wife.[34] And he killed Flavius Sabinus, one of his cousins,[35] because on the day

---

31. See 1.3. Sexual continence was advised for someone "in training" as a singer. In regard to Nero's training, see *Ner.* 20.1.

32. The historian Livy described the defeat of the Carthaginian general Hannibal and his brother Mago by the Romans in the Second Punic War. Pompusianus (also at *Ves.* 14) was apparently a threat because he obsessed over the grander moments in Roman history.

33. Thrasea and Helvidius were killed under Nero and Vespasian, respectively; see *Ner.* 37.1, *Ves.* 15. They opposed the principate on principle, on "philosophical" grounds.

34. The Trojan prince Paris deserted Oenone for Helen but later wanted her back. See 3.1 for Domitian's divorce of Domitia and her recall.

35. Titus Flavius Sabinus, the son of Domitian's cousin of the same name; see 12.3.

of the consular elections the herald made a mistake and announced to the populace not that he had been designated consul but that he would be emperor.

[10.5] Domitian grew even more brutal after he had put down the revolt in the military.[36] In his effort to hunt out those involved who were still in hiding, he mutilated many of the opposition by a new method of interrogation: he thrust burning wood into their genitals. He cut off the hands of some. Of the known conspirators, there is general agreement that only two were pardoned, a tribune of the senatorial class and a centurion. To make it easier to prove that they were innocent, they provided evidence that they were sexually indecent and for that reason could be of no value in the eyes of their general or their fellow soldiers.[37]

[11.1] Domitian's cruelty was not only extreme but devious as well, and he caught his victims off guard. The day before he crucified his steward, he called him into his chamber, had him sit on the couch next to him, and sent him away feeling safe and happy, having honored him by sharing his dinner with him. When he was at the point of condemning to death the consular Arrecinus Clemens, one of his close associates and trusted agents, he showed him the same favor that he always had—or even more. Finally, when they were riding in a litter together, Domitian spied the man who had informed against Clemens and said, "Should we hear what this nasty slave has to say tomorrow?"

[11.2] And in order to show greater contempt when he took advantage of men's silent endurance, he never pronounced a severe judgment without a preamble that hinted at clemency. As a result, there was no clearer indicator of a trial's grim outcome than its mild beginning. When he brought people accused of treason before the senate and began, "Today I will test how dear I am to the senate," he had no difficulty getting them condemned and even executed in the ancient manner.[38] [11.3] And then, appalled by the gruesome punishment, he interceded to lessen the opprobrium it would bring on him by saying (it will be of interest to know his exact words),

---

36. The revolt described at 6.2.

37. They played the female in male homosexual acts.

38. Stripped naked, fastened to a stake, and beaten to death; see *Cl.* 34.1, *Ner.* 49.2.

Let your devotion to me allow you, senators, to grant my petition, because I know that it is with difficulty that I will succeed in my request that you concede free choice in the manner of death to the condemned. There are two benefits: you will be spared an unpleasant sight, and all will know that I was present at this meeting of the senate.[39]

[12.1] Drained of resources by the expense of his building projects and entertainments and by the extra pay period for the army,[40] Domitian did indeed try to reduce the number of troops in order to lighten the expense of the military. But when he realized that this left him exposed to barbarian attack and still mired in his financial burdens, he felt no qualms about stealing and robbing in every way he could. He seized the property of men living and dead everywhere with the help of any available informer and any possible accusation. An allegation of any treasonous act or word of any kind against the emperor sufficed. [12.2] He confiscated the estates of people completely unrelated to him,[41] if so much as a single person testified that he had heard the deceased say, while still alive, that Caesar was his heir. Along with other taxes, he was very aggressive in exploiting the revenue available from the Jews. The treasury that held their funds was informed both of those who, although not registered as Jews, were living a Jewish life and of those who pretended that they were not Jews and so did not pay the tax levied on their nation. I remember that as a young man I was present at a crowded hearing when an imperial agent inspected a nonagenarian to see whether he was circumcised.

[12.3] From his youth, Domitian was not in the least humble but was insolent and uninhibited in what he said and did. When Caenis, his father's mistress, returned from Histria and offered him a kiss, as she usually did, he gave her his hand.[42] Resenting the fact that his

---

39. His presence will prove that it was he who was behind the mitigation of the penalty.

40. See 7.3.

41. Earlier he had been scrupulous about not accepting inheritances from strangers; see 9.2.

42. Histria was in the northeast corner of the Adriatic. Kissing was normal practice within the family. An extended hand invited a kiss from an inferior.

brother's son-in-law[43] had dressed his attendants in imperial white, he shouted, "Many rulers are not a good thing!"[44]

[13.1] And upon his accession to the principate, he did not hesitate to boast in the senate, "I gave power to my father and my brother; you have returned it to me,"[45] or to say, when he retrieved his wife after their divorce, "I have recalled her to her place on my *pulvinar*."[46] He enjoyed hearing the shout that went up at the feast he gave in the amphitheater: "Happiness to our master and our mistress."[47] And when at the competition held on the Capitoline[48] the entire crowd pleaded in a single voice for him to restore the status of Palfurius Sura, who had earlier been expelled from the senate and had just won the crown in the oratory contest, he did not dignify their request with a response but merely had the herald order them to be quiet. [13.2] With equal arrogance, when he was dictating an official letter to be signed by his procurators, he began like this: "Our master and our god orders that this be done." This established the precedent that he was not thereafter to be addressed by anyone in any other way, neither in writing nor in conversation. He did not allow statues to be set up for him on the Capitoline unless they were made of gold or silver and of a specified weight. He built so many huge passageways and arches decorated with four-horse chariots and tokens of his triumphs in all the sections of the city that someone wrote on one of them in Greek, "It is enough."[49]

[13.3] He held the consulship seventeen times, more than anyone before him, the seven in the middle sequentially. Almost all he served in title only, none longer than the Kalends of May and often only to the Ides of January. After he had celebrated two triumphs and

43. His cousin Flavius Sabinus (see 10.4), who was married to Julia, the daughter of his brother, the emperor Titus.

44. Homer, *Iliad* 2.204.

45. A reference to the fact that he was in Rome when the struggle for power ended but they were not; see 1.2–2.1.

46. The ceremonial couch for statues of the gods (and the emperor) but no doubt a reference to his "divine bed" as well.

47. The feast is described at 4.5. The words *dominus* and *domina*, master and mistress, imply a relationship to their subjects as slaves. Less pretentious emperors had not allowed the use of these titles; see *Aug.* 53.1, *Tib.* 27.

48. The mixed games; see 4.4.

49. In Greek, *arci* means "it is enough," but in Latin it means "arches."

had taken the cognomen Germanicus, he changed the months of September and October to Germanicus and Domitianus from his own names. He had succeeded to imperial power in the one and been born in the other.

[14.1] This behavior made him feared and hated by everyone, and in time he was destroyed in a plot formed by his friends and closest freedmen together with his wife. He had long had premonitions about the last year and day of his life, and even about the hour too and how he would die. Chaldean astrologers had predicted it all to him when he was a young man. His father made fun of him in public one time when he passed up mushrooms at a dinner party,[50] saying that he was badly informed about his fate because he was not afraid of a weapon instead. [14.2] And so, frightened and nervous, he was unduly upset by the least hint of something wrong. It is thought that nothing kept him from enforcing the edict he issued about cutting down vines[51] more than the pamphlets containing these verses that circulated widely:

> Even if you eat me to the root, still shall I bear grapes enough
> For wine to pour over you, goat, when you are sacrificed.[52]

[14.3] The same feeling of dread lay behind his refusal of an unprecedented and distinctive honor that the senate offered him—despite the fact that he was very eager for every such distinction: it was decreed that whenever he was consul, Roman knights chosen by lot, dressed in purple robes and carrying spears, were to go before him, walking between his lictors and his entourage.

[14.4] As the time drew near when Domitian was expecting danger, each passing day made him more apprehensive. In the colonnades where it was his custom to stroll, he lined the walls with phengite[53] so that he could see what was happening behind his back in the reflection from its polished surface. He rarely gave an audience to prisoners except in private and alone while holding their chains in his hand. To impress on his household that they must not venture to

---

50. Tradition held that Claudius had been poisoned by a dish of mushrooms; see *Cl.* 44.2.

51. See 7.2.

52. *Palatine Anthology* 9.75, a collection of Greek epigrams.

53. Light-colored translucent stone.

kill their patron—even for a good reason—he condemned to death
Epaphroditus, his secretary in charge of petitions, because it was
believed that he had, with his own hand, helped Nero commit suicide after he had been abandoned.[54] [15.1] Finally, he killed Flavius
Clemens, a cousin on his father's side, a man lazy beyond contempt.
Domitian had given public notice that he planned for Clemens' sons
to succeed him, and when they were still little boys he took their
given names from them and ordered one to be called Vespasianus
and the other Domitianus. On a sudden hint of suspicion, he killed
Clemens when his consulship was scarcely over. This murder especially hastened his own end.

[15.2] So many flashes of lightning were reported over a period
of eight months that Domitian cried out, "Now let him strike whom
he wishes!"[55] The Capitoline was struck and so were the temple
of the Flavians and his own house on the Palatine, even his very
bedchamber. The force of a storm tore the plaque bearing his name
from the pedestal of his statue as a triumphant general, and it landed
on a nearby tomb. A tree that had fallen when Vespasian was still
a private citizen[56] but then grown up again suddenly toppled once
more at that time. The oracle at the temple of the goddess Fortuna at
Praeneste had always, throughout his reign, when he asked her blessing on the new year, given him the same favorable response. This last
time, she foretold great evil and hinted at blood. [15.3] He dreamed
that Minerva, the goddess whom he served with blind devotion, left
her sanctuary and said that she could no longer protect him because
Jupiter had stripped her of her arms. But what alarmed him most
was the prediction made by the astrologer Ascletarion and what happened to him: When Ascletarion was accused and did not deny that
he had talked openly about events that his skill had permitted him
to see ahead of time, Domitian asked him how he himself would die.
The astrologer replied with assurance that he would soon be torn to
pieces by dogs. Domitian ordered him killed at once, and to prove
that the seer's skill was without foundation, had his body disposed
of with exceptional care. A sudden storm arose while this was taking
place, the funeral pyre collapsed, and dogs ripped the half-burned

---

54. For the part played by Epaphroditus in Nero's death, see *Ner.* 49.3.

55. Jupiter was the hurler of thunderbolts.

56. See *Ves.* 5.4.

corpse apart. The mime Latinus, who happened to have observed the incident as he passed by, told Domitian about it at dinner along with other stories of the day.

[16.1] The day before Domitian died, he ordered that some fruit that was being served be put aside for the next day and added, "Provided I can enjoy it." And turning to those next to him, he declared, "Tomorrow the moon will be blood-red in Aquarius[57] and will herald a deed of which the whole world will speak." At about midnight he grew so frightened that he jumped out of bed. Then in the morning he heard the case of a *haruspex* sent from Germany, who had predicted a change of government when asked about the lightning strike.[58] Domitian condemned him to death. [16.2] And when he scratched an inflamed wart on his forehead too hard and made it bleed, he said, "If only that's the end of it." He asked the time and was deliberately told that it was the sixth hour, not the fifth, the hour that he feared. Delighted by this information and thinking that danger was past, he was hurrying off to rest for a while, when Parthenius, his personal attendant, intercepted him, telling him that someone had very important business with him and was not to be put off. Accordingly, Domitian sent everyone else away and went into his chamber. And there he was killed.

[17.1] This is what has come to be known generally about the conspiracy and his death: When the conspirators were uncertain as to when or how they should approach him (in the bath or at the table), Stephanus, who was Domitilla's[59] steward and a defendant in an embezzlement case at that time, suggested a plan and offered his help. To avert suspicion he pretended that he had been injured, kept his left arm wrapped with a wool bandage for several days, and then, just before the critical hour, inserted a stiletto into the wrappings. Claiming that he had information about a conspiracy, he was ushered into the emperor's company and there surprised him and stabbed him in the groin as he was reading the papers he had just been given. [17.2] Wounded and struggling, Domitian was attacked

---

57. In the year of Domitian's assassination, 96 CE, the moon was in the astrological zone of Aquarius from the night of September 15/16 to the night of September 18/19.

58. Plausibly the strike on the emperor's bedchamber; see 15.2.

59. Domitian's niece, the daughter of his sister Domitilla, married to Flavius Clemens, whom Domitian killed; see 15.1.

by Clodianus, an adjutant; Maximus, a freedman of Parthenius; Satur, supervisor of the slaves who attended his bedchamber; and a gladiator from the training school. They inflicted seven wounds and hacked him to death. The murder was witnessed by a slave who was in the bedroom at his usual post to take care of the *Lares*, and he described it in greater detail: At the first stab wound, Domitian ordered him to hand him at once the dagger hidden under his pillow and call his attendants. But the slave found nothing near the head of the bed except the handle,[60] and furthermore, all the doors were barred. In the meantime, Domitian grabbed Stephanus, pushed him to the ground, and struggled with him for a long time, first trying to twist the weapon from him, then trying to gouge out his eyes, despite cuts on his fingers.

[17.3] Domitian was killed on the fourteenth day before the Kalends of October in the forty-fifth year of his age and the fifteenth of his principate.[61] Hired pallbearers carried his body on a cheap second-rate bier, and his nurse Phyllis arranged a funeral for him at her villa outside the city on the Latin Way. But she secretly took his ashes to the temple of the Flavians and mixed them with those of Julia, Titus' daughter, whom she had also reared.[62]

[18.1] Domitian was tall, had an unassuming expression, and blushed frequently. His eyes were large but his vision weak. He had handsome good looks, especially when he was young, and indeed, he was attractive in every aspect—except for his feet, which had toes that curved in a bit. Later in life, he was unappealing because he was bald and had a fat stomach and skinny legs (although these had become thin after a long illness). [18.2] He thought that his modest facial expression garnered him approval; he once boasted to the senate, "Up to now, I am certain that you have approved of both my thoughts and my countenance." His baldness distressed him so much that whenever someone else was laughed at or abused because of a bald head, he thought that it was he who was being made fun of. But in a little book, *On Hair Care*, written for a friend, he inserted these words of comfort for both of them: "Do you know how fair

---

60. Other narratives report that Parthenius had removed the blade.
61. September 18, 96 CE.
62. On Domitian's passion for his niece Julia, see chapter 22.

I am, and tall as well?[63] But the fate that my hair suffers is waiting for me too, and it is with fortitude that I bear the aging of my hair while I am young. Know you then: there is nothing more pleasing than beauty—or more fleeting." [19] He had little stamina and rarely went on foot when he was in Rome. On campaign marches he seldom rode on horseback but was normally carried in a litter. He had no interest in the weapons that legionary soldiers used but a great deal of enthusiasm for bows and arrows. A large audience would often watch him dispatch a hundred wild beasts of different kinds at his retreat on Mount Alba and intentionally pierce the heads of some so as to create horns of a sort with two arrows. Sometimes he aimed at a slave who stood at a distance holding up his right hand spread out as a target, and he was so skilled that all of his arrows went through the spaces between the boy's fingers without doing harm.

[20] His interest in the liberal curriculum flagged at the beginning of his reign, but he saw to it that the libraries that had been destroyed by fire were reconstructed at great expense.[64] He searched out texts everywhere and sent scribes to Alexandria to make new copies and correct the damaged ones. But he never made an effort to become acquainted with history or poetry or even the basic rules of composition. He read nothing but the commentaries and decrees of Tiberius Caesar. He used the talents of others to compose his letters, speeches, and edicts. But his conversation was not inelegant, and he sometimes said clever things: "I wish," he said, "that I were as handsome as Maecius[65] thinks he is." He said that the head of someone with a blend of red and white hair was "snow with mead poured over." [21] And a recurrent saying was, "Emperors are in a totally wretched situation. They are never believed when they say that they have discovered a conspiracy—unless they are killed."

Whenever he had the time, he amused himself with dicing, even on ordinary working days and in the early morning hours. He bathed during the day and lunched to satiety, so that at dinner he ate little more than a Matian apple[66] and took a small swallow from a flask.

---

63. Homer, *Iliad* 21.108.
64. The libraries at Alexandria were the most important in the ancient world.
65. Unknown.
66. An apple named after an authority on cooking.

He often held lavish banquets, but that ended early. They certainly did not last beyond sunset, and there were no drinking parties afterward, for the only thing he did until it was time to sleep was walk by himself, alone.

[22] Domitian's appetite for sex was enormous; he called his frequent intercourse "bed-wrestling," a kind of exercise program. There was a rumor to the effect that he plucked his partners' hairs himself and went swimming with low-class prostitutes. At the time when he was closely tied to Domitia, he was offered marriage to his brother's daughter, who was still a young girl.[67] He determinedly refused the match, but a short time later, after his niece was married to someone else, he seduced her on his own, even though Titus was still alive at the time. Then, when her father and husband were dead and she was left alone, Domitian had a passionate and open affair with her and even caused her death when he forced her to abort the unborn child conceived by him.

[23.1] Domitian's murder disturbed the populace little, but the military took it quite badly and immediately attempted to call him Divine. They were prepared to avenge his death but had no one to lead them. They did exactly this a short time later, however, when they insistently called for the assassins to be punished.[68] The senators, on the other hand, were so overjoyed that they fought their way into the crowded senate house and showed no restraint in abusing the dead emperor, calling him the nastiest and most insulting names possible. They ordered ladders brought in and the medallions with his portrait and the statues of him pulled down and hurled to the ground then and there as they watched. Their final measure was to vote that inscriptions containing his name be obliterated everywhere and that his memory be completely effaced.

[23.2] A few months before Domitian was killed, a crow croaked on the Capitoline, "All will be well."[69] Someone interpreted the portent thus:

---

67. On his wife Domitia, see 1.3, 3.1, and 10.2. The niece, Julia, was the daughter of his brother Titus (see 17.3) and the wife of his cousin Flavius Sabinus, whom he put to death; see 10.4, 12.3.

68. The following year, under the emperor Nerva, the praetorians killed Domitian's assassins.

69. It was believed that crows could imitate human speech.

> A crow that just now sat on the Tarpeian height[70]
> Could not say, "All's well." It said, "It will be."

Domitian himself is said to have dreamed that a golden hump grew upon his back, and that he considered it certain that this foretold happier and more successful times for Rome after his death. In truth, this came quickly to pass, for the emperors who followed displayed self-control and a sense of responsibility.

---

70. The Tarpeian Rock was a rock outcropping on the Capitoline Hill from which criminals were thrown to their deaths.

FAMILY TREES

The family trees of the imperial dynasties were very complicated with adoptions, marriages, and remarriages, often within the family. Only those individuals who play significant roles in the *Caesars* are included in the family trees on the following pages.

Individuals are given the names by which they are commonly known.

The names of the emperors appear in bold type.

Numbers in parentheses before or after a name indicate the order of marriages.

When a name is repeated because of marriage, the name appears in italics.

Julius Caesar and the Family of Augustus

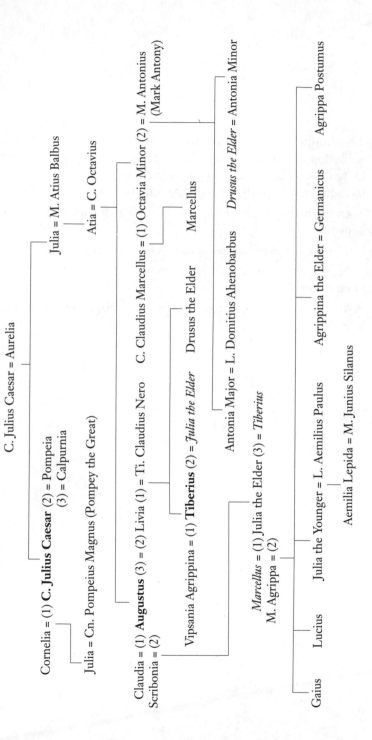

The Julio-Claudians

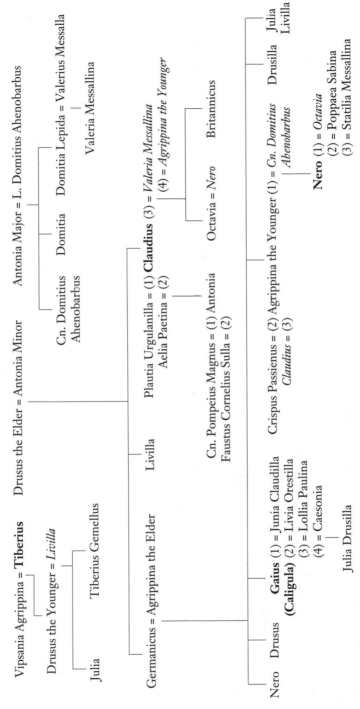

The Flavian Emperors

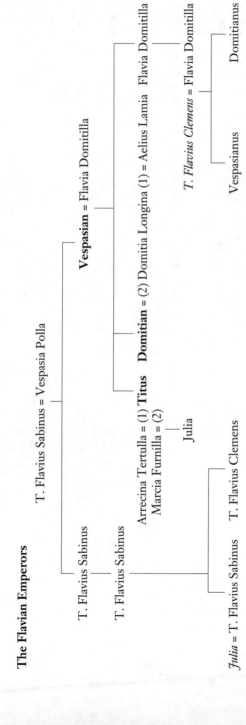

GLOSSARY

aedile   An elected official, second in the line of magistrates, responsible for public works and markets in Rome.

aerarium   The state treasury kept in the temple of Saturn. Also the name of the repository itself.

Atellan farce   Low comedy with stock characters, sometimes obscene and sometimes a vehicle for political satire.

augur   A priest, a member of the college of augurs who interpreted the flight of birds (augury).

auspices   The reading of the future from the behavior of birds. Only senior magistrates were permitted to "take the auspices."

auxiliaries   Military divisions recruited locally to supplement legionary forces.

Board of Fifteen   A college of priests charged with care of the Sibylline books.

Board of Twenty   Minor magistrates with various responsibilities. Appointment to the board was a precursor to candidacy for the quaestor-ship and the senatorial career that followed.

broad stripe   A clothing feature signifying rank. Senators and those eligible to compete for entry into the senate were permitted to wear a tunic with a wide stripe down the front.

censor   During the Republic, an official charged with conducting a census to determine senatorial and equestrian status; emperors assumed the role later on.

centumviral court   The "court of one hundred men" (*centumviri*), convened in sections to hear civil cases.

Circus Maximus   The most important racecourse in Rome.

civic crown   The honorific crown of oak leaves awarded for saving the life of a Roman citizen.

cognomen (pl. cognomina)   A third name added to the first and family names of a Roman citizen; it often differentiated branches of the family.

consul   The chief magistrate; two elected each year. A former consul was said to be a consular or of consular rank.

Corinthian ware   An alloy of copper and precious metals, popular for luxury goods.

cubit   A measure of length, about an English foot and a half.

curule chair   The ivory inlaid chair of state used by consuls and other high magistrates in their official capacity.

dictator   An official with absolute powers chosen for a limited period during times of emergency in the Republic.

dominus (**pl.** *domini,* **f.** *domina*)   "Lord," "master," a title specific for the master of slaves.

equestrian   Also called a Roman knight, a member of the social division just below the senators within the upper class.

essedarius   A gladiator who fought from a chariot with a driver.

fasces   A bundle of rods tied together and carried by lictors as a symbol of magisterial authority; the rods surrounded an axe when carried outside the city.

flamen (**pl.** *flamines*)   A priest assigned to the service of one particular deity or to an emperor deemed to be divine.

flamen dialis   A special priest of Jupiter.

Game of Troy   A display on horseback performed by boys of the upper class, connecting Rome (especially the Julian clan) with its alleged Trojan origin.

Gemonian Steps   Steps leading down from the Capitoline Hill where the bodies of executed criminals were publicly exposed.

genius   The divine spirit of a man.

gold ring   Sign of status for a senator or equestrian.

haruspex (**pl.** *haruspices*)   Etruscan soothsayers who predicted the future by examining the entrails of sacrificed animals.

hoplomachus (*oplomachus*)   A heavily-armed gladiator.

Ides   The name for the thirteenth day of the month or for the fifteenth of March, May, July, and October.

imperator   Title given to a victorious general by acclamation of his men and especially to emperors. Some emperors took it as a proper name.

Junian Latin   Irregularly freed slaves who had limited citizenship.

Kalends   The name for the first day of a month.

Lares   Tutelary deities of the hearth and household and of crossroads.

Latin rights   The limited citizenship given to Italian cities late in the Republic and sometimes to other municipalities or peoples.

legion   The basic infantry unit of the Roman army.

lex Papia Poppaea The name of the law of Augustus that freed married citizens with three legitimate children from certain restrictions.

liberal studies Language and literature but also law, philosophy, arithmetic, geometry, astronomy, and music, subjects that defined an educated man.

lictor An attendant who carried the *fasces* when he accompanied a consul or praetor in public and, in the empire, the emperor and other officials.

Lupercalia A festival celebrated on February 15. Young men sacrificed goats and wearing nothing but goatskins ran about striking bystanders with goatskin thongs.

magistrates Elected officials.

master of the horse Chosen second in command to a dictator during the Republic.

Mausoleum The tomb that Augustus built in the Campus Martius to hold his remains and those of his family.

military tribune A junior officer in a legion.

***murmillo* (pl. *murmillones*)** A gladiator who fought wearing Gallic armor.

narrow stripe A clothing feature denoting social class. Members of the equestrian order wore tunics with narrow bands of color.

Nones The name for the fifth day of the month or for the seventh of March, May, July, and October.

optimates The conservative political coalition of the late Republic.

ovation A lesser triumph awarded for minor military achievements.

pantomime A popular entertainment in which a solo dancer mimed a character from myth accompanied by music and a chorus.

patrician An inherited designation for some families of the aristocracy.

Pedian law A law directed specifically against the assassins of Julius Caesar.

Penates Guardian spirits of the house. The city of Rome had equivalent *Penates* worshiped in the temple of Vesta; they were supposed to have been brought to Rome by Aeneas.

plebeians All Romans who were not patricians, but also a term for the general population.

pontifex maximus The most important priesthood of the Roman state religion.

praetor The second highest of the magistrates; his duties included the oversight of the courts.

praetorian guard   The elite military unit stationed in and near Rome to protect the emperor; it was commanded by the praetorian prefect.

primipilaris **(pl.** *primipilares***)**   The rank of centurion in command of the first century of the first cohort of a legion. He held the prestigious title after his discharge.

principate   The name used for the imperial form of government; from *princeps*, "first man" or "leading citizen," as the emperor was called.

proconsul   The title of a governor or general with consular rank.

procurator   An imperial appointee, an agent who managed the emperor's property and other business.

propraetor   The title of a governor or general with praetorian rank.

pulvinar   A special couch on which images of the gods were placed or for the emperor himself; a *pulvinar* built into the Circus Maximus served as the imperial box.

quaestor   The first elected officer; election gave entry to the senate.

quaestor of Augustus   A few of the twenty quaestors elected each year designated as assistants to the emperor.

Quinquatria   A five-day festival in March that honored the goddess Minerva.

quinquennial   An interval or a period of five years, but with recurring events, usually four years since time was reckoned by counting both ends of a series.

retiarius **(pl.** *retiarii***)**   Gladiators lightly armed with tridents and daggers but without protective headgear. They had nets and fought in groups.

Roman knight   A member of the equestrian order.

rostra   the speaker's platform in the Forum.

Saturnalia   A December holiday of several days characterized by gift giving and license, including a temporary reversal of the slave–master relationship.

Secular Games   A special entertainment intended to usher in a new age and meant to be viewed only once in a person's lifetime.

secutor **(pl.** *secutores***)**   Gladiators armed with sword, shield, helmet, and a single greave.

sesterce   A monetary unit.

Sibylline books   Prophetic inscriptions that were held in great respect.

Sigillaria   The last day of the Saturnalia when gifts were exchanged; the word is also used for the small clay objects given as gifts and for the district where they were sold.

suffect consul   A replacement consul.

Thracian gladiator   A heavily-armed gladiator with a small curved sword and a small round shield.

toga of manhood (*toga virilis*)   The adult toga that replaced a boy's *toga praetextata* at a ceremony that marked his coming of age, usually when he was about fifteen.

toga praetextata   A toga bordered by a purple stripe worn by both ruling magistrates and underage boys.

tribe   A group into which citizens were divided for the purpose of voting.

tribunal   A raised platform on which the presiding officer sat at a trial.

tribune, tribune of the people   An officer elected from the plebeians, powerful during the Republic.

triumph   A victorious general's ceremonial procession into Rome.

triumvir   A member of a commission of three men that had no legal status. Two self-appointed confederacies were in effect at the end of the Republic, that of Caesar, Pompey, and Crassus, and that of Octavian (Augustus), Mark Antony, and Lepidus.

Vestal Virgins   The only female priesthood in Rome. They took a vow of chastity and served the goddess Vesta.

INDEX OF HISTORICAL NAMES

Included in this index are people Suetonius names more than once and those who may cause confusion because they share a name. A few others are identified as well, members of the imperial family, for instance, or particularly important historical figures who happen to appear only once. But all people, including many mentioned only in passing, are identified as they occur. This is sometimes done in footnotes, but Suetonius himself often performs the service ("Boter, his [Claudius'] freedman," *Cl.* 27.1; "Gaius Oppius and the rest of Caesar's friends," *Jul.* 52.2).

Roman citizens are listed by family name and can be located by cross-references from the name or names by which they are commonly called in the text (Sejanus = Aelius Sejanus, L.; Cicero = Tullius Cicero, M.). Some entries give multiple common names for the same person. One exception is the emperors who appear under the single name (in bold type) by which they have become historically known; their full names and imperial names follow. References for them are only to biographies not their own. The other exception is women who are listed under the name by which they are primarily designated in the text.

First names are indicated by the following standard abbreviations:

A.	Aulus	Mam.	Mamercus
Ap.	Appius	P.	Publius
C.	Gaius	Q.	Quintus
Cn.	Gnaeus	Ser.	Servius
D.	Decimus	Sex.	Sextus
L.	Lucius	T.	Titus
M.	Marcus	Ti.	Tiberius

Ennia Thrasylla (Naevia) (wife of
Macro) *Cal.* 12.2, 26.1
Epaphroditus (freedman of Nero)
Ner. 49.3; *Dom.* 14.4
Epidius Marullus, C. (tribune)
Jul. 79.1, 80.3

Fannius Caepio (conspirator
against Augustus) *Aug.* 19.1;
Tib. 8
Faustus Sulla = Cornelius Sulla
Felix, Faustus
Flavia Domitilla (wife of
Vespasian) *Ves.* 3
Flavius Petro, T. (grandfather of
Vespasian) *Ves.* 1.2, 1.4
Flavius Sabinus, T. (father of
Vespasian) *Ves.* 1.2, 5.2
Flavius Sabinus, T. (brother of
Vespasian) *Vit.* 15.2, 15.3;
Ves. 1.3; *Dom.* 1.2
Flavius Sabinus, T. (cousin of
Domitian) *Dom.* 10.4
Fonteius Capito (governor of
Lower Germany) *Gal.* 11
Fonteius Capito, C. *Cal.* 8.1
Fulvia (first wife of Mark Antony)
Aug. 17.5, 62.1
Furius Camillus (republican
dictator) *Tib.* 3.2; *Cl.* 26.1

Gaetulicus = Cornelius Lentulus
Gaetulicus, Cn.
Gaius = Julius Caesar, C.
(grandson and adopted son of
Augustus)
Gaius (Caligula), Gaius Julius
Caesar Germanicus, Gaius
Caesar Augustus Germanicus
Tib. 54.1, 62.3, 73.2, 75.2, 76;
Cl. 7, 8, 9.1, 10.1, 11.1, 11.3. 20.1,
26.3, 38.3; *Ner.* 6.2–3, 7.1, 30.1;
Gal. 6.2–3, 7.1; *Oth.* 6.1; *Vit.* 2.5,
4, 17.2; *Ves.* 2.3, 5.3; *Tit.* 1

Galba, Servius Sulpicius Galba,
Servius Galba Imperator Caesar
Augustus *Ner.* 32.4, 40.3, 42.1,
47.2, 48.2, 49.4; *Oth.* 4.1, 5.1,
6.1–3, 7.2, 10.1, 12.2; *Vit.* 7.1,
8.2, 9, 10.1; *Ves.* 5.1, 5.7, 6.2,
16.1; *Tit.* 5.1
Germanicus = Julius Caesar,
Germanicus

Halotus (taster for Claudius)
Cl. 44.2; *Gal.* 15.2
Hannibal *Tib.* 2.1; *Dom.* 10.3
Hasdrubal *Tib.* 2.1
Helvidius Priscus, C. *Ves.* 15;
Dom. 10.3
Helvius Cinna, C. (ally of Julius
Caesar) *Jul.* 52.3, 85
Hirtius, A. (ally of Julius Caesar
and Augustus) *Jul.* 56.1, 56.3;
Aug. 10.3, 11, 68; *Tib.* 5.
Hortensius Hortalus, M. (republi-
can orator) *Tib.* 47
Hortensius Hortalus, Q. (grandson
of the orator) *Aug.* 72.1; *Tib.* 47

Icelus (freedman of Galba)
Ner. 49.4; *Gal.* 14.2, 22

Juba I (king of Numidia, ally of
Pompey) *Jul.* 35.2, 59, 66, 71
Juba II *Cal.* 26.1
Julia (aunt of Julius Caesar)
Jul. 6.1
Julia (daughter of Drusus the
Younger) *Cl.* 29.1
Julia (daughter of Julius Caesar)
Jul. 1.1, 21, 26.1, 84.1; *Aug.* 95
Julia (sister of Julius Caesar)
Jul. 74.2; *Aug.* 4.1, 8.1
Julia, Flavia Julia (daughter of
Titus, niece of Domitian)
Dom. 17.3, 22

Pompeia (sister of Sextus
Pompeius) *Tib.* 6.3
Pompeius Magnus, Cn. (Pompey
the Great, triumvir) *Jul.* 19.2,
20.5, 21, 22.1, 24.1, 26.1, 27.1,
28.2–3, 29.2, 30.2, 34.1–2,
35.1–2, 36, 37.1, 49.2, 50.1, 56.1,
68.2–3, 69, 75.1, 75.4, 83.1;
Aug. 4.1, 31.5; *Ner.* 2.3
Pompeius Magnus, Cn. (son-in-
law of Claudius, husband of
Antonia) *Cal.* 35.1; *Cl.* 27.2,
29.1–2
Pompeius Magnus, Sex. (son of
Pompey the Great) *Aug.* 9, 16.1,
16.3–4, 47, 68, 74; *Tib.* 4.3, 6.3
Pompeius Rufus, Q. (father-in-law
of Julius Caesar) *Jul.* 6.2
Pompeius, Sex. *Aug.* 100.1
Poppaea Sabina (second wife of
Nero) *Ner.* 35.1, 35.3–5; *Oth.* 3.1
Porcius Cato Censorinus, M.
(republican statesman)
Aug. 86.3
Porcius Cato Uticensus, M. (repub-
lican opponent of Julius Caesar)
Jul. 14.2, 19.1, 20.4, 30.3, 53,
56.5; *Aug.* 13.2, 85.1, 87.1
Posides (freedman of Claudius)
Cl. 28
Ptolemy (king of Mauritania, son
of King Juba) *Cal.* 26.1, 35.1,
55.1
Ptolemy XII (Auletes) of Egypt
Jul. 54.3; *Cl.* 16.2
Ptolemy XIII of Egypt *Jul.* 35.1

Quinctilius (Quintilius) Varus, P.
Aug. 23.1–2, 49.1; *Tib.* 17.1–2,
18.1; *Cal.* 3.2, 31

Rufrius Crispinus (stepson of
Nero, son of Poppaea) *Ner.* 35.5

Sallustius Crispus, C. (republican
historian) *Aug.* 86.3
Sallustius Crispus Passienus, C.
(second husband of Agrippina
the Younger) *Ner.* 6.3
Salvius Otho, L. (father of Otho)
Gal. 6.1; *Oth.* 1.2, 2.1–2
Salvius Otho, M. (grandfather of
Otho) *Oth.* 1.1
Salvius Otho Cocceianus, L.
(nephew of Otho, victim of
Domitian) *Dom.* 10.3
Salvius Otho Titianus, L. (brother
of Otho) *Oth.* 1.3, 10.2
Scipio = Caecilius Metellus Piso
Scipio, Q.
Scribonia (second wife of
Augustus) *Aug.* 62.2, 63.1, 69.1
Scribonius Curio, C. (father)
Jul. 9.2, 49.1, 50.1, 52.3
Scribonius Curio, C. (son)
Jul. 29.1, 36, 50.1
Scribonius Libo Drusus, L.
Tib. 25.1, 25.3
Sejanus = Aelius Sejanus, L.
Seleucus (astrologer) *Oth.* 4.1, 6.1
Seleucus (grammarian) *Tib.* 56
Seleucus II (king of Syria) *Cl.* 25.3
Seneca = Annaeus Seneca, L.
Sergius Catilina, L., Catiline (con-
spirator of the late Republic)
Jul. 14.1, 17.1; *Aug.* 3.1, 94.5
Servilia (mistress of Julius Caesar,
mother of Marcus Junius
Brutus) *Jul.* 50.2
Servilius Casca, C. (assassin of
Julius Caesar) *Jul.* 82.1–2
Servilius Casca, P. (assassin of
Julius Caesar) *Jul.* 82.1–2
Servilius Isauricus *Jul.* 3
Servilius Isauricus, P. (republican,
father of fiancée of Augustus)
Aug. 62.1; *Tib.* 5
Sestilia (mother of Vitellius)
Vit. 3.1, 14.5

Silanus = Junius Silanus
Silius, C. (lover of Valeria
Messallina) *Cl.* 26.2, 29.3, 36
Silvanus = Plautius Silvanus, M.
Spiculus (gladiator) *Ner.* 30.2,
47.3
Sporus (slave, lover of Nero)
Ner. 28.1–2, 29, 46.2, 48.1, 49.3
Spurrina (soothsayer) *Jul.* 81.2,
81.4
Statilia Messallina (last wife of
Nero) *Ner.* 35.1; *Oth.* 10.2
Statilius Taurus, T. (general under
Augustus) *Aug.* 29.5; *Cal.* 18.1;
Ner. 35.1
Statilius Taurus Corvinus, T.
(conspirator against Claudius)
Cl. 13.2
Stephanus (assassin of Domitian)
Dom. 17.1–2
Suetonius Laetus (father of
Suetonius) *Oth.* 10.1
Sulla = Cornelius Sulla Felix, L.
Sulla (astrologer) *Cal.* 57.2
Sulpicius Galba, C. (grandfather of
Galba) *Gal.* 3.3, 4.2
Sulpicius Galba, C. (father of
Galba) *Gal.* 3.3–4
Sulpicius Galba, C. (brother of
Galba) *Gal.* 3.4
Sulpicius Galba, Ser. (great-grand-
father of Galba) *Gal.* 3.2
Sulpicius Rufus, Ser. (ally of Julius
Caesar) *Jul.* 29.1, 50.1
Sutorius Macro, Q. Naevius
Cordus (praetorian prefect
under Tiberius and Gaius)
Cal. 12.2, 23.2, 26.1

Terentia (wife of Maecenas)
Aug. 66.3
Terentius Varro, M. (officer under
Pompey) *Jul.* 34.2, 44.2

Terentius Varro Murena, A.
(conspirator against Augustus)
Aug. 19.1, 56.4, 66.3; *Tib.* 8
Terpnus (lyre player) *Ner.* 20.1;
Ves. 19.1
Thrasyllus (astrologer) *Aug.* 98.4;
Tib. 14.4, 62.3; *Cal.* 19.3
Tiberius, Tiberius Claudius Nero,
Tiberius Julius Caesar Augustus
Aug. 40.3, 51.3, 63.2, 65.1,
71.2–3, 76.2, 85.1, 86.2, 92.2,
97.1, 97.3, 98.4–5, 100.3, 101.2;
Cal. 1.1, 2, 4, 6.1–2, 7, 10.1, 11,
12.2–3, 13, 14.1, 14.3, 15.1, 16.1,
16.3, 19.3, 21, 28, 30.2, 31, 37.3,
38.2; *Cl.* 4.1, 5, 6.2, 11.3, 23.1,
25.3; *Ner.* 5.2, 6.1, 30.1; *Gal.* 3.4,
4.1, 5.2; *Oth.* 1.2; *Vit.* 2.2, 3.2;
Tit. 8.1; *Dom.* 20
Tiberius Alexander = Julius
Alexander, Ti.
Tiberius Gemellus = Julius Caesar,
Ti.
Tigellinus = Ofonius Tigellinus
Tillius Cimber, L. (conspirator
against Julius Caesar) *Jul.* 82.1
Tiridates (king of Armenia)
Ner. 13.1, 30.2
Titurius Sabinus, Q. (officer under
Julius Caesar) *Jul.* 25.2, 67.2
Titus, Titus Flavius Vespasianus,
Imperator Titus Caesar
Vespasianus Augustus *Ves.* 3,
4.6, 23.3; *Dom.* 2.1, 10.2, 13.1,
17.3, 22
Toranius (slave dealer) *Aug.* 69.1
Toranius, C. (Augustus' guardian)
Aug. 27.1
Tullius Cicero, M. (late republican
statesman and orator) *Jul.* 9.2,
17.2, 20.4, 30.5, 42.3, 49.3, 50.2,
55.1, 56.1, 56.6; *Aug.* 3.2, 5, 94.9;
Tib. 2.4, 7.2; *Cl.* 41.3
Tullius Cicero, Q. (brother of
Marcus) *Jul.* 14.2; *Aug.* 3.2

Valeria Messallina (third wife of
  Claudius) *Cl.* 17.3, 26.2, 27.1,
  29.3, 36, 37.2, 39.1; *Ner.* 6.4;
  Vit. 2.5
Valerius Catullus (lover of Gaius)
  Cal. 36.1
Valerius Catullus (republican poet)
  Jul. 73
Valerius Messalla, M. *Gal.* 4.1.
Valerius Messalla Barbatus, M.
  (father of Valeria Messallina)
  Cl. 26.2
Valerius Messalla Corvinus, M.
  (orator) *Aug.* 58.1–2, 74;
  Tib. 70.1; *Cl.* 13.2
Varro = Terentius Varro
Varus = Quinctilius (Quintilius)
  Varus, P.
Vatinius, P. *Jul.* 22.1, 28.3
Vergilius Maro, P. (the poet Virgil)
  Cal. 34.2, 45.2; *Ner.* 54; *Dom.* 9.1
Vespasia Polla (mother of
  Vespasian) *Ves.* 1.3, 2.2, 5.2
Vespasian, Titus Flavius
  Vespasianus, Imperator Caesar
  Vespasianus Augustus *Cl.* 45;
  Gal. 23; *Vit.* 15.1–2, 17.1;
  Dom. 1.3, 2.2, 15.2
Vespasianus (great-nephew and
  intended successor of Domitian)
  Dom. 15.1

Vibius Pansa C. (ally of Julius
  Caesar and of Augustus)
  Aug. 10.3, 11; *Tib.* 5
Vindex = Julius Vindex, C.
Vinius Rufinus, T. (ally of Galba)
  Gal. 14.2; *Vit.* 7.1.
Vipsanius Agrippa, M., Marcus
  Agrippa (general and Augustus'
  chief ally, husband of Julia)
  Aug. 16.2, 25.3, 29.5, 35.1, 42.1,
  63.1–2, 64.1, 66.3, 94.12, 97.1;
  Tib. 7.2, 10.1; *Cal.* 7, 23.1
Vitellius, Aulus Vitellius, Aulus
  Vitellius Imperator Germanicus
  Augustus *Oth.* 8.1, 9.1; *Ves.* 5.1,
  6.2, 6.4, 7.1, 8.2, 14; *Dom.* 1.2
Vitellius, A. (uncle of Vitellius)
  Vit. 2.2
Vitellius, L. (father of Vitellius)
  Vit. 2.2, 2.4, 3.2
Vitellius, P. (grandfather of
  Vitellius) *Vit.* 2.2
Vitellius, P. (uncle of Vitellius)
  Vit. 2.3
Vitellius, Q. (uncle of Vitellius)
  Vit. 1.2, 2.2
Vologaesus (king of the Parthians)
  Ner. 57.2; *Ves.* 6.4; *Dom.* 2.2